PENGUIN BOOKS

The War Against th

Patrick Barwise is Emeritus Professor of Management and Marketing at London Business School and former chairman of *Which?* His previous books include *Television and Its Audience*, *Simply Better* and *The 12 Powers of a Marketing Leader*.

Peter York is a cultural commentator, management consultant, author and broadcaster. His previous books include *The Official Sloane Ranger Handbook* and *Authenticity Is a Con*. He is the President of the Media Society.

The War Against the BBC

How an Unprecedented Combination of Hostile
Forces Is Destroying Britain's Greatest Cultural
Institution . . . and Why You Should Care

PATRICK BARWISE
AND PETER YORK

PENGUIN BOOKS

To Alex and Katy, Arthur and Anna – PB

To the late Juliette Jackson who contributed enormously
to this book, as to everything else – PY

PENGUIN BOOKS

UK | USA | Canada | Ireland | Australia
India | New Zealand | South Africa

Penguin Books is part of the Penguin Random House group of companies
whose addresses can be found at global.penguinrandomhouse.com.

Penguin
Random House
UK

Published in Penguin Books 2020

002

Text copyright © Patrick Barwise and Peter York, 2020

The moral rights of the authors have been asserted

Set in 11/13pt Dante MT Std
Typeset by Jouve (UK), Milton Keynes
Printed and bound in Great Britain by Clays Ltd, Elcograf S.p.A.

The authorized representative in the EEA is Penguin Random House Ireland,
Morrison Chambers, 32 Nassau Street, Dublin D02 YH68

A CIP catalogue record for this book is available from the British Library

ISBN: 978–0–141–98940–2

www.greenpenguin.co.uk

Contents

Introduction: 'You Don't Know What You've Got 'Till It's Gone'[1]

In his 2010 video *I'm Proud of the BBC*,[2] the musician and comedian Mitch Benn, formerly a staple of BBC Radio 4's topical *The Now Show*, lists some of the Corporation's marvels – its programmes and people. They're scrawled on hand-made cards – after the style of the Bob Dylan video for 'Subterranean Homesick Blues' – and carried by a small posse of distinctly ordinary adults and dancing children gathered outside the BBC's central London headquarters, Broadcasting House, and the – now abandoned – Television Centre in White City, west London. Pub rocker style, Benn isn't sleek and nor is his little film. But it's all from the heart.

The glories he lists stretch from *Newsround* and *Newsnight* to *Ab Fab*, from *Quatermass* to *The Two Ronnies*. Other programmes he cites include *Blackadder, Doctor Who, EastEnders, The Archers, The Thick of It, The Young Ones, Who Do You Think You Are?, Blue Peter, Panorama, Question Time* and *Yes, Minister*. The lyrics have a campaigning edge. 'I'm proud of the BBC, It's part of you and it's part of me', 'It's just this and lousy weather that holds us together' and 'We're not just listeners and viewers, it belongs to us.'[3] The song goes on for more than five minutes and there was clearly the material for much more. It's an extraordinary list in its sheer range of British glories and obsessions – famous prize-winning programmes of the *Blue Planet, Civilization* and *Monty Python* kind, and others that super-serve traditional British obsessions, such as *Gardeners' Question Time* or *Antiques Roadshow* – utterly timeless achievements, and others very much of their time.

Benn's point is that the BBC is the whole British nation in all its untidy variety and, at the same time, one of its glories. For anyone over forty – Benn is now fifty – this story taps into a rich stream of memories. For younger generations, the BBC is less central. That's one of the challenges it faces, but far from the only one.

In an interview, we asked Benn why he wrote the song. He told us, 'I had this feeling that not only were people tired of relentless criticism . . . they genuinely resented that the BBC couldn't really fight its corner because it's literally publicly funded . . . So I thought, I'm going to fight its corner for it.'

Is Benn's list of triumphs just playing on the BBC's past glories? Not if you list its new and continuing hits in the ten years since he released the song: from *Sherlock* to *Luther*, *Bodyguard* to *Citizen Khan*, *Fleabag* to *Strictly Come Dancing*, *Peaky Blinders* to *Killing Eve*, *Gavin and Stacey* to *The Great British Bake Off*, *Trust Me, I'm a Doctor* to *RuPaul's Drag Race UK* and Gareth Malone's choir series, with military wives and in schools, hospitals, companies, a housing estate and, most recently, a high-security prison for young offenders. And CBeebies. And on radio, *George the Poet*, *Desert Island Discs*, the *Today Programme* – it looks as if the BBC can still pull it off. At the September 2019 Emmy Awards in Los Angeles, it won another *six* major awards.[4]

The whole BBC is always there unless we're travelling abroad, which is the only time when we notice it – or rather, its absence. Or, as seasoned travellers will tell you, when they're away from the UK is when they appreciate the BBC the most – it's available in so many countries – it's a stabilizing presence. Usually, we just take it for granted. But, before very long, we may no longer be able to do that, unless, as a country, we start taking action.

This book is about why the BBC is in peril, why this matters and what we can do about it. Fortunately, ensuring that we and future generations can still enjoy the luxury of unlimited access to a strong, independent, properly funded BBC isn't that difficult or even that expensive, although it will involve confronting some powerful vested interests. If we want to save it, we can. The first step is to understand why the BBC still matters and the nature of the challenge it's facing – the topic of this book.

'It's Part of You and It's Part of Me'

What makes for national cohesion and 'national conversations' in today's world? We're more fragmented now. We've gone from jobs for life in giant factories and office blocks to freelance and zero-hours working lives, with less and less of the local and institutional glue we had from companies, trade unions, working men's clubs and round-the-water-cooler moments. We've moved away from the Victorian pubs, the giant cinemas, department stores and high streets – all the declining shared glories of the first mass age. All the things a generation of interwar intellectuals said were destroying the world at the time, and twenty-first-century intellectuals are sentimental about now that we're in a more individualistic world.

Who speaks for most of us – or at least tries to? The BBC is more than just a 'media content supplier', more than just positions on the TV Electronic Programme Guide (EPG) or the radio. Broadcasting like the BBC's is central to the country's understanding of itself and the rest of the world – and a big part of the world's understanding of Britain.

Small-town Vicar, Suburban Scotswoman

Radio 4's weekend morning show *Saturday Live* is co-presented by an RP (Received Pronunciation)-speaking middle-class English vicar, with a small-town parish in Northamptonshire, and a

Scotswoman, born in a genteel, leafy Glasgow suburb, with a reassuring, educated Scottish voice.

But *Saturday Live* is nuanced. The Reverend Richard Coles is an out, gay former rock star, once a member of Bronski Beat and co-founder of the Communards with Jimmy Somerville, who's written very candidly about his former life. And the nice Scots lady with the ready laugh is Aasmah Mir, the daughter of first-generation Pakistani immigrants. Some of the programme's stories are pretty full on about serious illness, addiction and bereavement.

The whole thing is *very* BBC, with its Auntie-like[5] uplift and its something-for-everyone tone, its evident concern not to be too metropolitan and its commitment to play on our shared granular popular culture; people and things that seem to hold the country together. But, whatever you feel about *Saturday Live*, it's doing the exact opposite of the tabloid newspapers' daily hate-ins or the dodgy bloggers' latest trolling campaign or conspiracy theory. *Saturday Live* pulls its 2.23 million listeners together in a civil, positive version of modern Britain.[6]

The Heart of British Broadcasting

The BBC's broad investment into making British TV and radio programmes is something we take as a given. But if it weren't here, who would make them? It wouldn't make commercial sense for anyone else to invest so heavily in creating original British content. The US giants like Netflix want internationally tradable programmes – 'content' – preferably with a long shelf life: big drama, big films, some comedy, some cartoons. Little or nothing small, live or local. And the UK's commercial public service broadcasters (PSBs) are either private companies with shareholders to satisfy (ITV and Channel 5) or, in the case of Channel 4, having to tread a delicate line to deliver its government-set public service remit while still covering its costs in an increasingly tough advertising market. They, and the UK pay-TV companies, are all key players in the unique – and still very successful – UK broadcasting ecology, competing against and feeding off each other. But the BBC is at the heart of this lively ecosystem – it's there for us all and, in terms of quality, it's still usually the one for the others to beat.

Despite the BBC's weaknesses – its timidity in the face of power, its rather odd current reading of the political continuum, its tendency to nannyism (all of which we will be looking at in this book), it isn't just a propaganda outfit.[7] Though it's had its propaganda moments, its original vision – known as Reithian, after its first managing director, Lord Reith – is for genuinely popular entertainment, reliable education and news. Real news as opposed to fake – news that's robustly resourced and delivered from around the world by intelligent people who know things and speak multiple languages and are actually there in Kiev, Kingston or Kuala Lumpur.

When the BBC was reporting on the Ukraine scandal that started the Trump impeachment inquiry, its man in Ukraine, Jonah Fisher – the one who got the scoop with the national prosecutor – had previously been the BBC's man in Eritrea, Sudan, South Africa, Nigeria and Thailand and, before that, its first correspondent in Myanmar. The BBC is the biggest broadcast news organization in the world, with two thousand journalists, fifty news bureaus and an annual budget of £350 million. This dedication to informed, impartial, on-the-ground reporting is more important than ever in today's world, and it's under threat – witness the current deep cuts in the BBC's news division.[8]

In 2010, two professors of communication at Westminster University, Jean Seaton, the BBC's then official historian, and Steve Barnett, co-author of the 1994 *Battle for the BBC*[9] wrote a piece for the *Political Quarterly*: 'Why the BBC matters: memo to the new parliament about a unique British institution'. In it, they say the BBC, like the NHS, needs to be nurtured rather than diminished. They go on to describe the BBC's benefits to the UK: creating informed democracy, representing us to the world, underwriting every original creative opportunity from Mozart to Monty Python, and making money for Britain from it. They describe music and children's programmes as a special part of that, and talk about the BBC as 'social glue': the BBC 'helps keep us together' and 'treats its audiences as intelligent, decent, national and in command'.[10]

'The Whole World of Knowledge and of Creativity Is On Offer'

At the 2015 Edinburgh International Television Festival, a world-class annual industry gathering, Armando Iannucci, the award-winning writer and producer of *I'm Alan Partridge* and *The Thick of It* (plus *Veep* in America), reminded his audience for the keynote MacTaggart Lecture just how huge an impact the BBC can have on each of our lives:

> That's what I remember from watching television when I was growing up in the 1970s and 1980s. The range in front of me. I could watch smart comedy like *Monty Python* and *Not the Nine O'Clock News*, but I also had Bruce and his *Generation Game*, *Morecambe and Wise* and no one to tell me only one type of show was for me and not the other. I loved it that I could glide from *Fawlty Towers* to a Horizon documentary on *Voyager*'s trip past Saturn. For a comedy and a space geek, that was satisfying, even if it seems a little embarrassingly sad talking about it now.
>
> But what I take from then is that British television said this: that everything, the whole world of knowledge and of creativity is on offer, is for you, all of you. No matter what your background, you were all equally welcomed to the most varied

content the world's best programme-makers could deliver. Yes, there were limits on the number of channels, and hours, but you didn't feel a limit on ideas and ambition.[11]

Yet despite the BBC's rich legacy, its continuing popularity and its centrality to British life, it – and much of what it represents – is at risk.

The BBC Is in Danger

The pressures facing the BBC include ever-increasing competition, technology and consumption trends; relentless attacks from a wide range of hostile players; disproportionate regulatory constraints; and deep funding cuts – much deeper than most people have realized. These are simultaneously increasing its costs, reducing its resources, limiting its ability to compete and innovate, and at least *attempting* (we'll see how successfully) to undermine its reputation for impartiality. These threats may even destroy the Corporation within a generation.

Five Challenges

Ever since the BBC's foundation almost a century ago, it has been routinely castigated for its supposed inefficiency and wastefulness, its public ownership and funding, and, especially, its alleged bias against the (often mutually contradictory) views of its many and varied accusers.[12]

Right now, however, we believe it is facing an unprecedented, and potentially lethal, combination of five hostile forces:

1. Consumption trends. The growing consumption of online 'subscription video-on-demand' (SVoD) services from Netflix, Amazon, YouTube (part of Google),[13]

Disney and others raises a question about the sustainability of the TV licence fee, which provides most of the BBC's funding and sets it apart from all other UK public and private broadcasters and media.[14]

2. Cost increases. Because of competition for content from SVoD services, real, inflation-adjusted programme costs are increasing for all British TV broadcasters while technology and distribution costs are also rising. SVoD increases consumer choice[15] but reduces UK broadcasters' ability to invest in original British programme content for British audiences.[16]

3. Attacks on its impartiality. In recent years, the volume and intensity of the attacks on the BBC's impartiality and trustworthiness have markedly increased, much amplified by social media and, in some cases, funded by 'dark money'. The right-wing attacks on the BBC came to a head in 2015 during the run-up to the renewal of the Charter under which the BBC operates, and have flared up again in the immediate aftermath of the 2019 election.

4. Disproportionate constraints on its ability to compete and innovate. The current BBC Charter, set by the government, aimed at striking a 'balance' between the interests of the British public and those of the Corporation's – mainly US-owned – commercial competitors. It includes extensive bureaucracy and regulation – severely limiting the BBC's ability to innovate and compete.

5. Funding cuts. The BBC's biggest challenge today, however, is lack of funding – due to the substantial cuts imposed by George Osborne in 2010 and the even worse ones of 2015, especially his decision to force the BBC to take full financial responsibility for the free TV licence concession for those aged above seventy-five from 2020–21 onwards.

By 2019, the real (inflation-adjusted) public funding of the BBC's UK services had already been cut by *30 per cent* since 2010.[17] Putting this another way, if the BBC's public funding had merely *kept pace with inflation* (still not enough to cover the increase in content and distribution costs), by 2019 it would have been *43 per cent – almost £1.4 billion* – higher,[18] leaving it well positioned to adjust to the other challenges, as it has done many times in the past. What puts it at unprecedented peril is the combination of these external pressures *and* sharply reduced resources, especially the Trojan horse that was taking responsibility for the free-TV licence concession for the over-seventy-fives.

How Did We Get to Here?

The TV licence concession began in November 1999, when Chancellor Gordon Brown announced that, from November 2000, every household with one (or more) members aged seventy-five or above – regardless of household size or income – would no longer have to pay for a licence, and the government would reimburse the BBC for the resulting loss of income. Despite the fact that the BBC welcomed the announcement,[19] it was clear to some, even then, that it might spell trouble later.[20] This type of concession, once given, is very hard to remove. And although the initial cost of £300 million per year[21] was small change in the context of the government's overall budget, it was inevitable that, with an ageing population, it would increase significantly over time – as indeed it has.

There was always a risk that, at some point, a chancellor less friendly to the BBC would seek to extricate HM Treasury from funding this concession. In 2010, George Osborne tried to do exactly that, but was faced down by Mark Thompson (the director-general) and Sir Michael Lyons (the chairman), backed by the trustees.[22] In 2015, however, at the second attempt, Osborne succeeded in forcing the BBC to take responsibility for the scheme.

We'll explore this in greater depth later on. But, in any case, coercing the BBC to fund free TV licences is an abomination. Free TV licences are a welfare benefit which should be funded out of general taxation.[23] The free TV licence concession has also been the subject of much misinformation – especially the claim that the BBC had agreed to continue it for all households with over-seventy-fives, which is not true. It is also widely believed that much or most of the cost could be covered by cutting the pay of the BBC's top managers and presenters. That, too, is untrue. A related, equally misleading, claim is that the BBC has over £5 billion in annual income to spend on programmes. In Chapter 4, we'll explain how this false claim was concocted in the *Daily Mail*.

Where Might This Lead?

If the recent funding cuts are not reversed or greatly mitigated, the BBC will, at best, survive for many years as a smaller and smaller part of a continually growing market, one increasingly dominated by US-based technology and media companies and their global content. At worst, its near century-old funding model will, at some point, break down, as more and more people try to avoid paying the licence fee as a response to a combination of BBC content and service cuts; resentment at subsidizing households with older members who watch and listen to it much more; the growing availability of global SVoD services; and the active encouragement of the BBC's enemies.

How and Why We Came to Write This Book

For the last few years, as patrons of the Market Research Society, the UK professional association for market researchers,[24] we've had the pleasure of handing out the awards at an annual event. As we chatted more generally, we found we were both appalled by the almost continuous and often dishonest attacks on the BBC within the UK and by the wider threats to its financial sustainability at a time when it's needed more than ever – with the country painfully divided by Brexit and the world awash with disinformation. So, in short, we decided to combine forces and write this book, offering our analysis of the five threats above, busting some of the biggest myths about the BBC, and offering what we see as a better way forward. We began in spring 2018 and had almost finished in late 2019. What then caught us by surprise was the new Beeb-bashing campaign after Boris Johnson's sweeping election victory in December 2019 – just as we were finalizing the manuscript!

The Latest Attacks since the December 2019 Election

During the election campaign, the would-be (and subsequently elected) Prime Minister Boris Johnson had already said the BBC should 'cough up' to cover the cost of free TV licences for all over-seventy-fives[25] – without, of course, saying which services he thought it should cut to cover the £745 million-and-growing annual cost. Since then, the BBC has been subject to a renewed wave of attacks in the *Sun*, the *Telegraph* and other Beeb-bashing papers.

But, perhaps more important still, the government indicated that it had set up a review of the BBC's funding and future, including whether licence-fee evasion should be decriminalized or the fee replaced with payment via subscription. Decriminalization was rejected in 2015 by the independent Perry Review commissioned by the then Culture Secretary – and now the ex-chancellor – Savid Javid (see chapters 5 and 10). However, in February 2020, Culture Secretary Baroness

Morgan, launching the new consultation on decriminalization, said 'the time has come to think carefully about how we
make sure the TV licence fee remains relevant in this changing media landscape'.[26] The government was not suggesting
Perry had got it wrong four-and-a-half years earlier, but, rather,
that the media landscape has changed *so much* (and, presumably, *unexpectedly*) that this conclusion was no longer valid. But,
at the time of writing, the government has still not explained
why the growth of Netflix and Amazon means licence-fee evasion should no longer be a criminal offence! Perhaps it thinks,
as Marie Antoinette might have said, 'If people can't afford the
licence fee, let them get a broadband connection, an iPad or
smart TV, and Netflix'.[27] Nor has it published the results of the
consultation, nearly five months after it closed.

As we'll explain, subscriptions are not a viable option, for
several reasons, the first of which is that the figures just won't
add up. They'd have to be *much* higher than the licence fee.
But what would be worse still is that the BBC would no longer
be a universal service shared by everyone. And when we actually get to it, will the government's review be as rational and
evidence-based as we might hope? According to recent reports,
the person leading it will be Dominic Cummings, former
campaign director of Vote Leave and now the Prime Minister's chief adviser.[28] In a fascinating exposé published in
January 2020, *The Guardian* revealed that back in 2004 Cummings created a media strategy for the Conservatives which
prioritized attacking the BBC and undermining its credibility
in a variety of ways: boycotting the *Today* programme on
Radio 4; introducing a Fox News type of broadcaster to move
the centre of political gravity to the right; removing the ban
on political advertising; and introducing right-wing phone-in
stations.[29] There was no pretence of a motive for these proposals other than party political advantage. Instead, the strategy
appears to have been based on the playbook developed by the

US Republican Party and its most powerful right-wing supporters. Cummings has never repudiated this plan, so we must assume it's what he still wants to do.[30]

Again, days before we finished this book, the BBC's director-general, Lord Hall, announced his unexpected resignation – and said that he would be leaving (before the end of his tenure) in summer 2020. The reason, so some people said, was that he wanted the existing BBC Board, under its current chairman, David Clementi (who can only remain in post until February 2021), to be able to choose his successor as director-general and avoid potential government pressure to make a particular, politically motivated appointment further down the track.

However, the main reason for Hall's early departure may have been his acceptance of the 2015 funding deal. As the full impact of the cuts became clearer, the BBC Board may have felt that only a new director-general – who, we now know, will be Tim Davie, currently running the BBC's commercial operations – could credibly fight the BBC's corner. The government is now (August 2020) recruiting Clementi's successor as BBC Chairman. This will presumably be a senior Conservative, but recent press reports suggest that the Prime Minister – perhaps in response to nervous pushback from his MPs (and doubtless despite the bloodthirsty urgings of Dominic Cummings) – is not planning to appoint someone to 'blow up' the BBC.[31]

Lastly, the book was already being copy-edited when the Covid-19 pandemic struck Britain, bringing in its wake all manner of misinformation and reminding the country of the BBC's importance as its most trusted information source. Audiences for the BBC's early- and late-evening TV news bulletins were up to double the average figures for 2019. There were also record online audiences for BBC News, CBBC, CBeebies, BBC Sounds and BBC Food.

What This Book Is, and Is Not

A final word: this book isn't an exhaustive analysis of the BBC, its programmes, its history or the way it's organized. Our focus is narrower: why the BBC matters; the fast-changing media landscape; the events and trends over the last ten years that have put it in its present predicament; its enemies, their possible motivations, their accusations and the evidence on these; its biggest mistakes; what the British public actually thinks about it; some of the wider global context; and, finally, the implications of all this for the UK government, the BBC itself and you, the reader.

We've written this book to try and ensure that people in Britain – and elsewhere – don't end up realizing what the BBC's value was only when it's gone. It's easy to take it for granted – for nearly a century it's always been there – but that doesn't mean its existence is a given. The BBC *could* be destroyed – or end up as just a minor sideshow like PBS in America. Because, just as almost everyone in the country uses it – in many cases, more than they realize – we think almost everyone has a reason to unite to ensure its long-term sustainability. If we lose it, it will be almost impossible to get it back.

1. *What, Exactly, Is the BBC?*

The BBC was launched in October 1922 as a private business, the British Broadcasting *Company*, by a consortium of radio manufacturers. Its commercial role, as the only UK broadcaster licensed by the General Post Office (GPO), which was responsible at that time for regulating the airwaves, was to drive consumer purchases of radios.[1]

In December 1922, the BBC – astonishingly – appointed as its general manager thirty-three-year-old Captain John Reith, a charismatic, six-foot-six-inches-tall Scottish Presbyterian Conservative with virtually no relevant experience but limitless self-belief, as he doubtless made clear at the interview.[2] The gamble paid off. Reith led the BBC until 1938 and it is still recognizably his creation. In particular, it was Reith who determined that its overall mission, even as a private company, should be public service, using its programmes to 'inform, educate and entertain' its audiences. This remains its mission today.

The initial funding for the service was provided from a royalty on the sale of radio sets from the six manufacturers in the consortium, but this proved insufficient as many listeners used unlicensed or home-made radios, and was soon replaced by an annual radio licence fee paid over the counter at post offices, broadly similar to today's TV licence fee. Any household with a working radio was legally required to have a licence.

Almost everything about the BBC – its funding, its scope and the nature and social and political effects of its programming – has always been contested, right from the start. For instance, concerns about its market impact go back to its foundation. To protect newspapers' revenue, it was banned from selling radio advertising and from presenting any news bulletins before 7 p.m. Initially, it was even required to source all its news from commercial wire services rather than setting up its own news-gathering operation.

In line with its mission, the BBC's programming was strongly skewed towards high culture. Reith believed that part of its role was to develop its listeners' tastes by offering them programmes *slightly* more demanding than they would have listened to if they'd had a choice. Even after the First World War, British society was still sufficiently deferential for this paternalistic approach to have been largely uncontroversial, although there was, as there always will be, a tension between challenging the audience and maximizing the number of listeners or viewers by giving them less demanding fare.

1927: The British Broadcasting Corporation

On 1 January 1927, the BBC became – as it still remains – the British Broadcasting *Corporation*, a statutory public Corporation with a Royal Charter[3] and therefore independent from direct government interference (although, as with all public institutions, especially public broadcasters, its relationship with the government and politicians is inherently problematic, as we'll discuss shortly).

The BBC Charter is reviewed every ten years or so. Under the current one, which runs from 1 January 2017 until 31 December 2027, the BBC:

- is governed by the BBC Board[4] and regulated by the communications regulator Ofcom;
- has five non-commercial divisions: Content (TV channels and programmes), Radio and Education, News and Current Affairs (including BBC Global

News), Nations and Regions and a group covering digital technology and services and functions such as research and development, finance, HR and property;

- has three commercial divisions: BBC Studios (TV production and international commercial activities), BBC World News (commercial TV news production and distribution) and BBC Studioworks (TV production facilities); and

- is funded by a combination of TV licence fees and the profits from its commercial activities.

The BBC is the original and archetypal public service broadcaster (PSB), that is, as a broadcaster managed and regulated to be universally available and to deliver explicit public service objectives in addition to those delivered by a purely commercial broadcaster, but editorially independent of government. Thanks to Reith, the BBC was a PSB under this definition even as a private company, as ITV and Channel 5 still are today. It is widely recognized as the most famous and prestigious PSB in the world; the biggest in terms of its international reach outside its home country, and, at least in broad terms, the model for PSBs around the world.

A PSB – Or a State Broadcaster?

A key issue is, inevitably, the BBC's relationship with the British government, especially the extent to which it really is an editorially independent PSB as opposed to a government-controlled state broadcaster. It is, of course, publicly owned and, as we've just described, it operates under a number of government-determined conditions – its periodically reviewed Charter and core funding, and much of its governance and regulation.

However, only the most paranoid conspiracy theorist would describe the BBC as a state broadcaster in the sense that, say, CCTV (China Central Television) or RT (formerly Russia Today) is a state broadcaster. CCTV is directly controlled by the Chinese state and the Communist Party (which itself controls the state) and explicitly works to their agenda.[6] RT is part of TV-Novosti, in principle an 'autonomous non-profit organization' but seen by almost everyone outside Russia as a government propaganda outlet and often accused of spreading disinformation, for example, about the Skripal poisonings in Salisbury.[6]

A closer case is the portfolio of international US-government-funded networks, such as Voice of America and Radio Free Europe, operated by the US Agency for Global Media (USAGM).[7] Long seen internationally as a US government propaganda vehicle, the USAGM is now also a domestic political issue because of two recent changes. First, since 2013, its services have been available within the US.[8] Secondly, since June 2020, its head has been Donald Trump's nominee Michael Pack, a conservative film-maker with close links to Trump's former chief strategist Steve Bannon (who we'll meet again in Chapter 14).[9] If Trump is re-elected in 2020, the chance of the USAGM *not* being widely seen as a Trump propaganda outlet is, in our view, close to zero.

As we'll discuss, the BBC has itself been repeatedly accused of peddling British state propaganda – or, at least, censoring information the UK government wanted suppressed – and not only by foreign demagogues and dictators. One critic was George Orwell, author of *Animal Farm* and *Nineteen Eighty-Four*, who worked there during the Second World War.[10]

George Orwell: From Catalonia to *Room 101*

In November 2017, a statue of Orwell was unveiled outside Broadcasting House, where he worked from August 1941 to November 1943.[11] Inscribed on the wall next to it is a quotation of his: 'If liberty means anything at all, it means the right to tell people what they do not want to hear.'[12]

Orwell is admired by people with strongly conflicting views – on the left and the right – who nevertheless often claim that, if he were alive today, he would agree with whatever it is they're saying.[13] (This includes his presumed views of the BBC now!)

He certainly hated his time working there during the war and resigned because he could no longer bear 'wasting my own time and the public money on doing work that produces no results'. However, that certainly doesn't mean he would have agreed with today's Beeb-bashers. His son, Richard Blair, present at the statue's unveiling, 'told reporters that although his father had a low opinion of public monuments in general, he might have made an exception: "I think secretly, shyly, he might have been chuffed"'.[14]

The BBC political journalist and presenter Andrew Marr said on Radio 4's *Start the Week* that the Orwell statue and quotation served as a challenge to today's BBC: 'We must do the job we do best, we must ask awkward questions, we must work harder'.[15] Orwell would surely have agreed. Let's look at how he ended up at the BBC in the first place and his legacy there.

In 1936, Orwell, a successful left-wing writer and critic and a self-described democratic socialist, approached Harry Pollitt, leader of the British Communist Party, to join the (Stalinist) International Brigade fighting Franco's Nationalists in the Spanish Civil War. However, Pollitt – astutely (and, in the event, correctly) – decided Orwell was 'politically unreliable' and turned him down,[16] so he ended up joining the much smaller (Trotskyist) *Partido Obrero de Unificacion Marxista* (POUM, or the (Spanish) Workers Party of Marxist Unification). By then, Stalin's secret police had already decided to 'liquidate' the POUM – their supposed Republican allies against Franco – which they did, with ruthless efficiency, during May and June 1937.[17]

Orwell, having been shot through the throat by a nationalist sniper, was lucky to survive and escape back to England. However, his powerful account of these experiences, *Homage to Catalonia*,[18] received mostly negative reviews, especially from left-wing reviewers, and initially sold just 638 copies.[19]

Unfit for military service because of serious respiratory problems (probably already including the TB that killed him in 1950),[20] Orwell worked at the BBC producing cultural broadcasts to India, where he had been born, with contributions from major figures such as T. S. Eliot, Dylan Thomas and E. M. Forster. He felt these broadcasts achieved little because their audiences were so small, but his main source of frustration was that, once the Soviet Union became Britain's ally after Hitler invaded it in June 1941, all negative media stories about the brutalities of Stalin's USSR were suppressed in the British media, including the BBC.

Reasonable people can disagree about whether Orwell was right to believe that the BBC should still have told the truth, the whole truth and nothing but the truth about Stalin's Soviet Union and the awkward fact that, until the June 1941 invasion, Nazi Germany and the USSR had been allies.[21] Britain and its empire and commonwealth had been losing the war, having stood alone against Hitler since the disastrous collapse of France during just six weeks from May to June of 1940, unable to match the Axis powers' military resources.[22] Nonetheless, the British had been able to reduce the military imbalance somewhat through their superior skills in code-breaking and spreading disinformation. The BBC was willingly used as a weapon in this information war, including by sending coded messages to resistance groups in occupied Europe which were embedded in its broadcasts.[23]

Meanwhile, Orwell had decided that fiction could be more powerful than facts in communicating the evils of totalitarianism.[24] From spring 1943, he started planning *Animal Farm*, which he completed in spring 1944, but was turned down by several publishers because of its clear attack on Stalin and the USSR. It was finally published in August 1945.

Four years on, in *Nineteen Eighty-Four*, his dystopian novel about what a Communist Britain might be like, Room 101 was the Party's basement torture chamber, where each prisoner was subjected to his or her own worst nightmare, fear or phobia.[25] The original Room 101 was alleged to have been the first floor BBC conference room used for politically vetting staff for far-left or far-right sympathies (on which Orwell doubtless had very mixed views).[26] *Room 101* was later the title of a BBC comedy show on radio (1992–4) and TV (1994–2007 and 2012–18) in which celebrities discussed their pet hates and tried to persuade the host to consign them to oblivion in an imaginary Room 101.

Orwell's experience at the BBC, and how it came to influence his fiction, which in turn influenced BBC programmes, is a good example of the type of cultural continuum the Corporation feeds into.

When the BBC Gets Caught in the Crossfire

We don't know how many people in Britain would have shared Orwell's view that the BBC (unlike British newspapers and book publishers) should have refused to censor its reporting and analysis of the Soviet Union after June 1941. But almost everyone would have agreed by then that the Third Reich had to be defeated. Overall, the BBC's role in maintaining morale and contributing to victory was non-controversial among the wider public.

The Corporation faces an even greater challenge when the country is deeply divided. In Chapter 9, we'll discuss the political minefield of Brexit and how the BBC has, and has not, managed to navigate it successfully. Previous such challenges include the

1956 Suez crisis, the Troubles and political violence in Northern Ireland, and Margaret Thatcher's industrial and labour market policies in the 1980s, especially the 1984–5 miners' strike.

But the most challenging case, at least until Brexit, was the 1926 General Strike, when the fledgling BBC was caught in the political crossfire. The facts of the General Strike, and the BBC's role in it, are well documented and not materially disputed.[27] But their interpretation is still contested nearly a century later.

The BBC's Reporting of the 1926 General Strike: Accurate – But How Impartial?[28]

The only newspapers available during the strike were the *British Gazette*, a government propaganda sheet, and the Trades Union Congress' *British Worker*. The agreement with the newspaper proprietors which prevented the still privately owned BBC from broadcasting news bulletins before 7 p.m. was temporarily waived. For the first time, it carried news bulletins throughout the day. The government pressurized it to act as a wireless version of the *British Gazette*, but Reith refused.

Winston Churchill, the hawkish chancellor, repeatedly advocated commandeering the BBC. He was overruled by the prime minister, Stanley Baldwin, and most of the Cabinet, but the threat of a government takeover was real throughout the strike. The *British Gazette* repeatedly attacked those parts of the BBC's output that were seen as unhelpful to the government, in a way we still see today.[29]

The outcome was a compromise. The BBC remained 'independent' – it was not commandeered by the government – but it was not wholly impartial. Its reporting was always accurate and it insisted on broadcasting the TUC's bulletins as well as those of the government. However, after Baldwin gave a broadcast to the nation – from Reith's own home and heavily coached by

him – Ramsay MacDonald, leader of the Opposition, was refused
the opportunity to put an alternative view. Reith had strongly
supported MacDonald's request, but was forced to back down
by Baldwin.

Reith's own allegiance was clear from his on-air comment
(after messages from Baldwin and the king) at the end of the
strike. It began, 'Our first feeling . . . must be one of profound
thankfulness to Almighty God, Who has led us through this
supreme trial with national health unimpaired'.[30]

Compare this to what Tom Mills says in his important account
of the BBC's political history, *The BBC: Myth of a Public Service*:
'the General Strike is a particularly *ignominious* episode in the
BBC's history, and it has rarely been quite so utterly subservient
to power, or so overtly partisan.'[31] Others might see this verdict
as unduly harsh in the circumstances.[32] Churchill's view was the
exact opposite of Mills': 'I first quarreled with Reith in 1926, during the General Strike. He behaved quite impartially between
the strikers and the nation. I said he had no right to be impartial
between the fire and the fire-brigade'.[33] This is an interesting parallel with Charlotte Higgins' view in her cultural history of the
BBC, *This New Noise: The Extraordinary Birth and Troubled Life of
the BBC*, that: 'The General Strike, the first great testing ground
for the BBC, showed how fragile its two great founding principles of impartiality and independence were in times of crisis or
conflict with the government'.[34] The BBC does not have an
unblemished record as an editorially independent PSB, and its
critics, including Orwell, often have good points to make. But,
typically, that didn't stop it from erecting a statue in his honour.

Accuracy and Impartiality

Mills' and Churchill's contrasting criticisms of the BBC's role
in the General Strike show the importance of distinguishing

between *accuracy* and *impartiality*. Where they differ is on
whether the BBC was *impartial*: Mills complains that it was not,
Churchill complains that it was, and should not have been. But
neither suggests that its coverage was *inaccurate*.

The BBC has almost never been accused of inaccurate reporting. The same is obviously not true of online media platforms
like Facebook and Twitter, which are exploited by a range of
state and non-state players for large-scale disinformation. But, to
a lesser extent, it is also not true of the right-wing tabloid newspapers (the *Sun*, the *Mail* and the *Express*) that are among the
BBC's most persistent enemies.

The BBC Today

If the BBC didn't already exist, we don't think it could be created today. Forcing almost every household to pay an annual tax
to fund a major new set of broadcast and online media services
is almost unthinkable, partly because the free market is now
seen as the default option for organizing everything, and partly
because existing media outlets would use their power to ensure
that such a potential new competitor was suppressed before it
ever got launched.

Luckily for us, the BBC had almost ten years as a TV broadcaster before the launch of commercial television in the UK – and
even this was highly regulated.[35] Sixty-five years later, we still
have a thriving mixed TV economy, albeit one in which most of
the revenue and three-quarters of the viewing now goes to commercial broadcasters.[36]

In contrast, in America, advertising-funded commercial TV
came first (as early as 1941)[37] and public service TV not until
thirteen years later, in 1954, ensuring that it never became a
major player.[38]

The media landscape in which the BBC operates is now

changing so fast that some people suggest that the Corporation cannot survive for long. It would be unrecognizable to Reith, and even Orwell might find much of it surprising (although perhaps not the scale of online personal data harvesting by both companies and states).

Nationalism versus Patriotism

As we will see, many of the criticisms against the BBC are politically and ideologically motivated. We are currently living through a period of widespread nationalism, including in Britain, with words like 'traitor', 'treason' and 'anti-British' regularly tumbling out of the mouths of the hard right. These are the same people who would love to see the BBC crumble.

With the 2019 UK election behind us, the Covid-19 pandemic still ongoing and Brexit continuing to cause rifts among voters – not to mention overshadowing all other issues that are important to people's lives, we turn again to Orwell, whose 1945 essay 'Notes on Nationalism' offers a perspective from an unthinkably (at least we hope it stays that way) different period when the rise of totalitarianism led people in Western democracies to ask: what does it mean to be patriotic? 'Nationalism', says Orwell, 'is the habit of identifying oneself with a single nation or other unit, placing it beyond good and evil and recognizing no other duty than that of advancing its interests.' He goes on to say that nationalism 'is not to be confused with patriotism'. The two could even be seen as conflicting ideas:

> By patriotism I mean devotion to a particular place and a particular way of life, which one believes to be the best in the world but has no wish to force on other people. Patriotism is of its nature defensive, both militarily and culturally. Nationalism, on the other hand, is inseparable from the desire for power.[39]

Although Orwell had been fiercely critical of the BBC and regarded his time spent there as wasted (but not actually harmful), we think he would have seen it as patriotically British, not as nationalistic propaganda like Soviet or Nazi broadcasting.

We'll return to these issues, and what we can do to keep the BBC a free-to-access, independent media service and broadcaster that touches all of our lives. But before we go any further, let's look at the media and technology context in which the BBC now operates.

2. The Media Landscape Today: A Netflix Universe?

'I say this in sadness,' reads the headline of an article by Stephen Glover in the 1 March 2018 *Daily Mail*, 'but unless the BBC gets its act together it may not be here in 15 years.'[1]

Glover – a co-founder of the centrist, or even the centre–left *Independent* in 1986,[2] but a *Daily Mail* columnist since 1998 – has written many Beeb-bashing articles there: in one, he criticized the appointment of 'former Labour cabinet member and "smoothie", James Purnell' as head of BBC Radio;[3] in another he describes a straw poll he had conducted among 'decent acquaintances' who had voted Labour in the 2017 general election: 'very few [had] the faintest notion of the disreputable causes [Jeremy Corbyn has] espoused . . . the terrorists he has succoured and the bloody hands he has shaken'. According to Glover, this knowledge gap 'must in large measure be attributed to the journalistic failures of the all-powerful BBC'.[4]

The tone of his 1 March 2018 article ('I say this in sadness, but . . . ') suggests mixed, rather than purely hostile feelings about the BBC – including genuine regret at the threats to it posed by the technology and consumption trends he discusses.[5] His article starts with two important questions, both highly relevant to this book: 'Can the BBC survive as a national institution commanding widespread respect? And, in an age of media behemoths such as Netflix, will the relatively small Corporation become irrelevant?' It describes these as questions that 'anyone who feels affection for the BBC, as I do despite everything' is bound to ask, adding, 'To say Auntie has an existential crisis is no exaggeration'.[6]

We will look at Glover's first question, about whether the BBC can survive as a national institution, at other points in this book. For now, let's take up his question about the current media landscape.

The US 'Media Behemoths'

Glover suggests that the BBC is becoming more remote from the public at a time 'when most young people aren't watching terrestrial television, or listening to radio news'. His last five paragraphs refer to Netflix, Comcast and Disney – 'ruthless American mega-companies that dwarf Auntie' – and raise the question of whether the 'fuddy-duddy, stuck in the past, intro-verted' BBC can survive.[7]

Well, we think the 'fuddy-duddy, stuck in the past, intro-verted' BBC is considerably better prepared than Glover and many others suggest to adapt to, and in some cases exploit, these trends (which are in reality a much more serious threat to the *Daily Mail* and other 'legacy' newspapers). Nevertheless, we agree that they pose very serious challenges and will require a skilful, vigorous, agile and continually evolving response – not only from the BBC, but also from other UK broadcasters, regu-lators and – most importantly – legislators, since the key issue is whether the Corporation will have the resources it needs to compete successfully in this new world.

What Is the Threat to the BBC?

Ever since the birth of Hollywood over a century ago, the US has been in a league of its own in global media. But the UK is also a major player – the world's second biggest exporter of TV programmes and the biggest exporter of TV formats (that is, the rights to make local versions of programmes such as *Who Wants to Be a Millionaire?*, *Top Gear*, *The Great British Bake Off*, *Strictly Come Dancing*, etc.).[8] As well as the BBC, there are several other global UK media brands such as *MailOnline*, *The Guardian* and the *Economist*, but the BBC is by far the most important – which is one reason why the war against it in the UK is so paradoxical.

The BBC, ITV and Channel 4 are still UK-owned,[9] as are most UK commercial radio stations, national and local newspapers[10] and small TV production companies. Foreign-owned TV companies in this market now include Sky (Comcast), Virgin Media (Liberty Global), Channel 5 (Viacom), most cable and satellite TV channels (A&E, Discovery, Disney, Fox, Paramount, Warner, etc.) and most large, independent TV production companies.[11]

However, US (and other foreign)[12] ownership of UK media may not in itself be a threat to the BBC. If anything, it strengthens the case for well-funded, British-owned media, including the BBC, to ensure a continuing supply of UK content for UK viewers and listeners. For instance, CBBC and CBeebies are now almost the only TV channels still showing British programmes for British children,[13] as opposed to the commercial children's channels from Disney, Paramount, Turner and others, where the content is mostly American and interrupted by frequent advertising breaks.[14]

The globalization of media also creates opportunities for the BBC. Most of BBC Studios' growing profits (reinvested in original UK content, supplementing the licence fee) are from international programme and format sales.[15]

The Subscription Video-on-Demand Invasion

Rather than globalization *per se*, the big new competitive threat to all UK broadcasters – not just the BBC – comes from online 'subscription video-on-demand' (SVoD) services and advertising-funded online video services from Facebook and YouTube. The first wave of these came from global *technology*, as opposed to media companies, especially the so-called FAANGs: Facebook, Amazon, Apple, Netflix and Google. These, too, are all US-based, but their main roots are in Silicon Valley (and Seattle, a two-hour flight to the north) – a quite different world to New York or Los Angeles, the traditional US centres of media and entertainment activity. All the FAANGs now have online TV/video services, although their business models and how we use them vary greatly.[16]

Netflix is the only 'pure' online TV firm among them: its business model is now entirely based on SVoD, making it as much a media company as a technology company. According to its chief content officer, Ted Sarandos, it aims to 'keep a foot firmly rooted in Silicon Valley and a foot in Hollywood'.[17] In contrast, Amazon's SVoD service is part of the Amazon Prime package for which UK members pay £9.99 per month, mainly for faster and/or free product delivery. Similarly, Apple's SVoD service is part of its broader 'ecosystem' of premium products (like the iPhone) and services (like Apple Music). Conversely, Facebook and Google are 'free' services funded by advertising. Facebook's business model is based on display advertising, including video, embedded in its social media services – Facebook, Instagram, Snapchat and WhatsApp. Google's main revenue source is online search advertising but it also owns YouTube, the dominant global video-hosting service, funded mainly by display advertising.[18]

Initially, the Hollywood studios saw royalties from these online streaming services as a welcome source of incremental revenue from their content, including their vast back catalogues. More recently, however, they have started seeing the FAANGs as competitors and have stopped signing new deals to supply them, devising ways to generate income directly from consumers instead.

At the time of writing, Disney is about to launch its family-focused S VoD service, Disney+, in the U K. Its recent $71 billion takeover of 21st Century Fox's entertainment business[19] also doubles (to 60 per cent) its stake in Hulu, another S VoD service based on general-audience T V shows. Hulu is currently available only in the US and Japan, but it is expected to launch in the UK in 2020, as may a version of Disney's ESPN+ US sports streaming service. AT&T (Warner Media/HBO) and Comcast (NBCUniversal) are also about to launch S VoD services.

In response to these changes, Netflix, Amazon and Apple are having to invest in their own, exclusive, original content – at enormous cost. Amazon and Apple have very deep pockets, filled elsewhere, but Netflix's continuing 'cash burn' (negative cash flow) – still hundreds of millions of dollars per quarter – is adding more and more to its already huge debt mountain. Some investors are sceptical about whether it will ever be able to repay this and generate dividends for its shareholders, especially since the S VoD market is now becoming so very crowded as the traditional media giants launch their own services.[20] Nevertheless, the chances are that this means most viewers will have more and more choice and this will increasingly be delivered online. And, meanwhile, the big US-based video-on-demand (VoD) services are already putting pressure on the BBC and other UK broadcasters.

How the VoD Services Are Driving Up Costs

All the FAANGs are now investing in content for their VoD services. Netflix alone invested an estimated $13 billion (£10 billion) in new programming in 2018.[21] Its priority is to create programmes with international appeal, especially drama, films and scripted comedy. According to Sarandos, 'our belief is that great storytelling transcends borders'.[22] Other key Netflix genres include documentaries, 'unscripted' reality shows such as *Queer Eye* and stand-up comedy.

Netflix does not yet show news, live events or sport, as these tend to have less international appeal and no shelf-life, so aren't suited to its consumer model – customers who download programmes from a library and watch them in their own time. However, some expansion into these genres is quite likely as broadband gets faster and cheaper, making large-scale simultaneous streaming smoother and more cost-effective.[23] Amazon Prime Video and Facebook Watch already show some live sports.[24]

Sarandos summarizes Netflix's growth model as 'More shows, more watching; more watching, more [subscriptions]; more [subscriptions], more revenue; more revenue, more content'.[25] This model reflects the classic business strategies and 'winner-takes-all' economics of technology platforms, with market leaders often enjoying ever-increasing advantage unless and until a radical new technology completely disrupts or replaces the market.[26] He could have added 'more data' to his explanation. Netflix has detailed data on subscribers' viewing. It mainly uses this to personalize which shows are most prominent on home screens: past viewing is much more reliable than demographics as a predictor of future viewing.[27] Netflix generates huge publicity around its so-called 'original content', which plays a disproportionate role in driving its relentless growth. In fact, according to TV analyst Ampere, Netflix's highly promoted 'original' programmes such as *The Crown*, *Orange Is the New Black* and the US remake of *House of Cards* account for only 8 per cent of its viewing hours.[28] But Netflix also uses a rather elastic definition of 'original', much exaggerating (at least, by implication) the proportion of content it commissions itself. For instance, *Bodyguard* was commissioned by the BBC and produced by an ITV subsidiary. Netflix then bought the rights for most overseas territories, where it markets the show as a 'Netflix Original'.[29]

The Impact on Costs: 'It's Not Just the Netflix Effect'

One British TV and film producer, speaking anonymously in late 2018, summarized the SVoD services' impact on content costs as follows:

> [Netflix has] inflated prices for established talent, so big-name writers, actors and directors can be paid very large fees to do TV shows. And the tendency has been to draw those people away from the terrestrial channels. So there is a . . . talent drain from the UK to America . . . Over the past year, [UK] costs have probably risen between 15 per cent and 20 per cent: and some of that is the Netflix effect. But it's not just the Netflix effect; it's also the Amazon effect; and other global players.[30]

These figures may be overstated but, directionally, there is no question that the SVoD services are bidding up the cost of content. The BBC and other UK broadcasters also now have to support a much wider range of technologies and distribution channels (both old and new) than before, to reach viewers and remain competitive against the FAANGs.[31] This further increases costs.

The net effect of these trends is that all UK broadcasters' like-for-like (real, inflation-adjusted) content costs, especially in genres such as premium drama, are rising fast, while they are also having to spend more on technology and distribution, and, to a lesser extent, marketing, in response to the ever-increasing level of competition. This is putting severe pressure on programme budgets and, in particular, making it harder for the PSBs to deliver their public service remits.

Differing Tax Burdens and Levels of Regulation

Because the FAANGs find it relatively easy to shift their (taxable) accounting profits offshore, they pay minimal UK tax on their earnings.[32] They are also relatively lightly regulated. This gives them a competitive advantage over the UK broadcasters, especially the PSBs, which pay UK tax and operate under multiple regulations: each PSB has a detailed remit, overseen by Ofcom, as part of its operating licence (in the BBC's case, the public purposes in its Charter). This covers the range of content (programme mix), the sources of content (London, other UK, imports), broad guidelines on diversity and so on.[33] Because it receives the licence fee, the BBC is even more tightly regulated than the other UK PSBs. For instance, it has a 50 per cent quota for non-London production (half of the network budget must be spent and half of the hours broadcast must be outside the M25). (The equivalent quota for ITV and Channel 4 is 35 per cent and 10 per cent for Channel 5.)[34]

The BBC's ability to offer new services or platforms or improve current ones is also significantly hampered by the current Charter, which requires its board to consider the impact on the rest of the market of all service innovations. This requires doing a formal 'public interest test' for any new service or any change to an existing service deemed by Ofcom to be 'material'. The question posed is whether, in Ofcom's view, the expected public value of the proposed innovation outweighs any expected negative impact on the BBC's competitors. For example, when in 2018 the BBC wanted to change iPlayer so that programmes would be watchable for longer, and that selected box sets and further archive content would be made available, it had to conduct a 'market impact assessment', open its proposals to feedback from anyone – industry or the public – who wanted to weigh in, and then wait *a year* until Ofcom allowed it to proceed with the service improvements. These merely brought the iPlayer into line with the rest of the market and viewers' expectations. The big competitors – Netflix, Amazon and so on – face no comparable regulation and update their platforms on almost a *weekly* basis.[35]

We'll be returning to the question of whether these concerns over the BBC's market impact are justified. But to say that this type of regulation to protect competitors is alien to Silicon Valley would be an understatement. In the words of Peter Thiel, cofounder of PayPal, 'Competition is for losers. If you want to create and capture lasting value, look to build a monopoly'.[36] Similarly, Facebook was built under Mark Zuckerberg's famous former motto, 'Move fast and break things'.[37]

The Potential Impact on the BBC

As discussed, although the FAANGs do not compete directly against the BBC for revenue – they have no access to the licence fee – they are already significantly driving up its (and other UK broadcasters') content, technology and distribution costs.

Additionally, SVoD players (both the FAANGs and traditional media companies) directly compete for subscriptions against pay-TV companies like Sky.[38] Similarly, Facebook and Google compete, a bit less directly, for advertising against ITV, Channel 4, and other commercial TV companies.[39] Therefore they are a much bigger *direct* threat to commercial broadcasters and other media funded by subscriptions and advertising than they are to the BBC.

In principle, a longer-term threat is that the proportion of homes with TV sets is falling as more people watch only on PCs and mobile devices. So far, the reduction in TV ownership has been small, from 96.4 per cent of UK households in 2011–12 to 95.3 per cent in 2019.[40] Over time, however, there are two reasons why the SVoD players are likely to become a bigger threat to the BBC's revenue.

First, the availability of SVoD services such as Netflix, with prices starting as low as £5.99 per month for the basic package (and even less for some other SVoD services),[41] may erode viewers' willingness to pay the £13.13 per month licence fee (figures are correct for 2020).

Secondly, although Stephen Glover's statement that 'most young people aren't watching terrestrial television' was overstated, the proportion of viewing going to non-broadcast sources, especially among younger viewers, is already substantial and seems likely to keep growing, putting further indirect pressure on the long-term revenue of *all* UK broadcasters, including the BBC.[42]

These are certainly threats, but it's important to remember the BBC has always been able to respond to technological changes – it has a long and strong record of engineering research and successful innovation. Like Netflix, it has always been a technology player as well as a media player. As we have seen, ever since its launch in 1922 by a consortium of radio-set manufacturers, a formal part of its role has been to help drive mass consumer take-up of new technologies, mainly through its content and services, supported by significant research and development.

The BBC has repeatedly been an early mover with new technologies, including television in the early 1950s, which took off with its televising of the Queen's Coronation in 1953, and, via BBC Two, colour TV in the 1960s.[43] Then it was personal computers (the BBC Micro) in the early 1980s, FM radio from the late 1980s,[44] the internet (BBC Online) and digital terrestrial TV (DTT) in the 1990s and online TV (the BBC iPlayer) since 2007. The BBC has also repeatedly had to adapt to increasing competition – most dramatically sixty years ago, in the mid and late 1950s, when the launch of ITV ended its television monopoly. The Catch-22 is that the more successfully the BBC competes – by innovating, engaging viewers, listeners and online users, and increasing the value for money it gives licence-fee payers – the more complaints there are from its competitors about its market impact. In fact, the reason why the UK commercial video on demand market was left largely open to the FAANGs is that when, early on in the new millennium – well ahead of the curve – the BBC, ITV and Channel 4 proposed a UK commercial VoD service, 'Project Kangaroo', it was short-sightedly blocked by the Competition Commission, the UK competition authority,[45] after intensive lobbying by the non-PSBs (Sky and Virgin Media) and some now long-forgotten SVoD start-ups (Babelgum and Joost).

Project Kangaroo

In 2007 the BBC, ITV and Channel 4 announced a proposed VoD joint venture codenamed Project Kangaroo. The aim was to create a single user interface and 'one-stop-shop' giving viewers online access to the three partners' archival content and, potentially, additional third-party content. About 90 per cent would be offered free, funded by advertising. The rest would be available to rent or buy.[46]

However, in June 2008, the government's Office of Fair Trading (OFT)[47] referred the project to the Competition Commission for an investigation into its potential impact on the market. The panel appointed to the case comprised a chartered accountant with an MBA, a banker specializing in corporate finance and energy markets, and a macroeconomist. None of them, to our knowledge, had any significant prior expertise in media, technology or audience/consumer behaviour.

To understand how they came to get things so wrong, you need a bit of background on the esoteric world of market regulation, where the competition authorities have to rule on whether a company has, or is likely to have, too much market power.[48]

Defining the 'Relevant Market'

In assessing a competition case, a key task is to define the so-called 'relevant market' within which each competitor's market share (and, by implication, market power) will be assessed: the bigger the 'relevant market', the lower each company's market share and the less need there is to worry about its market power because consumers are likely to have plenty of choice if they don't like any particular company's product or service. For example, a company with £100 million annual turnover would be seen as having a dominant – and worrying – 67 per cent market share if the relevant market is defined narrowly as only £150 million per annum. But if the market is defined more broadly, so that the total market size is £1.5 billion per annum, the company's market share would be only 6.7 per cent and unlikely to cause major anti-competitive problems.

To define the relevant market, however, the panel often has to make a difficult judgement about, essentially, which other brands consumers might buy if they didn't purchase the investigated company's one. For that judgement to be good enough to form the basis of a ruling, it needs to draw on a detailed understanding of real-world consumer behaviour within the particular context. For instance, one of the authors of this book acted as an expert witness in a competition case some years ago about 'impulse ice cream' – individual products such as Unilever's Magnum[49] sold in small convenience outlets for immediate consumption. The market definition hinges on issues around what consumers might buy if they didn't buy one of the Unilever ice creams: how likely would they be to buy confectionery or a soft drink, say, as opposed to a competitor's ice cream?

Unfortunately, it seems that no one on the Project Kangaroo panel had the necessary understanding of how audiences choose TV platforms and programmes. The panel therefore defined the relevant market extremely narrowly, excluding not only live and time-shifted[50] TV programmes, but also films, short-form videos, DVDs and – crucially – all non-UK content. They also saw little benefit in the PSBs offering a one-stop-shop for their archival content, deciding instead that viewers would be better off (despite the greater complexity and inconvenience) if the three partners ran competing services.

Leaving the Market Open to the FAANGs

On this basis, the panel blocked the new venture, explaining that, 'After detailed and careful consideration, we have decided that this joint venture would be too much of a threat to competition in this developing market and has to be stopped'.[51]

No one knows how successful Project Kangaroo would have been if it had not been blocked. But the Competition Commission's February 2009 decision left the UK SVoD market almost completely open to the FAANGs[52] until the November 2019 launch of BritBox, a joint venture between the BBC, ITV, Channel 4 and Channel 5 – broadly, Project Kangaroo by another name, ten years too late.[53] By then, Netflix, YouTube and Amazon had had plenty of time to build their dominant position in the UK market.[54]

The Constraint Is Funding

BBC Director-General Tony Hall spelt out the Corporation's broader response to the challenges discussed here in a speech to the Royal Television Society in September 2018, saying that the Corporation would: increase investment in quality British content across the full range of programme genres and keep reinventing services; the iPlayer would evolve more broadly from a catch-up service to a destination for all the BBC's long-form, short-form and live TV and video; and iPlayer radio would similarly become a go-to destination for audio content (BBC Sounds).[55]

He also said the BBC would invest more in content and services for children and young adults, sustain investment in BBC News and actively counter disinformation and fake news in the UK and globally. Finally, he pledged to increase commissioning outside London (already over 50 per cent) to ensure that the benefits are widely shared across the UK.

Technology developments, and consumers' response to them, are inherently unpredictable and hard to manage. Nevertheless, based on its long record of successful innovation, all the actions listed in Hall's speech are well within the BBC's capability, but they all need resources. The main constraint on the BBC's ability to respond effectively to the technology challenge is funding. Even in a world of proliferating distribution channels, the scarcest resource is still great programmes – the BBC's forte. As we'll show in Chapter 4 – and despite endless claims to the contrary – the BBC is extremely good at turning its limited income into great content. The problem is that its public funding has been massively cut – by 30 per cent in real terms between 2010 and 2019, with serious threats of further cuts to come – just as content and distribution costs are relentlessly increasing. The BBC can look for continuing efficiency gains and commercial income growth to soften the impact. But, as we'll see, there isn't much fat to cut: after two decades of year-on-year efficiency gains, the BBC is now firmly in the top quartile (25 per cent) of comparable organizations on the key efficiency measure of total overheads as a percentage of revenue – which is to say that it is, by and large, using the money it gets wisely. There will always be scope for further gains, but less and less each year. Having, rightly, first exploited the best opportunities for generating international revenue from its programmes and formats, it is now starting to find it harder to generate further increases in commercial income. The cumulative impact of the 2010 and 2015 funding settlements, which we'll describe more fully in Chapter 5, represents a more direct, and much bigger threat to the BBC than that posed by Netflix and the other US tech and media giants.

3.   'What Have the Romans Ever Done for Us?'

'All right, but apart from the sanitation, the medicine, education, wine, public order, irrigation, roads, a fresh water system
and public health, what have the Romans ever done for us?'[1]

To watch live television in the UK on any device, your household must have a TV licence. The current annual licence fee, for
those who have to pay it, is £157.50, equivalent to 43 pence per
day. That's £3.03 per household per week: enough to buy one
household member one pint of standard (not premium) lager or
bitter a week in almost any pub in the country – provided they
did not also want a packet of crisps.

Despite these low financial stakes – and the BBC's contrast-
ingly huge, central role in British culture, society, democracy
and international standing – much of the policy discussion
around it is about money and led by economists. There are also
some big myths about these issues. We'll discuss several of these
issues and explode the biggest myths. First, in this chapter, we
look at what households actually get for their 43p-per-day licence
fee. In the next one, we'll look at the closely related issue of how
efficiently the BBC spends the licence-fee income it receives.
Further on, in Chapter 10, we'll also look at the pros and cons of
the licence fee as a way of funding the BBC, including alternatives such as advertising and subscriptions. This is important
because, as we'll explain, the disadvantages of the licence fee
have been much exaggerated or misunderstood, while the disadvantages of replacing it with either advertising or subscriptions
are much bigger than most people realize. But for now, the question is what licence-fee payers get for their money under the
current system.

What Does the TV-Licence Fee Give You?

The 43p-per-day TV-licence fee gives everyone in the household unlimited access to:

- Six main national TV channels: BBC One, BBC Two, BBC Four, CBBC, CBeebies, the BBC News Channel, plus BBC Parliament
- Thirteen regional TV news programmes and some other regional programmes
- Ten national and forty local radio stations
- A wide range of online services including the BBC iPlayer and Sounds app, BBC Three (which, to save money, has been online-only since February 2016) and BBC Online, by far the most popular UK-owned website,[2] especially for news, sport and weather reports.

Households in Scotland, Wales and Northern Ireland receive additional services including the Welsh language BBC Cymru (TV and radio), the Scottish Gaelic BBC Alba (TV) and *nan Gaidheal* (radio) and, since February 2019, an additional English-language BBC Scotland TV channel.[3]

All these services are 'free at the point of use' for people in households with a current TV licence. But how many British households actually use them, and how much?

Usage of the BBC's UK Services

Households' usage of the BBC can be broken down into 'reach' (the percentage of households in which at least one person uses the BBC's services at all within a given time period) and 'user-hours per household' (the average total individual usage time per household over the same time period). Both are important:

household reach for fairness; user-hours per household for value for money.

Household Reach: The Myth of Households That Don't Use the BBC

Many critics' main objection to the licence fee is that it is compulsory: even households that don't use the BBC's services still have to pay for them. That's equally true for almost all tax-funded public services – schools, hospitals, social services – for all of which the amounts of money are, of course, much higher.

But, even more important, in the case of the BBC, the unfairness *in principle* of households paying the licence fee but getting no benefit from it turns out in practice to be almost entirely mythical because, even in a single week, 99 per cent of households consume at least some BBC services.[4] Even at the individual level, 91 per cent of people use one or more of the BBC's services in the average week.[5]

The licence fee gives the whole household access to all the BBC's UK services for a whole year. The idea that it disadvantages a significant number of households by forcing them to pay it without getting any benefit is complete nonsense.

User-hours per Household

The more practically relevant question is therefore *how much* benefit licence-fee payers get from it, relative to the cost. In thinking about this, a good place to start is the average weekly user-hours per household. Dividing the £3.03 weekly cost of the licence fee by this weekly usage measure gives us the cost per user-hour – a useful broad-brush indicator of the value for money of the licence fee for the average household.

31

Despite the growing competition from new online services (SVoD and commercial audio podcasts), in 2018–19, the average UK adult aged sixteen-plus in a household with a TV watched BBC Television for 7.6 hours, listened to BBC Radio for 9.55 hours and used BBC Online for 0.9 hours, giving a total of just over 18 hours a week consuming BBC services.[6] With an average of 1.93 adults per household,[7] this gives a total average of 35 adult user-hours per household per week, excluding consumption by household members aged under sixteen.

With a licence fee of £3.03 per week, this means the average cost per adult user-hour was therefore just 8.7p, with no charge for the under-sixteens. There aren't many things you can do for just under 9p per hour.

This is the overall hourly cost of consuming the BBC's services, averaged across the three media. But at least as important as this objective summary measure is the BBC's *perceived* value for money, on which we also have a lot of evidence. The strongest is from a study conducted in 2015.

Perceived Value for Money: The 2015 'BBC Deprivation' Study

No one likes paying taxes, but the TV licence fee is a partial exception: *most* people see it as providing good value for money – despite endless hostile stories over the years about the Corporation's alleged profligacy and inefficiency. And, the more time they have to think about it, the more likely they are to say that the licence fee offers good value. To test this, in 2015 the BBC commissioned market research agency MTM to explore how people's views of the value for money offered by the licence fee might change if they were 'forced' to spend some time without the BBC.[8] The study, described more fully in Appendix A, focused especially on the minority of households (28 per cent) who, in an initial survey, said that the licence fee – then £145.50, equivalent to 40p per day – did *not* offer good value for money.[9] After nine days with no BBC, and having then received a cash payment of £3.60 (i.e. 9 x 40p) in return, over two-thirds of these households[10] changed their minds and decided that the licence fee did represent good value for money after all.

The reasons they gave were that: they missed the BBC much more in their daily routines than they had expected; felt that it had unique content and services that they could not get elsewhere; realized that it provided a high level of quality versus the alternatives, more than they had previously appreciated; became frustrated at the amount of advertising on other services; were surprised by the range of BBC services (not all had known that BBC Radio and Online were included in the cost of the TV licence fee); and felt that the BBC played a more important role in UK life and the national conversation than they had realized.

For instance, in the initial survey, one participant who said that he would prefer to pay nothing and receive no BBC services explained that, 'I think it's awful because the way I look at it is that I pay for Sky already . . . I think it's unfair. Everybody is moving with the times, and the BBC still . . . expects us to pay £145, £149 yearly . . . for what?' As one of the two-thirds of initially anti-BBC respondents who changed their minds during the study, he commented at the end, 'That's for nine days? . . . £3.60 for nine days? That's peanuts really . . . In all honesty we do get a wealth of good programmes [and] it is an integral part of our everyday existence . . . It would be weird if there was [*sic*] no BBC channels.'[11]

So, even in pure consumer terms – that is, considering the BBC simply as a consumer service supplier – UK households get a lot of TV, radio and online content for their 43p per day (or for nothing if they have a free TV licence). In properly conducted surveys based on nationally representative samples, about 70 per cent say they see the licence fee as good value for money in response to a neutrally worded question – and, in the one study to date on those who initially disagreed with this, from 2015, two-thirds of them changed their minds after living without the BBC for just nine days.

The BBC's 'Citizenship' and Economic Contributions

However, the BBC isn't just a 'consumer service provider'. It is also one of Britain's most important social, cultural and political institutions. Its many 'citizenship' or 'public service' contributions are broadly summarized in its overall mission to inform, educate and entertain. The Charter sets out more fully the BBC's mission and public purposes, and sits alongside its Agreement – a kind of contract between the Culture Secretary and the BBC, with further detail on topics such as the BBC's funding and regulatory duties. The five public purposes in its Charter require it to: provide impartial news and information; support learning for people of all ages; show 'the most creative, highest quality and distinctive' output and services; reflect, represent and serve the diverse communities of all the UK's nations and regions and support the creative economy countrywide; and reflect the UK, its culture and values to the world.[12]

Many would argue that these wider public service contributions are even more important than its direct consumer value – although this begs many questions. What is indisputable is that, for a complete answer to the question 'What has the BBC ever done for us?' we need to incorporate these broader contributions. Moreover, the BBC does not exist in isolation: it sits at the heart of the UK's very successful and highly competitive, broadcasting ecosystem and the wider creative industries. It is by far the biggest investor in original British TV programmes and, especially, radio programmes, and in both formal and informal broadcast industry training: the training organization known as the Federation of Entertainment Unions (FEU) has described its staff training and experience as 'unrivalled'.[13] These contributions have helped make the UK the world's second largest exporter of TV programmes after the US, and the Number One exporter of TV programme formats.[14]

The BBC supports all the arts and creative industries, but it has a particularly important role in music. Through Radios 1 and 3, 6 Music, its five orchestras, three choirs, the BBC Big Band and its sponsorship and coverage of The Proms (the largest classical music festival in the world), the Glastonbury Festival (the largest green field music festival in the world) and televised events such as *BBC Young Musician of the Year* and *Cardiff Singer of the World*, it supports established and emerging musicians and composers across both classical and popular genres. In 1904, the German music critic Oscar Schmitz famously dismissed England as 'the land without music'.[15] This was somewhat overstated even then, but would be laughable today. We would argue that the BBC is the single biggest reason why.

Through its purchases of content and services, the BBC also makes a disproportionate contribution to the wider UK economy. In 2010, global accountancy and consulting group Deloitte estimated its 'Gross Value Added' (GVA) – the standard measure of an organization's economic contribution – at £7.7 billion in 2008–9.[16] By 2011–12, this had increased to £8.3 billion,[17] meaning that the Corporation generated about two pounds of economic value for every pound of the licence fee.[18] A 2015 study by Deloitte's competitor PwC using different measures and methodology suggests that this may even have been an underestimate, although the results are not directly comparable.[19] What is not in dispute is that the BBC contributes hugely to the UK broadcasting ecology and wider creative industries.

Finally, not all of the money from the licence fee goes to the BBC's UK services. Some of it is used to fund or subsidize the BBC World Service and a range of government activities. This goes back to an initial grab from the licence-fee pot by Chancellor Gordon Brown.

Gordon Brown's Raid on the BBC's Income to Fund Digital TV Switchover

In 2006, Brown 'top-sliced' the BBC's licence-fee income, diverting some of it to support households during the switchover from analogue to digital TV through a combination of an integrated communications campaign and the provision of free digital set-top boxes and advice to the elderly and vulnerable. Despite this additional burden and the £450 million cost of the planned move of a significant part of BBC production to Salford to boost the Greater Manchester creative economy, Brown did not award licence-fee increases above the rate of inflation.

The BBC-led digital TV switchover campaign was extremely successful. First, it enabled the old analogue TV distribution network to be switched off on time in October 2012. The Treasury (by then under George Osborne) then auctioned the released electromagnetic spectrum[20] for £2.34 billion.[21] The switchover campaign also came in well under budget – but, rather than allowing the BBC to invest the £334 million under-spend on programmes and services, Osborne 'repurposed' it to support another government project, broadband roll-out.[22]

The total estimated cost to the BBC of the TV switchover to digital was £600 million over six years from 2006 to 2012 – in other words the Corporation had roughly £100 million a year less to spend on broadcasting during this time.

The switchover to digital TV was a one-off project but it set a precedent – using licence-fee money for purposes other than funding the BBC's UK services – that has been followed by later governments.

The BBC World Service

Since 2014, the licence fee has provided the main income of the BBC World Service – formerly funded by the Foreign & Commonwealth Office as a part of the UK's foreign policy – at an annual cost of £325 million.[23] The World Service has a global weekly reach of 426 million viewers and listeners outside the UK – an increase of 50 million in a year[24] – and is valued around the world for trust, independence and reliability. The annual ranking of different countries' 'soft power' by Portland Communications, a political consultancy and public relations agency, still rates the UK as the best news source, despite the uncertainties created by Brexit. It specifically mentions the BBC World Service, alongside other institutions such as our top universities, as an important driver of this continuing reputational success.[25] The BBC World Service is highly effective at helping the UK government deliver its foreign policy objectives.

Other Government Activities Now Funded Out of TV Licence-fee Income

In 2020, the licence fee also provides most or all of the funding for the following: the Welsh language TV channel S4C (from 2022, the BBC will be paying the full £83 million annual cost);[26] BBC Monitoring;[27] the Local News Partnerships;[28] and a £60 million 'contestable' fund for children's TV (a contestable fund is one which allocates money in response to competitive bids), again 'repurposed' from the broadband fund. The BBC is now virtually the sole UK supplier of public service TV programmes for UK children. Commercial broadcasters and producers (potentially including Netflix and Amazon) will be able to bid for cash from the fund.[29]

However, as we'll discuss, by far the most expensive 'citizen-ship' benefit funded by those households paying the licence fee is the free TV licence concession for all the households that *don't* pay it. George Osborne's decision in 2015 to force the BBC to take responsibility for this concession for households was easily the most damaging example of the government raiding the BBC's income to fund a welfare benefit that should be funded out of general taxation.

Maybe Not as Wasteful and Inefficient as People Say?

We've seen how much households get for the 43p-per-day licence fee (or for nothing if they receive the free TV licence conces-sion); how much they use the BBC's services; how most people think the licence fee represents good value for money and even more so after living without the BBC for a few days; how the BBC also provides many public service benefits, sits at the heart of the UK broadcasting ecology and contributes significantly to the creative industries and the wider economy; and how it achieves all this, despite the licence fee now funding or subsidiz-ing the BBC World Service and a growing range of other government activities.

This remarkable value for money raises the question of whether the BBC is as spendthrift as it's portrayed by its enemies. Is the BBC really wasting your money? That's the topic of the next chapter.

4.   '£230,000 . . . on TEA'

A perennial criticism of the BBC is that it is bloated and inefficient, overpaying its executives and presenters and routinely wasting licence-payers' money. In this chapter, we'll test the validity of these charges with a detailed analysis of articles in Paul Dacre's *Daily Mail* in 2015 – part of the intensive right-wing attack on the BBC during the last Charter renewal – purporting to prove that the Corporation was every bit as bloated and inefficient as its critics claimed. Most such attacks are purely anecdotal, based on how much a particular executive spent on taxis, dinners or hotels, how many people the BBC sent to cover a music festival, or whatever. In contrast, this article was presented as a serious attempt to evaluate its overall efficiency, using real numbers.

'BBC Spends Less Than Half Its Cash on Programmes'

On 15 June 2015, the headline on page six of the *Daily Mail* was 'BBC spends less than half its cash on programmes: Critics demand inquiry into "staggering" waste' – to which the online edition added, '. . . as it's revealed £230,000 of licence-fee money was spent on TEA'.

The article that followed was by Katherine Rushton, the *Mail*'s media and technology editor and a prolific Beeb-basher, and Daniel Martin, its chief political correspondent. Its stand-out 'revelation' was that 'just £2.4 billion of [the BBC's] £5.1 billion annual budget went on "public service content" in the year to April 2014', most of the rest having been 'swallowed up by costs that included running its ostentatious buildings, middle-managers and services such as human resources and marketing'.

The Corporation also supposedly 'pumped money into its commercial arm, BBC Worldwide, and BBC Global News, producing content for audiences overseas'. But 'only £217 million was spent on the essential job of actually transmitting the programmes around Britain'. As we'll see, these statements are misleading in several ways. They include treating the £1.1 billion *turnover* (not the £174 million *profit contribution*) of the BBC's international commercial operations as if it were part of the 'budget' of its UK public service operation; 'forgetting' that a proportion of licence-fee income is 'top-sliced' to fund other government activities; and ignoring inconvenient facts such as that the BBC's overhead costs are actually *below* the industry average.

A large box headlined 'How They Fritter Away Licence Fee' listed seventeen examples of the BBC's alleged inefficiency and profligacy: the '£48,000 cost of a sofa and fake television studio set at [the BBC's new] Salford HQ', the revelation that '12 managers in BBC TV [had] the word "Controller" in their job title', and so on – including the Corporation's supposedly lavish expenditure on tea. The article included a photo of Tory MP Bill Cash with his mouth open and quoted him as saying, 'It's just mind-blowing. I can't begin to imagine how they can justify it. This revelation demonstrates the need for a radical overhaul of the BBC. The matter must be referred immediately to the Public Accounts Committee.'[1]

Furthermore, a comment piece in the same edition, under the heading 'BBC behemoth must be cut down to size', continued the attack:

BBC director of television Danny Cohen warns that if the licence fee is cut or frozen – measures being considered by

Culture Secretary John Whittingdale – the Corporation will be forced to slash the amount it spends on making programmes. Yet as we reveal today, only 47 per cent of the BBC's grotesquely bloated £5.1 billion budget is currently spent on providing shows for the British viewing public . . .

If Mr Cohen and his fellow BBC nabobs got to grips with this gross inefficiency, they would have more than enough cash to increase handsomely the amount they spend on programmes without the need for a licence fee rise.

But don't hold your breath. As long as the Corporation can levy what is effectively a poll tax on every TV-owning house in the UK – backed by the threat of draconian jail terms or fines for non-payment – where is the incentive for this most arrogant of state behemoths to change?[2]

As if this weren't enough, the article and comment piece were followed the very next day, 16 June, by another article – this time by the veteran journalist Max Hastings – headlined 'Decent TV shows? No, the BBC prefers splurging your cash on a bloated army of jobsworths'. Hastings' article uncritically repeated the previous day's claim that 'just £2.4 billion of [the BBC's] £5.1 billion annual budget was spent on making programmes' and added further allegations of excessive bureaucracy, political correctness, overpaid managers and overuse of management consultants. However, this article's tone was rather more sympathetic, concluding that we still need a strong BBC, but that it required a radical overhaul: 'All those who care passionately about the welfare and future of this great cultural institution recognise that it must reform itself, or have revolution thrust upon it'.[3] Both the comment piece and the article by Hastings based their criticisms on Rushton and Martin's analysis (and this was misleading in multiple ways, as a strong rebuttal by the BBC's finance director, Ian Haythornthwaite, made clear at the time).[4] So let's take a closer look at these claims.

Measuring Efficiency in a Creative Organization

The BBC is primarily a creative organization with, inevitably, a culture gap between content creators and managers – even though many of the latter started as the former. Programme makers have a particular aversion to management jargon, known at the BBC as 'Birtspeak' after John Birt, who, as director-general in the 1990s, introduced new – and much resented – organizational structures and processes, which led to significant efficiency savings. Characteristically, the Corporation's management systems have been exuberantly lampooned by the BBC itself in *W1A*, its spoof fly-on-the-wall documentary set inside Broadcasting House.[5]

Because every episode of every programme is unique and quality is subjective (although measurable in terms of audience perception), judging the BBC's efficiency is less straightforward than if it were producing smartphones, detergents or mortgages – standardized products closely comparable to those offered by competitors and with reasonably objective quality and value for money.

But because the BBC is publicly owned, accountable to Parliament, externally audited and regulated, and exceptionally transparent – *much* more so than most of its critics – we can nevertheless reach rather clear conclusions about its efficiency, both in general and relative to other organizations, including other broadcasters. In particular, because the claim of the headline in the Rushton and Martin June 2015 *Mail* article is so specific, we can certainly test its validity.

The Biggest Issue: Putting Licence-Fee Money into Programmes for the UK

The article's biggest error[6] was the crucial headline claim that the BBC had spent 'less than half its cash on programmes'. The clear impression given to readers was that the BBC spent less than half the money it received *from licence payers* on programmes available to them, instead squandering the rest on bloated overhead costs and the money it 'pumped' into 'producing content for overseas audiences'.[7]

The article's headline claim was derived by dividing the sum invested into making new content (programmes) by the BBC's UK Public Service Broadcasting (PSB) Group (that is, its non-commercial UK services, funded mainly by the TV licence fee) by the total revenue of the whole BBC – including that of its substantial, and very successful, international commercial operations. This was mixing up apples and oranges in a way that significantly distorted the analysis to make the BBC look much worse.[8]

Instead, the correct way to analyse how efficiently the BBC uses licence-payers' money is, first, to work out how much it actually spends making and then distributing the programmes and services available to them and, then, to express this as a percentage of the amount of licence-fee money it actually receives. (As we'll discuss, its commercial operations are also relevant – but not in the way the article suggested.) To reach really firm conclusions, you might then follow up this first-cut analysis with a more detailed one of how well the money had been spent, perhaps even down to the level of sofas, taxis, tea and whether the BBC's buildings are as unduly ostentatious as the *Daily Mail* suggests. But the starting point would be this simple ratio – as in the article, but using the correct numbers. If the overall efficiency ratios are good, it's hard to see how the amount spent on tea is a material issue. So, what were the correct numbers – and how do they compare with those in the *Daily Mail*?

What Percentage of the Licence-Fee Revenue Received by the BBC's UK PSB Group Did It *Actually* Spend on Content and Distribution?

Total licence-fee income in 2013–14 was £3.73 billion before collection costs. The BBC also earned £1.10 billion in revenue from commercial activities, mainly BBC Worldwide, and received £245 million in government funding for the World Service,[9] giving it a total group revenue of £5.07 billion. This is the figure used in the article to support its 'less than half' claim: the direct cost of content for the UK PSB group (BBC TV, radio and online services) was £2.41 billion,[10] which is indeed less than half of the £5.07 billion total group revenue – but 65 per cent of the £3.73 billion total *licence-fee revenue*.[11]

It gets worse – much worse. Beyond the elementary blunder – whether deliberate or unintended – of dividing the cost of UK PSB group investment into content by the *total* BBC revenue figure, the article also contained three other material errors, all of which distorted the figures to make the BBC look much worse:

- It failed to add in the £217 million distribution cost – in the article's own words, 'the essential job of actually transmitting the programmes around Britain'. The total direct cost of UK PSB content *and distribution* was £2.62 billion – actually 70 per cent of total licence-fee revenue
- Not all of the licence-fee revenue went to the BBC. Almost 8 per cent was 'top-sliced' to subsidize other government projects and activities, mainly broadband roll-out (at £150 million) and the Welsh language

channel S4C (£105 million, including £23 million for
content purchases), plus £30 million for investment into
local TV, the switchover to digital TV and BBC Monitoring. Collection costs were another £102 million
(2.7 per cent of total licence-fee income). The licence-fee
revenue *actually available to the BBC for its UK services*
after top-slicing and collection costs was only £3.34
billion. The £2.62 billion direct cost of UK content and
distribution was 78 per cent of this figure

- Finally, you can't run a broadcaster – or a newspaper –
without buildings (£141 million), technology
(£130 million), human resources departments and
training (£39 million). Including these essential infrastructure and support costs (£568 million), the BBC's
total expenditure on UK PSB content, distribution and
direct overheads was £3.10 billion – in fact, 93 per cent of
the licence-fee income it actually received.

In summary, far from spending 'less than half its cash on programmes', the BBC actually spent *93 per cent* of its licence-fee
revenue (after top-slicing and collection costs) on UK PSB content, distribution and essential infrastructure and support.[12]

The *Daily Mail's* 'less than half' claim was miles from the truth.

The BBC's Commercial Activities

The article also completely misunderstood or misrepresented
the contribution of the BBC's commercial activities. Far from
'pumping money' into these, as it claimed, the Corporation
actually received a financial contribution of £174 million *from*
them – a combination of direct payments for programmes and
dividends paid out of commercial profits – money it used to
boost its investment in UK content.

If there had been no BBC Worldwide (and therefore no financial contribution from it to subsidize the BBC's licence-fee income), the Corporation's investment in UK PSB content – which is what matters to licence payers – would have been lower, both in absolute terms and as a proportion of licence-fee revenue received. But it might well have been *higher* as a proportion of the total group revenue, the measure erroneously used in the *Daily Mail* article.

In 2018, the National Audit Office, which reports directly to the UK Parliament,[13] did an independent review of the BBC's commercial activities. It concluded that, 'The BBC's main commercial subsidiaries are significant businesses in their respective markets, creating important additional value for licence fee payers'[14] – the precise opposite of what the *Mail* article said. In fact, it was partly thanks to the contribution from its commercial activities that the BBC was able to invest so much in UK programmes as a proportion of the licence-fee revenue it actually received.

The BBC's commercial division also contributed to the Corporation's wider public purposes. First, in 2013–14, it paid £113 million directly to independent UK producers, on top of its £174 million contribution to the BBC.[15] Secondly, BBC Global News and BBC Worldwide helped promote the UK and its values to citizens of other countries.

Were the BBC's Overheads Too High?

We've seen that 93 per cent of the licence-fee revenue the BBC's UK PSB group actually received in 2013–14 (the year analysed in the June 2015 *Daily Mail* article) went into UK PSB content, distribution and essential infrastructure and support. However, this still leaves the question of how well the BBC controls its overheads – all those 'jobsworths', taxis and cups of tea listed by the *Daily Mail*. So, how high are its overheads compared to those in other comparable organizations?

The BBC's overheads include (i) content-supporting infrastructure costs such as studios, directly required to deliver its audience-facing services, and (ii) general overheads – other support costs such as those of the human resources and finance departments, which cannot be directly attributed to audience-facing activities.

An independent review for the BBC Board and Executive by accountancy firm EY reported that, in 2017–18, after twenty-plus years of relentless efficiency gains, the BBC's total indirect costs (combining (i) and (ii) above) had been reduced to just 17.8 per cent of its total costs[16] – the *eighth lowest percentage* in a sample of fifty-one mostly private sector, media and telecommunication companies. Also, general overheads ((ii) above) had been reduced to only 5.7 per cent of costs, the seventh lowest percentage in a sample of twenty-six organizations that reported comparable figures (regulated companies, government departments and charities).[17]

On both of these measures – especially the broader and more important total indirect costs – the BBC is now much more efficient than the average for organizations in both its industry and the public and non-profit sectors.

As we'll show later on, the BBC's low overhead rates partly reflect the inherent efficiency of the licence fee as a way of turning consumers' money into programmes, compared with other funding options such as advertising and subscriptions (both of which involve much higher income generation and customer support costs). But they are also the cumulative result of sustained year-on-year improvement and efficiency gains over many years. Examples include better procurement, simpler organizational structures and processes, new technologies such as fully digital ('tapeless') operations, and the 'Compete or Compare' framework in which, as far as possible, costs are tested against market prices either directly (by inviting commercial bids) or by benchmarking (comparing internal costs against estimates of what the equivalent market prices would be).[18]

Limited Scope for Further Efficiency Savings

The downside of these low overhead rates is that the scope for further efficiency savings is increasingly limited. As the BBC's director of television, Danny Cohen, and others too argued in 2015 – much to the scorn of the *Daily Mail* – the Corporation will have to make substantial service cuts in response to the triple whammy of (i) a frozen licence fee, (ii) taking on the cost of free TV licences for all households with members aged seventy-five-plus on Pension Credit and (iii) the escalating costs and other challenges raised by the growth of online TV, discussed in Chapter 2.

A Flurry of Beeb-bashing Articles

The 15–16 June 2015 articles weren't the only ones in the *Daily Mail* attacking the BBC during that period. The paper had already published at least six earlier that year, such as 'Fury after BBC splashes out £63,000 on cabs that went unused' (23 February, with a suitably enraged quotation from UKIP MP Douglas Carswell) and 'the incestuous luvvie clique who run it [the BBC]' (27 March).[19] Another, on 30 March, criticized the BBC's hiring of personal protection for Director-General Lord Hall after he received death threats in response to the sacking of Jeremy Clarkson, presenter of *Top Gear*, for punching the show's young producer and allegedly calling him a 'lazy Irish cunt', while filming on location.[20] However, this article was notable for a genuinely thoughtful and balanced comment from Philip

Davies MP, usually no friend of the BBC: 'Obviously the person who sent it is some kind of nutter. But you never know what these people are capable of. The BBC are in a difficult position. If they do nothing about it and something dreadful happens, they will be criticized. But if they take some action and nothing happens, they will be accused of over-reacting.'[21]

Feelings were running high. The right-wing blogger Paul Staines ('Guido Fawkes') had organized a petition to try to force the BBC to reinstate Clarkson, attracting extensive media coverage and a million signatures in just ten days.[22] This was delivered to the BBC by a man dressed as the *Top Gear* test driver, the Stig, riding a tank-like military vehicle.[23] But Clarkson was not reinstated. In fact, within four months he and his two co-presenters, Richard Hammond and James May, had signed a deal with Amazon Prime to create a new show, *The Grand Tour*, increasing their earnings by at least ten times compared with what they had been paid by the BBC. According to an industry source, 'Jeremy would be looking at £9.6 million a [12-part] series with the other two not far behind.'[24]

The *Mail* stepped up its attacks still further in July 2015, publishing at least eight more Beeb-bashing articles just in that month. One on 22 July – complete with quotations from Bill Cash, fellow Conservative MP Andrew Percy, and the TaxPayers' Alliance – berated the BBC for using '£20,000-a-DAY [*sic*]' photographer Rankin to take publicity shots of BBC World News presenter Yalda Hakim. Only near the end did it reveal that this was for a marketing campaign by the BBC's successful global commercial business and that the cost had been at approximately one-fifth of Rankin's normal (£20,000-a-day) commercial rate.[25] Although the *Daily Mail* was the newspaper most actively attacking the BBC around this time, there were also multiple attacks in the *Daily Telegraph*, the Murdoch press and the *Daily Express*, as well as from right-wing think tanks such as the TaxPayers' Alliance and the Adam Smith Institute.

The Context: BBC Charter Renewal and Funding Settlement

The background to this flurry of activity was that the BBC's then current Charter was about to end (on 31 December 2016) and its funding settlement from the government was soon to be agreed (which would be put in place from April 2017 onwards).

BBC Charter renewal may also explain one rather odd feature of Rushton and Martin's 15 June 2015 article: that, as well as being spectacularly misleading, it was based on the BBC's 2013–14 results – that is, the results for the year ending April 2014, nearly fourteen months earlier. These were indeed still the latest published figures – but those for the following year (2014–15) were released the very next day after the article's publication – 16 June 2015.

Any competent financial analyst or journalist without a hidden agenda would have surely waited a day for the new figures. We can only speculate as to why the *Daily Mail*'s editor at the time, Paul Dacre, was so keen to get the article and quotations from MPs (and the follow-up comment piece, and the Max Hastings article) published then, even with out-of-date information. Perhaps he already knew that the government was about to impose another deep cut on the BBC and felt it would be helpful for everyone to have the benefit of the *Daily Mail*'s wildly inaccurate analysis before the announcement?

We now turn to the political events that led to the BBC being forced to operate in this tough media landscape, hampered not only by significantly reduced funding (while its content and technology costs are rising sharply), but also by the restrictive terms of its current Charter. As we'll see, there seems to be a strongly ideological dimension to these restrictions.

5. Under Sustained Attack – Towards the Current Charter and Funding Deal

We've described how the BBC, like all established media, is in a tough market and technology landscape, facing new online competition, increasing content and distribution costs and fast-changing consumption trends. We've explained how it is also uniquely subject to relentless attacks on both its funding and its integrity by a wide range of actively hostile players – about whom more shortly.

But first of all, this chapter will describe the unprecedented assault on the BBC during the run-up to the last Charter renewal and funding deal in 2015–16. Instead of reinforcing the main British public broadcaster's ability to respond to the external threats it faced, ministers did the exact opposite, imposing additional constraints on it and deep further cuts to its already reduced income. It is these events, above everything else, that have put the BBC into its current weakened state, as the online competition keeps growing and the new government and its supporters continue their endless onslaught on its funding and editorial independence.

Autumn 2012: Heading towards Charter Renewal

We'll start in the early autumn of 2012, with the BBC's ten-year Charter due to end in December 2016 and the Corporation in apparently good shape for the forthcoming negotiations about the next one.

Under Director-General Mark Thompson, the BBC had steadily

increased its content investment since 2004, thanks to broadly level real funding, continuing year-on-year efficiency savings[1] and growing commercial revenue. It had launched three successful new digital services in response to emerging technology opportunities: the iPlayer online catch-up service; the Freesat free-to-air satellite TV joint venture with ITV; and the YouView hybrid (digital terrestrial and online) TV joint venture with the other public service broadcasters and three telecommunications providers. These investments had enabled it to increase its reach and the perceived quality and value for money of its services, while also moving significant production away from London to new, state-of-the-art studios in Glasgow (2007) and Salford (2012) as part of its remit to support broadcasting in the nations and regions.

On 17 September 2012, Thompson stepped down as director-general, moving to New York to become president and CEO of *The New York Times*, with an annual remuneration of up to $10.5 million (£6.7 million) – ten times his (much criticized) £671,000 final annual salary at the BBC.[2]

George Entwistle: Into the Maelstrom

The BBC Trust[3] chose George Entwistle as Thompson's successor. Despite over twenty years' experience producing and commissioning current affairs, arts and science programmes, Entwistle had had only eighteen months' senior management experience (as director of the BBC's TV channel portfolio) and none in crisis management. The timing could not have been worse. Within three weeks, he was engulfed in the BBC's biggest crisis in decades – the massive scandal about alleged sexual abuse on its premises by Jimmy Savile and other presenters.

In December 2011, BBC Two's *Newsnight* had decided not to air an exposé on Savile. The journalists had taken the story to

ITV, which, on 3 October 2012, showed a programme based on their work. On 22 October, BBC One's *Panorama* broadcast an episode highly critical of the earlier decision to pull the *Newsnight* programme from the schedule. The next day, Entwistle struggled through a hostile two-hour grilling on this by the House of Commons select committee which oversees the Department for Digital, Culture, Media and Sport (DCMS).[4]

On 9 November, the crisis deepened even further when it emerged that another recent *Newsnight* programme, on paedophilia, had wrongly (albeit inadvertently) implicated Lord McAlpine, a former senior Conservative politician. The following morning Entwistle admitted to John Humphrys on the BBC's Radio 4 *Today* programme that he had not known about this highly incendiary – and, in the event, mistaken – programme until after it was transmitted. Later that day, he resigned, after just fifty-four days as director-general.[5] Several other senior managers had also either recently left the BBC or were on temporary leave due to their involvement in decisions connected to the Savile scandal, leaving something of a leadership vacuum close to the top.

Davie and Hall: Steadying the Ship

The BBC Trust appointed Tim Davie, director of its audio and music department, as acting director-general after Entwistle's departure. Davie led the BBC capably for just under five months before moving on, as planned, to BBC Worldwide in April 2013. (As we go to press, Davie is about to take over again, but this time as permanent director-general, starting September 2020.) Tony Hall (Lord Hall of Birkenhead) then became the new and permanent director-general of the BBC. He had been chief executive of the Royal Opera House since 2001 and, before that, an experienced producer and leader in BBC news and current affairs.

As so often at the BBC, exactly what drove these events is highly contested.[6] What is not in dispute is that Davie and Hall steadied the ship after Entwistle's resignation and that Hall and the Trust soon had to navigate two more media storms: one about pay-offs to departing executives, including Entwistle, the other about the Digital Media Initiative (DMI), a failed IT project. As a result, the BBC Trust introduced a £150,000 cap on severance payments and cancelled the DMI. But the very worst of all the scandals, the one which everyone remembered, was the Savile story.

We'll return to these controversies in Chapter 12, but the immediate point is that when Tony Hall took over as director-general on 2 April 2013, the BBC's enemies had plenty of sticks with which to beat it. This wasn't the ideal time to be facing the ordeal of negotiating the next decade-long Charter and – broadly in parallel – funding settlement. (The Charter and funding deal are closely connected – each needs to take account of the other – but the two processes are separate. They are also slightly out of sync: in 2016–17, the Charter ran to the end of the calendar year (31 December 2016), but the funding deal to the end of the financial year (31 March 2017).) These negotiations promised to be longer and tougher than ever, and the BBC went into them with a weakened reputation.

The Charter Renewal Process

The formal Charter renewal process started in October 2013 with a 16-month 'root-and-branch' inquiry into the BBC's future by the House of Commons Culture, Media and Sport Committee. The next step was a DCMS consultation paper (a 'green paper'), followed by one giving the government's proposals (a 'white paper'), which were then debated in Parliament. The Charter was finalized by the Culture Secretary in December 2016.[7]

The breadth and depth of the DCMS Committee inquiry's 'terms of reference' (its stated aims and limits) were unprecedented. They included questions about the BBC's underlying purposes; its scale, scope and remit; its performance under the then current ten-year Charter; its funding; its use of internal versus external production; its commercial activities; and its governance, regulation and accountability. Almost everything was up for grabs.

The Corporation had good reason to be nervous, not only because of the recent scandals and upheavals and the far-reaching questions raised by the sixteen-month inquiry but also because of the views of some of the individual members of the DCMS select committee: for example, those of its chairman, John Whittingdale, and another member, Philip Davies, who were both council members of The Freedom Association (TFA). TFA had only two main policies: leaving the EU ('Better Off Out') and replacing the TV licence fee with subscriptions ('Axe the TV Tax').[8] Also, the inquiry's specialist adviser, Ray Gallagher, had worked for James Murdoch for fifteen years as director of public affairs at Sky, the BBC's most hostile and powerful competitor.

An Opening Shot from Conservative Party Chairman Grant Shapps

As the inquiry started in October 2013, Grant Shapps, Chairman of the Conservative Party and minister without portfolio, opened the attack on the BBC in a *Sunday Telegraph* interview which was 'understood to have been made with the knowledge of Downing Street'.

Shapps accused the BBC of a culture of 'waste and secrecy' which 'sometimes . . . crosses the mark over into bullying'; of resistance to change ('they really need to show that they get it and come into the twenty-first century'); biased news coverage; and needing to win back public trust after many scandals. He called for it to become 'fully open' to the National Audit Office and to Freedom of Information (FoI)[9] laws. He threatened that, unless it became more transparent and rebuilt public trust, it could face a cut in the licence fee, or have to compete with other broadcasters for a share of that revenue.[10]

A BBC spokesman responded, 'Mr Shapps is right that transparency is key to the BBC's future. So is its freedom from political pressure', adding that the BBC's own TV and radio programmes held its executives to account;[11] that it had dealt with 1,600 FoI requests in 2012 and already appeared in front of sixteen parliamentary committees in 2013; and that it gave the National Audit Office 'full access to everything except editorial decisions'.[12]

Given his colourful personal history, Shapps was, in any case, not best placed to criticize the BBC for a lack of transparency. According to *The Guardian*, he had continued selling a get-rich-quick scheme under the name of 'Michael Green' for at least a year after his election to Parliament without declaring this activity,[13] and then aggressively denied having done so – supporting these denials with legal threats – until faced with undeniable evidence.[14] In 2015, he was also accused of covertly using a 'sock-puppet' account to tamper with his own and several Conservative colleagues' Wikipedia pages.[15] Furthermore, in 2018, he was forced to resign as co-chair of the All-Party Parliamentary Group on Blockchain (a cross-party group of MPs with an interest in 'blockchain' technology)[16] after the *Financial Times* uncovered an undeclared conflict of interest.[17]

His charge about 'bullying' within the BBC looked almost equally hypocritical when he was forced to resign as Conservative chairman in 2015 after a young party activist committed suicide after allegedly being bullied by a campaign aide appointed by Shapps.[18] He continues as MP for Welwyn Hatfield in

Hertfordshire (and, in July 2019, Boris Johnson appointed him as Secretary of State for Transport).

The Conservative Attack Gathers Pace

The Conservatives had started as they meant to go on. After Shapps' initial attack in the *Sunday Telegraph* from his position as party chairman, and apparently with Number Ten's endorsement, they quickly built a wider 'case to answer' against the BBC, especially in the *Telegraph* papers. This appeared to follow a script dictated by the Corporation's enemies and competitors.

One such target was its severance payments to executives.[19] A second was the licence fee: an article by Rob Wilson MP, parliamentary private secretary to Chancellor George Osborne, called for it to be scrapped and for the BBC's activities to be narrowed down to focus on 'core public service broadcasting'.[20] Wilson also referred to a *Sunday Telegraph* poll purporting to show that '70 per cent of voters believe that the BBC licence fee should be abolished or cut'. The paper reported that the poll had been conducted by ICM, a respected research company, but said nothing about the wording of the question used to achieve this remarkable result.[21]

Yet another *Telegraph* target was a BBC charity, BBC Media Action – financially, a separate entity, not licence-fee supported – which had received EU funding for a project training journalists in countries in Eastern Europe and North Africa where conflict was ongoing, such as Algeria, Belarus, Egypt, Russia and Ukraine. The article reported that: 'MPs said the extent of the charity's dependence on money from Brussels could undermine the credibility of the BBC's coverage of controversial European issues, including EU enlargement'. It did, however, admit that the charity also received funds from other sources, including the government's own Department for International

Development and the US State Department. However, there was no suggestion that funding from these sources might lead the BBC into broadcasting unduly positive coverage of the UK and US governments: apparently, only EU funding brought such risks.[22] There were numerous, similar attacks in the other, regular BBC-bashing papers: the *Sun*, the *Express* and, especially, the *Daily Mail*.

The BBC didn't have to be paranoid to see all this as a coordinated assault on its funding, scope, scale and news coverage in the run-up to Charter renewal. Its chairman, Lord Patten – one of Shapps' predecessors as Conservative Party chair – claimed that it got 'bashed more than [Syria's] President Assad'.[23] As always, the DCMS Committee inquiry also enabled other vested interests to have a go at the BBC. Some wanted it to put more money into particular types of content, such as the arts, or into particular parts of the UK, such as Scotland. Others, for obvious commercial reasons, wanted it to compete less vigorously in areas such as popular entertainment and online news. For a range of reasons, many of these lobbyists argued that the BBC should invest more in programmes for smaller audiences, and less in popular entertainment shows like *Strictly Come Dancing* and *The Great British Bake Off*. As we'll see, this made little sense to most viewers and listeners. Regardless, it became one of the dominant themes of Charter renewal.

The DCMS Select Committee's February 2015 report[24]

While the committee's February 2015 report on its sixteen-month inquiry rightly acknowledged the recent scandals and the governance issues they raised, it was far from the hatchet job many had been expecting (and some had been hoping for). On funding, it concluded that there was no better immediate alternative to the licence fee (which was, from then on, to include those who were only watching online, closing the iPhone loop-hole). However, it argued that there was a strong case for decriminalizing non-payment of the licence fee. In the longer term, it recommended either a levy on all households or a move to subscriptions.

Furthermore, to improve and clarify the BBC's regulation and accountability, the committee called for it to have an external regulator, a Public Service Broadcasting Commission (PSBC). This would, among other things, determine the level of public funding for the BBC – i.e., in the short term, it would set the licence fee.[25] In addition, it stated that Ofcom should be the final arbiter on competition issues, the 'terms of trade' between the BBC and independent producers and complaints about BBC content; while the National Audit Office should be its external auditor, with unrestricted access to its accounts.[26]

But the report's most important conclusions were about the BBC's scope and scale.[27] Reflecting the idea that the BBC should avoid competing in the popular entertainment arena, the report said that, although the Corporation's scope and scale would largely be determined by its funding level, it should 'reduce pro-vision in areas that are over-served or where the public service characteristics of its output are marginal or where others are bet-ter placed to deliver excellence and better value for money'.[28]

Behind this rather opaque wording was a radical challenge to the BBC's long-established Reithian mission to inform, educate and *entertain*. In free-market circles, there is a quasi-religious belief that the market, with no intervention from government, will provide all the entertainment viewers and listeners want;[29] and that the BBC's sole role is to supplement this with informa-tion and education that the market won't sufficiently provide. In Chapter II and Appendix E, we'll return to this so-called 'market failure' argument[30] and test it both conceptually and against the evidence on the BBC's actual market impact and the implica-tions for UK audiences.

The July 2015 Funding Settlement – Again, No Public Consultation

The BBC's finances had already been weakened by the 2010 funding deal. This earlier funding deal, reducing the BBC's real (inflation-adjusted) licence-fee income after top-slicing to pay for these other activities –

all of which were above and beyond its commitment to UK services for licence-fee payers – had been imposed with no published analysis, no public consultation and no parliamentary discussion.[31]

It had seemed heartening for the BBC that the February 2015 DCMS Committee report strongly criticized the way the 2010 settlement had been imposed upon the Corporation and recommended: 'No future licence-fee negotiations must be conducted in the way of the 2010 settlement: the process must be open and transparent, licence-fee payers must be consulted and Parliament should have an opportunity to debate the level of funding being set and any significant changes to funding responsibilities.'[32] (The 2010 funding agreement was due to end just a little over three months later than the Charter, by 4 April 2017; but the two were to be considered in parallel.)

However, on 7 May 2015, David Cameron's Conservatives unexpectedly won a general election with a narrow majority of twelve – although the polls had predicted another hung parliament. In the resulting ministerial reshuffle, Sajid Javid was promoted from Culture Secretary to Business Secretary and John Whittingdale – chairman of the DCMS Committee since 2005 – was promoted from the backbenches to replace him as Culture Secretary. Thus it was that, on 6 July 2015, just under two months after his appointment, Whittingdale found himself on the floor of the House of Commons announcing the new BBC funding deal. This had once again been agreed by George Osborne behind closed doors with no published analysis, no public consultation and no parliamentary debate – a carbon copy of the widely criticized 2010 process, which Whittingdale's own committee, in the strongest terms, just five months earlier, had said should never be repeated.

This was shocking enough. But the substance of the deal was even worse than the 2010 one, for both the Corporation and most households. The 2015 settlement forced the BBC to take responsibility for deciding whether to continue funding TV licences for every household which included one or more members aged seventy-five-plus – regardless of household size or income. The cost of this concession to the taxpayer in 2013–14, the most recent reported year, had been £608 million, about a fifth of the BBC's then licence-fee income.[33] If it were continued, the cost would relentlessly rise every year because of the UK's ageing population.[34]

One of the DCMS select committee's recent recommendations had been that licence fee income should be used 'only for the purpose of broadcasting or the production of public service content'. Forcing the BBC to fund free licences, which was clearly a welfare benefit – or get the blame for phasing them out – went directly against this recommendation.[35]

The 2015 Green Paper

The Charter review process was led by John Whittingdale in his new role as Culture Secretary, supported by his special adviser on media, Carrie Symonds.[36] It reflected both his free-market thinking and his extensive knowledge of UK broadcasting, acquired over ten years as chairman of the DCMS Committee. To his credit, and in striking contrast to Osborne's 2010 and 2015 funding deals, there was extensive analysis, research and both public and parliamentary consultation.

On 15 July 2015, just nine days after announcing the new

funding deal, Whittingdale launched a detailed consultation paper ('green paper') which invited the public and interested parties to submit answers to nineteen questions relevant to the BBC Charter's renewal.[37] He and the DCMS also commissioned two independent reviews – one on the BBC's market impact and distinctiveness, one on its governance and regulation – and a programme of public opinion research by the market research firm GfK.[38]

Whittingdale's Obsession with the BBC's Market Impact

Whittingdale's consultation questions covered a wide range of issues. But the dominant theme – accounting for eleven of the nineteen questions[39] – was the need for the Corporation to be smaller, narrower and more 'distinctive' in order to minimize its impact on the rest of the media market. The implication is that the government was putting the concerns of the BBC's powerful commercial rivals before those of the British public.[40]

In a press release, Whittingdale appeared to regard it as *self-evident* (that is, requiring no justification) that the BBC, as a publicly funded body, should not offer services that could be provided by the free market: '[It] should . . . not stray into areas that can and should be left to commercial providers . . . It is pointless and wasteful having an organization receiving that kind of public funding competing with – and potentially crowding out – other providers.'[41] In the same vein, George Osborne, while confirming his intention to transfer responsibility for free TV licences for the over-seventy-fives to the BBC, had said that 'You wouldn't want the BBC to completely crowd out national newspapers'.[42]

Further reinforcing the impression that the government was prioritizing the interests of the BBC's competitors and planning to cut it down to size to reduce its market impact was the composition of a panel Whittingdale appointed in July 2015 to advise him on Charter renewal. Almost all of the eight panel members were leaders or former leaders of the BBC's competitors or suppliers.[43] And although the panel would be meeting five or six times, Whittingdale said that he would not be publishing anything on its deliberations, on the grounds that it would merely be 'providing views . . . not making recommendations, it is a sounding board, if you like'.[44]

The statements by ministers, the questions in the green paper, the composition of Whittingdale's advisory panel and the terms of reference of the market-impact study he commissioned all suggested that the government's *top* priority for Charter renewal was to minimize the BBC's impact on its competitors. Part of the justification for this was the claim that it was both too big and relentlessly expanding. But was this actually true?

How Big Is Too Big?

As Whittingdale introduced questions on the BBC's scope and scale into the consultation, his green paper showed its significant (although not huge) expansion between 1994–5 and 2014–15.[45] However – as he and his advisers must have known – almost all of this expansion had happened under the *previous* Charter of 1997–2006 when, as part of its remit, the BBC had agreed to introduce new digital services to help drive the take-up of digital terrestrial television (DTT), digital audio broadcasting (DAB radio) and the internet, to support the government's digital strategy and give licence-fee payers more for their money.

Over the most recent five years, from 2010 to 2015, its scale had already been reduced by Osborne's 2010 funding cuts. Budgets and the total number of staff were down and, to save money, BBC Two was no longer showing first-run daytime programmes and BBC Three was to be a broadcast channel no longer. The next funding settlement (of July 2015) would inevitably force further cuts upon the Corporation. It is inconceivable that Whittingdale did not know most or all of this. Further, as the green paper itself said, the context of the BBC's expansion was one of greatly 'increased choice for audiences'.[46]

The reality was that the BBC's *share* of total income, services and audiences had been declining for decades. One recent, credible estimate – which has, so far, proved highly accurate – was that BBC TV's share of total industry revenue would fall from 22 per cent in 2010 to 17 per cent in 2016 and 12 per cent by 2026.[47] It hardly shows a pattern of an ever-expanding BBC 'crowding out' the competition. For BBC Online, the market definition wasn't all that clear, but its revenue share was, again, obviously small, and declining overall, although it was still a significant player in online news, weather and sport coverage.

The green paper's bald assertion that the BBC was relentlessly expanding was therefore demonstrably untrue: in fact, thanks to the 2010 and 2015 funding cuts, it was – for the first time in its long history – getting significantly smaller, in absolute terms, and even more so relative to the rest of the expanding market. The green paper also described it as 'the world's largest PSB'.[48] This too was – at best – highly misleading. Two other PSBs – Japan's Nippon Hōsō Kyōkai (NHK) and Germany's Arbeitsgemeinschaft der öffentlich-rechtlichen Rundfunkanstalten der Bundesrepublik Deutschland (ARD) – receive more public funding than the BBC, and ARD is also bigger overall.[49] (The green paper simply ignored NHK[50] and disaggregated the regional parts of the ARD system[51] whose public funding[52] is 40 per cent higher and total income 15 per cent higher than the equivalent figures for the BBC.)[53] These misleading claims about the BBC's supposed expansion and relative size were used to justify the green paper's focus on its market impact as the main issue in its Charter renewal, requiring major additional changes.

Responses to the Green Paper Consultation

The twelve-week public consultation ended on 8 October 2015. Clearly reflecting the importance of the BBC to the British public, there were 192,000 responses. The DCMS had to draft in help from other departments to go through them.[54] Even with this help, it took almost six months to publish a summary.[55]

Both the volume and the content of the responses must have been a shock to those hoping to reduce the scope of the BBC. Despite the distortions and hostile framing of most of the green paper's questions, just over 97 per cent of responses still supported the BBC providing all types of content to everyone, versus only 2.4 per cent saying that it 'should not seek to be universal'. Eighty-one per cent said it was serving its audiences well or very well, versus only 6.3 per cent saying it was not doing so or could improve.

Clear majorities also said that: the BBC's content was of high quality and had the right genre mix; it provided good value for money; its expansion had been justified in the context of greater consumer choice; by raising standards, it had a *positive* impact on the market; it should keep playing a leading role in the development of new technology; and it should continue to be funded by the licence fee. (The deviations from these majority views were mostly from organizations with a commercial vested interest in reducing its scale. There were also some demographic patterns in the individual responses, with those who were younger, less well off, or from ethnic minorities or some of the nations and regions still being generally positive, but somewhat less so than the average. (We'll return to these persistent demographic differences in Chapter 13.))

Only a small minority said that the BBC's content was not of a sufficiently high quality (8.2 per cent) and even fewer said it had a negative impact on the wider market (3.3 per cent) or was unjustifiably crowding out competitors (0.5 per cent).[56]

The government was under no legal obligation to take any notice of the consultation responses but, given their number and the overwhelming support they gave to the BBC, simply ignoring them could have been politically damaging.

More Support for the BBC

Even worse for the opponents of the BBC, in spring 2016, the Corporation received further support from five more UK-wide reports related to Charter renewal.[57]

A report by the DCMS Committee under its new chairman, Jesse Norman MP, described the BBC as 'an extraordinary national and global institution' and 'a beacon of enlightened values of openness, freedom of thought, toleration and diversity'.[58] It issued a strong criticism of the process of the 2015 funding deal and did not even think it necessary to discuss the BBC's alleged negative market impact.

The House of Lords Select Committee on Communications was, if anything, even more positive, titling its report 'BBC charter review: Reith not revolution'.[59] It described the Charter review as 'an opportunity to ensure that the BBC remains the keystone of British broadcasting, plays a central role in the wider [UK] creative industries . . . and continues to be respected across the world'.[60] It, too, was highly critical of the 2010 and 2015 funding settlements and dismissed the suggestion that the BBC's scale or scope should be reduced and that it should not compete in popular entertainment:

> We have not heard a compelling case for a significant reduction in the scale or scope of the BBC and note it remains, in global terms, a comparatively small player. The BBC should not be restricted to providing content which the commercial market does not provide. Instead it must continue to be a universal broadcaster providing content to inform, educate and entertain.[61]

To get the public's view, the market research firm GfK, commissioned by the DCMS, conducted two large-scale surveys and sixteen focus groups representative of the UK population. Among other results, clear majorities among the survey respondents welcomed the BBC's expansion over the previous twenty years and agreed that it should 'continue to expand to take full advantage of developments in technology' (with the proviso that it should not add any more channels), and that the growth of commercial services 'shows that the BBC is not crowding out the competition'. Similarly, the focus group participants simply assumed that the BBC should provide programmes that would entertain as well as inform and educate. Like most viewers and listeners (as opposed to the BBC's competitors, its political enemies and a few free-market economists) they just took it as a given that it should provide all manner of different programmes to serve licence-fee payers across the country.[62]

The Market-Impact Study from O&O and Oxera

Neither the green-paper consultation responses, nor the two parliamentary committee reports, nor the GfK research gave *any* support to Whittingdale's apparent view that the BBC's scope should be narrowed to reduce its market impact. He did, however, get some extremely limited support for this view from the market-impact study he had himself commissioned from the media, sport and entertainment consultancy Oliver & Ohlbaum, supported by the economic consultancy Oxera. This suggested that some shifts away from popular entertainment on BBC One, BBC Radio and BBC Online would, albeit very marginally, benefit the BBC's commercial competitors and *might* have a small positive net impact on the overall market – but on nothing like the scale to justify the green paper's treatment of this as the most important issue in Charter renewal.[63]

Finally, a review of the BBC's governance and regulation by Sir David Clementi, a former chairman of Virgin Money and Prudential, and previously a deputy governor of the Bank of England, commissioned by Whittingdale in September 2015, recommended that the BBC should be governed by a new unitary board and regulated by Ofcom, replacing the BBC Trust, which had previously combined both functions.[64] It was against this background that Whittingdale finally presented the government's proposals for Charter renewal in a May 2016 white paper.

A BBC for the Future: A Broadcaster of Distinction

The white paper's subtitle echoed Whittingdale's obsession with the BBC's 'distinctiveness', a rather slippery term (the implications of which we shall discuss later). But, presumably in response to the clear and consistent message of the consultation and reports, the proposals included no big moves to reduce the Corporation's scope and scale beyond those already being forced by the funding cuts.

The most important of its proposals were about governance and regulation. These largely followed Clementi's recommendations, with responsibility for governance going to a single BBC Board (rather than this being shared between the BBC Trust and the BBC Executive) and external regulation by Ofcom (instead of the BBC Trust). It was widely felt that the new structure made it clearer who was responsible for what. Other measures focused on ensuring even greater transparency and accountability by increasing the ability of Ofcom, the National Audit Office and the Board to hold the Executive (the top management team) to account. The BBC would be forced to publish still more detailed figures on remuneration and expenses and to conduct an extensive market impact evaluation of any proposed new service or – in Ofcom's view – 'material' change to an existing one.

There were also further requirements for diversity, impartiality, external commissioning, out-of-London production and support for local journalism and other partnerships.

Another 'small' proportion of the licence-fee revenue (i.e. on top of what had already been top-sliced) was to be diverted to a new 'contestable' fund,[65] independent of the BBC, which would allocate money to commercial broadcasters for public service content projects in response to bids. The aim would be to create 'new opportunities for others to provide the best [PSB] content in the UK and enhance plurality'. (This potentially signified the start of all PSB funding being put up for grabs, the great dream of some free-market enthusiasts.)[66]

However, there were also two important proposals to safeguard the BBC's political independence. First, the new Charter would run for *eleven* years (i.e. until 2027) instead of the usual ten, with mid-point reviews of both the Charter and the funding deal in 2021–2.[67] The aim was to ensure that the next Charter renewal did not coincide with the most likely date of a general election.[68] Secondly, the white paper stated that there should be a new, far more open, public process for setting the licence-fee level.

Astonishingly, the white paper did not even mention the impact of free TV licences for the over-seventy-fives. The whole Charter renewal debate had been framed to suggest that the BBC would be lucky not to be cut down to size even further. And the impact of the 2010 and 2015 funding cuts on UK viewers, listeners and producers was not even part of the government's stated agenda.

New Government, New Minister, New Charter, New Chairman

The white paper was published on 12 May 2016. Exactly six weeks later, on 23 June, the UK voted for Brexit. The following morning, David Cameron announced his resignation as Prime Minister.

On 13 July 2016, Theresa May became the new Prime Minister. The next day she sacked six of Cameron's cabinet members in what the *Telegraph* called a 'brutal cull'.[69] John Whittingdale was one of them, returning to the backbenches after just fourteen months as a minister. His successor as Culture Secretary was Karen Bradley. In December 2016, she introduced the new (current) eleven-year Charter, which was to run from 1 January 2017 until 31 December 2027. In January 2017, she selected Sir David Clementi as the BBC's new chairman. On 3 April 2017, at the start of the BBC's 2017–18 financial year, Ofcom became the Corporation's first external regulator.

Where Did This Leave the BBC?

The long, bruising process of Charter renewal had consumed much of the BBC leadership's time and energy over more than three years, starting with the disastrous events of late 2012. Given this hostile background, the 2016 Charter was less restrictive than it might have been.

Much of the credit for this outcome should go to BBC supporters – individual viewers and organizations – who took the time to write in with responses to the consultation's questionnaire. As Culture Secretary, John Whittingdale had surely wanted the BBC to be smaller, more 'accountable' and more 'distinctive', reflecting his obsession with its market impact and his overall political and ideological viewpoint. But, to his credit, he led an open, democratic and evidence-based Charter renewal process, and did not ignore the public's response, nor the various parliamentary committee reports and commissioned studies, all of which showed that limiting the BBC to focus only on public service content which would provide information and education –

but not entertainment – would be both unpopular and irrational. The idea was, therefore, largely shelved, as were some of the other hostile proposals that had been mooted.[70]

Conversely, the 2015 funding deal imposed by George Osborne (with no published analysis, public consultation or parliamentary scrutiny) is a disaster for the BBC – and, increasingly, its viewers, listeners and independent programme suppliers. Thanks to continuing efficiency savings and an increasing contribution from its commercial operations, it has so far largely managed to protect its programme budgets from the full effects of Osborne's cuts. But as its real funding continues to fall while real content and distribution costs keep rising, it will increasingly need to reduce programme budgets and, most likely, start cutting services.

It is perhaps not a coincidence that, in contrast to the open, democratic and evidence-based Charter renewal process led by Whittingdale, Osborne's two highly destructive funding deals were both imposed behind closed doors. Bad processes usually create bad outcomes. However, the BBC also has many enemies outside of government. Let's turn now to a wider discussion of who they are, what they say about it, and how they pose a threat to the future of a strong, independent BBC able to deliver its public-service mission to Britain and the world.

6. 'The Addams Family of World Media'

The James MacTaggart Memorial Lecture is the keynote, the big plenary, the absolute centrepiece of the Edinburgh International Television Festival – the most important annual gathering in British TV-land. On 28 August 2009 it was still being held in the McEwan Hall, the University of Edinburgh's graduation hall – a marvel of late Victorian Scottish philanthropic architecture lavishly paid for by the brewer and politician William McEwan. It has high-minded exhortations everywhere and feels distinctly churchy.

The MacTaggart was the night that really mattered in the three-day weekend event and people made an effort to sort-of dress up (as dressed up as TV people can manage). There were dinners afterwards, the most important being the one the festival committee gave for the main speaker.

That year the speaker was thirty-six-year-old James Murdoch, younger son of Rupert, who'd himself done the MacTaggart exactly twenty years earlier, in 1989. James was, so everyone said at the time, the favoured son and heir. He was certainly important in the media world: chairman and former chief executive of Sky, the dominant UK pay-TV platform, and chief executive of News International, the largest UK newspaper group, comprising the *Sun*, the *News of the World*, *The Times* and the *Sunday Times*.

One of the authors of this book, Peter York, was there that evening and recalls how Murdoch Jr's voice belied his heritage: 'It had a rather reedy, Manhattan-preppy sound, with MBA top notes, the product of the Ivy League preparatory Horace Mann School in New York and then Harvard. You couldn't hear Australia at all, nor his birthplace, Wimbledon.' Standing in front of a British broadcasting crowd, he simply sounded like a wealthy East Coast American.

The speech itself confirmed just how American he was, although he had a Scottish mother, was born in Britain and still held a British passport.[1] Once into his stride, he spoke clearly, confidently and with evident feeling. He had a shocking tale to tell. Over the next forty minutes, he described the UK broadcasting system as a hopeless, over-regulated basket case, with limited choice for consumers; 'unaccountable institutions' (the BBC Trust, Channel 4 and Ofcom); regressive taxes and policies that 'penalize the poorest in our society', notably the BBC licence fee; the promotion of 'inefficient infrastructure' (digital terrestrial television, which supports the popular free-to-air Freeview service in competition with Sky's pay-TV service); and many other faults.

In UK public service broadcasting, 'the customer does not exist', he declared. The right word for it was 'authoritarianism'. British broadcasting was the 'Addams Family' of world media – a reference to Charles Addams' gothic horror family, a satirical macabre inversion of the ideal twentieth-century American family.

James and the Giant BBC

Murdoch's speech raised many of the issues we discuss in this book: the speed of technological advance and its implications; the disadvantages of the TV licence fee and how it compares, in his view, unfavourably, with pay TV; and the BBC's supposed lack of accountability, trust and impartiality. Even the title of his speech was 'The Absence of Trust'.

Murdoch was especially incensed about the BBC's scope, scale and market impact. He came back to this again and again: 'Dumping free, state-sponsored news on the market makes it incredibly difficult for journalism to flourish on the internet';

the BBC should not be in the business of 'competing with professional journalists'; and 'the threat to independent news
provision is serious and imminent'.

This speech exemplifies several aspects of the war against the
BBC. Rupert and James Murdoch have been among its most ardent
and persistent enemies for many years. They control the UK's largest newspaper group and enjoy good (and largely opaque) access
to senior ministers. Their views on broadcasting policy matter.

Although their attacks on the BBC have doubtless been significantly driven by their commercial interests, they also appear
to have a strong ideological bent. For instance, James' MacTaggart speech, referring to Orwell's *Nineteen Eighty-Four* (published
exactly sixty years earlier), said: 'As Orwell foretold, to let the
state enjoy a near-monopoly of information is to guarantee
manipulation and distortion ... Yet *we have a system in which
state-sponsored media – the BBC in particular – grow ever more dominant* [emphasis added]'.[2] When he was forcefully questioned
about this on the following day, he testily insisted to an incredu-
lous audience that his references in the speech to Orwell's
warnings about dominant state-sponsored media were fully justified because the BBC was 'a public institution owned by the
taxpayer', resulting in 'unaccountable, self-perpetuating growth
over generations'.[3]

Also in his sights were the rules requiring broadcast news to
be impartial. The effect 'is not to curb bias – bias is present in all
news media – but simply to disguise it ... It is an impingement
on freedom of speech and on the right of people to choose what
kind of news to watch'.

What Guarantees Independence?

James Murdoch's alternative was a system based on a free market
that trusted people to make sensible choices, with intervention to

occur 'only on the evidence of actual and serious harm to the interests of consumers', and he argued that there should be a 'much, much smaller' BBC, leaving it largely to the market ('choice-driven television' – i.e. pay TV) to provide the programmes people really wanted.

Essentially, Murdoch's ideal model was the UK newspaper market or, at least in some respects, the US television market. Both are largely deregulated, with minimal government intervention of any kind and, certainly, no significant publicly owned competitor like the BBC or Channel 4. In his speech he claimed, 'The free press . . . is noisy, disrespectful, raucous and quite capable of affronting people . . . But it is driven by the daily . . . choices of millions of people. It has had the profits to be fearless and independent.' He went on to argue that, because of digital convergence (with previously separate media increasingly all using the internet),[4] different outlets were now barely distinguishable from each other ('We no longer have a TV market, a newspaper market, a publishing market'). Why should broadcasting be regulated any differently from the press?

His concluding words were, 'The only reliable, durable and perpetual guarantee of independence is profit.'[5]

The View from 2009

Naturally, this speech reflects its particular time and context. In 2009, the BBC had recently enjoyed several years of growing real revenue from licence-fee increases to fund the launch of its digital TV services BBC Three, BBC Four, CBBC and CBeebies and drive the take-up of digital television, in line with its Charter. As well as launching these channels in order to increase consumers' incentive to invest in a digital TV or set-top box, the BBC was also tasked with leading – and funding – the communications campaign for the switchover to digital TV and the help scheme for vulnerable consumers. The government's aim in this was both to increase choice (since the switch to digital transmission would allow more universally available terrestrial TV channels) and to allow analogue TV signals to be switched off in late 2012, releasing valuable electromagnetic spectrum it could then auction off.

In the event, the BBC-led campaign (featuring Digit Al, a friendly cartoon character created by Aardman Animations) delivered digital TV switchover on time and 23 per cent below budget. However, as we saw in Chapter 1, the 'underspend' of £334 million of licence-fee revenue did not go back to the BBC: the government transferred it to the Treasury, on top of the £2.34 billion raised from the spectrum auction.

Meanwhile, advertising-funded commercial TV companies were under pressure because the financial crisis had led to a 12 per cent fall in annual TV advertising revenue since 2007 – 17 per cent in real (inflation-adjusted) terms.[6] Because TV production and distribution costs are largely fixed (that is, they don't go down just because the broadcaster is getting less advertising revenue) the impact on profit was severe. Understandably, many in the Edinburgh audience from the hard-pressed commercial sector shared Murdoch's resentment of the BBC's guaranteed licence-fee income.[7]

Most also agreed that the industry was over-regulated – although, to be fair, it's hard to find an industry that thinks it's under-regulated. (Many of the bankers whose recklessness had caused the financial crisis insisted, even after the crash, that the problem had been one of over-regulation.) However, most would have disagreed with Murdoch's view that the requirement for broadcast news to be impartial should be dropped. And, above all, the independent producers – the largest group in the Edinburgh audience – disagreed with Murdoch on his view that the BBC should be 'much, much smaller'. With fewer commissions from commercial TV companies, the last thing they needed was also fewer from the BBC, their other main UK revenue source. This was especially true for producers of factual and children's programmes: it's possible they may have resented their dependence on the BBC for commissions, but they certainly did not want to see its funding, and their income, cut to placate Rupert and James Murdoch.

Moreover, James Murdoch's audience was also completely alienated by his cultural and political remarks. Some of his references – such as describing the BBC as presenting 'state-sponsored news' and comparing it to *Pravda* (the Russian Communist newspaper) – struck them as so culturally tin-eared as to provoke giggling. People wondered how many ordinary Brits he'd actually met – people who weren't his neighbours, bankers, lawyers or employees and didn't share his worldview. Had he even heard about the 'mixed economy' or the innovations of Attlee's post-war Labour government? Come to that, had he actually read *Nineteen Eighty-Four*?

The View from 2019

Ten years on, the speech feels out of touch in several respects. Even at the time, Murdoch's suggestion that the government had, or was close to having, Orwellian control of information was, literally, laughably over the top. Almost as hyperbolic was his claim that the BBC was 'ever more dominant': Sky's fast-growing annual revenue in the UK and Ireland was already over £5.3 billion in 2009[8] – a year-on-year increase of 8.2 per cent to almost double the £2.7 billion licence-fee funding of BBC Television that year.[9] Just nine years later (in September 2018) Sky was sold to the US media giant Comcast for over £30 billion.

Another strikingly dated feature of the speech is that, although it repeatedly refers to a converged 'all-media market', its *only* reference to the big US technology companies – who, unlike the BBC, really have become dominant in the last ten years[10] – is an evidence-free and (in our view) highly implausible claim that the reason why Google attracts such a high share of UK advertising revenue is the over-regulation of our 'tightly restricted commercial television sector'. We are not aware of anyone else having ever made this claim.

Today, analysts and policy-makers all agree that it's Google, Facebook and the other advertising-funded US technology giants who pose the most 'serious and imminent' threat to UK newspaper journalism – so much so that, in March 2018, the government commissioned the economist and journalist Dame Frances Cairncross, former rector of Exeter College, Oxford, specifically to review the long-term financial viability of the press in the light of this threat.[11] Neither the BBC nor the regulation of TV advertising was even mentioned in the terms of reference setting out the aims and scope of the Cairncross Review.

The speech's uncritical acceptance of free-market ideology would also probably be less widely shared today, even in the USA. To support its case, Murdoch rather bizarrely invoked Darwin, arguing that his theory of evolution by natural selection implied that markets, too, should be unmanaged, and he likened public service broadcasting to the faith of creationism, as a 'belief in a managed process with an omniscient authority' (with Ofcom, presumably, cast as God).[12]

James Murdoch's portrayal of the BBC was nothing short of horrific, and – like many horror stories – sparing with the facts. For instance, rather than ignoring viewers' and listeners' preferences, as he suggested, the BBC is highly audience-focused and, therefore, competitive – which is, presumably, the real reason why he was attacking it. In 2009, the populist backlash against neoliberal global capitalism – triggered by austerity and growing inequality – had hardly begun. But even today, many of the

79

attacks on the BBC reflect free-market thinking that struggles with the idea of a popular and successful public service broadcaster funded by a compulsory licence fee. A BBC-equivalent in the US is culturally almost unthinkable (although, with five or six times the BBC's actual budget and access to the Hollywood studios, it could make some wonderful programmes . . .)

What James Didn't Say

There were also many relevant issues Murdoch's speech *didn't* mention. Some of these were commercial.

Most obviously, it didn't mention Sky's and News International's clear commercial vested interest in what he was arguing. (He may have felt such a declaration unnecessary, since everyone there would know that Sky and News International would benefit if there were lighter regulation, less competition from the BBC and no digital terrestrial television (DTT) offering free-to-air viewing. Companies are fully entitled to argue their case and it's normal for them to frame it in socially beneficial terms and in a one-sided way.) For instance, James Murdoch was under no obligation to talk about the social, economic and consumer benefits of DTT: releasing the analogue TV spectrum to help fund public expenditure, and increasing the range of universally available free-to-air channels. And mention them he most certainly did *not*.

The speech was also part of a wider effort by the Murdochs to persuade newspapers around the world to charge for their online content.[13] As James said, newspapers find it hard to fund quality journalism on the internet. The main reason is that their revenue per reader from online display advertising is only a small fraction of the equivalent figure for print display advertising.[14] But the alternative business model – erecting a paywall and charging online readers – is almost impossible for mass-market newspapers like the *Sun*, and, even for broadsheet-style quality newspapers, much harder if their competitors are not also doing the same.[15]

Murdoch was correct in saying that UK commercial TV advertising is 'tightly restricted': unlike in the US, broadcasters are limited as to how many minutes per hour of commercial airtime they are allowed to sell. However, he omitted to mention that the rules are significantly *more* restrictive for the three commercial public service broadcasters (ITV, Channel 4 and Channel 5) and therefore actually *favour* Sky and the other non-PSB broadcasters and channels competing against them.[16]

'Fearless, Independent Journalism'

As well as these unstated commercial points, there were also several others missing from James Murdoch's speech. First of all, the Murdochs' commitment to 'fearless, independent' journalism did not stretch to China. Ten years earlier, as part of Rupert Murdoch's attempt to build a business there, he had dropped BBC World Service Television from the Star TV network when the Chinese government expressed unhappiness with the BBC's coverage of its human rights record. As he explained, China has 'distinctive social and moral values that Western companies must learn to abide by'. He had already directly instructed HarperCollins, which he also controlled, not to publish Chris Patten's book on his experience as the last governor of Hong Kong, as it too included some criticisms of the Chinese authorities (his actual words were: 'Kill the fucking book'). Having been forced to write off a significant advance on Patten's book, HarperCollins then had to write off another, for a biography of Deng Xiaoping, which had been commissioned from Deng's own daughter.[17]

Secondly, the 'noisy, disrespectful, raucous free press' (a.k.a.

the 'professional journalists' against whom James Murdoch argued that the BBC should not be competing) specifically included News International's *Sun* and *News of the World*. As we now know, at the time of his 2009 speech (called 'The Absence of Trust', remember) the *Sun* and – especially – the *News of the World* had been conducting large-scale phone hacking for several years while under his leadership. News International's initial claim that hacking was done by only one person working for a rogue *News of the World* reporter had already been exposed as untrue seven weeks earlier, by Nick Davies in *The Guardian*.[18]

Thirdly, a few years earlier, the 2003–4 Hutton Inquiry had held a high-profile investigation into the events leading to the death of UN weapons inspector Dr David Kelly. Central to these events was a BBC Radio report in May 2003 which quoted Kelly, without naming him, and claimed that the intelligence dossier used to justify the second Iraq War had been 'sexed up' under pressure from the government. Kelly committed suicide after the government named him as the source of the BBC story. Lord Hutton's report on these events, seen as a whitewash by most of the UK public and media, exonerated the government and heavily criticized the BBC, leading to the resignation of both its then chairman, Gavyn Davies, and director-general, Greg Dyke – the only such double resignation in its history.

Whatever one's views of the 2003 invasion of Iraq – all 175 of Rupert Murdoch's 'fearless and independent' editors around the world supported it[19] – these events are hard to reconcile with the speech's portrayal of the BBC as a state propaganda vehicle and its references to *Pravda* and *Nineteen Eighty-Four*.

The US Market: Myth and Reality

Finally, the speech's description of James' favoured system for TV, the US market, was also highly misleading. TV news in the

US does indeed have no impartiality requirements, which would almost certainly be argued to be against the constitutional right to free speech and a free press.[20] This lack of impartiality regulation had enabled News Corporation to set up the popular – and hugely profitable – Fox News. Despite its former slogan 'fair and balanced' (dropped in 2017 after being endlessly mocked),[21] Fox News has an unashamedly right-wing Republican agenda and played a significant role in the 2016 election of Donald Trump.[22] The contrast between the notoriously biased Fox News in the US and the much more balanced Sky News in the UK, both owned by the same parent company, illustrates the value of UK regulation of broadcast news and current affairs – a value that the British public strongly appreciates.

Despite this lack of impartiality regulation, the reality is that, in terms of ownership and control, the US television market is actually *more* tightly regulated than the UK's. (In particular, if we return to the context of James Murdoch's speech, that of 2009, anyone controlling more than 25 per cent of a TV channel or even a local radio station there still had to be a US citizen.[23] That's why Rupert Murdoch had to become an American in 1985, when James was twelve, in order to take over the Metromedia TV stations that became the Fox network.)[24]

The US also has tight restrictions on the ownership of different media within the same local market. If these had applied in Britain, they would have prevented News Corporation from its simultaneous market leadership in both newspapers (News International) *and* pay TV (Sky). Naturally, James' speech mentioned none of this.

7. Rupert, Paul and the Gang

In this and the next chapter, we'll meet a motley selection of the BBC's enemies in the UK.[1] Some have been around forever, others are new; some are high-profile, others are less well known or even shadowy.

The BBC's enemies actively seek out and publicize negative stories about it, drawing on any evidence and arguments they can find to build a plausible case against it. And they return to the attack again and again. Some even seem to have made it into a full-time job. The newspapers listed below have run literally *thousands* of anti-BBC stories in recent years. There's one free-market think tank which has published a major report or book calling for radical cuts or changes in its funding at least once a decade since the 1960s. Another attacker is an author, a former BBC correspondent, who has written three books in the last twelve years telling viewers and listeners not to trust it.[2]

This isn't about occasional criticisms. Everyone in Britain complains about the BBC from time to time. Later on, we too will criticize it for some big mistakes. But these chapters are about those people whose attacks are persistent and give every appearance of being deliberately damaging. Many also seem to be *strategic* – driven by commercial or political motives which are often underpinned by free-market ideology: the BBC's continuing popularity is hard for free-market ideologues to bear.

However, this hostility is not always calculated – some of it also seems to come from the heart. Paul Dacre, former editor of the *Daily Mail*,[3] has often shown a *visceral* hatred of what he sees as the left–liberal culture and social attitudes of the BBC undermining traditional British family values and society.

The BBC's UK enemies include hostile newspapers and politicians who draw on research by free-market think tanks and News-watch – a specialist organization devoted almost entirely to monitoring and attacking the BBC's news and current affairs coverage of the EU and Brexit. There are also a host of hostile websites, YouTube channels and trolls of varying degrees of respectability. Some are entirely dedicated to attacking the BBC. The low barriers to entry in digital and social media mean the list is almost endless. It is often impossible to trace who is really writing the comments and who, if anyone, is funding them – and also, who is reading, endorsing and sharing them. They're designed to make you think almost everyone hates the BBC.

Although we've necessarily had to be highly selective, the examples we've picked are representative of this wider BBC-attacking 'industry'. In this chapter we'll look at some of the BBC's traditional media enemies: the UK's most powerful right-wing papers, focusing mainly on Rupert Murdoch, the most powerful and persistent of them all, and Paul Dacre, the BBC's second greatest media enemy during his twenty-six-year reign at the *Daily Mail*.

The Murdoch Empire

Rupert Murdoch's hostility to the BBC goes back over fifty years, at the very least to when he bought the *News of the World* and the *Sun* in 1968–9. Its roots may go back even further, to whatever early experiences led to his lifelong antipathy towards the British Establishment, including the monarchy as well as the BBC. (The paradox is that, although he was born in Australia, he went to Oxford[4] and his newspaper proprietor father, Sir Keith Murdoch, was knighted.)

Whatever the reason, Murdoch's animosity seems to have

been fully formed by the time of his political alignment with Margaret Thatcher in the late 1970s and his 1983 acquisition of the company that became Sky.[5]

In 1989, just seven months after the – very risky – launch of Sky, he gave the keynote MacTaggart Lecture at the Edinburgh International Television Festival. Like James in 2009, Rupert framed his speech ('Freedom in Broadcasting')[6] within the broader context of British history, politics and economics. The general thrust was an assault on public service broadcasting – ITV, as well as the BBC – and an argument for a 'market-led TV system' like the USA's.

Murdoch's UK tabloids, the *Sun* and the *News of the World* (now the *Sun on Sunday*) whose editorial policies he closely controls, have routinely assaulted the BBC, focusing on celebrity scandals, lurid stories of corporate excess and occasional attacks of the vapours about particular programmes. What may be more surprising are the methods sometimes used by Murdoch's *Sunday Times* – Britain's highly respected, top-selling broadsheet Sunday newspaper – to dig up or concoct hostile stories about the BBC.

The *Sunday Times* and the 'Gentleman Blagger'

'Barclays bankers who blew £44,000 on dinner'; 'Shop giant pays Blair's top fixer £100,000'; ' "Pirate" pays £15m for Lloyd Webber home'; 'Millionaire Eurosceptic gave Brown trust £50,000'; 'Four-homes Prescott faces censure over flat'; and 'Prescott's son may cash in as council homes go cheap'. These are some of the headlines that John Ford, known as the 'Gentleman Blagger', garnered for the *Sunday Times*. His story is the stuff of legend (with a book apparently in preparation).

Ford told us that, as a struggling writer and actor, he did not go looking for his dream job – it found him. During 1994, out of work and living in Brixton, he bumped into an old university friend who claimed to be working in the intelligence business. Remembering Ford's skill at mimicry, the friend gave him an office, a phone, a script – and an entry into the secret world of *blagging*, persuading people to give you their secrets by lying to them, impersonating 'insiders' and creating urgent deadlines in order to transfer secret documents.

In 1995, with Ford now working for a Croydon-based investigation agency, his bosses revealed to him that they were providing 'research' for the *Sunday Times*. Soon, Ford became an adept and proficient blagger, handling weekly requests from Murdoch's News International.

A series of scoops for the paper made possible by Ford meant that he swiftly became its blagger of choice. After uncovering the war chest that had just been raised to fight New Labour's imminent election campaign, he was approached to work for all corners of the *Sunday Times* newsroom. The operations were always secret and carried out remotely in order to leave no traceable link between Ford and the paper. He was utterly deniable. The paper had him on its books as a freelance contributor, but, in reality, he was, in his own words, 'a one-man crime wave' specializing in document theft. His victims were 'generally high-profile, celebrities and politicians'.[7] In fact, at the 2012 Leveson Inquiry into phone hacking by the press, another of Ford's victims, former Prime Minister Gordon Brown, said that blaggers had been 'impersonating me to get bank information, we had blagging by lawyers, we had what is called reverse-engineering of telephones ... and, even now, I'm afraid, the editor of the *Sunday Times* has come to your inquiry and said that he had evidence of something he was never able to prove and there was no public interest justification for the intrusion and the impersonation and the breaking into records'.[8]

Some of Ford's scoops were about the BBC. Whereas Murdoch's *Sun* and *News of the World* mainly offered salacious stories and gossip about presenters and celebrities, the *Sunday Times* focused on exclusives about management crises, financial disasters and alleged political bias. Its headlines read 'Revealed' or 'Secret memo', as opposed to the tabloids' 'Fury', 'Shocking' or 'Scandal'.

Ford's first big BBC scoop for Nick Hellen, the *Sunday Times* media editor, was a front-page story on 12 February 1995, which carried a great headline, supposedly quoting the Corporation's then director-general: 'Birt tells the BBC: "We're boring, biased and bourgeois"'. (It was based on a 'leaked' internal BBC report on a programme strategy review led by executives Liz Forgan and Alan Yentob.)[9] In reality, according to Ford, there was no 'leak'. He'd stolen the report, making a simple interception at the printers. He had called them, pretending to be a member of BBC staff, and said he needed a proof copy dispatched to him on the Friday before publication, apparently 'to check for revision'. The report was collected in a taxi and delivered to a cab office in Croydon. Ford picked it up and sent it to News International in Wapping. There were champagne celebrations for him and the rest was history.

In February 1996, another *Sunday Times* story, 'BBC to move into pay TV Channel' by Nicholas Hellen and Nicholas Fox disclosed that a further 'leaked' BBC report outlined plans for a satellite pay-TV service to rival Murdoch's BSkyB.[10] Had someone at the BBC really leaked it, or maybe inadvertently revealed it? No: once again, John Ford had blagged it – stolen it, using deception rather than forced entry.

This is how he did it. Having identified the report's authors, he contacted the BBC's internal report production staff, convinced them he was working with the authors and, with a mixture of charm and authority, again persuaded them to hand the report over to Reception for immediate collection by an innocent taxi driver, whom he'd already booked. Eager and nervous, Ford took the report, cycled to Wapping, and handed it over to Security to make its way to the newsroom, there to be spun and rewritten before the 2 p.m. Saturday copy deadline. Ford told us that he'd refined his technique down to an art form. The BBC was one of his key targets over many years.

BBC Radio: A 'New Front' in Rupert Murdoch's War

In 2018, the Murdoch group sold its 39-per-cent share in Sky to the US media giant Comcast in a deal that valued the business at £30 billion.[11] For the first time in years, Murdoch was no longer competing against BBC TV. However, this did not lead to any noticeable reduction in his war against the Corporation, because, in 2016, News UK (which had changed its name from News International in 2013) had acquired the Wireless Group, which owns Virgin Radio, talkSPORT and other commercial radio stations in the UK and Ireland – all competing for listeners against BBC Radio. Thus it was that, in late 2017 (perhaps the move was timed to coincide with Ofcom taking over as the BBC's regulator)[12] – News UK awarded Kent University's Centre for Journalism a £25,000 research grant to 'assess the delivery of BBC Radio 5 Live's public service commitment'. Perhaps unsurprisingly, the resulting study damningly concluded that only 45 per cent of Radio 5 Live's output was serious news and current affairs, far short of the 75-per-cent requirement in the BBC's operating licence (and the 76 per cent claimed by the BBC itself).[13] *The Times* duly reported this finding as emerging from 'an academic study'.[14] The study's lead author, Professor Tim Luckhurst, a former BBC Radio 5 Live assistant editor, defended the work as a 'detailed and meticulous piece of pure academic research', including a 'practical, real-world definition of what constitutes news and what constitutes current affairs' which '[a]cademics [had] been seeking . . . for nearly 50 years'.[15]

Despite these bold claims, as far as we know, the research was only published as a short report,[16] rather than a peer-reviewed paper – the normal channel for academic research.[17] In other words, the Luckhurst team had marked its own homework (and given it an A+). According to *Private Eye*, Luckhurst (a 'self-styled leading expert on broadcasting' despite having 'published nothing authoritative' on it) presented the report at a working breakfast of the all-party parliamentary media group[18] in January 2019. The only other contributors at the event were the Wireless Group and News UK – both Murdoch-owned – with no one from the BBC invited to reply.[19] The *Financial Times* neatly summed up this incident under the headline 'Rupert Murdoch's News UK takes a potshot at BBC radio'.[20]

This was not to be News UK's only assault on the BBC. Eight months later, in September 2018, the Wireless Group demanded that Ofcom investigate how the BBC acquires sports rights for Radio 5 Live. However, Ofcom rejected this request, arguing that the Wireless Group had failed to identify any changes in the BBC's acquisition of sports rights since Charter renewal, and that the BBC's activities in this market posed 'no material harm to consumers'.[21]

In January 2020, News UK announced plans to launch Times Radio, clearly in competition with BBC Radio 4 – so the Murdoch empire's attacks on the BBC look likely to continue.

Six Secret Meetings with Osborne in 2015

We have seen how Rupert and James Murdoch have repeatedly argued, either personally or via their media outlets, that the BBC should be 'much, much smaller', with Rupert explicitly citing PBS in America as a model for the UK to emulate. (You may also recall from Chapter 2 that Sky was also part of the industry lobby which successfully persuaded the Competition Commission to block Project Kangaroo, the proposed SVoD joint venture between the BBC, ITV and Channel 4.) But Murdoch also lobbied at the very top of government.

In the eight weeks between the Conservatives' unexpected election victory of 7 May 2015 and the announcement of the BBC's funding deal on 3 July, George Osborne had six meetings with News UK – including two with Rupert Murdoch himself. What Murdoch and his executives said at those six meetings remains secret. But, given his track record, and the outcome – a second set of deep and damaging cuts within five years of the last – we can reasonably assume that his fingerprints were all over the cuts. The *Sunday Times* broke the news of the funding deal on Saturday, 5 July 2015 – two days *before* its announcement in Parliament the following Monday. On 8 July, *The Times* praised Osborne for reining in the BBC, especially BBC Online, with the claim that: 'an overwhelmingly dominant state-funded news organization is inimical to the genuine and robust diversity of views on which a true democracy depends'. The *Sun* even claimed that the deal was too generous.[22]

Rupert and James Murdoch have led some very successful businesses. But they don't like competition, and they will do everything in their considerable power to reduce it.[23] It's clear that Rupert Murdoch's papers will keep on attacking the BBC for as long as it is in his vested interest for it to be weakened.

Some Policy-Makers Agree with Rupert and James

Of course, there's no great mystery about why a company – especially one as powerful, aggressive, feared and well connected as the Murdoch organization – might do whatever it can to increase its profits through reduced competition, lighter regulation or lower taxation. Nor is it surprising that politicians around the world have often found it expedient to help it in return for supportive newspaper stories and editorials – and to avoid hostile ones.[24] Having said that, the BBC is hugely popular and provides remarkable value for money; it also creates a mass of public service and reputational benefits to the UK and makes a significant economic contribution as a major customer for independent producers and a significant exporter in its own right. It sits at the heart of our very successful broadcasting ecology and wider creative industries. One might therefore expect policy-makers – other than for reasons of political expediency – to give short shrift to the Murdochs' transparently self-serving arguments for less competition from the BBC. But the evidence is that some, such as John Whittingdale, and perhaps even George Osborne, *genuinely believe* that reducing the Corporation's funding, scope and scale is in the public interest. As we saw in Chapter 5, Whittingdale, as chair of the House of Commons DCMS Committee (and perhaps even still as Secretary of State) was a council member of the Freedom Association, whose *only* policies were Brexit and abolishing the TV licence fee; and the BBC's market impact was by far the biggest issue in his 2015 Charter renewal green paper.

A Complete Dog's Breakfast in the *Sun*

After the BBC Board's decision in June 2019 to restrict free TV licences to households with at least one person aged seventy-five or above in receipt of Pension Credit, the *Sun* published four articles in four months attacking the decision.[25] The editorial line was that, as part of the 2015 deal, the BBC had agreed to take on the cost of free licences for all over-seventy-fives; that it had now reneged on the deal; and that it could easily cover the cost if it weren't so inefficient and didn't overpay its managers and senior presenters. None of these claims was true.

The last of these articles, from 8 September 2019, is especially striking. Under the headline 'BBC blows more than £745m on presenter pay hikes and buildings while axing free TV licences for millions of OAPs', it appeared at first glance to be a detailed and wide-ranging analysis of the BBC's accounts. It claimed to show that, by reducing wastage and inefficiency, the BBC could save enough to cover the full cost of giving a free TV licence to *every* household with one or more members aged seventy-five-plus: 'The annual amount needed by 2021–2022 to keep the cherished perk is £745 million – the exact sum we found has been frittered away'. The Tory MP Peter Bone was duly quoted as saying the figures were 'disgraceful' and that 'The BBC is mismanaging its accounts and now over-seventy-fives are having to pay'.

You may remember that in Chapter 4 we looked at a *Daily Mail* article from 2015 which purported to show that the BBC spent 'less than half of its money on programmes'. Although, as we saw, this claim was miles from the truth, this article was, at least, based on a coherent, if badly flawed analysis. In contrast, the *Sun* article was such a complete dog's breakfast that it is impossible to do a rational analysis of it. At its heart is a list of seventeen random examples of supposed BBC 'waste', a mish-mash of one-off historical costs incurred over the previous *decade* (for a variety of reasons – from the payment of costs in law suits to capital expenditure) and recurring annual costs. These are then added up, as if they were all annual expenditure, to produce the £745 million (per annum) figure in the headline which led Peter Bone to claim that the BBC was mishandling its money.

If we home in on the detail of the article we can see that the most important (and largest) listed item was the £187.5 million-per-year cost of the BBC's ten-year recovery programme to eliminate its pension-fund deficit. Like many, perhaps most, organizations both public and private, the BBC had a pension-fund deficit (because the insurance companies had misjudged how long people would live and how far their invested money would go, having been caught by surprise by the 2008 world financial crash). We'll assume the *Sun* was highlighting this mainly to illustrate what it saw as the BBC's incompetence – and the size of some senior management pension pots – rather than suggesting that the Corporation should try to renege on its pension obligations.

Moreover, many of the annual costs itemized in the *Sun's* 8 September 2019 article are part of the BBC's government-set remit: £32 million per year for BBC Scotland and £9 million per year for BBC Alba (a Scottish Gaelic-language free-to-air television channel). Other items falsely recorded as annual expenses encompassed the payouts for wrongful accusations – to Lord McAlpine in 2013 (£185,000, plus costs) and to Sir Cliff Richard five years later in 2018 (£2.5 million, including costs). The article *did* note that the BBC's legal expenses were largely covered by insurance.[26] But it failed to mention that the total cost of these cases was completely dwarfed by that of News UK's own payouts to its phone-hacking victims – by May 2019, it stood at a figure of £400 million, possibly with more to come – at least 200 times the net cost to the BBC of settling the McAlpine and Richard cases.[27]

A final, ironic point about the Murdoch empire is that, like other popular newspapers, the *Sun* relies heavily on the BBC as a source of celebrity gossip and stories. In fact, at the time of writing, in late September 2019, four of its top five 'BBC' stories are about *Strictly Come Dancing*. Other BBC programmes that frequently feature in the *Sun's* stories include *EastEnders*, *Doctor Who* and *The Graham Norton Show*.

Paul Dacre and the *Daily Mail*

From 1992 to 2018, Paul Dacre, as editor of the *Daily Mail*, was the BBC's second most powerful media enemy after Rupert

Murdoch. Over the twenty-six years of his editorship, the *Mail* ran endless Beeb-bashing articles, often as front-page stories. For Dacre, famously an absolutist editor, this was personal. He clearly hates – it is the only possible word – the 'metropolitan liberal elite', whom he sees as snobbish, hypocritical, posturing and unpatriotic, unlike his solid, honest, conservative, unpretentious, provincial, Middle England readers.[28] He sees the BBC's culture and management as a prime symbol of what he hates – although, even for Dacre, it's a bit more complicated than that.

Over the last ten years of his tenure, Dacre's attacks on those he disapproved of became more and more extreme. As well as the BBC, his targets included the Leveson Inquiry, the EU, Labour politicians, *The Guardian* and prominent Remainers.[29] In 2016, he notoriously labelled judges who gave a correct, Brexit-related ruling (i.e. one that has not since been successfully legally challenged) as 'enemies of the people'.[30] (We wonder what Orwell would have made of that.) According to an analysis by Liz Gerard, a former *Times* journalist who undertook research on *Daily Mail* headlines for this book, from 2008 to 2018 there were: 'More than 4,000 news stories with BBC in the headline or subhead [including] about 500 front-page stories [and] 2,500 opinion columns and leaders'. The recurring themes were bias, profligacy, pampered stars and the failure to make enough new programmes.[31]

The *Mail*'s attacks on the BBC were not restricted to its own activities. If there was a viewpoint the paper didn't approve of, it attacked both that viewpoint *and* the BBC for reporting it – or, as Dacre's *Mail* would have it, for 'fomenting misconceptions'. Conversely, the paper also condemned the BBC for *failing* to report stories (apparently forgetting that all news organizations make editorial decisions on what to cover and that none can do everything). Dacre's *Daily Mail*, with its majority female readership, also made much hay of the BBC's gender pay-gap row – but reported on its own, minimally, only when legally required to do so. (For the record, the BBC's median pay gap[32] was 7.6 per cent in 2018, less than half the *Mail*'s, at 15.4 per cent. The *Mail*'s median *bonus-pay gap* between genders was 26.7 per cent,[33] versus zero for the BBC.)[34]

The World according to Dacre

As an editor, Paul Dacre was notoriously ungregarious. He didn't give interviews[35] and was hardly ever on television – except, looking a very unhappy bunny, when giving evidence to the Leveson Inquiry in 2012.[36] He preferred to send his lieutenants out to explain or defend the *Mail*'s most controversial stories. He seemed nostalgic about both the old Fleet Street days (when the press – national and local – was rich from advertising, confident and, as he saw it, fearless and independent) and an imaginary 1950s Middle England with almost universally shared, honest, 'small c' conservative values. But the dark side of this nostalgia of his was a narrow nationalism and various, endlessly repeated right-wing obsessions and phobias – wicked foreigners, benefit scroungers, teenage 'thugs', a criminal justice system that's too soft, and so on (spoofed in the popular '*Daily Mail* Song' YouTube video).[37] The paper's tendency to play to its readers' prejudices goes right back to the mantra of Alfred 'Sunny' Harmsworth, who founded it in 1896: 'The British people relish a good hero and a good hate'.[38]

The BBC and the 'Subsidariat'

Like James Murdoch, Dacre saw profit as both the reflection of quality[39]and, more controversially, the only basis for independent journalism. Therefore, his pet hates were the loss-making

Guardian and the publicly funded BBC, both part of what he called the 'Subsidariat' – organizations which, to his mind, existed outside the 'real world' of the profit motive. As he said in his Hugh Cudlipp Memorial Lecture[40] of 2008:

> It's my contention in this lecture that the Subsidariat, dominated by the BBC monolith, is distorting Britain's media market, crushing journalistic pluralism and imposing a mono culture that is inimical to healthy democratic debate . . . Now before the liberal commentators reach for their vitriol – and, my goodness, how they demonise anyone who disagrees with them – let me say that I would die in a ditch defending the BBC as a great civilising force. I, for one, would pay the licence fee just for Radio 4 . . . But, as George Orwell said, 'to see what is in front of one's nose requires constant struggle'. And what is in front of one's nose is that the BBC, a behemoth that bestrides Britain is, as Cudlipp might have put it, TOO BLOODY BIG, TOO BLOODY PERVASIVE AND TOO BLOODY POWERFUL [capital letters in original].

Dacre presumably put a lot of thought into this high-profile reflection on his long career in journalism and his comments do register praise for the BBC as a 'civilising force' and for Radio 4 in particular.[41] But his description of it as part of the 'Subsidariat' was simply wrong, revealing him to be a victim of the very problem described in his quotation from Orwell. The BBC is not 'subsidized' like a commercial business that can't pay its way: its Charter *does not allow it* to sell advertising or subscriptions. Rather than being an unprofitable business, it is something completely different – a public institution deliberately financed mainly by the licence fee, an earmarked tax, supplemented by the significant contribution from its profitable international commercial operations. And his idea of the BBC's overall 'dominance' was also years out of date by 2008. Sky, in particular, was already much bigger financially (although smaller in terms of UK reach and consumption) – and is even more so today. The media sector has grown and the BBC is, increasingly, a smaller part of a larger whole.

Dacre was a brilliant and inspired editor, one who followed his intuition about what would resonate with readers, rather than being a slave to market research, and he was rightly recognized as such by his peers. But you have to wonder how this virtual recluse – with his £2.7 million final annual remuneration,[42] his house in Belgravia, his chauffeur-driven car and his 17,000-acre estate in Scotland – really kept up with the lives and worldviews of ordinary people,[43] or whether he was still running on impressions he formed as a younger man during the 1970s when he worked on the *Daily Express* in Manchester and Belfast.

From Dacre to Greig: Still No Quarter for the BBC?

When Dacre left the *Mail* in November 2018, just before his seventieth birthday, his successor was the altogether more clubbable, apparently socially liberal and certainly elite Geordie Greig, former editor of both the *Mail on Sunday* and the long-established society magazine *Tatler*. There was no love lost between Dacre and Greig. The editorial line of Greig's *Mail on Sunday* – on issues up to and including Brexit – was often the opposite of that taken by Dacre's *Daily Mail*, and many people believed this largely reflected the two editors' mutual animosity. Their feud continued even after Dacre had left.[44]

There was therefore much speculation, and nervousness in some quarters, about how the *Daily Mail*'s editorial positions would change under the new regime.[45]

Greig significantly altered the paper's stance on Brexit[46] and dialled down the hysteria more generally. But there has been little, if any, sign of a reduction in its hostility towards the BBC – although, like all the Beeb-lambasting papers, both the *Daily Mail* and *Mail on Sunday* continued to feature a mass of BBC programmes and stars in their main pages and 'what to watch' columns.

And the Rest – Other Anti-BBC Newspapers

The *Daily Express*, now a shadow of its former self as the leading mid-market, Middle England newspaper, moved vociferously further to the right under Richard Desmond, its owner from 2000 to 2018.[47] It was the only national newspaper to back UKIP in the 2015 election and a constant, if somewhat unfocused enemy of the BBC under Desmond, with headlines like 'Songs of Praise in Calais EXPOSED – this is how the BBC is spending YOUR cash'.[48]

In February 2018 the Express Newspapers group was acquired by Trinity Mirror (now Reach plc), owners of the left-leaning *Daily* and *Sunday Mirror* and the *Sunday People*. The *Express* is now being closely watched for signs of change.[49] However, as with Greig's *Daily Mail*, the initial signs are that the *Express* will continue to castigate the BBC. For instance, it was at the fore-front of the press attacks on the BBC for limiting the free TV licence concession solely to households with over-seventy-fives on Pension Credit, and a key sponsor of the Age UK petition after the BBC's decision – while not making it clear to its readers that Age UK was primarily blaming the government, *not the BBC*, for the problem.[50] The *Daily* and *Sunday Telegraph* are owned by the famously reclusive Barclay brothers, who also own the – increasingly conservative – *Spectator* magazine.[51] The *Telegraph* also criticizes the BBC on a constant basis, but in a more considered style than the *Sun*, *Mail* and *Express*.

The media we've discussed here – the Murdoch papers, the

Mail, the *Express* and the *Telegraph* – are where the majority of people in Britain see the various charges laid against the BBC, especially its supposed inefficiency, bloatedness and bias, but also, sometimes, both the real and the imaginary disadvantages of the TV licence fee and, occasionally, at least in the 'quality' papers, the suggestion that the BBC does things that would be better left to the free market.

Some of the material for all this – and the shocked rent-a-quotes from backbench MPs – comes from research by the journalists themselves, not all of it nearly as rigorous as one might hope. But behind most of the headlines and political statements is a stage army of backroom boys (and, yes, they are mostly boys) of varying degrees of respectability, tirelessly developing arguments to pillory the BBC. Let's now meet a few of them up close and personal in the following chapter.

8.   In Which We Meet . . .

In her book on US political funding, *Dark Money*, Jane Mayer describes how, when businessman Robert Brookings founded the Brookings Institution in 1916, he mandated that its mission must be 'free from any political or pecuniary interest' and, although he was a Republican, that its board should include scholars from many viewpoints to ensure an ethic of 'disinterestedness'.

According to Mayer, 'The same ideals animated the Rockefeller, Ford, and Russell Sage Foundations, as well as most of academia and the elite news organizations . . . like *The New York Times*, which strove to deliver the facts free from partisan bias'.[1] She then describes the extraordinary growth over the last fifty years of right-wing US think tanks and pressure groups, mainly funded – often covertly – by billionaires and generous tax breaks.

Brookings' spirit of impartiality seems like a lost world in this network of right-wing 'research' groups, lobbyists and 'astro-turf' organizations,[2] whose mission is invariably to drive tax cuts and deregulation and to roll back the state. They include the American Enterprise Institute, the Cato Institute, several Koch foundations, the Manhattan Institute, the Center to Protect Patient Rights, Americans for Prosperity and *hundreds* more.

Britain has nothing on a comparable scale, but we too now have a growing roll call of right-wing think tanks sharing many of the same aims and characteristics. It's a world most people know nothing about – a smaller bubble within the Westminster bubble they see every day on the TV news. But, as in America, it now has a significant impact on our politics and media.

Each UK right-wing think tank has its own emphasis, but they tend to have several points in common, including being opaquely funded, an aversion to being described as a right-wing think tank, scepticism about government regulations, the scientific arguments about man-made climate change and the EU – and hostility to the BBC, with an emphasis on reducing its scope and funding and abolishing the TV licence fee. The Institute of Economic Affairs, Adam Smith Institute, Tax-Payers' Alliance, New Culture Forum and Centre for Policy Studies, in particular, have repeatedly produced ammunition for right-wing newspapers and politicians to use in their attacks on the BBC. News-watch, which is less well known and a monitoring organization rather than a think tank, essentially does nothing else. In the rest of this chapter, we first discuss these UK right-wing think tanks and how their attacks on the BBC fit into their other work. There is nothing comparable on the left.

We focus on the Institute of Economic Affairs (IEA), the main *economic* right-wing think tank, the New Culture Forum, the main *cultural* one, and News-watch. We then briefly summarize the role of lobbyists in spreading and reinforcing messages which are helpful to their clients, including those attacking the BBC. Finally, we review some of the less respectable players working constantly to attack and undermine the BBC – a plethora of online trolls, bloggers and conspiracy theorists that have sprung up like mushrooms in the new world of digital and social media. As we've discussed, the systematic attacks on the BBC are overwhelmingly from the right, so this chapter is about the right-wing players making these attacks.

We start in the rather rarefied world of the UK right-wing think tanks. It's all rather cosy: most of them are near neighbours or even housemates.

The House in Tufton Street and the Illiberal
Metropolitan Elite

Fifty-five Tufton Street, SW1 – a stone's throw from the Palace of
Westminster, Number Ten and the Whitehall departments of
state – is Right-Wing-Policy Central. From the outside, it's a
pleasant enough, largeish town house in the Brewers' Georgian
style. But inside, it could become dangerously overcrowded,
with a significant health-and-safety problem because of its large,
constantly shifting population of up to ten different right-wing
institutes and forums – the cream of what we might call the
illiberal metropolitan elite. They include Civitas, the Global Warming Policy Foundation, Leave Means Leave, the New Culture
Forum and several others,[3] notably the TaxPayers' Alliance,
probably the most powerful pressure group in the country,
mainly through its network of well-placed alumni.[4]

Their near neighbours include the Adam Smith Institute,
only a three-to-four-minute walk away at 23 Great Smith Street;
the IEA, still closer at 2 Lord North Street; the Centre for Policy
Studies, just down the road at 49 Tufton Street; and Policy
Exchange, a couple of blocks further away, at 8–10 Great George
Street. All these think tanks are classified by independent analysts like Transparify, Sourcewatch and Who Funds You as
having a lobbying – or, in the US term, 'advocacy' – approach to
their work, unclear funding sources and strong links to their
American right-wing counterparts.[5]

For instance, the IEA is part of the International Affairs
Group of the Atlas Network of think tanks[6] and receives American funding through a US subsidiary. Now that politics is
increasingly international, so too is the 'advocacy' think-tank
family: they all know each other and their American counterparts and their approaches are similar.[7] Though most people
will never read any of their reports, their work lies behind

thousands of articles and stories making the case for free markets, tax cuts and policies favouring specific commercial interests, especially the fossil-fuel industry. They prefer not to be front-page news themselves, but they definitely help create it.

They are also characterized by all-out support for Brexit, their initiatives on this front typically being coordinated by political strategist Matthew Elliot. Elliott founded the TaxPayers' Alliance in 2004, at the age of twenty-six. He founded Big Brother Watch in 2009 and the Conservative Friends of Russia in 2012 – we think the irony of founding both Big Brother Watch and Conservative Friends of Russia is probably deliberate – and then Business for Britain in 2013. But he is best known as co-founder (in 2015, alongside Dominic Cummings) and chief executive of Vote Leave. He has a strong US right-wing network through his American wife, Sarah, herself chair of Republicans Overseas UK and an ardent Trump supporter,[8] and also through Westminster Brexiteers like Boris Johnson, Michael Gove and Liam Fox.[9]

For the avoidance of doubt: yes, this *is* a sort-of conspiracy. It involves multiple players with overlapping aims; most of their funding (and, therefore, the links between their activities and their funders' vested interests) is hidden; and they appear to coordinate their messages. Direct evidence for this last point comes from a whistleblower, Shahmir Sanni, who formerly worked at the TaxPayers' Alliance. According to Sanni, the Tufton Street think tanks, despite their distinct brands and missions, act as one on issues such as Brexit – and also on threats to the safety of the pack, like Sanni himself.[10] He claims that, during his time there, the TaxPayers' Alliance and eight other organizations at, or linked to 55 Tufton Street, had regular fortnightly meetings to share aims.[11]

A Venue for Beeb-Bashing

Downstairs at 55 Tufton Street is devoted to receptions and events – a smart mini-conference suite where, depending on the evening, journalists and supporters can meet, say, Nigel Farage or former Thatcher cabinet minister Lord Lawson, or hear what new nefarious activities the BBC's been up to, under the auspices of whichever think tank has the stage.

Robin Aitken – the author of *Can We Trust the BBC?* (2007), *Can We Still Trust the BBC?* (2013) and, in case you didn't get the message, *The Noble Liar* in 2018 – has presented his work here more than once. He claims he was virtually the only Conservative at the BBC when he worked there as a journalist. Aitken's contemporaries contest this, pointing to John Humphrys, Andrew Neil, Jeremy Paxman, Robbie Gibb and others. Nevertheless, he doubtless gets a lot of sympathetic tutting from the Tufton Street audience whenever he says this, most recently in March 2020, being interviewed – twice – by Peter Whittle of the New Culture Forum for its YouTube channel.[12] As always, he discussed what he and many others see as the BBC's systematic left-wing bias.

If the newspapers are looking for anti-BBC messages, they are spoiled for choice: almost every right-wing think tank in and around 55 Tufton Street has attacked the Corporation. Nonetheless, nearly all of them have had speakers repeatedly invited to *Question Time*, *Today*, *Newsnight* and other BBC current affairs programmes – which in turn has provoked some criticism of the BBC.[13]

Let's look at the pre-eminent UK right-wing think tank (a label it, naturally, rejects): the Institute of Economic Affairs.

The Institute of Economic Affairs

The name sounds highly impressive and disinterested: 'Institute' has gravitas and 'Economic Affairs' suggests something weighty, discussed by high-powered, politically neutral, senior academics. And, indeed, the Institute's history *is* impressive. It was the first of the post-war right-wing think tanks that have flourished on both sides of the Atlantic, and funded in the USA by a weight of financial support which is revealed in detail in Jane Mayer's *Dark Money*.[14] It was founded by the Etonian businessman and battery-chicken-farm pioneer Antony Fisher in 1955.[15] It is widely credited with helping create much of the thinking, rhetoric and public acceptance of Thatcherism. It is probably the most respected member of the Tufton Street cluster because of its long association with the arguments for free markets, low taxes, privatization and deregulation.

The Institute of Economic Affairs' Covert Aims and Funding

In *Dark Money*, Jane Mayer describes how concealing the Institute's true aims goes right back to its foundation, sixty-five years ago, as a tax-deductible – and therefore supposedly non-partisan – charity[16] by Anthony Fisher and his partner Oliver Smedley:

> Smedley wrote to Fisher, saying that they needed to be 'cagey' and disguise their organization as neutral and non-partisan. Choosing a suitably anodyne name, they founded the grandfather of libertarian think tanks in London, calling it the Institute of Economic Affairs. Smedley wrote that it was 'imperative we should give no indication in our literature that we are working

to educate the public along certain lines which might be inter-preted as having a political bias. In other words, if we said openly that we were re-teaching the economics of the free market, it might enable our enemies to question the charitableness of our motives.'[17]

Despite the IEA's charitable status, in 2013 it emerged that at least some of its funding came from the tobacco giants Philip Morris, Japan Tobacco and British American Tobacco.[18]

Five years later, in early summer 2018, a sting organized by Greenpeace secretly filmed a meeting between its director, Mark Littlewood, and an undercover reporter from Greenpeace's investigations unit posing as a consultant for a US agriculture investor. (Littlewood and the undercover journalist's conversa-tion was detailed in a 2018 *Guardian* article – which also has a weblink to clips from the original video, which you can see for yourself.)[19] Littlewood was recorded promising to introduce the consultant and his client to an agriculture minister so that they could say, 'Minister, I'm really keen to bend your ear about beef'. He said that the IEA had already arranged for the owner of an 11,000-acre cattle ranch in Oklahoma to meet the then Brexit minister Steve Baker and, with the director of an Oklahoma think tank, to visit the Department for International Trade and meet a senior civil servant.

He added that 'The people running our international trade team are talking to [Gove] . . . every three or four days . . . along with David Davis, Boris Johnson, Liam Fox'.[20] He also made a pitch to the so-called 'consultant' for research funding for a pro-posed study on post-Brexit farming, which was to focus on how 'changes in technology, genomics and chemicals could benefit the British countryside'. The aim would be to 'get these ideas into the bloodstream of Defra' (the UK Department for Envir-onment, Food and Rural Affairs, then led by Michael Gove). The cost would be £42,500, including £5,000 for a private lunch with a minister, 'quite possibly' Gove himself. Littlewood went on to say that, although – of course – donors could not influence the results of the study, its conclusions would be consistent with the Institute's free-market position: 'There is no way this report is going to say the most important thing we need to do is keep American beef out of our market in order to prop up our beef farmers, in fact exactly the opposite.' He also suggested the study might propose allowing the UK sale of US chlorine-washed chicken, 'as long as it was labelled'.

The same *Guardian* article tells us that 'In lengthy exchanges with [them], the IEA said there was "nothing untoward about think tanks having a collaborative approach with politicians"', and that Littlewood described his job (to the BBC *Today* programme) in this way: 'My job is to meet other free-market people to try and persuade them to give me some money so my institute can conduct free-market research so that we can influence debate and opinion in society'.[21] Fair enough. We did rather wonder what free-market research with the intention of influencing debate and opinion might be! But, given that the IEA enjoys charitable status – meaning that its purpose(s) must be only for the public benefit – surely the public has a right to know who is funding it and their commercial or political agenda, especially if some of the funding is coming from outside the UK?

For instance, the IEA's former associate director, American Kate Andrews (who recently moved to the *Spectator* to become its economics editor), is a high-profile advocate of 'reforming' the NHS by introducing more market-based service delivery. (She often appears on BBC programmes like *Question Time* and *Newsnight*.) Clearly, there are businesses, mainly in the US, with a vested interest in her success, but who it was funding her campaigning has never been revealed.

The IEA's Sustained Attacks Against the BBC

A striking feature of the IEA, the Adam Smith Institute, and, to a lesser extent, all the think tanks in the Tufton Street cluster, is that, whatever the question, the answer is always the same: *less* government, *less* tax, *less* regulation, *more* market.

That does not, in itself, mean that the answer is necessarily wrong: each case needs to be analysed on its own merits. But it does mean that complex social and economic policy choices are sometimes reduced to the level of a generic introductory lecture on microeconomics without analysing the specific practicalities and trade-offs. As we'll see, this is certainly true of the IEA's long-running campaign for replacing the TV licence fee with subscriptions.

Much of the IEA's thinking on the BBC was developed by the late Professor Alan Peacock, who chaired the committee set up by Margaret Thatcher in 1985 to investigate advertising and other alternatives to the licence fee as sources of long-term funding for the BBC.[22] (We'll discuss the Peacock Committee and its legacy further in Chapter 10 and Appendix C.)

By the late 1980s, much of the IEA's work on broadcasting was led by the economist Dr Cento Veljanovski, former economic adviser to the Peacock Committee. Dr Veljanovski has been advancing much the same arguments ever since, including as a co-author of the IEA's wide-ranging, 170-page, 2016 report: 'In focus: the case for privatising the BBC', its most ambitious attack on the BBC yet.[23] This report, published during the run-up to Charter renewal, develops two main arguments.

The first is that funding the BBC through the licence fee is no longer sustainable because of technology changes and the emergence of new global players like Netflix and Amazon Prime – a kind of technological determinism, the idea being that the BBC is being swept away in a tsunami of new technology and *there's nothing we can do about it*.

The second is that the Corporation's news coverage is biased in many ways and that this particularly matters because of its scale, as by far the biggest and most trusted UK news supplier.[24] The report does not discuss *why* the British public relies on, and puts its trust in, such a supposedly biased source. Given the IEA's belief in the near-infallibility of markets and consumer choice, its reticence on this point is understandable.[25]

The report also seeks to explain the BBC's alleged left-wing bias, attributing it either to unconscious left–liberal groupthink[26] or, perhaps, its journalists and editors deliberately pushing a left-wing agenda.[27] We discuss the evidence on both the IEA's arguments – the non-sustainability of the TV licence fee (a genuine issue) and the BBC's alleged bias (largely a myth) – in the next two chapters.

Despite dabbling in the BBC's organizational culture in its 2016 report, the IEA generally sticks to economic arguments, as its name suggests. In contrast, the New Culture Forum – again reflecting its name – focuses on the *cultural* dimension of the right's struggle for dominance.

The New Culture Forum

The New Culture Forum (NCF)[28] is much younger than the IEA – it was founded in 2006 – and much smaller: it has published just eight reports and six books, its main focus being on live events at 55 Tufton Street, disseminated through videos on its YouTube channel and through wider press coverage. It is in the 'culture wars' business, fighting against what it sees as the dominance of left–liberal forces in our media and cultural institutions. Its mission statement argues that:

In the last quarter of the twentieth century, the Right decisively won the important economic arguments. But in the so-called 'culture wars', the liberal Left have dominated. The triumph of cultural relativism and political correctness in the opinion-forming fields of the media, academia, education and culture has meant that these attitudes have become even more deeply entrenched. What started out as a counter-culture has become the reigning orthodoxy.[29]

Some of the NCF's publications and presentations aim to show the BBC's cultural bias in favour of what it terms the 'Left' – a slightly vague and shifting mixture of explicitly left-wing organizations and causes and other more elusive targets, such as modern public art, which can be seen as left-wing prox-ies ('cultural Marxism').[30]

The NCF's broadcasting policy work – and that of its Tufton Street housemate Civitas – resonates with the editorials in those newspapers most critical of the BBC – the *Mail*, *Express*, *Sun* and *Telegraph*. Two of its eight published reports are specifically about the BBC's alleged political and cultural biases. As with the *Daily Mail*, a key claim is that the BBC is seeking to 'impose' a set of liberal cultural values that are alien to most ordinary people. The charge is that the Corporation constantly reflects the worldview of the 'metropolitan liberal elite' and is out of touch with everyone else, especially working- and lower-middle-class people, particularly outside London. Its values are said to be internationalist – and, therefore, unpatriotic. (The NCF's director, Peter Whittle, is the author of *Being British: What's Wrong with It?*[31] Until late 2018, he was a senior UKIP figure – and its candidate for London Mayor in 2016.)

As with the IEA, the NCF presents the BBC's senior editorial people as over-educated, overpaid metropolitans, contemptu-ous of traditional values and unthinkingly in favour of a checklist of politically correct policies, such as unregulated immigration, multiculturalism, LGBTQ+ rights and unfettered identity politics of all kinds.

News-watch

Closely related to the BBC's right-wing critics, and extremely important in the context of this book, is News-watch. Its website says that it 'monitors public service programmes to examine whether – as required by law – they deliver impartiality and political balance'.[32] However, since its foundation in 1999, its two full-time researchers have, in practice, largely ignored the other PSBs, targeting their efforts entirely on the BBC, and mainly on just one issue – its coverage of the EU and Brexit.

News-watch's foundation (originally as Minotaur Media Tracking) may have been inspired by that of the much larger Media Research Center (MRC) in the US,[33] launched in 1987 by L. Brent Bozell III, chairman of the National Conservative Political Action Committee. The MRC is the very model of a right-wing US advocacy organization funded by mysterious money (its reported annual revenue was $11 million in 2018). Unlike News-watch, its aim is to monitor and criticize the output of *all* the 'liberal' US mainstream media. Its slogan used to be the rather chilling 'We watch the liberal media so you don't have to,' but this has now been dropped.[34]

One sign of how News-watch sets about its research on 'impartiality and political balance' is the 'Contact Us' message on its website. As we went to press in 2020, this still read: 'If you'd like to alert News-watch to examples of EU bias in BBC News and Current Affairs reporting during the 2016 Referendum Campaign, for use in our ongoing research, you can do so using our new *BBC Complaints* website. For other inquiries, please use the contact form below.'[35]

This rather gives the game away. News-watch is not a neutral monitoring organization: it *actively solicits* examples of what its supporters think is biased BBC coverage (and in this context, 'bias' is, invariably, pro-EU and anti-Brexit).

News-watch's Founders, Funders and Fellow Travellers

News-watch was set up by its director, David Keighley, a former BBC local radio producer and later a BBC and TV-am public relations man, and Kathy Gyngell, widow of Bruce Gyngell, founder of TV-am and a close friend of Margaret Thatcher. Kathy Gyngell also co-founded and co-edits the Conservative Woman website,[36] which regularly attacks the BBC alongside other familiar targets – *The Guardian*, the EU, climate change activists, political correctness and so on. Typically, one recent article (12 March 2020) asks, 'Coronavirus: is the cure worse than the disease?'[37] (By the time you read this, you should know the answer.)

News-watch does not reveal its funding sources but an investigation by openDemocracy revealed several supporters in addition to Gyngell.[38] These included Arron Banks, the Brexit Bad Boy – whose Leave.EU website encouraged visitors to send it donations – and also the rather mysterious Institute for Policy Research, which funds several right-wing think tanks but is so self-effacing that it does not have a public website.[39] openDemocracy also reported that News-watch had conducted research for Migration Watch, Global Britain, the Centre for Policy Studies and several of the most ardent Eurosceptic MPs.

David Keighley's sympathies were directly on display in a November 2017 speech on 'BBC bias' he gave to the Traditional Britain Group (TBG).[40] TBG ('home to the disillusioned patriot') has given a platform to many far-right and racist speakers over the years, including the American white supremacist

Richard Spencer, far-right speakers from Germany, Sweden, Austria, Hungary and our very own Katie Hopkins.[41] In 2013, TBG called for Doreen Lawrence, mother of the murdered teenager Stephen Lawrence, and others from ethnic minorities, to 'return to their natural homelands'.[42] Keighley started his speech by saying how pleased he was not only to have been invited but also to have found, chatting to the group's members, how much they shared his views on the BBC. He recounted a little of his own story, bringing it rapidly to 1999, when, in an apparently chance conversation, Lord Pearson of Rannoch, founder of UKIP, asked him to help put the spotlight on the BBC's bias. Out of this came Minotaur Media Monitoring, the first iteration of News-watch. You can see the whole speech on YouTube.[43]

News-watch's Impact and the Quality of Its Research

For years, News-watch's – invariably critical – reports on the BBC's impartiality have been widely and uncritically cited by right-wing think tanks, newspapers and politicians. If you see a headline about the BBC's anti-Brexit bias, it will very likely be based on a News-watch report. The quality of this research appears to be less than its impact. News-watch's methodology remains something of a black box, making it well-nigh impossible for other researchers to replicate or test its findings. Its website says that:

> We work by logging, transcribing and analysing representative programmes over extended periods, and producing longitudinal analysis based on statistical findings.
>
> By necessity, this is a detailed and very thorough process that over the past 15 years has involved the line-by-line analysis of millions of words and the writing of dozens of detailed reports, most of which are archived and accessible through this site.

This begs a number of questions, discussed in the next chapter. Independent academic studies of the BBC's news and current affairs coverage reach very different conclusions. So too does Ofcom, now the BBC's regulator, which is therefore also attacked by News-watch in some of its reports, although the BBC is still its main target.[44] Despite its limitations as a research organization, however, News-watch has been extremely successful in generating press coverage hostile to the BBC and helpful to the Eurosceptic cause.

Lobbyists

In their book *A Quiet Word: Lobbying, Crony Capitalism and Broken Politics in Britain*,[45] Tamasin Cave and Andy Rowell remark on the proliferation of paid lobbyists, their cynical use of think tanks as 'wonk whores', their increasing bias to the right, and their focus on a particular cluster of concerns that reflect their clients' interests.

David Cameron famously described lobbying as 'the next big scandal waiting to happen'.[46] Lobbyists are very discreet. As invisibly as possible, they take their clients' aims and concerns – the relaxing (or tightening) of regulations, the gaining of endorsement from government, the ability to win government contracts or acquire public assets through privatization – to the key decision-makers and influencers.

Lobbyists' role is to develop, marshal and disseminate material supporting their clients' cause, which is often expressed later by third parties, apparently unconnected with the lobbyists' original – usually commercial – clients: It is much better to have your talking points made by an apparently disinterested politician, celebrity, expert or think tank, and then picked up by the media to reach a bigger audience.

Lobbyists can be a funnel for donations, commissioning a sympathetic think tank to write a report supporting their clients' position. Or they can get their clients to donate to a politician's favourite charity. The US lobbying business – clustered around K Street in Washington – turns over billions per annum[47] and dispenses truly immense influence and cash in a country with few limitations on political spending.[48]

The British lobbying business is slightly more modest but is increasingly influenced by American and international owners and clients. Lobbyists acting for commercial competitors of the BBC see the think tanks as a *very* useful platform for their views. (Rupert Murdoch is a special case, acting as his own lobbyist with back-door access to Downing Street – literally – and resenting having to wait in line in Brussels.)[49]

Westminster has a largely unacknowledged population of influencers working inside the policy maelstrom with parliamentarians, civil servants, ministers and their 'spads' (special advisors), party researchers, think tankers and political and some specialist journalists. Nobody knows how effective this process is, but, following the trend in America – albeit on a much smaller scale – it's attracting ever more money as new sectors become big spenders and the techniques of influence become ever more sophisticated.[50]

Right-wing Websites and YouTube Channels

There are now websites, like Biased BBC, entirely devoted to visceral attacks on the Corporation. Right-wing YouTube channels include both general British alt-right ones like The Iconoclast ('British Nationalist, Anti-EU, Pro-Nation State, Anti-Mass Immigration, Pro-Personal Responsibility, and bloody handsome to boot') and dedicated ones such as Ban the BBC and TV Licence Resistance.[51] Then there are the trolls: a massive-seeming stage army of hostile online commentators who attack the BBC using similar predictable 'talking points' and lines of attack, often under jokey pseudonyms. This is a wildly partisan, virulent and mostly unaccountable world peppered with right-wing dog-whistle phrases such as 'cultural Marxism', 'political correctness' and much worse.

Ban The BBC ('A constant reminder that life would be so much better without the BBC's TV Licence Gestapo') has its own You-Tube channel and blog, where it repeatedly urges readers to refuse to pay the licence fee and constantly criticizes the BBC's supposed inefficiency, left-wing bias, political correctness and so on.[52]

What is sinister about this is that this loose online throng appears to have achieved significant scale, and probably influence too, without getting much attention from mainstream media – including the BBC itself – or mainstream politicians. To judge by the comments on these sites and channels, and those responding to articles attacking the BBC, especially in the *Daily Mail*, Britain is full of people who really hate the BBC and are furious about what they claim are its abuses. But these comments are hard to evaluate directly. How representative are they really? What are their origins and real motives? Are they bots, multiple postings from geeks, or all genuinely from ordinary people simply having their say? Their style, favourite phrases and talking points certainly often seem oddly similar. But no one seems to know.

A Dedicated Anti-BBC Online Player

David Vance, the founder of the Biased BBC website,[53] turns out to be a colourful character formed in the politics of Belfast and the right-wing Traditional Unionist Voice,[54] which broke away from the mainstream Democratic Unionist Party in 2007 on the grounds that the DUP was unduly flexible and pragmatic – not a universally shared view. Vance's blog, 'A Tangled Web', founded in 2004, was reported as having been closed by its host for numerous instances of hate speech directed at Palestinians and other groups.[55]

Vance's new multi-platform vehicle Altnewsmedia,[56] formed in 2017, says it 'provides an alternative to the fake news mainstream media narrative', but denies any political affiliation. On Twitter, however, he has been a little more candid, telling his followers that 'Donald Trump "wants EU to break up in wake of Brexit vote". So do I! Let's bury the tyranny' and that '17.4 million people voted to end the tyranny of the EU'.[57]

On his YouTube channel, Vance supports Tommy Robinson, 'a man more sinned against than sinning' in speaking out against 'the (mainly) Muslim rape gangs who infest our cities'.[58] It's not difficult to imagine that the BBC's polite coverage looks decidedly liberal and PC from where David Vance is standing.

A Home-Grown Conspiracy Site

For seasoned British commentators, much of this online comment from people like Vance may seem palpably – even comically – of the American fringe and unlikely to have much impact over here. Maybe that's right. But the paranoid approach is gaining ground in the UK. It has already been used by the alt-right site 21st Century Wire and its presenter, the excitable Patrick Henningsen.

In 2013, a *Panorama* programme showed the aftermath of a chemical weapons attack on Aleppo civilians by the Assad regime in August that year. According to Henningsen and his fellow speakers at the 'Media on Trial: The Truth about Syria' London event on 19 October 2017, the *Panorama* programme was fictional and the BBC had staged the aftermath of the attack. Media Bias/ Fact Check, an organization that rates bias in the news, places 21st Century Wire in its 'conspiracy–pseudoscience' category.[59] But how many people believed Henningsen's version of events? Or, perhaps more likely, were unsure *which* version to believe?

The new populist alt-right has largely given up on the cara-pace of seemingly respectable academic-style analysis that think tanks like the IEA use in their attacks on the BBC. Instead, they are part of a 'disruption' narrative that proposes total war on the Old Order (recall the Trumpian cries against Hillary Clinton: 'Lock her up! Drain the swamp!'). In this context, the BBC's history and even its funding matter far less than they do to its traditional enemies. What matters more to this new breed is that whatever *they* believe, the BBC is against it. To them, the BBC is just another mainstream media fake news outlet, part of a wider conspiracy against ordinary, decent British people. The question is whether this new movement and its media can com-mand or influence a significant percentage of the UK electorate, as it has in the US, with its very different history, enthusiasm for conspiracy theories and its long tradition of what *New York Times* journalist Kurt Andersen calls 'going overboard, letting the sub-jective entirely override the objective, acting as if opinions and feelings were just as true as facts'.[60] It's the Trumpian approach, pre-emptive media de-legitimization.

Political analysts like the author of *Revolt on the Right*,[61] Robert Ford, acknowledge that something like the Trump base – *imper-vious* to most factual counter-argument – exists in most Western European countries. That base carries with it a considerable potential for hostility to a wide range of established British insti-tutions, including the BBC.

We just don't know how many UK citizens really subscribe to this hostility to mainstream media, nor how many share the new attraction to what Donald Trump's spokeswoman Kellyanne Conway, with unintended humour, called 'alternative facts' – the kind the President deploys in his tweets and speeches.[62] Many of the comments in this online world of smoke and mirrors are designed to give the impression of a huge groundswell of feeling against the BBC amongst 'ordinary people'. As we shall see, however, the polls – so far – tell a different story.

9. 'Bolshevism', Brexit and Bias

It is often suggested that the BBC is attacked equally by the right and the left, with those on the right accusing it of left-wing bias, and the opposite on the left – like a football match, with 'both sets of fans taking turns to abuse the referee, convinced that he's biased in the other team's favour'.[1]

However, this cosy idea – the 'symmetrical illusion' – is incorrect when it comes to the war against the BBC described in this book: politicians, journalists, think-tankers and others attacking it *as part of their day job*, often because their organization has a political or commercial vested interest in weakening it, cowing it or undermining its credibility to the public – which is almost invariably greater than their own. In reality, as we've already noted, there are many more of these organized professional attacks from the right than from the left – even more than we thought when we started our research.

Right-wing critics' explanation for this imbalance is, presumably, that because in their view the BBC's coverage has a constant left-wing and anti-Brexit bias, it inevitably, and justifiably, attracts criticism mostly from the right. However, as we'll see shortly, this claim is not supported by the most reliable evidence.

Instead, we think the main reason for the asymmetry in the scale and persistence of organized attacks on the BBC from the right and the left is the *imbalance in resources and outlets* between them. The BBC's critics on the right are, in general, much better funded, often with 'dark money' (like most of the right-wing think tanks discussed in the last chapter). But they are also better able to disseminate their claims because, as we'll show, right-leaning newspapers have far more combined UK readership and influence than left-leaning ones and still play a big role in setting the political agenda.

However, as well as this 'asymmetric warfare' difference, we think there are three other factors driving the greater scale of organized attacks on the BBC from the right.

Ideology, Commercial Rivalry and the 'Silent Majority' Illusion

First of all, there's ideology: many on the right object as a matter of principle to the whole idea of a large-scale PSB funded by a compulsory licence fee. Those on the left have no such objection in principle.

Secondly, there's commercial rivalry: although many on both the left and the right have a political interest in bullying the BBC,[2] those with a *commercial* vested interest in diminishing it (exemplified by Rupert and James Murdoch) are mostly on the right.

Finally, those on the right seem more likely to assume – without looking at the evidence – that most people agree with them about the BBC's biases. Look at the *Telegraph* letters page or the online comments in the *Mail* whenever the issue arises, which it often does. We call this the 'silent majority' illusion.

'We Are the Many and They Are the Few'

The 'silent majority' illusion was perfectly illustrated in a recent article by the US-born *Sunday Telegraph* columnist Janet Daley.[3] Under the heading, 'The BBC is panicking at the public's rejection of its arrogant Left-liberal worldview', Daley gleefully described '[t]he crisis in confidence at the BBC – and make no mistake, it is a full-blown, all alarm bells ringing, catastrophic crisis'. She ends, 'But the truth has finally hit. To adapt a notorious Corbynism, we are the many and they are the few, and it is time we were given our proper place in respectable conversation'.[4]

It's unclear whether Daley really believes that 'we' people with right-leaning views – including herself, with a regular column on a national newspaper! – are unable to make their voices heard in modern Britain. Given the right's advantage in resources and outlets, our hunch is that this preposterous claim was largely rhetorical. But on her stated belief that those rejecting the BBC's 'arrogant Left-liberal worldview' are 'the many not the few', we have no reason to doubt her sincerity.

However, she is mistaken. In reality, the public has not 'rejected' the Corporation's 'worldview' of politics and events. On the contrary, the BBC remains, by far, the place where they are most likely to go for trusted news coverage – far more likely than they are to go to the *Telegraph* or any other newspaper.

Apart from the odd – in both senses – conspiracy theorist, no one seriously questions the *accuracy* of the BBC's news and current affairs coverage.[5] The contested issue is its *impartiality* – its choice of which topics to cover, how its journalists frame and discuss those topics, the selection of commentators (politicians, experts, the general public, etc.) representing different views, and how they are introduced and questioned. All of these involve editorial judgements that are open to challenge. The BBC's TV, radio and online journalists make literally *thousands* of these judgements every day.

The public is divided over how well the BBC delivers on its commitment to 'due impartiality'. In line with the football referee analogy, those on the right do tend to think it leans to the left, but a roughly equal number on the left see it as biased towards the right, while a large minority in between sees it as broadly impartial, if a bit pro-Establishment.

Right, Left and the 'Brexit Turn'

Although most of the organized attacks on the BBC are from the right, it is also frequently criticized by the left, especially the further left, often as part of a wider critique of mainstream media.

Further, in a recent turn, disagreements about Brexit have also now led to it being criticized – for virtually the first time ever[6] – by people in the centre of the political spectrum who would normally be its natural supporters. They have no problem with its funding, governance, market impact or general impartiality. But, on this specific issue, they believe that – despite endless Brexiteer claims to the contrary – in reality, the BBC's coverage has systematically *favoured* pro-Brexit voices by giving them a disproportionate amount of airtime and by insufficiently challenging their claims, especially false claims. Brexit cuts across traditional left–right party lines and the BBC has, perhaps inevitably, been caught in the crossfire.

In the rest of this chapter, we first look at the right-wing charges against the BBC, and then at those from the left, and how they are not quite a mirror image of each other. To illustrate both perspectives, we invited two prominent critics of the BBC, one on the right, one on the left, to review each other's books; we summarize their reviews below. We then look at the academic evidence on the BBC's supposed left-wing bias and relate it to the imbalance in the combined readerships of left- and right-leaning newspapers. Finally, we explore the evidence on the BBC's EU/Brexit coverage: is its coverage really biased in favour of staying in the European Union and hostile to Brexit, as it is said to be? And is there any truth in the idea that it glosses over some difficult political issues?

'Pinkoes and Traitors':[7] The Right-Wing Case

The main right-wing case against the BBC is that it has an institutional left-wing bias, reflected in its programming. This has been repeated endlessly in books, newspaper articles and think-tank reports for decades, now amplified, more raucously, by anti-BBC blogs and YouTube channels.

These attacks focus mainly on the choice and treatment of interviewees on the BBC's news and current affairs programmes. The obsessive level of granular detail can be mesmerizing. They count the number of interviewees categorized (by them) as left- or right-wing in a given news item or on, say, a *Newsnight* panel. They look at how these people are introduced and questioned by presenters. Did Emily Maitlis give the Tory a rough ride while letting the Labourite off too easily? Was the film package edited to give an unfairly negative impression of the right-winger or unduly flatter the leftie? Were they given equal airtime? These questions are endlessly monitored. Almost invariably, the BBC is found to be at fault.

Additionally, the right-wing attacks now also involve a checklist of more elusive *cultural* bogeymen, such as the BBC's alleged obsession with multiculturalism and political correctness (or, now, 'wokeness').[8] Here the critics see bias in the characters and issues in a drama, the focus of an arts programme like *Imagine*, or the line-up of contributors to a comedy panel – such as *QI*, *Have I Got News for You?* or *Mock the Week* – or even a chat show like Graham Norton's. The BBC's choices at every level are constantly being accused of left–liberal, politically correct bias. Here's an example.

James Delingpole on Bodyguard

In a September 2018 *Spectator* review, its TV critic James Delingpole described the hugely successful BBC drama *Bodyguard*[9] as full of 'PC bollocks'.[10] Delingpole is also London editor of the alt-right US news organization Breitbart, and, therefore, a kind of witchfinder-general for smelling out political correctness over here. His objection to *Bodyguard* was that it presented women and ethnic minority members in powerful roles to, as he saw it, an absurdly unrealistic, politically correct degree: a senior politician – the Home Secretary! – and a senior police officer were both women; two other senior officers were from ethnic minorities (a mixed-race woman and a British south Asian man); and a bomb disposal expert was a London-accented Anglo-Chinese man!

Delingpole's indignation says more about him than about *Bodyguard*'s supposed misrepresentation of today's Britain. At the time of transmission, we had a female Prime Minister, a Muslim Home Secretary and Mayor of London, and a recently departed female Home Secretary.[11] Meanwhile, the Met was led by a lesbian commissioner with several ethnic minority officers in her top team, including the head of counter-terrorism.[12] *Bodyguard* was fictional, but its writer, Jed Mercurio, seems to have been more in touch with reality than James Delingpole.

'If You Think the BBC Is Too Woke, Wait 'Till You See Netflix'

In March 2020, Damian Reilly took a very different view in another *Spectator* piece. He argued that the US online TV services – constantly praised by free-marketeers as harbingers of a utopian future with little or no PSB – are, in reality, much *more* PC and woke than the BBC: 'If you think the BBC is too woke for you, just wait until you sample wokeness as beamed into your sitting room by Netflix – maker of programmes like Dear White People ("students of colour navigate the daily slights and slippery politics of life at an Ivy League college that's not nearly as 'post racial' as it thinks")'. He also asked readers to 'imagine the outcry if the BBC refused to make programmes in places whose abortion laws they didn't agree with, as Netflix recently threatened to do in the state of Georgia'.[13]

The right-wing charge that the BBC uniquely portrays an unrealistically PC world is therefore wrong on both counts. The BBC does indeed often seek to show women, people of colour and gay people in a positive light, but not in the grossly distorted way claimed by Delingpole. And there's no evidence that its coverage of these issues differs from that of other UK broadcasters – which actually appear to be less PC than the free-market US streamers.

The 'Bolshevik Broadcasting Corporation'[14]

There have always been accusations of left-wing BBC bias, but they increased markedly under Margaret Thatcher's 1980s Conservative government. Party Chairman Norman Tebbit, her closest lieutenant, was so obsessed about it that she eventually had to rein him in.[15] No copywriter, Tebbitt called the BBC the *Stateless Person's Broadcasting Corporation* because of what he saw as its unpatriotic coverage of the Falklands War.[16] In reality, the BBC's and MoD's careful reporting won the propaganda war for Britain while giving away no military secrets.[17] UKIP and the Brexit Party are, if anything, even more hostile than most right-wing Conservatives: the 2019 UKIP manifesto promised to end the licence fee and sell off the BBC,[18] while the Brexit Party said it would 'phase [it] out'.[19]

Part of the right-wing case is that everyone at the BBC shares a left–liberal worldview, making it *institutionally* left-wing. This draws especially on the work of Robin Aitken, the former BBC journalist we met in the last chapter.[20] His thesis is that the Corporation's 'monoculture' of unquestioned left–liberal secularism is constantly reflected in its news coverage, which, in turn, has largely destroyed traditional Conservative and Christian British values.

His books clearly come from the heart, being based on two very personal factors. The first is his background as a traditional, upper-middle-class practising Catholic, educated at a private Catholic boarding school. This, he confirms, is the basis of his social and political conservatism and moral outlook. The second factor – central to his case against the BBC – is his own experience there.

Starting as a local radio reporter in 1978, and then taking on a wide range of roles at BBC News, Aitken constantly felt as if he was the only Conservative in the village. He was, he says, shocked by what his BBC peers held as self-evident. At BBC Scotland, this included *hatred of the English*. And back in London, so he said, it included *hatred of the Tories*. This experience eventually led him into an ongoing battle with the Corporation's bureaucracy. He felt his views and concerns were patronizingly dismissed rather than engaged with. But the BBC didn't sack him: instead, after twenty-five years there, he took voluntary redundancy in 2004 and started work on a book about his experience, *Can We Trust the BBC?*, published in 2007. The *Daily Mail* serialized a 2,500-word excerpt,[21] but it had limited impact.

Five years later, however, the Savile and McAlpine scandals and the resignation of George Entwistle as director-general enabled Aitken to publish a revised edition of his book in 2013, now titled *Can We (Still) Trust the BBC?* This gained more traction, partly because of the timing: it offered the BBC's right-wing enemies material for their attacks on it during Charter renewal. As you may remember from the previous chapter, at the time of publication of his third book, *The Noble Liar*, in 2018, he had been taken up by the 55 Tufton Street network and right-leaning media. Over the years, he has also published numerous articles on 'BBC bias' via Conservative outlets.[22]

For all that, Aitken does not say much about how the 'monocultural' worldview at the BBC translates into actual editorial choices and therefore leads to the systematic left-wing biases in its output usually claimed by its right-wing enemies. He also largely ignores the organizational power structures that Tom Mills – whose left-wing critique of the BBC we examine shortly – cites. (Mills argues that, *at senior decision-making levels*, the BBC always follows the Establishment of the day on the big issues. In Aitken's view, however, the DGs and BBC governors were always easily subverted by the lefties at the coal face.)

The Left's Case

The left's case against the BBC is not simply a mirror image of that of the right. It is smaller-scale, and more episodic and reactive than the persistent and systematic right-wing attacks. There is no left-wing site equivalent to News-watch – or even Biased BBC – which are entirely devoted to delegitimizing its news and current affairs coverage. Nor do people on the left object in principle to a public service broadcaster or worry about the BBC's market impact – since they aren't commercial competitors.

However, the left wing of the Labour Party has been highly critical of the BBC, especially its coverage of Jeremy Corbyn. There was, for example, the *Newsnight* 'Hatgate' incident. In March 2018, 'left-wing firebrand' – his own description – Owen Jones (whom BBC News and Current Affairs clearly have on speed-dial and helicopter service, with seven appearances on *Question Time* over the last seven years) claimed that a picture of Jeremy Corbyn on a *Newsnight* background had been altered to suggest that Corbyn was a 'Russian stooge'.[23] Later, John Clarke, another Corbyn supporter, tweeted, 'The BBC actually photoshopped Jeremy Corbyn's hat to make it look more Russian for this smear on Newsnight. Let that sink in. The BBC is being used as an anti-Labour propaganda machine'.[24] It was claimed later that two million people read this accusation.

The programme's acting editor, Jess Brammar, replied, saying, 'By all means criticise Newsnight. That's healthy, and we will always welcome people like @OwenJones84 coming on the show to criticise us from our own studio. But no one photoshopped a hat'. Two days later, the hat reappeared on BBC News Online, with a strong denial and the original photograph of Corbyn in the hat at a King's Cross protest in 2016, adding that he'd worn it many times and that they'd used the same Red Square backdrop for Gavin Williamson, the then Conservative Defence Secretary. Laura Pidcock, a Corbynite Labour MP, then tweeted that the hat *had* been photoshopped to look more Russian. *Newsnight* presenter Emily Maitlis weighed in, saying, 'This is what we're dealing with, Peeps'.[25]

As Donald Clarke said the following week in the *Irish Times*, 'Hatgate illustrated how "so many of us treat prominent news sources like a Rorschach test. This person sees a manifestation of unreconstructed Stalinism. Another chap detects the malign influence of the neo-liberal establishment. You see a bunny?" '[26]

Jeremy Corbyn's unreconstructed dress code has often been a matter for right-wing comment – his Lenin cap had been a constant – and arguably That Hat picture could be said to be *less* ideological and more 'touristy'. But the particular venom of John Clarke's tweet echoed his earlier retweeting of an anti-Semitic tweet – without checking its full text or origins – from a Holocaust-denying, Hitler-supporting conspiracy theory site in New Zealand.[27]

Tom Mills, whose book *The BBC: Myth of a Public Service* we mentioned in the first chapter,[28] is also a good representative of a robustly critical left-wing view of the BBC. A lecturer in sociology and policy at Aston University, Mills described himself to us as a 'socialist Labour supporter'. In an openDemocracy interview with Ian Sinclair, shortly after his book's publication, he summarized its thesis: that the BBC likes to play it safe – which means that, in recent years, it has shifted to the right:

Ian Sinclair: Is the BBC independent and impartial?

Tom Mills: [. . . The BBC] isn't independent from governments, let alone from the broader Establishment . . . Governments set the terms under which it operates, they appoint its most senior figures . . . and they set the level of the licence fee . . . So that's the context within which the BBC operates, and it hardly amounts to independence in any substantive sense . . .

What happens is the editorial policy is defined at the top of the BBC – which is the most politicised section of the Corporation, given that senior executives have to periodically negotiate with governments over its funding, its Charter and so on, and senior editorial figures have to respond to constant complaints over its reporting – and that policy then cascades down the hierarchy, in rather complex and uneven ways . . .

Ian Sinclair: A key issue seems to be the BBC's working definition of impartiality. How would you define this?

Tom Mills: . . . I think the most straightforward way of putting this is that *the BBC will aim to fairly and accurately reflect the balance of opinion amongst elites* [emphasis added].[29]

The View from All Sides

It is interesting to see how Mills (and others) characterize the instatement of John Birt as director-general at the BBC in 1992. This happened after the former director-general, Alastair Milne (father of Jeremy Corbyn's communications supremo, Seamus Milne), was forced to resign by the Thatcher-appointed BBC chairman Marmaduke Hussey for – as Mills sees it – 'representing the more independent spirit of the BBC's programme making':

[Birt] was an out-and-out neoliberal who wanted not only to introduce stronger editorial controls over BBC journalism, but also to radically shift its institutional structure and culture away from its 'statist' character and in a more neoliberal, business-friendly direction. This was resented by BBC staff and the Corporation went through a quite unhappy period.[30]

John Birt, now Lord Birt, provides some support for both Aitken's and Mills' views in his memoir, *The Harder Path*. He describes how, as deputy director-general and head of news and current affairs (from 1987 to 1992) and then as director-general (from 1992 to 2000), he introduced tighter editorial controls at the BBC, especially on controversial programmes that might provoke unnecessary run-ins with the government. His 'mission to explain' policy meant programmes were rigorously pre-planned and double-checked, making for a tighter organization which was much less prone to slip-ups. However, for those on the right, Birt would probably be seen as a typical representative of the left–liberal Blairite BBC, although they might afford him some grudging respect for his successful initiatives to increase its efficiency and strengthen its business coverage.

Aitken and Mills Review Each Other's Books

We were so struck by the contrast between Aitken's and Mills' readings of the same institution that we asked them to critique each other's books on the BBC for us. Their reviews reflect striking differences in how they see the BBC: Mills is forensic in his analysis of its power structures and history, while Aitken focuses on his own experience. Mills accuses Aitken of fuzzy thinking, and Aitken charges Mills with 'viewing the world through an orthodox Marxist lens'.

'There is nothing', Aitken complains of Mills' book, 'that addresses how the BBC, over the last fifty years, has helped mould and shape public attitudes in Britain along "progressive" lines ... the old serviceable Christian morality has been dismantled. It bears absolutely no relation to my lived experience of working at the BBC.'

Conversely, Mills accuses Aitken of failing to do any 'institutional analysis' of the BBC: '[He] moves from one anecdote to another. This leads to a number of misunderstandings ... His conception of the political spectrum as spanning socially conservative and liberal attitudes completely ignores anything to the left of Peter Mandelson'.

It's an ink-blot test.

Blues under – or Even in – the BBC Bed?

Mills' book also takes up – more fully and with more evidence – a position originally stated by the journalist Mehdi Hasan in the *New Statesman* in 2009: 'The charge that (the BBC) is left-wing has been repeated so often that it goes almost unchallenged ... if anything it is a bastion of conservatism'.[31]

Hasan complained that the prevailing debate was between the right-wing view (exemplified by Paul Dacre at the *Daily Mail*) that the BBC was strongly left-wing and the centre–left view (exemplified by *The Guardian*'s Polly Toynbee) that it was constantly striving for fairness and balance. He was puzzled that the idea that the BBC might be *more* sympathetic to a Conservative worldview than a left-wing one never actually came up for discussion. Hasan's argument was that, in reality, many of the top BBC political journalists and editors were Conservatives.

His first example was Andrew Neil, central to the BBC's political coverage and on air for four hours a week at the time. He pointed out that, four years earlier, Neil had given the IEA's fourteenth annual Hayek Lecture,[32] which argued for a free-market, libertarian view of society, fully in the spirit of the eponymous economist[33] and the IEA's mission.

Hasan's other examples were the BBC's political editor, Nick

Robinson, a former chair of the Young Conservatives;[34] Robbie Gibb, then the editor of BBC Two's weekday show *Daily Politics* (which ran from 2003 until 2018), who had previously worked for Conservative MP Francis Maude and went on to become Theresa May's head of communications; Guto Harri, the BBC's former chief political correspondent, who, from 2008, worked as communications director for Boris Johnson when he was Mayor of London; the rumbustious free-marketeer, Jeff Randall, the BBC's first business editor, who went on to work at the *Telegraph* and Sky; and three – according to Hasan, right-leaning and unduly pro-US – former Washington correspondents. He argued that, whatever may or may not have been the *general* culture within the BBC, these key *political* news posts were all held by right-leaning journalists and editors.

Left-wing *Guardian* journalist and author Owen Jones returned to this theme in 2014, arguing that the right's constant claim that the BBC is a den of socialism is 'a campaign based on myths and deception . . . It is extraordinarily clever; it allows the Right to police the BBC to make the Corporation fearful of crossing certain lines', while, in reality, 'the BBC is stacked full of right-wingers'.[35] In 2018, he went on to argue that double standards were applied to the BBC's left- and right-leaning journalists. Singling out Andrew Neil and Robbie Gibb, he wrote:

> Imagine this. The BBC appoints a prominent radical leftist, a lifelong Bennite, the chairman of the publisher of a prominent leftwing publication no less, as its flagship political presenter and interviewer. This person made speeches in homage of Karl Marx calling for the establishment of full-blooded socialism in Britain . . . They appear on our 'impartial' Auntie Beeb wearing a tie emblazoned with the logo of a hardline leftist think tank. Their BBC editor is a former Labour staffer who moves to become Jeremy Corbyn's communications chief. They use their Twitter feed – where they have amassed hundreds of thousands

of followers thanks to a platform handed to them by the BBC – to promote radical leftist causes.

This would never happen. It is unthinkable, in fact. If the BBC establishment somehow entered this parallel universe, the British press would be on the brink of insurrection.[36]

His point, of course, is that this imaginary situation is pretty much a mirror image of the BBC's use of Neil as its top political presenter and interviewer, with Robbie Gibb as his editor. Jones accepts that 'Neil skins politicians alive across the political spectrum' but adds that 'he reserves his ideological assaults for the left'. There was also evidence of a significant right-wing bias in the choice of guests invited to appear on the show. This evidence, from an analysis by the left-wing writer Alex Nunns, is important because it is simple, numerical and transparent. As always, exactly how individuals are classified involves some judgement. But even allowing for this, it is clear that right-wing contributors were greatly over-represented on the programme.[37]

More importantly, Jones is surely correct that it would be almost unthinkable for the BBC to appoint left-wing versions of Andrew Neil and Robbie Gibb to lead such a high-profile news discussion programme – and that, if it *did*, there would be a huge political and media backlash, even if the new appointee gave tough interviews across the political spectrum. Aitken's claim that almost everyone at BBC News shares a set of unthinking left–liberal assumptions has been strongly, repeatedly and persuasively contested. However, given the demographics of those working there, his related claim that most of them are *socially* liberal (e.g. on issues like abortion and gay marriage)[38] may well be correct, although this has never been researched, as far as we know.

But the BBC's journalists are supposed – indeed *required* – to leave their personal views at home; so the key question is therefore whether the programmes they create really *are* biased towards the left.

Academic Research on the BBC's 'Left-wing Bias'

Although a comprehensive review of the academic research on the BBC's bias or impartiality is beyond the scope of this book, Appendix B shows the methods and results of the main recent studies, focusing especially on research at Cardiff University's School of Journalism, Media and Culture, the largest academic group working on impartiality in UK broadcast media. We here summarize some of the main findings and conclusions.

The BBC's References to Think Tanks

Some of the most telling evidence on the BBC's impartiality comes from two contrasting studies on which think tanks are mentioned in its news and current affairs coverage. The first, by economist Dr Oliver Latham at the Centre for Policy Studies (CPS) – part of the right-wing Tufton Street cluster we met in the last chapter – looked at the think tanks cited on BBC Online News over the three years after the 2010 election. The second, by the Cardiff University group, looked at think-tank citations on over 30,000 BBC TV news and current affairs programmes in 2009 and 2015. So, not looking at *exactly* the same issue – but *almost*.

The 2013 analysis by the Centre for Policy Studies used an ingenious statistical measure to rank the forty-one think tanks mentioned in its sample on a spectrum from left to right, based on how often they were cited by *The Guardian* and the *Telegraph*, respectively. The assumption is that think tanks mentioned more by *The Guardian* are more likely to be left-leaning and those mentioned more by the *Telegraph* are more likely to be right-leaning. The problem is that this does not distinguish between articles that mention a think tank to praise and publicize its work and those designed to attack it and discredit it. Unsurprisingly perhaps, this somewhat flaky method led to some marked anomalies in the ranking. The most extreme example – acknowledged by the author – was that of the clearly left-leaning Institute for Public Policy Research (IPPR), which the analysis ranked as further to the right than the Adam Smith Institute, the CPS itself and other staunchly right-wing think tanks.

The CPS study's main result was that the think-tank citations on BBC Online were slightly more highly correlated with those in *The Guardian* than with those in the *Telegraph*.[39] On the basis of this small difference, it concluded that, 'In a statistical sense, the BBC cites . . . think tanks "more similarly" [*sic*] to . . . The Guardian than [to] The Telegraph', while still making no distinction between positive and negative citations.[40] These conclusions were enthusiastically picked up and publicized – with no questions about their validity – by the *Sunday Times*, *Mail* and *Telegraph*,[41] as well as in some more surprising places, such as the Derby County Football Club Fans' online forum.[42]

In contrast, the 2017 Cardiff study used multiple sources of evidence[43] to categorize the sixty-seven think tanks in its sample as left-leaning, neutral or right-leaning. The result was much more robust than the Centre for Policy Studies' ranking, with *no* big anomalies within it, just a few borderline cases.[44]

On this basis, there was a broad balance between mentions of left- and right-leaning think tanks in 2009, but a clear bias towards the right by 2015.[45] In the authors' words, 'When Labour was in power [in 2009], the BBC's use of think tanks was relatively even-handed, but when a Conservative-led coalition was in power [in 2015],[46] the centre of gravity [in BBC coverage] shifted to the political right'.[47]

This conclusion was consistent with an earlier Cardiff study of the BBC's coverage of politically sensitive topics under Labour and the coalition government.

BBC Coverage of Sensitive Topics

In 2012–13, as an input to a major review of the Corporation's news and current affairs output for the BBC Trust, the Cardiff University group did a content analysis of its TV, radio and online coverage of three sensitive topics – immigration, the UK in relation to the EU and religion – in 2007 and 2012.[48] They found that the BBC consistently gave the most coverage to voices from the two main political parties, especially the governing party, but with some asymmetry: under Labour, government voices had only slightly more airtime than the Conservatives; but under the Conservatives, government voices dominated by a wide margin.

The Dominance of Conservative Voices on The Papers during 2017

The BBC's news coverage also includes its daily TV show *The Papers*, a late-night studio discussion of the next day's front pages with a host and two guests, usually journalists,[49] and a brief, largely factual, written summary on BBC News Online.

A study of *The Papers* by two London-based academics during the 2017 general election campaign[50] found that stories in Conservative-supporting papers accounted for about 70 per cent of the coverage.[51] The authors argued that this imbalance was in breach of the Ofcom rules requiring broadcasters to take account of past and present electoral support in their coverage of political parties and their policies.[52]

In the BBC's defence, one might argue that the dominance of Conservative voices on *The Papers* was merely a reflection of the Conservative papers' domination of the market, discussed shortly. However, the imbalance on the show was, arguably, even greater than in the newspaper market (although that depends on the measure of market dominance). There is certainly no evidence that the programme took any account of the level of electoral support for the different parties.

Although this study was for only one programme during one election, its results are consistent with those of a larger-scale Cardiff University study of how newspapers drove the TV news agenda during the previous election, in May 2015.

How Newspapers Determined the TV News Agenda in 2015

As newspapers' circulation, revenue and resources decline under pressure from online media, especially Google and Facebook, it is tempting to assume that their political influence is being drastically reduced. However, this ignores their continuing role as agenda-setters,[53] including for broadcast news.

In 2015, the Cardiff University group looked at how UK television news broadcasters[54] decided which election-related issues and stories to cover during the general election campaign. They did a content analysis of TV and newspaper coverage and semi-structured interviews with senior broadcast news editors. They summarized their findings as follows:

> Our analysis of the major evening TV bulletins shows issues where the Conservatives were seen as strong, such as the economy and a potential Labour–Scottish National Party coalition, were among the dominant themes. And while the broadcasters are required to seek balance, the right-wing press was responsible for pushing Tory-friendly issues to the forefront of TV news.
>
> In over 2,000 news items between 20 March and 6 May, the main topics addressed by broadcasters were 'horse-race'

coverage – notably in how close a contest it was meant to be between Labour and the Conservatives – a possible [Labour–SNP] coalition government, the handling of the economy and levels of taxation. Between them, they made up 43% of the entire TV news agenda. In contrast, Labour's campaign issues – the NHS or housing for instance – were covered far less. While there was some variation between the broadcasters, social policy issues were not widely reported anywhere . . .

[The coverage] consolidated the dominant narrative of the campaign as a close contest between the two main parties and drew attention to the SNP's potential coalition power. And it meant most policy issues, with the exception of the handling of the economy, were marginalized.[55]

There was little difference between the different TV broadcasters' coverage. But, if anything, the BBC's was marginally *more* in line with the Conservative-supporting newspapers' agenda than were those of ITV, Sky, Channel 4 and Channel 5.

The academic research reveals a consistent pattern: the BBC's political coverage is dominated by representatives of the two main political parties, especially whichever is in power, but with a bias towards *Conservative* voices and issues. This persistent tendency to favour the Conservatives holds sway across: TV references to left- versus right-leaning think tanks in 2009 and 2015; TV, radio and online coverage of immigration, the UK and EU, and religion in 2007 and 2012; front-page stories discussed on *The Papers* (and including the choice of guests), both on TV and online, in 2017; and the topics on *BBC News at Ten* during the 2015 election.

The claim that the BBC's news and current affairs coverage systematically leans to the left is simply untrue. In reality, it tends to favour whichever of the two parties is in power, but with a general bias towards Conservative views, voices and issues. This pro-Conservative imbalance is not huge, but it has increased in recent years.

A key part of the context for the infinitely repeated (but false) claim that the BBC's news coverage leans to the left is that of the UK national newspaper market, which itself has a marked imbalance to the right. As we've seen, this still matters because of newspapers' role in driving the wider political agenda, including on the BBC. However, it is somewhat contested, with some on the right downplaying it and some on the left overstating it. So, what are the facts?

The Right-Wing Imbalance in UK National Newspapers

The newspapers' political positions are widely agreed by analysts and well understood by the general public. A February 2017 YouGov survey found that 44 per cent of British adults considered the *Daily Mail* to be 'very right wing'. At the other extreme, 16 per cent said *The Guardian* was 'very left wing'.[56] Combining the responses for each of the eight papers studied[57] into a single summary measure, YouGov reported the following: that, in line with the football referee analogy, respondents' answers depended somewhat on their own self-defined political positions:[58] those on the right tended to see *The Guardian* and *Mirror* as more left-wing and the *Express* and *Mail* as less right-wing than the average respondent; and vice versa for those on the left.

But respondents across the whole political spectrum agreed that *The Guardian*, *Mirror* and *Independent* were left of centre and the *Sun*, *Times*, *Telegraph*, *Express* and *Mail* were right of centre. This included those who had voted Conservative, Labour, Liberal Democrat or UKIP in 2015, and Leave or Remain in 2016,[59] as well as representing all geo-demographic groups[60] in the analysis.

So, in terms of public perceptions, a majority of UK newspapers (five out of eight) are agreed by most people to be right of

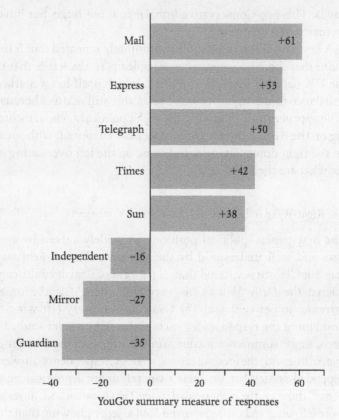

Figure 9.1
Public Perceptions of UK Newspapers' Political Leanings
Source: YouGov, February 2017

centre. They are also *all* seen by the average respondent as further from the political centre (scores of +38 to +61 on YouGov's summary measure) than *any* of the left of centre papers (scores from −16 to −35). In other words, the British public sees the 'centre of [political] gravity' of the national press as being well towards the right.

The Imbalance in Readership

The left–right imbalance is, if anything, increased when we factor in the different papers' readerships. Using the 'daily unduplicated print and digital reach' – the total number of people reading each paper in print and/or online on the average day – the combined readership of the left-leaning *Guardian*, *Mirror* and *Independent* was 12.8 million in September 2019. The combined readership of the right-leaning *Sun*, *Times*, *Telegraph*, *Express* and *Mail* was 21.7 million, with a difference between the two groups of nearly nine million daily readers.[61]

The imbalance is greater yet if we consider only *print* readers, who tend to read articles for longer, and more carefully, than online readers, most of whom are looking at small screens (often on the move). The combined print readership figures were only 1.53 million for the left-leaning papers[62] versus 7.06 million for the right-leaning ones, 4.6 times as many.

Again, these readership figures make no distinction between papers that are only slightly left- or right-leaning and those that are further from the political centre. Since – at least in the public's view – the five right-leaning papers are all further from the centre than any of the left-leaning ones, the huge imbalance in their combined print readership, understates still further the extent to which, in terms of their impact, the 'centre of gravity' of the newspapers is towards the right.

Whichever metric one chooses, we think this media imbalance, combined with right-wing players' greater resources for developing *content* (and reinforced by free-market ideology, commercial vested interests and the 'silent majority' illusion) explains why there are so many more organized attacks on the BBC from the right, despite the evidence that, in reality, its coverage tends to favour the Conservatives.

The 'Brussels Broadcasting Corporation': Is the BBC's Coverage Really Pro-EU and Anti-Brexit?

In recent years, the other main charge against the BBC, often from the same people who accuse it of left-wing bias, is that – in line with its general liberal, metropolitan outlook – it is systematically *pro-EU and anti-Brexit*.

The Key Role of News-watch

The main evidence cited to support this claim comes from News-watch, which we met in the last chapter. As we saw, News-watch was set up in 1999[63] by its director, David Keighley, and Kathy Gyngell, who appears to have provided or raised most of the funding. And, although its stated mission is to monitor the overall impartiality of all the PSBs,[64] in practice, it appears to focus solely on the BBC and almost entirely on its coverage of the EU and Brexit.

It has certainly been productive, as you can see from its archive.[65] For instance, over the two-and-a-half years from the June 2016 EU referendum till January 2019, it published *eleven* major reports – with a total of 1,583 pages – covering eighty-one hours of the BBC's Brexit coverage.[66] Its overall conclusion was that, 'the BBC has put Brexit under sustained negative attack since the Referendum, through inequality in the time given to interviewees, choice of story, and "bias by omission" '.[67]

News-watch's research raises two questions. First, how reliable is its methodology? Secondly – and more important – is its invariable conclusion that the BBC is pro-EU and anti-Brexit actually correct?

As you may recall from the previous chapter, News-watch works by 'logging, transcribing and analysing representative programmes over extended periods, and producing longitudinal analysis based on statistical findings'.[68] We assume this must involve David Keighley and News-watch's senior researcher, Andrew Jubb, first deciding which programmes to record and transcribe; then reading through the transcripts and classifying the topics and speakers into pro- and anti-EU camps;[69] and finally analysing the results, mainly in terms of the percentage of air-time allocated to voices they deem to be pro- or anti-EU.

Although News-watch claims to use 'accepted academic principles', its detailed methodology – how it decides which programmes to monitor and, especially, whether a contributor is pro-Brexit, anti-Brexit or neither (the key issue) – has never, to our knowledge, been published. Nor, as far as we know, have any of its results ever been published in a peer-reviewed academic journal.[70] Keighley appears to have no academic research training or experience, while Jubb's seems to be limited to an undergraduate degree in English and media studies, 'with a strong focus on media bias, politics and representation'.[71] We are, essentially, asked to take their methodology, results and competence on trust.

The limitations of this methodology were pointed out by Dr Oliver Latham in his 2013 Centre for Policy Study's review of references to left- and right-leaning think tanks on BBC Online News (which we discussed earlier on): 'even these studies rely on subjective judgements as to which periods to study and deciding what constitutes, for example, a pro-EU or anti-EU voice'.[72]

We think the real mission of News-watch is to generate a limitless stream of material to be used in Eurosceptic 'hit jobs' on the BBC's coverage of the EU and Brexit. This view is based on the identity of News-watch's 'founders, funders and fellow travellers' (discussed in the previous chapter), its active soliciting of examples of pro-EU BBC bias, its ignoring of the other PSBs and news issues, its consistently critical output, and the way its output is then disseminated by the BBC's right-wing enemies. Perhaps coincidentally, this is also completely in line with the discrediting proposed by Dominic Cummings in his New Frontiers blog of 2004.[73]

The War Against the BBC

News-watch follows a long line of groups set up by the Conservatives to monitor the BBC and provide material for party political attacks on it. As long ago as 1947, Winston Churchill, having been recently ousted as Prime Minister by Clement Attlee, set up a six-person unit at Conservative Central Office under John Profumo – yes, *that* John Profumo – who had lost his seat in 1945. Each week, on the day the *Radio Times* was published, they were told which programmes to monitor. Profumo later boasted that 'we made a great deal of headway with the BBC – it had its effect'.[74] A similar unit was set up by Norman Tebbitt in the 1980s and revived in the 1990s.[75]

In our view, News-watch is neither a politically neutral research organization, nor even one that delivers on its stated mission to monitor the general news coverage of all the PSBs. Given the opacity of its detailed methodology, its researchers' minimal relevant academic training, and its failure over twenty years to publish any of its research in a peer-reviewed outlet, one does not have to be a mad conspiracy theorist to suspect that the subjective judgements it makes, highlighted by Oliver Latham of the Centre for Policy Studies, are biased towards producing the hostile results those funding it are looking for. This impression is further reinforced by its recent run-ins with both the courts and Ofcom.[76] It is neither publicly accountable nor transparent to any degree; we suggest you look at its website and decide for yourself how much you trust it as a source of evidence.

But, whatever News-watch's agenda may be, the key question is: are its results valid? Is the BBC really biased pro-EU and anti-Brexit?

The 2004–5 Wilson Review of the BBC's EU coverage

In 2004, the BBC governors commissioned a panel under former cabinet secretary, Lord Wilson of Dinton, Master of Emmanuel

148

College, Cambridge, to assess the impartiality of the BBC's EU coverage, in response to claims that it was systematically pro-EU, anti-withdrawal and too Westminster-centric, and had failed to increase the public's understanding of the EU. The five-member panel was 'sort-of' balanced: of the three members explicitly involved in European issues, two were active Euro-sceptics and one an active EU supporter.[77] They received written submissions from a wide range of stakeholders and spoke to some of them.

In January 2005, the Wilson panel reported that the BBC's coverage was widely perceived as pro-EU, although there was disagreement about the extent of this. It argued that, although there was no deliberate pro-EU bias in the Corporation's cover-age, there was nevertheless a problem, caused by five factors: the BBC's 'institutional mindset'; 'over-simplified polarization of the issues and stereotyping'; the 'Westminster prism' (over-emphasizing the main UK parties' views); 'ignorance' (journalists being simply out of their depth on some of the technical details); and 'omission', meaning that the BBC should have given more coverage to 'the importance and relevance of the EU in the political and daily life of the UK'.[78]

It concluded that, 'Sometimes being attacked from all sides is a sign that an organization is getting it right. That is not so here. It is a sign that the BBC is getting it wrong, and our main con-clusion is that urgent action is required to put this right.'[79]

The BBC vowed to do better and set up a committee under its new head of news, Helen Boaden, to develop new policies and guidelines.

Although the Wilson panel relied on public, stakeholder and its own members' *perceptions*, rather than actual content analysis of the BBC's EU coverage, it raised genuine issues which remain challenging. But how does its portrayal of the BBC's coverage – never mind News-watch's highly critical portrayal – stack up against the evidence from other sources?

BBC 'Treats Assad Better Than the EU'

One piece of evidence on this comes from Media Tenor, a Zurich-based commercial media research agency.[80] In April 2016, it presented the results of an extensive analysis of the EU coverage on British television. It claimed that British TV – and the BBC in particular – had consistently failed to present a balanced view of the EU or give sufficient coverage of how it affected the UK.[81]

It went on to report that, over the previous fifteen years, about a third of 102,772 reports on the EU on BBC One's *News at Ten* had been negative and only about 7 per cent positive. An additional comparative analysis of 46,737 stories on *News at Ten* and BBC Two's *Newsnight* in 2015, about two totally different subjects, the EU and three international 'strongmen' leaders, found that the balance of BBC coverage was much more negative for the EU than it was for China's Xi Jinping, Russia's Vladimir Putin and even Syria's Bashar al Assad. Media Tenor's methodology was not perfect. It involved researchers watching BBC news reports on the EU and assessing whether they were positive, negative or neutral, taking into account both the topic (for example, whether EU membership was leading to higher or lower UK unemployment) and the language used. So, although its results are, in our view, more reliable than News-watch's, because they covered *every* relevant story on the BBC's flagship news programme over an extended period of time (which meant they used a huge sample, with no 'cherry-picking'), it still involved subjective judgements about which reports were pro- and anti-EU.[82]

For research that minimizes these limitations, we again need to look at academic studies, similar to those on whether the BBC's news coverage is systematically biased to the left or right. Unfortunately, there has been less academic research on the Corporation's coverage of the EU than its potential left- or right-wing biases, but the Cardiff University group has done two major studies that bear directly on this issue (see Appendix B for further detail).

Cardiff University's Studies on the BBC's Coverage of the EU and the Referendum

First, as already discussed, in 2012–13, the Cardiff group did a content analysis for the BBC Trust of the Corporation's TV, radio and online coverage of three sensitive topics in 2007 and 2012. One of these three was the EU.

In both years (and in line with Media Tenor's research) the EU was framed largely in negative terms as a threat to British interests. It was mainly viewed through the prism of political conflict between Labour and the Conservatives, or as a football in Tory infighting. Like the conclusions of the Wilson Review, the Cardiff study concluded that there was virtually no rounded debate about the multiplicity of ways in which the relationship between the EU and the UK affected Britain. Conversely, Euroscepticism was very well represented through the voices of Conservative politicians, although UKIP received little airtime. There were only a few voices – mostly those of business representatives – arguing for the benefits of EU membership in either year (2007 and 2012).

Next, in 2016, Cardiff University's Stephen Cushion and Justin Lewis did a content analysis of the five TV news broadcasters' main evening bulletins[83] over the ten-week EU referendum campaign (15 April to 22 June 2016).[84] Their conclusions were a strong indictment of *all* the broadcasters (there was no material difference between the BBC's and the other broadcasters' coverage):

> [W]hile broadcasters understandably balanced the airtime granted to official Leave and Remain actors, they did not consider or scrutinize the veracity or weight of opposing arguments [. . . W]e also found broadcasters did not reflect the full range of party political opinions and left little space for analysis beyond politicians and campaigners ... the Conservative case for Remain was featured prominently, [but] a more left-wing case for EU membership – despite intense campaigning by many

senior Labour, Liberal Democrat, SNP, Plaid Cymru and trade union figures – was side-lined.

[C]overage was dominated by statistical tit-for-tats, with rival camps trading numerical claims with little journalistic arbitration or attempt to consult or interpret expert opinion ... Strikingly absent ... was coverage that explained how the EU worked, the nature of international trade, or the economic role of EU immigration and its impact on public services.[85]

Ultimately, the evidence on the BBC's EU coverage is mixed. As you will recall, since 1999, News-watch has published report after report claiming a marked and systematic pro-EU bias. In 2004, the Wilson Review, based on public, stakeholder and its own (marginally Eurosceptic) perceptions, largely agreed (and the BBC responded with new policies and guidelines). However, the Media Tenor study in 2016, based on a very large, comprehensive sample, found that, in reality, the EU had been discussed in principally *negative* terms on the BBC's flagship *News at Ten* over the previous fifteen years. This general picture of *negative* EU reporting is confirmed by the Cardiff studies on the BBC's TV, radio and online EU coverage in 2007 and 2012, and that of the Brexit referendum on *News at Ten* in 2016.

The balance of the evidence is that, in the words of Cardiff's Mike Berry, 'The BBC tends to reproduce a Conservative, Eurosceptic, pro-business version of the world, not a left-wing, anti-business agenda'.[86] However, the evidence on its EU coverage is less clear-cut than that on the false accusation that its news and current affairs coverage is systematically left-wing.

The BBC and the Problem of 'False Balance'

One of the biggest sticking points over the BBC's Brexit coverage has been the idea of *false balance*. The charge is that the Corporation, worried by being constantly accused of anti-Brexit bias by the Leave camp, gave almost as much airtime to the small minority of relevant experts – notably economists – supporting Leave, as to the large majority supporting Remain, but without informing the audience of the actual balance of expert opinion. Viewers and listeners were therefore given the misleading impression that the experts were split roughly down the middle.

False balance was a fairly constant complaint during the Brexit referendum campaign. It provoked a sharp response from the BBC's then head of news and current affairs, James Harding, in *The Guardian*. He pointed out that interviewers had challenged Leavers' claims, such as the one which appeared on the famous red bus and alleged – at least by implication – that Brexit would release an extra £350 million a year for the NHS, and also that Andrew Neil had tackled Nigel Farage's false figures on immigration.[87]

Harding's article, in its turn, provoked Hugo Dixon, of the independent fact-checking agency Full Fact, to point out that 'there were many times when [the BBC's journalists] didn't [challenge interviewees] . . . I paid special attention to its agenda-setting Today programme . . . and noted many cases of inadequate challenge'.[88]

Brexit isn't the only subject on which the BBC has been accused of false balance. Another example relates to climate change. In August 2017, Lord Lawson, founder of the Global Warming Policy Foundation (one of the think tanks at 55 Tufton Street) made two important incorrect statements about the science of climate change on the *Today* programme, both of which went unchallenged. The first was that there had been no increase in extreme weather events. The second was that mean global surface temperature had slightly declined over the previous ten years. Two complainants felt that the BBC's initial response to their complaint had been insufficiently clear-cut and escalated it to Ofcom, which agreed that the two statements were incorrect and that the BBC, in introducing Lord Lawson, should have said that his view of climate change ran counter to the weight of scientific opinion.[89]

Two final points. First of all, insofar as the BBC seems to have generally framed the EU in negative terms, one reason may be that, once again, it tends to follow the agenda set by the (overwhelmingly Eurosceptic) UK newspapers. Secondly, News-watch has never even raised the question of whether the BBC's EU coverage is more Europhile than that of the other British broadcasters. Nor was the Wilson Review asked to consider this question. In contrast, the Cardiff studies discovered no material difference between the BBC's and other broadcasters' EU coverage, and Media Tenor found the BBC to be marginally *more* negative than the rest.

The misleading singling out of the BBC by those accusing it of left-wing and/or pro-EU bias probably reflects three things, in combination: the importance to those on the Eurosceptic right of reducing its credibility (because of its prominence in UK news and the high trust in which it is still held by the British public); a feeling that – because of its public funding – it may be more easily cowed than other broadcasters; and some of its critics' other commercial, political and ideological agendas.

Avoiding Sensitive Stories

A related issue appears to be the BBC's recent tendency to avoid a number of – possibly linked – sensitive stories. The first of these relates to Vote Leave's activities during the 2016 Brexit referendum campaign.

We spoke to investigative journalist Carol Cadwalladr about how two planned *Panorama* programmes – on Vote Leave's breach of spending limits, and nefarious use of Facebook data through Cambridge Analytica – came to be dropped.[90]

Cadwalladr told us that, after some initial contact with ITN (for *Channel 4 News*) and the *New York Times*, she and two young whistleblowers, Shahmir Sanni and Christopher Wylie, had met the editor of *Panorama*, Rachel Jupp. They were very impressed with her and gave her all their material – a mass of evidence, including some lengthy filmed interviews. Their expectation was that there would be two *Panorama* programmes on different aspects of the Leave campaign's alleged cheating. But three months later – in February 2018 – *Panorama* told them it would not run either film because 'the evidence was not strong enough'. Cadwalladr's impression was that this decision had been made at a senior level.

On 30 July 2019, one of the whistleblowers – Shahmir Sanni, who we met in the last chapter – tweeted that he had been invited to BBC Radio 4 and had recorded a contribution to a profile of Dominic Cummings, but added, 'I've been told they're not going to run it'.[91] Although individual contributions often end up not being used, that doesn't mean they've been censored. However, Sanni's tweet provoked a long trail of comments, with people claiming that the BBC had been taken over by conservative forces. Three months later, in a series of tweets on 1 November, Sanni claimed that the BBC *had* (among other things) deliberately censored the story, 'refusing to cover the Cambridge Analytica or Vote Leave scandal because it involved friends and former colleagues of several editors at the BBC'.[92]

Journalists we spoke to, both inside and outside the BBC, understood its caution about breaking such a politically charged story which also featured specific accusations. But they expected the Corporation to give the story a full-spectrum investigation and the coverage it warranted once it was in the public domain.[93] Particularly because many of the same players – notably, Cambridge Analytica and Steve Bannon, with additional evidence of potential Russian involvement – were involved in comparable meddling in the US presidential election just four and a half months later.[94] They were surprised when, as they saw it, the BBC ducked the issue. People were starting to say that the BBC was avoiding political 'hot potatoes', especially anything that might call into doubt the conduct of the 2016 Brexit referendum, and therefore the legitimacy of its outcome. As these concerns grew, and Cadwalladr's revelations progressed in parallel with other media stories about Russian meddling in the US election, so did the conviction that the BBC was avoiding anything that might bring it into conflict with the, now-dominant, vocally Eurosceptic right wing of the Conservative Party.

A number of BBC employees described to us, off the record, a climate of fear, with senior managers demanding they should be constantly careful not to provoke the government or the Tory right. Some also claimed that, over the last ten years, the BBC had recruited several right-wing Brexit supporters to positions of power in news and current affairs who had become gatekeepers, actively managing the news agenda and coverage. It's unclear exactly how and why this alleged recruitment process is supposed to have worked.

We heard plausible explanations from BBC people for its avoidance of 'difficult' stories – that they didn't clear the burden-of-proof bar, or that they were competing for airtime with more important stories. This was the typical response to questions about the BBC's failure to cover Boris Johnson's alleged links to the American global right-wing linkman Steve Bannon at a time when revealing those links might have damaged Johnson's prospects in the Conservative leadership election.[95]

Another story that the BBC is frequently said to have avoided is that of President Trump's hard-right agenda – the changes his administration was making to taxes and regulation, appointments to the Supreme Court, attacks on Obamacare and the Environmental Protection Agency (EPA) and so on[96] – instead providing colourful three-minute packages about his personality, style, tweets, speeches and latest scandals.

John Sweeney's Travails

In November 2019, the allegation that the BBC was sitting on potentially contentious stories was brought into stark relief by an explosive *Sunday Times* article by the paper's political editor, Tim Shipman. Based on claims by John Sweeney, a controversial former *Panorama* and *Newsnight* investigative reporter who had recently left the Corporation, it argued that 'BBC bosses have been accused of pulling the plug on politically sensitive reports into the close links between leading politicians and Russia'.[97]

Earlier that month, Sweeney had written an open letter 'as a reluctant whistleblower' to Sharon White, the chief executive of Ofcom, asking for an investigation into 'a number of [BBC] films relating to the far right, Russia and Brexit [that] were not broadcast'. He went on to say, 'BBC management, led by Director-General Lord Hall, has become so risk-averse in the face of threats from the far right and the Russian state and its proxies that due impartiality is being undermined'.[98]

Sweeney's list featured prominent figures whose Russian links were being 'censored' by the BBC; they were mainly, but not all, from the right. They included not only Tommy Robinson, Arron Banks and Boris Johnson (allegedly seen as a security risk when he was Foreign Secretary), but also Lord Mandelson and Seamus Milne. Sweeney also highlighted BBC employees who, he claimed, were compromised by their relationships with Russian or other commercial interests.

Andrew Adonis' Lonely Mission

Andrew Adonis, Lord Adonis of Camden, a prominent centre–left critic of the BBC, refers to its 'Farageization'. Adonis is a former Blairite technocrat who became the first chair of the Tory government's National Infrastructure Commission, an executive agency tasked with advising government on how to ensure that the country develops the infrastructure (roads, railways, broadband) it needs over the long term. He has gone further and been more public with his criticism of the BBC than most. As a former BBC supporter, he wrote an open letter to Lord Hall, saying this:

> It is my belief that your coverage has been fundamentally corrupted on Brexit because of your desire to conciliate the government and pro-Brexit campaign on the fundamental question of leaving the European Union. You have accepted the government's view that the decision is irreversible, when that is not in fact the case either in law or in public debate.
>
> I believe there is also a problem of bias even when the BBC does cover the 'binary choice', as in the constant high-profile coverage you give to Mr Nigel Farage, including his 32nd appearance on Question Time last month and the major coverage you gave to his 'fish' protests more recently, at which few besides journalists were present.[99]

As a result of this, the Brexiteer online mob trolled Adonis, saying he was appointed because of his connections: an unelected placeman criticizing an elected politician (Farage, as a longstanding MEP and former party leader). And, according to Adonis himself, the BBC privately appealed to him not to attack it, while others who largely agreed with him nevertheless also urged caution.

His response, in *The Guardian*, was this: 'There are those who find such criticism of the BBC, and of its editorial decisions, distasteful. "Careful, Andrew," they say to me, even as more often than not they agree with the substance of my case, "you don't want to damage Auntie, we could end up with the Beeb being run by Murdoch!" Well I certainly want no such thing. But recently, and particularly on the issues surrounding Brexit, it has frankly been hard to see what difference it would make.'[100]

The BBC's 'Sins of Omission'

Nick Cohen – a notable left renegade and vocal critic of Corbyn's Labour Party and another former BBC supporter – has persistently criticized it for ignoring Carole Cadwalladr's revelations of 'Brexit cheating' and Russian interference in the 2016 referendum. In a June 2018 *Guardian* article, he wrote:

> For months you'd be forgiven for thinking its editors have not let its reporters cover Russia/Brexit ... I've defended the BBC against Scottish Nationalists, Corbynistas, Remainers and the Brexit right. But how can anyone defend a news organisation that prefers staged confrontation to reporting?[101]

The following month, in the *New York Review of Books*, he told Americans, 'I doubt you will have grasped the extent of [the BBC's] journalistic cowardice in covering the 2016 referendum that decided to take Britain out of the European Union and its aftermath ... The BBC's report of the scandals around the Brexit referendum is not biased or unbalanced: it barely exists.'[102] This provoked a reply from James Stephenson, an editor on the BBC News and Current Affairs programmes.[103] He ignored Cohen's claim of Russian interference and gave a very different account of the history of the aborted *Panorama* programme on Referendum-meddling than that of the *Guardian* journalist who had originally broken the story. Political commentators reported growing incredulity and disappointment that Cadwalladr's *Observer* revelations warranted so little BBC attention.[104] The charge was not that the BBC had crudely censored all mentions of the story, but rather that it sought to minimize them and then failed to give them the authoritative coverage and analysis they warranted, not at all in line with the BBC's Birt-ist 'mission to explain'.

The BBC's response to these sorts of charges is often the 'symmetrical' one: because people on both sides see reports they don't like we must be getting it right. The right's regular response is simply a rubbishing of the other side: that out-of-touch Remainers can't understand or accept the referendum result, so they have to believe in Russians under the bed and sinister social media manipulation. But very few people address what has truly been a key issue (and still is): that of the BBC avoiding difficult subjects.

The Russian Connection

The problem for the BBC has been not just that the same approach, with the same cast of characters, appeared to feature in the American election, but that it is so widely *acknowledged* in the mainstream US media that there was Russian meddling. It is well documented – from the Mueller report to *The New York Times*.

In 2018, Jane Mayer of the *New Yorker* examined Russian meddling in both the Brexit referendum and the US election four-and-a-half months later. In one article,[105] she summarized Kathleen Jamieson's forensic analysis in *Cyberwar: How Russian Hackers and Trolls Helped Elect a President* of how the Russians had successfully interfered in the US election.[106] In another, she raised a very important question: whether the UK had been the 'petri-dish' for the later Russian interference in the US election.[107] Angry Remainers have told us that the BBC continues to ignore these stories when even mainstream American media like the *New Yorker* have given them this major coverage.

As we've seen, the endless right-wing and Eurosceptic claims that the BBC's news and current affairs coverage is systematically biased against them (that is, to the left, and in favour of the EU) are not supported by the facts: the most reliable evidence suggests, if anything, the opposite, on both counts.

Nor, as we'll see, have these attacks succeeded in persuading the British public to agree with those making them, apart from people who already share these views. But they may have

intimidated the BBC into ignoring some of the most important –
and politically explosive – stories of the last few years. Reflecting
on her curious relationship with the BBC, in 2019 Carol Cadwalladr, who wrote the original Cambridge Analytica story,
told us that the omission was so important precisely because the
BBC still defines mainstream news: 'If it isn't on the BBC, it
hasn't happened.'

10. 'Worse Than Poll Tax'

In the last chapter, we discussed the many, mostly right-wing criticisms of the BBC's programmes, especially its news coverage, which is characterized as left-wing, anti-Brexit and excessively politically correct. We'll now turn to the other main target of right-wing attacks: the television licence fee as a method of funding the BBC.[1]

The fact is most people don't seem to be all that fussed about having to pay the TV licence fee. At most, they may see paying it as a bit of an annual chore and they may be rather vague about exactly where the money goes and what it funds apart from BBC television.

But to some people, mainly on the right, it's a *huge* issue. For instance, it's a perennial target for the IEA, the Adam Smith Institute,[2] the TaxPayers' Alliance and many of the anti-BBC blogs. And it features centrally in the latest wave of attacks since the December 2019 election.

Right-wing attacks on the licence fee last came to a head in the run-up to the renewal of the BBC Charter in 2016. In October 2014, John Whittingdale, then still chairman of the DCMS select committee, described it in an article in the *Daily Telegraph* as 'worse than poll tax ... because under the poll tax,[3] if you were on a very low income you would get a considerable subsidy'. Whittingdale certainly knew about the poll tax, as he was Margaret Thatcher's Political Secretary at the time.[4] He would have remembered its political impact – how it had led to massive riots, splits within the Conservative Party and, indirectly, Mrs Thatcher's downfall. On top of its political impact, the poll tax was also much bigger financially than the TV licence fee, costing the average household about ten times as much. Additionally, the then Culture Secretary, Sajid Javid, was also quoted in the same *Telegraph* article saying that the Conservatives might cut the licence fee if they won the next election, as £145.50 was 'a large amount of money' for many families, and the BBC's funding might need fundamental reform to reflect changing technology and viewing habits: 'nothing is ruled out'.[5] This raised the question of how the licence fee could be improved upon. One issue was whether non-payment of it should continue to be punishable by law.

Should Licence Fee Evasion Be Decriminalized?

As with all taxes, licence-fee evasion is a criminal offence. The maximum penalty is a fine of £1,000, although the average is about £170.[6] Contrary to widespread belief, no one goes to prison for not paying the licence fee, but up to several dozen are jailed each year, for an average of twenty-five days, for failing to pay the resulting fine, although there appear to be no data on how many of them also have other unpaid fines.[7] The main arguments for decriminalizing non-payment are that almost all of those prosecuted are struggling financially, and often in other ways; about 70 per cent are women, including many single mothers; and the threat of prison seems disproportionate.[8] It is also sometimes wrongly claimed that it would significantly ease the pressure on magistrates' courts. This is an emotive topic that unites many on both the left and the right, although perhaps for different reasons.

The 2014–15 Perry Review

As part of the political and media assault on the BBC during the last Charter review, a new decriminalization campaign was launched in March 2014 by Andrew Bridgen MP, an energetic Eurosceptic Tory backbencher. His proposal attracted cross-party support from more than 150 MPs.[9] Only Deputy Prime Minister Nick Clegg, on behalf of the Liberal Democrats, publicly expressed caution, saying it might increase evasion and force the closure of BBC services.[10] In October 2014, Culture Secretary Sajid Javid appointed David Perry QC, a top criminal barrister, to conduct an independent review.[11] Perry's July 2015 report noted that the costs and problems to do with the licence fee had been much exaggerated. For instance, although licence-fee cases did, as claimed, represent a substantial proportion of magistrates' overall court *cases* (11.5 per cent in 2013), they took up only 0.3 per cent of court *time*, because most defendants pleaded guilty by post. It recommended against decriminalization, describing the system as 'broadly fair and proportionate [and providing] good value for money (both for licence fee payers and taxpayers)'.[12] We agree. The government accepted the recommendation then, but Boris Johnson's government has now revived the idea of decriminalizing licence-fee evasion.

'If at First You Don't Succeed . . . ': the 2020 Consultation on Decriminalizing Licence-Fee Evasion

In February 2020, the government launched a new consultation on decriminalization.[13] This was widely seen as part of Dominic Cummings' personal war against the BBC – an issue on which the PM was said to be 'significantly less gung-ho'.[14] Despite its possibly murky origins, the consultation document is very clear and well worth a read. It appears to be a delicious mixture of the political (presumably written by ministers or their special advisers) and the rational (presumably written by DCMS officials). There was no suggestion that Perry had given the wrong answer in July 2015, so the government's challenge was to come up with a plausible cover story for revisiting the issue less than five years later. You can decide for yourself how well it succeeded. The government's broad, and rather vague, justification for the new consultation was that 'the broadcasting landscape has changed [since the Perry Report]'.[15] This was presumably a reference to the rapid growth of online streaming and all that, although there was no attempt to explain *why* these trends were relevant to the decriminalization issue beyond a general feeling of technological determinism, like saying 'Now we have planes, we no longer need trains'.

A blog post ('Let them Eat Netflix') by the New Weather Institute, a left-leaning environmental virtual think tank, estimated that, for a household with a digital TV but no broadband, the monthly cost of renting a smart TV and subscribing to a cheap broadband package and the most basic Netflix package would be almost three times the cost of the licence fee. It concluded, 'for the great majority of those most in need in society struggling to pay the TV licence fee, online TV is out of their reach and completely irrelevant. Unless the government can offer a more credible explanation, the only reasonable interpretation is that this consultation is simply part of its wider attack on the BBC since the election'.[16] The only specific changes since the Perry Report that the consultation document mentions are, first, that a TV licence is now required to watch or download content on the BBC iPlayer, and, secondly, the BBC's decision to limit free TV licences to households with one or more members aged over seventy-five and in receipt of Pension Credit, saying that, 'The Government recognises the value of free TV licences for the over seventy-fives and believes they should be funded by the BBC'.[17] We're curious to know when the government, using the same logic, plans to force the energy companies to take over the cost of winter fuel payments for the elderly – about £2 billion per annum.[18] The consultation closed on 1 April 2020. At the time of writing, the government has published neither a summary of the responses nor its proposals on decriminalizing licence-fee evasion.

All this begs the question: why is the 43-pence-per-household-per-day TV licence fee so controversial? What makes it so terrible in the minds of so many? And, if people have been criticizing it for decades – which they have – why do we still have it?

Pros and Cons of the Television Licence Fee

Perhaps surprisingly, given his criticism of it, one of the best and most balanced analyses of the licence fee is by Whittingdale's own DCMS Committee. Four months after his comment, the committee report included an excellent summary of the licence fee's pros and cons. The advantages listed were that it was simple, secure, predictable and associated in people's minds with paying for the BBC; it helped maintain the Corporation's independence from commercial and political pressures; and it generated enough income for the BBC's services to be universally available at no extra charge. None of these is, as far as we know, contested.

The licence fee's disadvantages, according to the DCMS Committee, were that it was regressive ('all pay the same regardless of income or size of household'); it gave households no choice ('it is compulsory for TV homes that do not use the [BBC's] services'); it was 'expensive to collect' and suffered from a 5.5 per cent evasion rate; and 'homes that watch only catch-up TV online, listen to radio and/or use BBC online get a free ride'.[19]

How valid are these claimed disadvantages in practice?

'All Pay the Same'

As a flat tax for all households, regardless of household size or income, the licence fee is indeed regressive in its 'one size fits all' approach; it is not 'a large amount of money' for most households, but it is for some. Those with one or more members aged seventy-five-plus who are also on Pension Credit get it for free, but there are many poor, mostly younger households which do not.

However, if considered not as a tax, but as a price for a set of services, the licence fee is no more unfair than any other price: everyone pays the same amount for the same product for pay TV, refrigerators, baked beans and restaurant meals. In fact, as a single set of services for a single price, the licence-fee-funded BBC is *more* egalitarian than most things, and always has been. As Reith wrote in 1924 (using the language of the time): 'Most of the good things in this world are badly distributed . . . Wireless is a good thing, but it may be shared by all alike, for the same outlay, and to the same extent . . . there is no first and third class'.[20]

A Compulsory Charge

As we saw in Chapter 3, the fact that households have to pay the television licence fee even if they do not use the BBC's services is a disadvantage in theory; but not in practice, because the evidence is that, even if such households exist *at all*, their number is tiny: remember that *in a single week* in 2015 (the only time this has been measured) 99 per cent of TV households consumed at least some BBC services. The suggestion that a significant number do not use *any* of these services in the course of a whole year is nonsense.[21] Needless to say, those objecting to the licence fee on the grounds that people have to pay for it even if they use no BBC services have never felt the need to provide any evidence that such people exist.[22]

Collection Costs, Evasion and Free-Riding

The other supposed disadvantages of the licence fee are equally mythical.

The cost of collecting it was £103 million in 2018–19, just 2.8 per cent of the £3,690 million total licence-fee income.[23] (As we'll see, alternative funding methods like subscriptions and advertising involve *much* higher collection costs.) Evasion of payment, estimated at 5.5 per cent, is somewhat higher and this may increase in future with the growth of changing consumption patterns, especially among younger viewers and listeners. However, as the DCMS Committee noted, before the BBC took over TV licensing from the Home Office in 1991, collection costs were 6 per cent of licence-fee income and the estimated evasion level 10 per cent[24] – a total of 16 per cent, almost double the level in 2015.[25]

The Catch-22 is that taking over collection of the payment from the Home Office has reduced evasion, but shifted the blame for the suffering caused by enforcement directly onto the BBC – and this is enthusiastically exploited by bloggers and right-wing politicians and journalists (many of whom rarely show similar concern for poor people struggling to pay other taxes and bills). Lastly, the free-riding iPlayer loophole has now been addressed, at least in principle.[26]

The practical – as opposed to ideological and/or mythical – disadvantages of the licence fee therefore come down to just two: it is regressive *when seen as a tax* (but egalitarian as a single price for a single set of services equally available to all); and there is still some evasion of payment.

Alternative Ways of Funding the BBC

Whatever the licence fee's pros and cons, the real-world policy question is whether there is a better alternative. The DCMS Committee discussed four options: advertising, subscriptions, a revised licence fee (or another earmarked tax) and general taxation.[27]

Most discussion has focused on the first three of these: advertising, subscriptions and a revised licence fee or another earmarked tax. However, general taxation remains a potential fourth option.[28] Let's take a look at the four options and what we see as the best solution.

Advertising

Advertising[29] is the option that has been explored in most detail, because, in 1985, Margaret Thatcher appointed a committee under Professor Alan Peacock, a leading free-market economist, to investigate it. The committee's brief also asked it 'to consider any proposals for securing income from the consumer other than through the licence fee'.[30]

The Peacock Committee sat for over a year and its report runs to 223 pages. (Its wider legacy is discussed in Appendix C). It firmly rejected advertising as a form of funding for the BBC, for two reasons. First of all, the evidence was that most of the BBC's advertising income would be captured from that of other advertising-funded broadcast and print media companies, severely damaging them and reducing their ability to invest in content. Secondly, advertising funding would give the BBC an incentive to prioritize advertisers' needs over those of viewers and listeners. Therefore, despite Margaret Thatcher's enthusiasm for advertising on the BBC, her government accepted the recommendation not to take it further.

We agree with both of the Peacock Committee's reasons for rejecting advertising on the BBC, but we note that there are two further reasons for doing so which, as far as we know, are not even mentioned in its report.

The first and most obvious further reason for rejecting BBC advertising is consumer preference: audiences much prefer not to have their viewing and listening interrupted by commercials. It seems hard to believe that, in the course of fourteen months of deliberations – and despite the primary focus of its brief being on whether the BBC should carry advertising – the committee did not even discuss this aspect of what audiences wanted. But, unless we have missed something in its report, that really does appear to be the case.

The second additional factor the Peacock Committee seems not to have considered is less obvious and more technical, but equally important: the substantial hidden overhead costs of broadcast advertising. Companies' investment in TV and radio advertising campaigns includes creative agency fees, media agency fees and commercial production costs. We estimate that, conservatively, these amount to about 13–15 per cent of the total cost to the advertiser of a typical broadcast campaign.[31] The equivalent trading costs for digital advertising are unknown, but certainly much higher, i.e. at least 30 per cent of the total cost.[32]

Advertising funding also involves significant *internal* costs for the broadcaster. Consider Channel 4, which operates in very competitive markets and is generally seen as a 'tight ship' without excessive overheads. Its £85 million 'cost of sales' (that is, the cost of its commercial sales operation) was 8.7 per cent of its £975 million revenue in 2018.[33]

If we combine all these hidden overhead costs for advertising funding, the total is in the order of 20 to 25 per cent of the advertiser's campaign investment[34] – up to three times the total amount the BBC has to spend on its collection of the licence fee *and* loses from evasion of payment.

The arguments against advertising on the BBC are so clear that no serious policy analyst has ever, to our knowledge, proposed it since the Peacock Inquiry in the 1980s. There are still occasional attempts to revive it, but these are unable to withstand proper scrutiny. The twenty-one-page section on funding in the DCMS Committee's 2015 report barely even considers it, beyond quoting the BBC's view that, in line with Peacock's analysis, 'an advertiser-funded BBC could change its priorities and would have significant consequences for commercial broadcasters and the revenue available for investment in content'.[35]

A significant minority of the public still supports an advertising-funded BBC, however, perhaps seeing it as costless – apart from forcing them to put up with commercial interruptions to their BBC viewing and listening.[36] But many more prefer the licence fee, rejecting advertising mainly because they think it might force the BBC to be more commercial in its programming.[37]

Subscriptions: A Recurring Theme

The Peacock Committee defined its brief very broadly and made several recommendations, beyond the main question of whether the BBC should be wholly or partially funded by advertising.[38] The one which was to prove the most influential over the long term was that 'British broadcasting should move towards a sophisticated market system based on consumer sovereignty' with the licence fee eventually being replaced by subscriptions. To enable this, every home would need what is called conditional access (CA) technology, so that access to each service, including the BBC, could be limited to only those households which have paid for it. In 1986, only homes with cable TV had CA technology, although satellite pay TV was also on the way. The committee therefore recommended a three-stage strategy under which, within twenty years or so, every home would have installed CA technology to support the 'sophisticated market system'. Their idea was that there would be a multiplicity of suppliers (including a subscription-funded BBC, as the licence fee would have been phased out).[39]

Although there are many options (including those whereby consumers pay for individual programmes),[40] the main policy debate has been about whether to replace the compulsory TV licence fee with monthly subscriptions for those choosing to pay for the BBC's services, although the proponents of this have always been remarkably vague about the details. Ever since the Peacock Inquiry, there has been a steady stream of think-tank white papers, newspaper editorials, comments from MPs and taxi drivers and so on calling for the TV licence to be replaced by subscriptions and the BBC to 'earn its keep'. These appeals have been revived since the 2019 election. They still sometimes refer back to the 1986 report, which has acquired something of the status of holy writ at the IEA in particular. Most of these calls – although not all – are from the right, especially free-market think tanks, often also recommending partial or total BBC privatization.[41] Given the repeated calls for the BBC to be funded by subscriptions, the 2013–15 DCMS Committee naturally looked closely at this option.[42]

There were two arguments in favour of subscriptions put to the DCMS Committee by David Elstein, the principal witness arguing for a 'more immediate' move to this option.[43] The first was that it would end the compulsory licence fee. This is obviously true by definition. But whether one regards it as an advantage is more an ideological issue than it is a practical one; as we've seen in reality, the number of households paying the annual licence fee and not directly benefiting from the BBC's services as consumers is negligible.

Elstein's second argument in favour of subscriptions was that they would increase choice, with the BBC offering a range of packages at different price points, and being given an incentive to develop a more 'premium' product, such as high-cost drama, sports and arts programmes and documentaries.[44] However, he offered no evidence or analysis to support this second claim. His reticence is not unique: as far as we know, *none* of those proposing subscription funding for the BBC over the last thirty-five years has ever published any evidence-based analysis of the practicalities and the expected benefits to UK viewers, listeners and online users – not even a hypothetical illustration of what the numbers *might* be. Subscription funding for the BBC is essentially a faith-based policy: its proponents see no need to discuss what it would actually mean in practice, except in the very vaguest terms.[45]

The DCMS Committee heard four arguments against replacing the licence fee with subscriptions. The main witness making these arguments was Patrick Barwise, one of the authors of this book. He argued that switching to subscriptions would fundamentally change the nature of the BBC; the BBC would no longer be a universal service; it might reduce the overall investment in content (especially UK-originated content); and most households would be worse off.[46]

There are many unknowns, discussed more fully in Appendix D,[47] but our analysis suggests several reasons why replacing the licence fee with subscription funding would lead to a worse outcome for most UK households, independent producers, the BBC itself and the pay TV companies too.

Firstly, it would risk changing the fundamental nature of the BBC by giving it a financial incentive to prioritize programmes which, relative to their cost, would be attractive to as many subscribers as possible – especially larger, middle- or high-income households who would be better able to pay. Resisting this pressure would be a challenge, but not necessarily insuperable: a combination of governance, regulation and the BBC's public service culture could limit the extent to which the financial incentives were allowed to change its priorities. We would portray this issue as a risk, but potentially manageable.

Secondly, a subscription-funded BBC would, by definition, no longer be a universal service. Most supporters of public service broadcasting, including ourselves, see universality as crucial, especially in today's world of increasing discord, disinformation and 'echo chambers'. (However, this too is an ideological issue – in fact, it is almost a mirror image of some other people's objections to the licence fee being compulsory.)[48]

The other arguments against subscription funding are about its probable financial impacts. According to our analysis, it would reduce the BBC's (and pay TV companies') programme investment and the value for money of British TV and radio for the great majority of households.

As already noted, to enable subscriptions, someone – presumably UK consumers in the long run – would have to pay for 'conditional access' technology on every device used to watch BBC TV, so that – as with commercial pay TV – only those who had paid would be able to see the programmes.[49]

Beyond this medium-term implementation issue, however, there are three further inherent long-term financial problems with subscription funding. In summary: it would first, by definition, reduce the BBC's 'revenue base' (that is, the number of homes funding it); secondly, it would substantially increase overheads to cover marketing, billing and customer service costs; and thirdly, it would reduce pay-TV companies' revenue and content investment.

Even if we could magically – overnight and at zero cost – introduce conditional access technology on every device capable of receiving BBC services (and register every potential user), and even if we ignored the social benefit of the BBC's universality, these problems would still remain. There are many unknowns, but one thing we can say with absolute certainty is that, for a subscription-based system to maintain the same level of content investment by the BBC, the average price would need to be *much* higher than the licence fee.

Therefore, the onus should surely be on those advocating subscriptions to publish some concrete proposals on how they would address the practical challenges, and at least some hypothetical illustrations of how they think the subscriptions might be packaged and priced, what the consumer take-up might be and what this might mean in terms of revenue, additional overhead costs, market impact, content investment, choice and value for money. Show us we're wrong!

Because of the many practical problems and other disadvantages of subscription funding, the 2015 DCMS Committee, like every previous one, rejected it as a short-term option: 'There currently appears to be no better alternative for funding the BBC in the near term other than a hypothecated tax or the licence fee.' However, they added – rightly, in our view – that the licence fee was becoming harder to sustain because of changes in technology, services and audience behaviour. They warned that 'we do not see a long-term future for [it] in its current form'.[50]

A Household Levy?

The DCMS Committee's preferred approach was to replace the TV licence fee with a universal household levy (i.e. regardless of whether the household has a TV set), similar to the one introduced in Germany in 2013.[51] This also seemed to be the model backed in 2015 by the BBC itself, John Whittingdale as Culture Secretary, and the economist Helen Weeds.[52] The levy would not be linked to the ownership of a TV set, since a growing proportion of viewing of BBC TV (and virtually all consumption of BBC Radio and BBC Online) is on other devices.

The current German system is a universal flat fee paid by every household, company and public institution, with exemptions for some welfare recipients, for those with second homes and students. Evasion is minimal and, because of its simplicity, the collection costs are also low.

We agree that a device-independent household levy is likely to be a better long-term option than the licence fee. Linking the BBC's funding to the ownership of a TV set is anachronistic. We assume this will be one of the main options examined in any future review of long-term funding for the BBC. Ireland recently announced a switch to a similar system, starting in 2024.[53]

The main problem of switching from the licence fee to a household levy may be the politics of the transition (doubtless reinforced by Beeb-attacking newspapers doing their best to maximize the resistance), and there would inevitably be some losers – especially the *very* few people who genuinely watch no television and the rather larger number who claim not to, and possibly really believe that they don't. There will also be political questions about what is included and how to make the cost of the levy more equitable. One option would be to collect the levy alongside the council tax and in proportion to it, which would enable it to be modified from a single flat rate. This is the system used in France.[54]

An Earmarked Tax

There are other options for replacing the licence fee with another sort of earmarked tax, such as the current Labour Party proposal to fund the BBC out of a sales tax levied on technology companies.

Another interesting option would be a small levy on electricity consumption, which would mean bigger and richer households (who use far more electricity) would contribute the most. Italy moved to this system in 2016.[55] We think this may well be the best option for generating the BBC's long-term core funding.

One aim of switching to a levy on council tax or electricity bills would be to address the long-standing – and valid – criticism that the fixed-rate licence fee is one-size-fits-all. But, typically, the *Daily Mail*'s response to a recent suggestion that these options should be considered focused entirely on the negative impact on better-off households: the headline was, 'People with big houses could be forced to pay higher TV licence fee under "progressive" BBC proposals'. Similarly, the *Express'* was: 'BBC licence fee shock: bizarre new fee system could see YOU paying more'.[56] (As usual, the *Express* article also included links to stories on several popular BBC shows: *Sherlock, Killing Eve, Countryfile, Antiques Roadshow* and Charlie Brooker's *Wipe*.)

Ensuring the BBC's Long-term Financial Sustainability

As well as finding a better model for the BBC's core funding, there are several other ways to help ensure its financial sustainability. The BBC already generates far more commercial revenue than any other publicly funded broadcaster in the world, and initiatives such as its BritBox SVoD joint venture with the commercial PSBs (discussed in Chapter 2) have the potential to increase this further, thus creating more money to invest in new programmes, although we do not see its market potential as big enough to make a huge difference.[57]

What about further efficiency savings? As we discovered in Chapter 4, the BBC is already very efficient in terms of its low overheads and the high proportion of its income invested in content. Its efficiency programme is increasingly running up against diminishing returns but, of course, there will always be some scope for a little more. The BBC and the commercial PSBs can also be supported by increasing their prominence[58] and by increasing the number of listed sporting events[59] for which broadcast rights must be offered to free-to-air broadcasters at a 'fair and reasonable' price.[60]

What the Fee or Levy Should Cover Beyond the BBC

Over time it should be possible to phase out the use of licence-fee revenue for all purposes other than funding the BBC (including the World Service) and a few limited and closely related media activities, such as S4C, the contestable fund for children's TV, and support for local journalism, perhaps capped at a statutory maximum total of, say, 5 per cent of licence-fee revenue. In the past, the BBC has been forced to pay for too many other government projects unrelated to its role. The BBC's handling of the switchover to digital TV was a government project which enabled the Treasury to auction the released analogue TV spectrum and keep the £2.34 billion proceeds. The government's roll-out of rural broadband is another government project subsidized by the BBC, which significantly benefits its deep-pocketed SVoD competitors, such as Netflix and Amazon. Neither of these should have been funded from the licence fee, and nor should *any* free TV licences for the over-seventy-fives: this is a welfare benefit which, if justified, should be funded out of general taxation, as Age UK has demanded.[61]

With a household levy, licence fee or any other earmarked tax, we need a politician-proof way of setting its level and preventing governments from raiding the BBC's funding to pay for other things, as Gordon Brown and George Osborne both did repeatedly as chancellor. The same principle applies to the option of funding the BBC out of general taxation.

Is There a Politician-proof Solution?

The main advantage of paying for the BBC out of general taxation is that the amount handed over would no longer be regressive (as richer people pay more tax than poorer people). It would also minimize collection costs (or, at the very least, pass them on to HMRC), although what the impact upon evasion of payment might be is unclear.

The big disadvantage of this strategy is the risk to the BBC's editorial independence from politicians progressively cutting – or (overtly or implicitly) threatening to cut – its funding, as the DCMS Committee noted had happened in Australia, Canada and the Netherlands. The question is whether, in the light of those countries' experience, it is possible to develop a politician-proof system that minimizes these risks.

Well, the BBC's editorial independence is already protected by its reputation and now by its external regulation by Ofcom. However, at the same time, its current arrangements have not protected its funding from the cuts forced on it by George Osborne in 2010 and 2015. In whatever way the BBC is funded over the long term – whether through the licence fee, another earmarked tax, such as a household levy, or general taxation – we need a statutory framework to prevent a repetition of this disgraceful process.

In February 2016, the House of Lords Select Committee on Communications proposed a framework explicitly designed for this purpose.[62] Similarly, the House of Commons DCMS Committee recently called for the government and the BBC to 'set out [steps] to ensure that the licence fee negotiations in 2021 are conducted in a wholly different way [from the process in 2015], with a sensible timescale, parliamentary oversight and involvement of licence fee payers'.[63]

The obvious model to explore in developing a politician-proof solution for the UK is the KEF, the German independent commission that, every four years, sets the level of the household levy and its allocation between its PSBs. We return to this in the Conclusion, where we discuss the future.

11. 'The Scope of Its Activities Is Chilling'[1]

A striking feature of UK broadcasting policy is how many of the proposals aim to make the BBC *less* popular, competitive and agile, to reduce its impact on the rest of the market. The underlying idea behind these restrictions is that the BBC's *only* role should be to address 'market failures' by providing public service programmes that the market won't supply because they're not commercially viable.

We here explain why, in our view, this 'market failure idea' is completely wrong, especially in a world increasingly dominated by global technology companies with vastly deeper pockets than the BBC, no such constraints and, of course, absolutely no commitment to a UK public service remit. The idea of market failure, as reflected in the current BBC Charter, is wrong both in principle and in practice. In principle, because policy should aim to maximize the UK public interest, not to balance it against the commercial interests of the BBC's – mostly non-UK – competitors. And in practice, because the BBC's actual impact on its competitors has been found to be much less than they claim, again and again. Its impact on *their* willingness and ability to invest in content is either minimal or even slightly positive (by forcing them to spend *more* on programmes to attract audiences).

Nonetheless, the Corporation is still a big, successful player and its role in its markets does need to be monitored. Part of its remit should certainly be to collaborate with and support other media, such as local media enterprises and start-ups, to help mitigate the growing democratic deficit in local communities. However, based on the consistent evidence across multiple studies, the BBC's negative market impact should not be one of the central, dominant issues for its funding and regulation. This emphasis does not serve British audiences or the public good.

The regulatory constraints on the BBC's ability to compete and to innovate at speed are, naturally, supported by many of its competitors – notably, as we've seen, Rupert and James Murdoch. In contrast, for those who, like John Whittingdale, support the restrictions despite having no such commercial vested interest, the reasons seem to be largely ideological.

These regulatory burdens on the BBC, like the 2010 and 2015 funding cuts, aren't based on any evidence. In fact, the evidence is that they are *against* the interest of both the UK public and UK producers. But, before we consider this, we first note that the 'market failure' argument also has a fundamental fault because it assumes a clear distinction between public interest programmes and commercial programmes. Let's look at an (admittedly extreme) example of the problem.

Bake Off: Who Knew?

The first episode of *The Great British Bake Off* aired on BBC Two on 17 August 2010. This certainly appeared to be a classic, worthy but dull public service programme – an amateur baking competition! – shown at the time of year when TV audiences are at their very lowest. The coverage the next morning was, indeed, dire. Lucy Mangan in *The Guardian* commented on 'the humourlessness that pervaded the proceedings'. In her view, 'competitive baking [is] a contradiction in terms' and 'Once you've seen one person cream butter and sugar together, haven't you seen them all?'[2]

The *Daily Telegraph*'s review, by Iain Hollingshead, was even more scathing. It began, 'There was a moment three-quarters of the way through The Great British Bake Off (BBC Two) when you expected the picture to topple forward and hit the floor as

the cameraman finally gave up the will to live'. Hollingshead
sneered that the contestants ('about whom we knew little and
cared even less') were being deliberately wound up to say how
much they wanted to win, 'as if anyone really cares which amateur baker is slightly less bad than the other'.[3]

Of course, we all know now that viewers loved *Bake Off*. It
appealed to a huge number of people, going well beyond those
interested in baking (although it has also greatly increased the
number of those who are),[4] and went on to be a blockbuster success, transferring to BBC One after four seasons and, in 2015,
becoming the highest-rated programme in Britain, when seven
of the top ten most-watched TV broadcasts of the year were
Bake Off episodes.[5] The original programme was being shown in
almost every country in the world, and twenty were also making their own versions.[6] The show was then acquired by Channel
4 after the BBC refused to pay the new price demanded by the
production company, Love Productions (itself 70 per cent owned
by Sky), which was rumoured to be £25 million per season,
almost four times what the Corporation had been paying. (The
BBC, despite its funding cuts, was said to have offered £15 million.)[7] Love Productions claimed that it had turned down even
higher offers from Netflix and ITV.[8]

Bake Off – and *Celebrity Bake Off* – still attract massive newspaper and social media coverage and have even generated
some widely discussed scandals. In the notorious Bingate incident during series five, contestant Iain was shown throwing
away his Baked Alaska because it had not fully set. Initially,
suspicion for causing this fell on another contestant, Diana,
who had indeed briefly removed Iain's effort from the freezer
to put in her own. But it later emerged that the real culprit was
a third contestant, Luis, who had recklessly exposed Iain's
Baked Alaska to ambient air for several minutes by leaving the
large freezer door open while piping his own effort, which had
already set. Bingate sparked a furious Twitter campaign with

the hashtag #justiceforiain, over 800 complaints to the BBC and even a discussion on *Newsnight*.[9]

The point is not that we should, with the wisdom of hindsight, berate the critics for misjudging *Bake Off* so badly. It is that, in the creative industries, 'Nobody knows anything'.[10] Love Productions had spent five years unsuccessfully pitching *Bake Off* to broadcasters and the presenters Mel Giedroyc and Sue Perkins had turned them down once already before they were won over.[11] It's easy, *in retrospect*, to see many reasons why viewers find *Bake Off* so engaging: the personalities (judges, presenters and contestants) and their relationships; the drama and jeopardy, with almost constant time pressure on the contestants and uncertainty about the quality of what they will produce before the clock runs down; the possibility of another drama like Bingate at any moment; all combined with the comforting, underlying associations of English summers, cakes, marquees and the upper-middle-class senior judge Mary Berry (now replaced by Prue Leith).[12]

But when the show was launched, no one could see its potential. At that point, presumably, even John Whittingdale and James Murdoch would have been more than happy for the BBC to commission such an innocent, minority-interest show. The logic of their rather Alice in Wonderland position, however, is that, once *Bake Off* became a blockbuster, the BBC should have stopped broadcasting it because it might have then started to 'crowd out' commercial competition.

The first lesson to be learned from the *Bake Off* example is that, with a creative product like TV programmes, the sheep-and-goats distinction between public service and commercial content, so appealing to some economists and other tidy-minded people, is much too black-and-white for the real world, especially since commissioning decisions on new shows have to be made in advance based on, at best, an educated hunch about the probable audience response. According to one of our sources, *Bake Off* was, in fact, developed and commissioned partly on the basis of audience research suggesting that, during recessions, 'northern' values (authenticity, home and hearth, manual hard work and skill) come to the fore, replacing 'southern', London-centric values associated with boom times ('loadsamoney', empty fame and bling). But, even with these insights, commissioning it was a gamble – part of the BBC's role as what former Culture Secretary Tessa Jowell called 'venture capital for the creative industries'.

The second lesson is that, even if and when we know for certain that a programme is popular enough to make it commercially viable, it is far from obvious that the public would benefit from the BBC *not* showing it. Suppose the BBC had been forced to stop showing, say, *Strictly Come Dancing*, because its success was, apparently, hurting commercial broadcasters. If the show had simply gone off the air, the public would have been understandably furious. But even if, instead, it had been snapped up by ITV or (as happened with *Bake Off*) Channel 4, it is still hard to see any benefit to the public – and *forcing* this to happen in the interests of 'fair competition' would seem completely bizarre. Even worse for viewers than the show being snapped up by ITV, Channel 4 or Channel 5 (all of which are, like the BBC, universally available) would be if it were bought by a pay TV or SVoD company so that only that company's subscribers were able to see it (at a much higher cost per viewer) and watching it would no longer be an experience shared by so many people in different social groups across the country.

The *Bake Off* example illustrates the real-world problems of trying to limit the BBC to supplying public service programmes that the market will not provide. But, aside from these practical implementation problems, the underlying question is: why would you want to do this anyway?

Why, John, Why?

As we noted in Chapter 5, John Whittingdale appeared to regard it as self-evident that the BBC, as a publicly funded body, should not offer services that might have been provided by the market. But the only rational justification for limiting the BBC in this way is that it would somehow actually *benefit the British public*.[13] This is the claim we'll be testing here. It may sound implausible, but how, at least in theory, *might* it happen? The key assumption behind the idea that reducing the BBC's scope, scale and funding would be in the public interest is that the revenue of commercial media would be so much higher that their content investment would increase by more than enough to replace the reduction in the BBC's content investment. Since content is what media consumers value, cutting the BBC's funding and stopping it from showing more popular entertainment programmes would, on this basis, benefit the British public.[14] So, if that's the theory, what are the facts?

The first attempts to explore the BBC's market impact were as part of the performance reviews of its new digital services during the run-up to Charter renewal in 2006. Culture Secretary Tessa Jowell commissioned reviews of *BBC News 24* and the Corporation's other new digital TV, radio and online services.[15] Those reviewing digital TV and radio were also able to draw on a separate assessment by Ofcom.[16] None of these reviews found any evidence that the BBC's new digital services were materially crowding out commercial media revenue and content investment. On the contrary, they all, although to varying degrees, concluded that the BBC's market entry had helped drive the take-up of digital technology, benefiting consumers by making the markets more competitive – and potentially also benefiting commercial media by creating new market opportunities – but that the BBC might pose a risk of crowding out some commercial revenue further down the line. They also reported that uncertainty about the timing and positioning of new BBC services *might* have discouraged some commercial investment and innovation – but concluded that this was unlikely to be an issue in the future, as the BBC was planning no more major new services.[17] In simple terms, the whole story about the BBC significantly crowding out commercial content investment was a myth.

Ten years later, however, the BBC's market impact was a much bigger political issue in the run-up to the next Charter renewal in 2016, especially after John Whittingdale became Culture Secretary in May 2015. As we discussed in Chapter 5, this new emphasis led to *four* larger-scale quantitative studies of the BBC's market impact. (Appendix E describes their methods and results.) Just like the earlier, smaller-scale reviews ten years earlier, *all four* of the quantitative studies made during 2013–16 concluded that, in reality, the BBC has little, if any, crowding-out effect on content investment by UK commercial media, especially on original UK content.[18] The implication is that the funding cuts and other constraints imposed on the BBC have reduced the BBC's content investment without materially increasing investment by its competitors. The net effect of the 30-per-cent cut in the real public funding of the BBC's UK services since 2010 has been strongly negative for most British viewers, listeners and producers, reducing total UK content investment,[19] choice, value for money and the other public service contributions in its remit.

BBC Online: Too Big for Its Boots?

The main, and perennial, complaint about the Corporation's market impact *beyond* broadcasting is that BBC Online, by offering high-quality, trusted news, sport and weather reports for free and with no advertising, lessens newspapers' and magazines' ability to generate online advertising (a key reason why James Murdoch and Paul Dacre have claimed that the BBC is too big). As we saw in Chapter 7, however, the 2019 Cairncross Review on financially sustainable journalism rejected calls from News UK and others that the BBC's online coverage should be significantly cut back. Based on the research evidence, Cairncross was unconvinced that BBC Online posed a significant threat to commercial providers. Instead, she argued that 'curtailing the BBC's news offering would be counter-productive [because] the BBC offers the very thing this review aims to encourage: a source of reliable and high-quality news, with a focus on objectivity and impartiality, and independent from government'.[20]

Some newspaper publishers complain that it is not so much the *scale* of BBC Online which is problematic as much as the fact that, like BBC TV and Radio, it includes 'soft' news on sport and celebrities, gives recipes, etc., as well as hard news on political events, natural disasters and so on.

As discussed in Appendix E, Oliver & Ohlbaum and Oxera estimated that making BBC Online less popular by eliminating such soft news *might* increase the advertising revenue of commercial online services, including newspapers, by something between £3.2 and £8.2 million a year. That might sound like a lot, but, to put this in perspective, total UK online advertising expenditure in 2018 (dominated by Facebook and Google) was £13.44 *billion*,[21] between 1,600 and 4,200 times Oliver & Ohlbaum and Oxera's estimate of the increase in newspapers' combined advertising revenue if BBC Online were to be cut down.[22] Technology and consumption trends are putting newspapers under pressure everywhere around the world, including the US and many other countries, which have virtually no competition from public broadcasters' sites. The impact of BBC Online on UK newspapers' revenue is minimal in the context of these wider trends.

BBC Jam: Children's Education – or Publishers' Profits?

In Chapter 2, we criticized the decision by the competition authorities to block Project Kangaroo, the PSBs' proposed SVoD venture, in 2009, leaving the UK market completely open to the big US tech companies for almost ten years. Equally egregious was the closure of BBC Jam, a free online learning service for children and schools, two years earlier. It is worth looking at in detail, as it offers a stark illustration of how a combination of free-market ideology and well-funded industry lobbying can lead to an outcome that, in our view, cannot conceivably have been in the public interest.

In November 1999, the newly appointed director-general of the BBC, Greg Dyke, gave a lecture in the City of London in which he outlined a vision making 'educating the nation' a top priority for the BBC.[23] The lecture, sponsored by the *Spectator* and Zurich Financial Services, was welcomed by both the then Education Secretary, David Blunkett, and the *Spectator*'s editor, Boris Johnson, who said, '[It] could not be more timely . . . Greg Dyke's plans for BBC television and radio will, over time, have a deep impact on audiences in Britain and beyond'.[24]

In turning Dyke's vision into reality, the BBC focused on exploiting the new opportunities created by digital technology and the New Labour government's billion-pound investment into computers in schools. In 2000, it conducted a public consultation which, not surprisingly, found strong public support for the idea of a free BBC-backed online learning service for children and schools. The BBC also participated in the government's 2001 Curriculum Online consultation, engaging closely with the Education Department and with industry.[25]

In May 2002, the BBC submitted a proposal to DCMS for a Digital Curriculum, a free, licence-fee-funded online learning service for five- to sixteen-year-olds, linked to the National

Curriculum. To protect commercial publishers of educational material for children, the funding would be capped at £150 million over five years, and 60 per cent of the budget would be allocated to minority and non-core subjects, such as languages and geography;[26] the service would cover a maximum of half the curriculum in any one subject; and each year the BBC would publish its commissioning plans for the following three years to give the commercial suppliers advance notice of its content investment.[27]

Criticism of the proposal came from two very different places. To some teachers, educationalists and the NUT teachers' union, the BBC, in its enthusiasm for online learning, was cutting its investment in traditional TV programmes for schools by too much and, because of differences in IT access and skills in different schools and homes, risked increasing educational inequalities.[28] Conversely, the Digital Learning Alliance (DLA), a pressure group representing educational software and content companies, based its objections on the standard commercial arguments that the BBC proposal represented unfair competition and would damage their revenue, limit their ability to invest and, they – somewhat implausibly – claimed, actually *reduce* choice for schools.

In response, in June 2002 the BBC made the significant further concession that half the content budget would be allocated to external providers (such as the DLA members). Nevertheless, the commercial educational suppliers still objected. Research Machines (RM),[29] Granada Learning, Reed Elsevier, Rupert Murdoch's HarperCollins and the Adam Smith Institute led the charge, claiming that the service would be a one-size-fits-all monolith, represented 'backdoor nationalization of the UK educational content marketplace' and would significantly reduce choice. RM and others also sought, unsuccessfully, a judicial review and for both the Office of Fair Trading *and* the European Commission to block the proposal on competition grounds.

The industry lobby managed to persuade the government to provide long-term funding to support schools' purchases of commercial online learning material, compensating for the supposed adverse impact of the proposed BBC service. The government initially committed £50 million to this eLearning Credits (eLCs) scheme.

In 2003, Culture Secretary Tessa Jowell gave the BBC Digital Curriculum ministerial approval, but only on the basis of the 'strongest ever' conditions.[30] At the same time, the government announced that the funding for the eLCs scheme would be increased to £300 *million* over the four years from 2003 to 2006 – double the BBC's total proposed investment in its Digital Curriculum of £150 million over *five* years.

The BBC service, branded BBC Jam, launched in January 2006 with just 10 per cent of its planned content. (The aim was to launch the full service in September 2008.) However – despite the limited scale of the BBC's proposed service, the multiple constraints imposed on it, the BBC's commitment to commissioning half the content from external suppliers, the evidence of public support, PwC's conclusion that it would actually *increase* the market for commercial online educational content, services and software, and the introduction of a funding scheme with double the total BBC Jam budget which guaranteed extra purchases of commercial products – the BBC Trust suspended the service in March 2007, eighteen months before it was even fully operational.[31] To John Whittingdale's DCMS Committee, the decision to suspend BBC Jam was praiseworthy, 'an encouraging sign of real change' in the BBC's approach to activities that might damage the commercial sector.[32] Teachers felt otherwise.[33]

The evidence, in retrospect, is that the industry's arguments were either complete nonsense or *almost* complete nonsense. In line with the wider evidence that the BBC's TV, radio and online news services have, in reality, had little if any crowding-out impact on commercial media, an academic study in 2012 claimed that the commercial online learning suppliers had made 'no significant investment' in more online educational content during the five years since the suspension of BBC Jam, suggesting that its market impact had been 'negligible'.[34] Similarly, a retrospective impact assessment, in 2010, of the BBC's other educational activities by the consultancy FTI, commissioned by the Trust, found that they had not, in economist-speak, 'substantially foreclosed competition'.[35]

However, the closure of BBC Jam *definitely* deprived schools and schoolchildren of access to a free, high-quality resource, and online educational publishers' profits were clearly boosted by the £300 million of public money invested in the eLCs Scheme introduced to protect them from the impact of BBC Jam on their revenue. They *may* then have been very slightly further boosted by the suspension of the BBC's service – or perhaps not, if PwC's assessment (that BBC Jam would benefit them by driving the market forward) was correct.

To us, the outcome was unquestionably – and predictably – against the public interest.

The BBC's 'Distinctiveness': Another Fetish?

One consequence of the disproportionate emphasis on minimizing the BBC's market impact, epitomized by the BBC Jam example, is the insistence on the need for its programmes and services to be 'distinctive', a rather slippery term. The title of Whittingdale's 2016 white paper – 'A BBC for the future? A broadcaster of distinction'[36] – exemplified this, subliminally implying that the BBC should be *distinguished* (meaning 'excellent' – who could disagree with that?) more than it should be *distinctive* (meaning 'different from its commercial competitors' – because *they* would rather have less competition).

Despite some people's obsession with 'distinctiveness', the Great British public is, very sensibly, unconvinced. As we'll see in Chapter 13, the public places a high value on all the public-service elements in the BBC's remit *except* 'distinctiveness', which it rightly sees as a bit strange and, at best, only marginally relevant. The reality is that the BBC's 'distinctiveness' was introduced into public discourse by its commercial rivals to encourage policies that made it less competitive. David Mitchell hit the nail on the head when he commented on the Oliver & Ohlbaum and Oxera report in 2016:

> 'More distinctive' is just a way . . . of saying 'less successful'. [T]his report makes the strategy of those commercially or ideologically opposed to the BBC startlingly clear. An overt challenge to the corporation's existence remains politically infeasible . . . The first step, then, is to turn it into something that fewer people would miss – and eventually, over time, to make it so distinctive that hardly anyone likes it at all.[37]

'Distinctiveness' is, at best, a red herring. At worst, it is a dis-guised way of weakening the BBC, as Mitchell suggests. The idea that reducing the funding, scope and scale of the BBC might be in the public interest is based on an assumption that it crowds out *so much* content investment by commercial media that the net effect is to reduce the total amount of UK media content investment. That said, not only have those advocating this idea never offered any evidence to support it, but also the consistent evidence shows that it is not the case. *None* of the many formal studies to date, both those made during 2002–4 and 2013–16, has found evidence of a significant negative market impact, or crowding out of commercial content investment, by the BBC. That includes the very substantial 2016 Oliver & Ohlbaum and Oxera study commissioned by John Whittingdale himself, the politician most associated with the idea that the

BBC should be smaller and more 'distinctive' to reduce such crowding out.

It is simply implausible that the cumulative 30-per-cent funding cuts forced on the BBC in 2010 and 2015, and the bureaucratic processes introduced in the 2016 Charter to limit its ability to compete and innovate, have enabled and encouraged commercial broadcasters to increase their content investment (compared to what it would have been without the cuts imposed upon the BBC) so much that the net effect has been to increase total content investment – never mind investment in UK-originated content and, therefore, UK producers' revenue. In other words, the cuts and constraints have unambiguously reduced choice and probably value for money for British viewers and listeners, as well as UK producers' revenue.

The market impact studies reviewed in Appendix E also discussed the BBC's *positive* market impacts, such as driving the take-up of new technology and, especially, forcing commercial broadcasters to 'compete on quality' through innovation and investment in programme-making. For a complete analysis of the BBC's net impact on the range, quality and value for money of the TV, radio and online services available to UK consumers, we need to allow for these positive market impacts as well.

As we have already seen in Chapter 5, the British public does not share the obsession with the BBC's market impact; you may recall that 97 *per cent* of the green-paper consultation respondents supported the idea of the BBC providing all types of content to everyone. A clear majority also said that its expansion into digital services had increased consumer choice; that, by raising standards, it had a positive net impact on the market; and that it should continue to play a leading role in developing and popularizing new technology.

'Four Legs Good, Two Legs Bad'[38] or 'Just Because'

Given the consistent evidence presented here that the BBC does not, in reality, materially crowd out commercial provision – and the public's justified scepticism with the claim that it does – why are some people, including policy-makers with no commercial vested interest, so obsessed with the Corporation's market impact?

One explanation might be that they have been bamboozled or intimidated into supporting the BBC's powerful rivals' case. Another is that they would like to see it weakened because they genuinely (although, in most cases, wrongly) believe that its news and current affairs coverage is biased against their particular viewpoint, as we've discussed. There may be a grain of truth in both of these explanations. But, in our view, this is more about ideology than about conspiracy or *realpolitik* – and the big underlying issue is that the BBC is publicly funded. The assumption here is that anything the market *can* do, it should be allowed to do, with as little government interference as possible[39] and certainly without competition from a public service, which is automatically assumed to be less efficient, effective, innovative and customer-focused simply *because* it's publicly owned and funded. Recall John Whittingdale saying that there were areas that should be 'left to commercial providers' because 'It is pointless and wasteful having an organization *receiving that kind of public funding* competing with – and potentially crowding out – other providers [emphasis added]'.[40] We think this is the main assumption underlying the 'market failure' argument at the heart of this chapter.

As we have shown, from a rational, public interest perspective (and also in the public's own view), it is certainly not 'pointless and wasteful' for the BBC to show popular entertainment programmes like *Strictly* and *Bake Off* in competition with commercial broadcasters. On the contrary, it is highly benefi-cial, increasing choice, quality, innovation and value for money.

But the BBC's public funding is clearly a crucial issue for many. As far as we know, none of them has ever spelled out *why* its publicly funded status means that it shouldn't compete with com-mercial players, beyond perhaps saying that such competition is 'unfair' because, unlike commercial broadcasters, the BBC does not have to 'earn its keep'. The irony is that, as we saw in the previ-ous chapter, if the BBC really did 'earn its keep' by competing for advertising or subscription revenue – as many of the same people advocate – it most surely *would* have a significant market impact.[41]

In a world with Netflix and Amazon, and given that the BBC is significantly smaller than it was ten years ago, the continuing emphasis on its market impact is even more disproportionate. The priority now should be for the Corporation to use its limited resources to deliver its remit as efficiently and effectively as pos-sible, without being perpetually hobbled to demonstrate that its services are somehow distinct and different from those provided – or which might conceivably be provided – by its commercial rivals.

The idea that the BBC somehow does *not* have to earn its keep is ludicrous. It does. The main reason why it has managed to thrive (albeit on a somewhat smaller scale now) with sharply reduced funding in such competitive markets and within a con-sistently hostile environment is its continuing success in meeting the needs of viewers, listeners and online users. It is precisely this success that leads to so much hostility from some of its rivals.

Finally, even if the BBC's licence-fee funding is in some slightly obscure sense 'unfair' (and its prohibition from generat-ing subscription and advertising revenue, and the relentless scrutiny and attacks under which it operates, somehow not 'unfair') – so what? The only rational policy criterion is the wider public interest.

12. 'To Err Is Human'[1]

In previous chapters, we've looked at a wide range of accusations against the BBC: that it is 'shockingly' wasteful and inefficient, but nevertheless dominates its markets and ruthlessly crowds out commercial media; that the licence fee is an unfair, regressive tax and has many other disadvantages; and that BBC programmes, especially in news and current affairs, are either consistently biased to the left and anti-Brexit, or alternatively, if anything, increasingly 'Establishment' and give right-wing and pro-Brexit voices *more* than their fair share of airtime.

As we've seen, although there always will be room for improvement, overall the evidence is that some of the perennial criticisms are simply wrong and the others are much overstated. A few – especially the charges of systematic bias – are also mutually contradictory.

Nevertheless, the BBC – like every organization – does get things really, really wrong from time to time. This chapter is about its biggest mistakes in the last ten years or so. Some raised difficult questions about its leadership; others look, in retrospect, like the inevitable prat-falls made by all great institutions of any scale – but with two big differences. The first is that the BBC's mistakes are much more visible than most organizations' and are gleefully seized on by its enemies. The second – crucial, but not widely realized – difference, as we'll now discuss, is that, although the BBC is much smaller in terms of its *finances* and *people* than the biggest companies and government departments, the extraordinary volume and range of its original *output* and the scale of its *consumption* by viewers and listeners are much higher, giving it an astonishing number of opportunities to make editorial mistakes and upset its customers every single day. Let's look at the numbers.

The Scale of the BBC's Output and Consumption

The BBC's six UK-wide TV channels[2] broadcast for a combined total of about eighty hours per day. Its ten national radio stations broadcast for a total of 200 hours per day, mostly live. On this basis, the BBC broadcasts a total of about 280 hours per day of original UK-wide TV and radio programmes. Assuming an average programme length of forty-five minutes, that's over 370 original, UK-wide programmes every day – an average of fifteen unique, UK-wide programmes every hour – many of them live. That excludes the much-larger number of regional and local programmes, as well as everything on BBC Online. What could possibly go wrong?

The scope for problems is, if possible, even clearer if we look at consumption. As we saw in Chapter 3, the average UK adult consumes BBC services for about eighteen hours per week – over two-and-a-half hours per day.[3] Once again assuming an average programme length of forty-five minutes, that's equivalent to twenty-four programme choices every week or 3.4 per day. With 52 million UK adults,[4] that's 178 million BBC programme choices by UK adults every day. Adding in consumption by 14.7 million children and teenagers, *the UK public chooses the BBC brand at least 200 million times a day*. That's an astonishing number – far more than for any other product, service or media brand. It's a well-known axiom that you can't please all of the people all of the time; and every single one of those 200 million daily brand choices is an opportunity to disappoint or offend *someone*.

In addition to the BBC's huge scope to get things wrong

editorially, it also, like every organization, has plenty of opportunities to make commercial and managerial mistakes: for
instance, we'll discuss an IT project that failed and an acquisition project that ended up losing millions. Beyond these, a
perennial area for criticism – much of it confused or disingenu-
ous, and often hypocritical, but some of it valid – is how much
the BBC pays its top managers and presenters and now, in a
related area, its gender pay gap too.

In the rest of this chapter, first we discuss the BBC's biggest
and most damaging scandal for many years: the revelations
about Sir Jimmy Savile, and the *Newsnight* programme which
inadvertently led to Lord McAlpine being falsely 'outed' as a
paedophile. We then look at its other, more straightforward, editorial misjudgements and its commercial and managerial
mistakes over the same time period.[5] Finally, we discuss its most
recent controversy, about its handling of Naga Munchetty's on-
air comments on some of President Trump's tweets.

How Jimmy Savile Hid 'in Plain Sight'

When the BBC disc jockey and presenter Sir Jimmy Savile died,
aged eighty-four, in October 2011, a nation mourned. Everyone
stepped up to polish his halo, focusing especially on his extensive work for charity and for the NHS. Charles Moore wrote
later in the *Daily Telegraph* that at the time Savile was eulogized
as a 'proper British eccentric' by the writer and comedian Ricky
Gervais, termed a 'real character' by former deputy prime minister John Prescott and a 'ray of sunshine' by the presenter Carol
Vorderman – and that the *Daily Mail* had said he was 'working
miracles for 1,500 children'.[6] Hundreds lined the streets as his
body was driven to his funeral in Leeds Cathedral.[7] In his hom-
ily, Monsignor Kieran Heskin said that 'Sir Jimmy Savile can

face eternal life with confidence' and 'God [would] "fix it" that Jimmy would [find] a place in heaven'.[8]

Less than two years later the Metropolitan Police and NSPCC[9] reported that at least 214 alleged sexual offences attributed to Savile had been identified over a 50-year period across 28 police force areas, including 126 indecent acts and 34 rapes.[10] Savile, it turned out, had been the subject of five police investigations in his lifetime, none of which had led to prosecution.[11] How could he have gone for so long without being prosecuted, while allegedly committing so many terrible crimes? Had people at the BBC and elsewhere turned a blind eye?

Commander Peter Spindler, head of the police inquiry, powerfully summed up Savile's life-long wrongdoing when he said that he had 'groomed a nation'.[12] This Leeds-born, former nightclub proprietor had won over much of the Establishment: the royal family, the NHS, the BBC, the *Daily Mail* and many others in the media, major charities and politicians as well, including Margaret Thatcher, who forced through his knighthood at the fifth attempt and against the advice of her civil servants.[13] Savile's other honours included a papal knighthood, the Cross of Merit of the Sovereign Military Order of Malta (Knights of St John) and honorary doctorates at Leeds University (in law!) and Bedfordshire University.[14] Rumours – or even evidence – of his criminality never seriously dented his reputation: he was probably the best-loved celebrity in Britain, after the Queen Mother.[15] Prince Charles led the tributes when he died.[16]

While attitudes were different in the 1970s and 1980s, the trust placed in Savile as a top BBC celebrity almost certainly helped him to go unchallenged. (Other key factors seem to have been his network of powerful supporters and the way he frightened victims into not reporting him.) Although it was never possible to put him on trial, most people now believe he was a prolific, cynical and probably psychopathic serial abuser.[17] Reports of specific incidents from a large number of people and organizations, including multiple, different NHS institutions, show clear, repeated patterns of abuse, in particular of vulnerable young people.[18]

The Newsnight Report That Wasn't

Rumours about Savile's activities started circulating long before he died, but it was only after his death in October 2011 that BBC *Newsnight* journalists Meirion Jones and Liz MacKean began to investigate claims that he had sexually abused children. They prepared a filmed report based on interviews with former pupils from Duncroft Approved School for Girls in Surrey. One alleged victim was interviewed on camera, while others agreed to have their stories told anonymously. The report was scheduled to be broadcast on 7 December 2011 – but it was cancelled at the last minute.

Worse still, the BBC then showed two programmes – effusive tributes to Savile – over the Christmas 2011 period. Some people claimed at the time that the BBC had deliberately shelved the *Newsnight* report in order not to compromise those tributes. Later evidence suggests that this was not the case, but rather that, in what became known as the 'just the women' issue, the *Newsnight* editors had dropped the report because they felt it did not pass the journalistic bar as there were no 'authorities' corroborating the stories of the women who had stepped forward to say they had been abused.[19] Their testimony was doubtless given less weight because Duncroft had been an approved school (a boarding school, to which children and teenagers could be sent by a court, either for a criminal offence or because they were deemed to be beyond the control of their parents or guardian). Its own former headmistress later said that some of Savile's alleged victims there were 'no angels' and had 'traded sex for cigarettes'.[20]

Disgruntled, Jones and MacKean took their story to ITV,

where it eventually went out on 3 October 2012 as *Exposure: The Other Side of Jimmy Savile*. Ahead of the broadcast, the BBC denied that it had failed to take action against Savile: 'The BBC has conducted extensive searches of its files to establish whether there is any record of misconduct or allegations of misconduct by Sir Jimmy Savile during his time at the BBC. No such evidence has been found.'[21] But after the ITV programme, the floodgates opened and the BBC immediately had to issue a new statement: 'We are horrified by allegations that anything of this sort could have happened at the BBC – or have been carried out by anyone working for the BBC. They are allegations of a serious criminal nature which the police have the proper powers to investigate.'[22] Jeremy Paxman, who had pressed hard to cover the story on *Newsnight*, described the decision not to do so as 'pathetic'.[23] The BBC endorsed this judgement (and showed that it was willing and able to correct itself) in its *Panorama* programme of 22 October 2012, which condemned its earlier decision not to air the *Newsnight* programme on Savile.

As we saw in Chapter 5, all this blew up immediately after the inexperienced George Entwistle took over as director-general in September 2012. During his brief tenure, Entwistle launched two investigations: the Pollard Review (led by Nick Pollard, former head of Sky News) into the editorial decision not to air the *Newsnight* programme, and a much longer and more wideranging investigation (led by the High Court judge Dame Janet Smith) into the culture of the BBC, which, over many years, had apparently allowed Savile's alleged predatory behaviour to occur largely unreported – and where it *was* reported, not investigated.[24]

The Pollard and Smith Reports

On 18 December 2012, Nick Pollard reported that, in his view, the *Newsnight* investigators had been right: there was clear evidence that Jimmy Savile had been a paedophile. He argued that the BBC's 'rigid management chains' had made it 'completely incapable of handling the Savile case'.[25] Liz MacKean, one of the two journalists involved, alleged that *Newsnight* editor Peter Rippon had tried to kill off the Savile story by making 'impossible editorial demands'.[26] In Pollard's view, Rippon's decision to drop the original investigation had been 'taken in good faith', but both it and the way it was taken were flawed.[27] In 2015, MacKean was named journalist of the decade by the LGBT rights charity Stonewall.[28]

Dame Janet Smith's report, released over three years later on 25 February 2016, concluded that Savile had probably sexually abused seventy-two people at the BBC and raped eight. These crimes had taken place at 'virtually every one of the BBC premises at which he [had] worked'. Smith stated that some BBC staff members were aware of complaints against Savile, but did not pass the information on to senior management due to the 'culture of not complaining'. She also reported, 'The management structure of the BBC was not only hierarchical, but deeply deferential' and that '[s]taff were reluctant to speak out to their managers because they felt it was not their place to do so'. She described an 'atmosphere of fear' still existing at the BBC and added that, 'All the problems of reporting [wrongdoing] were compounded in the case of the Talent [celebrity performers]. One witness told me that the Talent were more important than the BBC's own values.'

Her report noted that Savile's crimes on NHS premises appeared to have been on an even larger scale, but added that this in no way exonerated the BBC over its failure to prevent his predation on children and young people in its care over many years.[29] Unsurprisingly, the Smith report on Savile's activities at the BBC attracted vastly more press coverage than the *forty-four* reports on his much more extensive activities on NHS premises.[30]

Why had the *Newsnight* team failed to break one of the biggest news stories of the year? Partly because they felt the evidence was insufficient, but also, according to Pollard, because they did not realize how big the story would be and its potential impact on the BBC: the exposé had not even been on the Managed Risk Programmes List (a register of upcoming programmes seen as potentially risky, which had been set up three years earlier). Jones and MacKean *had* understood its significance but, for whatever reasons, they were unable to communicate this successfully to the top of the editorial hierarchy.

The underlying organizational problem with the BBC which Savile's crimes revealed was even more serious: the presenter had apparently been able to work there for many years while repeatedly abusing, and in some cases even raping, large numbers of young people. Liz Dux, a lawyer for some of the victims, told *Panorama* in October 2012: 'The stories that I'm hearing from some of the victims are that they *did* report the abuse and that no action was taken'.

Furthermore, it transpired that when allegations *were* reported, they were not properly investigated. In 1973, the Radio 1 controller Douglas Muggeridge asked his press officer, Rodney Collins, to find out if the rumours about Savile were true. Collins said he found no evidence of any *newspaper or police investigations* about Savile (as opposed to direct evidence of his alleged wrongdoing). The culture at that time at the BBC, and in society more generally, assumed that 'These things happened' and were no one else's responsibility. Former BBC reporter Martin Young said he once found Savile in a camper van, lying on a bed with a teenage girl, both of them clothed. Asked if he thought about reporting it, he replied: 'No, never even crossed my mind. And I'll take my share of the blame for that'.[31] This negligence went on for years: only after the Smith Review in 2016 were regulations put in place to ensure that children in audiences always came to the studio with an adult.

The Savile scandal showed serious, systematic weaknesses in

the BBC's editorial and managerial processes and culture, and the effects were not short-term: in an interview three years later, Meirion Jones, one of the two reporters who originally exposed Savile's behaviour, alleged that 'Everyone on the right side of the Savile argument has been forced out of the BBC'.[32] In his view, those who made the decision not to air the story had kept their jobs, while people like himself and his fellow investigator, Liz MacKean, had been forced out.

Too Hasty: Inadvertently – and Wrongly – Outing Lord McAlpine as a Paedophile

Things soon got even worse for the BBC when a *Newsnight* programme inadvertently led to former Conservative Party treasurer Lord McAlpine being incorrectly outed on Twitter as part of a paedophile ring in North Wales. On 2 November 2012, Iain Overton, head of the small, not-for-profit Bureau of Investigative Journalism,[33] tweeted: 'If all goes well, we've got a *Newsnight* out tonight about a very senior political figure who is a paedophile'. This incendiary tweet was based on a series of misunderstandings, including a wine-fuelled, dinner-jacketed conversation as Overton and others unwound after speaking at an Oxford Union debate on politics and the media.[34] But, despite its shaky basis, naturally the rumour went around media London in an instant. Despite the attention that such a programme might attract, Director-General George Entwistle had not been briefed about it and due care was not taken with the story. The *Newsnight* team had been weakened after the Savile story: its previous editor, Peter Rippon, was, in effect, under suspension, and its most experienced investigative reporter, Meirion Jones, was off preparing his testimony for the Pollard inquiry on how his and Liz MacKean's (completely accurate) investigation into Savile had been suppressed.

The reason why the paedophilia allegation had not been put to Lord McAlpine by the *Newsnight* team was because he was not to be named on its programme; its focus (despite Iain Overton's tweet suggesting otherwise) was on failings by the police and an official inquiry, not on the identity of the alleged abuser(s). Furthermore, its main claims had already been made twelve years earlier in a documentary on Radio 5 Live.[35] However, having been part of the Oxford Union discussion, on the day of transmission Michael Crick from *Channel 4 News* mistakenly assumed that McAlpine *would* be identified in the programme. He then called McAlpine and tweeted a public warning: 'Senior political figure due to be accused tonight by the BBC of being paedophile denies allegations + tells me he'll issue libel writ against BBC'.[36]

It was too late to stop transmission. The programme went ahead. It was largely based on an interview with Steve Messham, the alleged abuse victim at the care home. He said he had been taken in a car and abused more than a dozen times by what the programme termed 'a prominent Thatcher-era Tory figure'.[37] *Newsnight* appeared to have scored a journalistic coup, recovering some of its reputation after not showing the Savile story – despite online complaints that it had 'bottled' giving the alleged abuser's name.

Within a few hours, however, the supposed abuser had been 'outed' on Twitter as Lord McAlpine. But this was a case of mistaken identity, a fact which had been known by journalists for more than fifteen years: Messham's claims had been examined and rejected by an official inquiry in 1997.[38] Lord McAlpine's cousin Jimmie McAlpine, a prominent local businessman, was the one originally named by former inmates of the care home in Wrexham as the subject of rumours, although there was no evidence of sexual abuse. *The Guardian* published evidence that exonerated Lord McAlpine[39] and within twenty-four hours his accuser had retracted his statement and apologized. The McAlpine fiasco, following so soon after the scandal over Jimmy

Savile, was a disaster for the BBC, leading to Entwistle's resignation on 10 November 2012, with immediate effect. Although *Newsnight* had not actually named Lord McAlpine, this fiasco had seen it swing from one wrong end of the editorial spectrum to the other. With regard to Savile, it was too cautious. In the case of Lord McAlpine it failed to apply due diligence. In the October 2012 *Panorama* programme that laid into the BBC for its mishandling of Savile, which helped to make George Entwistle's position untenable, its World Affairs editor John Simpson described this combination as the BBC's 'biggest crisis for over 50 years'.[40]

However, although these were the Corporation's worst editorial and/or managerial errors in recent years, they were not the only ones. For instance, the event that came to be known as 'Sachsgate' briefly created a comparable media storm in 2008.

'Sachsgate' – Whose Responsibility?

In October 2008, comedian Russell Brand and TV presenter Jonathan Ross had been due to call the veteran actor Andrew Sachs, who had played the Spanish waiter Manuel in the sitcom *Fawlty Towers* many years earlier, for a Radio 2 show Ross and Brand were making together. When Sachs didn't answer, they left a series of four lewd phone messages about Brand's relationship with Sachs' granddaughter Georgina Baillie, a member of the band Satanic Sluts Extreme.

In the first of these messages, Brand was interrupted by Ross shouting out, 'He fucked your granddaughter!' Brand and Ross then tried to apologize, but each time made it worse. Brand later said that listening to those calls was like hearing 'two idiots dancing towards a canyon'.[41] However, the show was not live – it had been pre-recorded – but the producers had not taken the opportunity to remove this section before the broadcast.

Over the next week, the BBC received just two complaints from the show's 400,000 listeners,[42] but there was no wider reaction. Then, on 26 October, the *Mail on Sunday* ran a story strongly criticizing Brand, Ross and the BBC.[43] After other newspapers and some anti-BBC politicians picked up the story, it escalated into a media and political storm, briefly eclipsing UK coverage of the global financial crisis and the impending election of the first black US president.[44] The number of complaints to the BBC rose over the following weeks from two (from listeners to the show) to 44,790.[45]

As a result, Russell Brand, Lesley Douglas, controller of Radio 2 and David Barber, the head of specialist music and compliance at Radio 2, all resigned,[46] but Jonathan Ross refused to do so. The BBC issued a formal apology to Sachs and on 30 October it suspended Ross without pay for twelve weeks. The Corporation was subsequently fined £150,000 by Ofcom.

Even at the time, some people felt that the reaction had been excessive. This included members of a 15,000-strong Facebook group who threatened to protest outside the BBC in support of Ross and Brand and also Georgina Baillie herself. In a Channel 5 documentary, Baillie said 'it's way out of proportion what happened . . . a world without Jonathan Ross and Russell Brand would be a very sad, dull place'.[47] The former BBC journalist Tim Luckhurst wrote that Brand and Ross had been the wrong target: 'Holding Brand and Ross to account for being facile, arrogant and foul-mouthed is silly. That is what they are for. The real scandal is that the producer and his line manager cleared the show for broadcast.' He argued that the BBC's belt-and-braces approach to editorial decision-making had led to both excessive bureaucracy and ambiguity about where responsibilities lay. In Luckhurst's view, the producers who had allowed the show to go ahead should have been immediately held to account for their mistake.[48]

On 21 November 2008, the BBC Trust said that the phone calls were a 'deplorable intrusion with no editorial justification' and that the failures lay in mistakes made by BBC editorial and compliance management. The BBC Executive echoed this view, stating that the incident was a 'very, very serious failure where editorial judgement . . . seriously let the BBC down'.[49] In response, the BBC set up a register, the Managed Risk Programme List (although, as we saw, the *Newsnight* programme on Savile three years later was not seen as sufficiently important to go onto this list. A perennial leadership challenge in large organizations is that formal risk management systems are only as good as the way they are used at an operating level).

After 'Sachsgate', fifteen MPs signed a House of Commons motion calling for Brand and Ross to be no longer funded by the licence fee.[50] To his great credit, Shadow Culture Secretary Jeremy Hunt refused to participate, saying that politicians should stay at arm's length from the BBC's operational decisions.[51]

The BBC's Coverage of the Cliff Richard Police Raid

In 2014 Dan Johnson, a north-of-England correspondent for BBC News, received an anonymous tip-off about a truly sensational story: that Sir Cliff Richard was being investigated for historical child sexual abuse and the police were planning a house search for evidence. To keep the story from getting out early, the police promised to let Johnson know when the search was to take place. Accordingly, on 15 August 2014, in order to get the most dramatic footage of this exclusive story, the BBC hired a helicopter to fly over Cliff Richard's Berkshire mansion during the raid. No arrests were made, however, and Sir Cliff was never charged.

In 2018 Sir Cliff won £210,000 in damages from the BBC after a judge ruled that it had violated his privacy in a 'serious way and also in a somewhat sensationalist way'.[52] The singer had also settled out of court with South Yorkshire Police for £400,000 before the start of the trial, although the judge ruled that the police could be responsible for 35 per cent of any further damages. It was a landmark ruling that, broadly, split opinion between celebrities arguing that their privacy should be protected even when they were under police investigation, and journalists, such as Ian Murray of the Society of Editors and Tim Shipman of the *Sunday Times*, who agreed with the BBC's director of news, Fran Unsworth, that it created a significant and unwelcome shift against press freedom. Even Tom Newton Dunn, political editor of the *Sun*, supported this view, saying that the ruling was 'madness' and the BBC was 'just doing its job'.[53] Roy Greenslade, in *The Guardian*, described the ruling as a chilling blow to press freedom: 'This sets a precedent whereby a celebrity's right to privacy trumps the public's right to know'. After spending £1.9 million in legal costs, the BBC decided to rest its case. It remains unclear whether it might have won on appeal. Former chairman Lord Patten felt that the BBC would be 'crazy' to do so. In contrast, former director-general Mark Thompson, speaking on *The Media Show*, believed it would be 'very much in the public interest ... Of course [the BBC] will be looking very closely at the potential cost and the likelihood of success, but how much is freedom of the press worth? In my book it is worth a lot'.[54] Typically, the *Daily Mail* managed to have it both ways, gleefully reporting the judge's criticisms of the BBC while also quoting legal experts who argued that his judgement could have 'worrying consequences' for press freedom.[55] In our view, it was the sensationalist *style* of the coverage that looked wrong for the BBC.

Covering the Royals: Too Sycophantic or Insufficiently Respectful?

The BBC has to tread a particularly delicate line in its coverage of the royal family. The degree of sensitivity is illustrated by the so-called 'Queengate' incident in 2007. A *trailer for the press launch* of a documentary on the royals (i.e. neither the actual programme, nor even a promotional trailer aimed at potential viewers) had been edited out of sequence. Peter Fincham, the controller of BBC One, wrongly told the journalists at the launch that it showed the monarch walking out of a photo session 'in a huff'. He resigned after it emerged that, in reality, the film showed her *before* the photo session began. In fact, both the programme and trailer had been made by an independent production company, RDF Media, whose chief creative officer, Stephen Lambert, also took the decision to stand down from his job. A review into the incident by former BBC executive Will Wyatt blamed 'misjudgements, poor practice and ineffective systems'. The BBC had been 'slow to appreciate the magnitude and import of the mistake'. Fincham had known the trailer misrepresented the Queen at 7 p.m. on the evening of the press screening, but a correcting statement was not put out until the following day. By that time, the news of the Queen 'storming out' had already become a big story. According to Wyatt, it was this delay in admitting the error that was the BBC's key mistake.[56]

Different audiences and generations have different – and, in some cases, strongly opposed – views of how the BBC should cover royal events. The balance between these views has also shifted through the years. At the time of the Queen's Silver Jubilee in 1977, support for the monarchy was very high and the BBC's traditional approach of respectful celebration and unquestioning loyalty was accepted by almost everyone except a small minority of – mostly, but not entirely, left-wing – republicans. (Even the *Sun* enthusiastically joined the celebrations, despite Rupert Murdoch's lifelong republicanism.)[57]

Twenty-five years later, with the June 2002 Golden Jubilee, times had changed. Roger Mosey, then head of TV news, sent a staff directive instructing those covering the events to avoid sycophancy, and the approach was less adulatory. Nevertheless, some years later, in 2008, the self-confessed republican-turned-monarchist Jeremy Paxman criticized the BBC for the 'fawning tone of voice' of its royal coverage. He specifically condemned the detailed preparations that had been made for announcing the death of the Queen Mother in March 2002, saying: 'it was unclear if the BBC was announcing this as a piece of news or as mourner-in-chief'.[58] (However, at the time, the BBC had been criticized for showing *insufficient* respect because news presenter Peter Sissons had announced the Queen Mother's death wearing a burgundy rather than a black tie.)[59]

By the time of the Queen's Diamond Jubilee in 2012, the BBC had updated its approach further, recruiting younger and more diverse presenters to try to make the event more accessible and inclusive, hoping to reach beyond the traditional audience of the monarchy's – mostly older – supporters. The result was a fiasco, generating over 2,400 complaints.[60] In the words of presenter Michael Buerk:

> With barely an exception, [the presenters] were cringingly inept. Nobody knew anything and nobody cared. The main presenter couldn't even work out what to call the Queen . . . The Dunkirk Little Ships, the most evocative reminders of this country's bravest hour, were ignored so that a pneumatic bird-brain from Strictly Come Dancing could talk to transvestites in Battersea Park. I was so ashamed of the BBC I would have wept if I hadn't been so angry.[61]

The presenter Fearne Cotton responded by saying that she loved her job and wouldn't be doing it if she wasn't good at it.[62]

The Diamond Jubilee debacle illustrates two editorial dilemmas the BBC constantly faces. First, like all news media, it has to take risks. By definition, some of these turn out to be mistakes; but what distinguishes it from all other UK media is the level of scrutiny it faces and the extent to which it gets pilloried for any real or perceived missteps. The second conundrum is that it urgently needs to engage younger viewers and listeners – not least because of the technology and consumption trends we discussed in Chapter 2 – but it also needs to retain the support of older viewers and listeners.

We now turn from the BBC's editorial mistakes to its commercial and managerial ones. However, despite the growing scale of its business activities (and therefore, inevitably, risk-taking) to reduce the impact of funding cuts on its ability to invest in programmes, the Corporation has made only one material commercial mistake over the last twenty years (or, possibly, ever): the 2007 acquisition of Lonely Planet.

Lonely Planet

The BBC's acquisition of Lonely Planet in 2007 illustrates another perennial dilemma it faces. When it diversifies into new areas, it is invariably challenged by incumbent commercial interests. But if it *doesn't*, it is accused of complacency and a failure to adapt to changing technologies and audience trends – often by politicians and journalists with absolutely no management experience themselves.

In 2007, BBC Worldwide acquired 75 per cent of the travel guide publisher Lonely Planet for £130 million, to support its 'ongoing migration from a traditional book publisher to a multi-platform brand'.[63] Lonely Planet's main business was still printed guidebooks and phrasebooks, but it was also creating some TV programming for Discovery Networks and its website hosted the popular Thorntree online community for international travellers. BBC Worldwide planned to make all of the guidebooks fully accessible online (as well as in print: 'a guidebook for the bag when travelling'), launch a Lonely Planet magazine and expand its TV programming, and boost distribution across BBC and third-party channels worldwide, while also increasing the BBC's portfolio of online content brands and its operations in Australia and America.[64] A senior BBC source told us that another aim was to use Lonely Planet as an 'umbrella brand' for all the Corporation's travel-related content on all its platforms. Tony and Maureen Wheeler, who had founded Lonely Planet in 1972 (after Tony Wheeler had completed his MBA at London Business School and both had made the overland trip from Britain to Australia), agreed to stay on as advisers until 2011.[65]

At the time, the deal was widely criticized by rival publishers, including some long-term supporters of the BBC such as Tony Elliott, founder of the London listings magazine *Time Out*.[66] In March 2009, the DCMS Committee, chaired by John Whittingdale, published a report on the BBC's commercial operations, including BBC Magazines (which is part of BBC Worldwide). Commercial publishers argued that the BBC enjoyed an unfair advantage due to lower content development costs (e.g. through its free access to popular characters and cartoons) and easier or cheaper trade and consumer marketing (because of its strong, trusted brand and the ability to promote its magazines on air).[67] However, the DCMS Committee acknowledged that licence payers benefited from the income generated by the BBC's commercial operations, including its magazines.[68] The committee's conclusions on Lonely Planet were carefully balanced:

It is right that the BBC should exploit its intellectual property, including by allowing the publication of magazines using the BBC brand, in order to generate returns for the licence fee payer. However, the BBC must take due care not to distort the market, and it should not buy new brands – as it did with Lonely Planet – to enter new markets . . . New BBC magazines should only be launched if there is a clear link with core BBC programming, and where the public value of launching a magazine outweighs any adverse impact on the existing marketplace.[69]

The BBC Executive and Trust agreed that similar acquisitions would not be sought out by the Corporation's commercial arm in the future, except in 'exceptional circumstances'.[70]

In the event, the Lonely Planet acquisition was a disaster. A scathing review by the BBC Trust (which had been seeking to rein in BBC Worldwide's risky expansion for some time) criticized many aspects of this saga: overoptimistic revenue and margin forecasts at the time of the deal (with insufficient analysis of the possible impact of a faster-than-expected decline in book sales and underestimation of the likely backlash from commercial publishers); the structure of the deal, which enabled the Wheelers to sell the remaining 25 per cent of the business in 2011 at the 2007 price, regardless of market conditions; poor integration of Lonely Planet into BBC Worldwide (perhaps reflecting the difference between their cultures), including a failure to manage conflicts between Lonely Planet and BBC Worldwide and the BBC's existing travel activities; and poor execution of the difficult process of turning Lonely Planet into a (mainly) digital media business (in part, because of delays in the relaunch of the BBC's Global News and US websites). In 2013, BBC Worldwide sold the business to US-based NC2 Media for £50 million, representing a loss of nearly £80 million.[71] The only mitigation was that, at the time of the acquisition in late 2007 (just before the 2008 financial crash), many other media companies had made similar, or even bigger mistakes: ITV had lost £150 million on Friends Reunited and News Corporation over $500 million on MySpace.[72]

The Lonely Planet fiasco reflected both commercial ineptitude (the price paid and the structure of the deal) and managerial incompetence (the numerous weaknesses in executing the post-acquisition strategy). Nonetheless, it remains the BBC's only material commercial mistake during the last fifteen years.

We now turn to the biggest purely managerial mistake it has made recently, an example of something many organizations have suffered – an IT project that went wrong. IT projects have a notoriously high failure rate: one estimate is 30 per cent.[73] The following project, launched in 2008, turned out to be one of those.

The Digital Media Initiative

The BBC's Digital Media Initiative (DMI), launched in 2008, was an ambitious £98 million project designed to make all its film and video archives available to programme makers online, creating a more flexible and efficient workflow across the Corporation, saving significant time and money and making the BBC more agile. Initially, a £79 million contract was given to Siemens (with whom the BBC had a technology framework agreement set up) to undertake the project. When Siemens failed to deliver, the project was taken in-house, but still failed.

The DMI was cursed by two issues: insufficient prior agreement on the requirements between the chief technology officer John Linwood and senior production executives, and unclear responsibilities and governance during the project's execution. As Brian Glick wrote later in *Computer Weekly*, 'DMI was not the first major IT project to founder on the rocks of disagreements between business and IT leaders . . . But few IT projects have to bear the public scrutiny that the BBC does, and the embarrassment of seeing its dirty technology linen washed in public'.[74]

The DMI was first reviewed by the National Audit Office in 2011. The evidence from key BBC people, including then Director-General Mark Thompson, convinced the NAO, and then the House of Commons Public Accounts Committee

(PAC), that the Corporation had been right to take the work in-house and that the project was now proceeding effectively, despite a poor start.

But when the PAC revisited the project after Lord Hall had cancelled it in May 2013, its report was highly critical of both the BBC's management of the project and its earlier representations in 2011. Dame Margaret Hodge, the committee's chair, introduced the report, as follows: 'The BBC's Digital Media Initiative was a complete failure. Licence fee payers paid nearly £100 million for this supposedly essential system but got virtually nothing in return.'

She continued, 'The BBC was far too complacent about the high risks involved in taking it in-house. No single individual had overall responsibility or accountability for delivering the DMI. Lack of clearly defined responsibility and accountability meant the Corporation failed to respond to warning signals that the programme was in trouble. The BBC Trust demonstrated similar complacency in its poor oversight of the Executive's implementation of the DMI.' She also criticized the BBC for failing to mention in its evidence to both the NAO and the PAC a 2010 report by the global consulting company Accenture highlighting concerns about the DMI project. She said this lack of openness had contributed to the committee's false impression of the progress of the DMI at that point.[75]

In a further twist, the BBC's former head of IT, John Linwood, brought a case against it for sacking him for the failure of the DMI. The BBC lost the case at a cost of half a million pounds.[76] However, in May 2016, the NAO reported that: 'The BBC has learnt from the failure of its Digital Media Initiative (DMI), and taken a number of steps to strengthen its oversight of projects.'[77]

It's a familiar story of organizational ambition and over-confidence and miscommunication between IT specialists and those representing their users. The difference in the BBC's case was that it was played out in public with two reviews by the NAO, another by the PAC and loud recriminations all round.

Problems with Pay

The Lonely Planet acquisition and the DMI project were both one-off cases where the BBC's management got things wrong. But in today's competitive media market, and in the hostile climate described in this book, the Corporation's biggest – and never-ending – managerial headache is remuneration. Its challenge is to remain competitive in hiring, rewarding and retaining the best people, especially top presenters, when market rates are constantly increasing and its inflation-adjusted public funding has been cut by 30 per cent since 2010. It is also, rightly, expected to set an example through its equal pay and diversity policies. Meanwhile its enemies actively seek out and relish any payment that can – regardless of the context – be presented as excessive, on the grounds that the Corporation is publicly owned and funded by the compulsory licence fee and should therefore, presumably, pay less than the market rate.

It is sometimes suggested that no one at the BBC should be paid more than the prime minister's salary, currently £150,000 a year – as if that were a relevant yardstick for a broadcaster in the creative, technical and executive talent markets in which the Corporation has to compete with UK commercial broadcasters and, increasingly, US media and technology companies.[78] In 2016, the DCMS Committee argued that the BBC should be forced to publish all salaries – for both stars and managers – above this level.[79] In 2019, a petition to Parliament again used the same metric. It sought to amend the BBC Charter to ban the Corporation from paying anyone more than *twice* the PM's salary, on the grounds that: 'The BBC is a public service and should not pay excessive salaries. Paying anyone over £1.5m a year to watch and comment on sport or present a 3 hour radio show is too much. Alternative talent could be found at lower salary levels ... Publicly funded bodies have shown disregard for financial discipline and the BBC may be the worst'. However, the petition, which ran for six months, attracted only thirty-four signatures.[80]

The pressures on BBC remuneration come from a combination of rational and emotional factors, often pulling in different directions. At an emotional level, reflected in the wording of the petition above, paying anyone '£1.5 million a year to watch and comment on sport' for one three-hour period does indeed seem far too much to many licence payers. But, rationally, the same licence payers want as much value as possible from their fees. As we've seen, it is simply wrong to suggest that the BBC 'disregards financial discipline', despite endless claims suggesting that it does. It is true that '[a]lternative talent could be found at lower salary levels' – but unlikely that viewers and listeners would, in general, like the result.

In reality, BBC remuneration levels are, if anything, below current market rates, as recently reported by the National Audit Office,[81] although you are unlikely to read that on the front page of the *Telegraph*, *Mail*, *Express* or *Sun*. This is reflected in recent defections to commercial broadcasters by former BBC stars such as Chris Evans, Eddie Mair, John Pienaar, Phoebe Waller-Bridge and – shortly before we went to press – *Saturday Live*'s Aasmah Mir, who we met in the Introduction and has now joined Rupert Murdoch's Times Radio. The Corporation has so far – just – managed to square this remuneration circle, because it is one of the UK's strongest brands. It is a place where many people would love to work; however, its pay is never going to match that of its commercial rivals. As a media organization, it also operates in a wide range of very different talent markets. So, managing executive, presenter and other employees' pay and conditions is always going to be challenging, especially for the highest-paid presenters who – mainly *because of* their exposure on the BBC – are famous brands in their own right, and are represented by agents who fully exploit their market power.

Celebrity Pay

Celebrity pay has been one of the BBC's biggest challenges in recent years. Jonathan Ross' £16.9 million three-year deal, signed in mid-2006, became a focus for particular criticism after Sachsgate in 2008.[82] In 2010, the BBC paid its top presenters a total of £54 million.[83] By 2015, a review by media consultants Oliver & Ohlbaum found that this had been reduced by 29 per cent, thanks to a more relaxed approach to exclusivity, being willing to let top stars leave and simply paying less. Presenters were also appearing on more programmes for the same level of pay. The Oliver & Ohlbaum review also pointed out that, although some household names, such as Susanna Reid and Chris Moyles, had left the Corporation for more money elsewhere, the BBC had still 'maintained the quality of output for licence-fee payers'.[84]

In 2018–19, the BBC transferred part of the pay of many of its top stars to its commercial business, BBC Studios, which sells programmes to other broadcasters, and whose profits, as we saw in Chapter 4, *support* the UK public service broadcasting group by supplementing its licence-fee income. This move provoked a furious response from the *Sun*, which ran a long article under the heading 'British broadcasting cover-up: BBC "hiding top stars' sky-high salaries" after axing free licences for over-75s', complete with photos of Graham Norton, Gary Lineker, Claudia Winkleman and a dozen other top presenters. There were also lists of the BBC's 'Top 10 Cover-Ups' (i.e. those earning the most from BBC Studios), the top twenty highest-paid BBC stars and the top five pay increases; an indignant quote from the TaxPayers' Alliance and a slightly more measured one from a spokesman for Prime Minister Theresa May; boxed text ('It's Match of the Pay') on the salaries of the *Match of the Day* presenters; and a one-minute video repeating the key points in the article. A furious boxed-text item headed 'THE SUN SAYS' linked the pay story to the BBC 'stripping OAPs of their free TV licence', arguing that, 'The BBC is now indefensible. It needs total reform . . . Whole sections should be shut, including its website.'

Needless to say, the article did not mention News Corporation's commercial vested interest in weakening the BBC. But, in the middle of all the carpet-bombing, it did include a brief comment from the BBC which explained that: 'BBC Studios operates on a commercial footing, where it competes for business with other broadcasters and isn't underpinned by the licence fee. The Government agreed it should be on a level playing field with independent companies who are not required to disclose pay.' It also quoted BBC Chairman David Clementi explaining that critics who said the Corporation could afford to carry on funding free licences for all over-seventy-fives if it cut back on stars' salaries were wrong. Even putting a £150,000 ceiling on stars' salaries would save only £20 million – versus the £745 million annual cost of free licences for all over-seventy-fives.[85]

There will always be a tension for the BBC between attracting the best talent and minimizing its enemies' ability to claim it is squandering licence payers' money.

Executive Pay-offs and Transparency

Another genuine challenge – and topic for attacks on the BBC – is executive pay. On his appointment as director-general in 2012, Tony Hall immediately responded to the controversy over big money severance pay-offs to senior executives by limiting them in future to £150,000. He said he wanted a BBC in tune with the times and said it could no longer be 'tone deaf' to public opinion.

However, in 2017 he announced that having to disclose individual stars' salaries amounted to a 'poacher's charter' and, far from reducing costs, was likely to inflate them.[86] The BBC operates within a commercial world, where there is usually much less transparency about pay: if the owners of the *Daily Mail* or the *Sun* think they would save money and increase their profits by publishing the pay of all their star writers and senior managers, why don't they? Forcing the BBC, including BBC Studios, to do the equivalent for its top presenters and executives is likely to make it less able to compete with commercial broadcasters and technology companies with no such requirements, *reducing* value for money for licence payers. We credit at least some of those calling for more and more BBC pay transparency, such as the TaxPayers' Alliance, with sufficient sophistication to realize this. In other words, we think the TPA's motivation is malicious as well as ideological! However, one unintended consequence of the BBC's pay transparency rules is likely to be beneficial over the long term, both at and well beyond the BBC: the revelations about the gender pay gap.

A Moral Issue: the BBC's Gender Pay Gap

In January 2018, in an explosive open letter 'to the BBC audience', Carrie Gracie, the Corporation's highly respected China editor, resigned 'with great regret'. She said the BBC had a 'secretive and illegal pay culture' and was facing a 'crisis of trust' after the publication of individual stars' pay revealed that almost two-thirds of those earning more than £150,000 were men.

Gracie wrote: 'In thirty years at the BBC, I have never sought to make myself the story and never publicly criticised the organization I love. I am not asking for more money. I believe I am very well paid already – especially as someone working for a publicly funded organization. I simply want the BBC to abide by the law and value men and women equally.'[87]

The BBC had claimed that there was 'no systemic discrimination against women' and that its 9.3 per cent gender pay gap,[88] which it was seeking to reduce, reflected differences in seniority (i.e. that there were more men in higher-paid senior positions), and was already well below the UK average of 18.1 per cent.[89] However, Carrie Gracie's complaint was that, based on her own and other women's experience, there *was* systematic discrimination at the BBC because she was being paid less than her male counterpart *for the same level of job*. According to a *Guardian* editorial, its managers could not grasp that her case was about equality, not money.[90] Discrimination is a moral, as well as a legal, issue and, as a nation, we expect the BBC to operate at a high moral standard.

Naga Munchetty and the Impartiality Rules

Our final example illustrates the complexity of some of the issues through which the BBC has to steer.

BBC Breakfast is a live, daily, three-and-a-quarter-hour breakfast show with the familiar format of two presenters chatting informally to studio guests in the MediaCity studio in Salford, interspersed with filmed reports and over-the-air interviews on the day's featured items, news, sport and weather. On 17 July 2019, the presenters, Dan Walker and Naga Munchetty, were reporting on Donald Trump's recent statement that four Democratic congresswomen of colour should 'go back to the totally broken and crime-infested places from which they came'.[91] Three of the women were born in the US, and the fourth was born in Somalia, but came to America at the age of ten.

Munchetty is a British-born woman of colour herself, with parents from Mauritius and India. Walker asked her how she felt on hearing Trump's comment and whether she'd experienced this sort of remark. She responded, 'Every time I have been told, as a woman of colour, to go back to where I came from, that was embedded in racism ... And I imagine a lot of people in this country will be feeling absolutely furious that a man in that position feels it's OK to skirt the lines with using language like that ... And it is not enough to do it just to get attention. He's in a responsible position – anyway, I'm not here to give my opinion.'[92]

One solitary viewer wrote a letter of complaint. That letter didn't try to defend Trump against the charge of racism (difficult as that would have been),[93] but, under a heading which said, 'Blatant political bias from both presenters', its writer complained that:

> Dan Walker, whilst interviewing a guest about President Trump's recent tweets, repeatedly expressed incredulity that anybody could defend Trump's tweets. Very unprofessionally, he then asked Naga Munchetty for her personal opinions on this news story! She foolishly complied and launched into an attack on Trump, including stating that she was personally 'furious' about his comments.
>
> These two presenters have never made any secret of their left-wing and anti-Trump bias, but usually in more subtle ways, such as eye-rolling and looks of exasperation when reporting on news stories. However, personal commentary on controversial news stories is surely going too far ... They are employed as presenters and not as political commentators.[94]

The complaint was passed to the BBC's Executive Complaints Unit, which partially upheld it on the grounds that Munchetty's comments had breached the Corporation's editorial guidelines. David Jordan, its editorial standards director, told the *Today* programme that Trump's *comments* had indeed been racist – and

Munchetty had been within her rights in describing them as racist and in explaining how, as a person of colour, she felt when told to 'go home', but that she had breached the impartiality guidelines in suggesting that *Trump* was a racist.[95] Understandably, all hell broke loose. Over the next few days, absolutely everyone had something to say, most of them supporting Munchetty and accusing the BBC of censorship. Prominent broadcasters (both of colour and not), including Sir Lenny Henry, Krishnan Guru-Murthy, John Sargeant and Emily Maitlis, said that the position Jordan had taken was unfair, a suppression of free speech and an instance of blaming the victim, since it was Dan Walker who had started the discussion.[96]

On 27 September 2019, sixty broadcasters of colour wrote to *The Guardian* to say that censuring remarks which were calling out racists was wrong, and that the stance the BBC had taken over this issue could prove to be the thin end of the wedge for future employment of BAME individuals. Women broadcasters were angry that the woman had taken the rap when it was a man who had introduced the controversial topic and solicited a response. A couple of 'veteran' voices – Alastair Stewart from ITV News and Andrew Marr from the BBC – said that both of the presenters shouldn't have had that conversation – neither of them, any of it – in the first place, because those were the rules.[97] This was true, but didn't address how those who had held such a conversation should be treated once it *had* taken place. Then, after a complaint was filed with the BBC's regulator by Labour MP Chi Onwurah about the same *BBC Breakfast* show, Ofcom got involved too.[98]

On 30 September, BBC Director-General Lord Hall weighed in, changing the whole situation. He said he'd reviewed everything and listened to the responses. He told BBC staff that Munchetty's words had been 'not sufficient to merit' the ECU's partial uphold of the complaint. The BBC, Hall said, should not be impartial about racism. He added that Ms Munchetty was an 'exceptional journalist and presenter' and that he was 'proud that she works for the BBC'.[99]

The whole thing was disastrous on every level, suggesting the BBC was out of touch with public opinion (and its own employees too), and that, in an overly rule-bound way, it had blamed the *woman of colour* for expressing a widely held view. Then it had changed its mind when there was a public storm. Everyone had a go. Even the (then) Trump-loving ITV presenter Piers Morgan said Naga Munchetty should have been allowed to express her views.[100] (Not everyone agreed. Newswatch's David Keighley wrote in an article on the Conservative Woman website that the 'BBC censures presenters – but not very much' and went on to describe Munchetty's comments as 'an attack on Donald Trump'.)[101]

On 7 October Ofcom published its report.[102] It had received eighteen complaints about the programme. A majority of complainants had objected to the ECU's earlier ruling which had partly upheld the original complaint to the BBC. A further two complaints had objected to the director-general's overruling of the Executive Complaints Unit. Based on a detailed analysis of the context (a magazine-style news programme featuring informal exchanges between the presenters commenting on news items) as well as the specific comments that had been made, Ofcom concluded that the programme had *not* been in breach of the impartiality rules. It did, however, criticize the Executive Complaints Unit's lack of transparency. Ofcom's Kevin Bakhurst, group director for content and media policy, said, 'We'll be requiring the BBC to be more transparent about its processes and compliance findings as a matter of urgency'.[103]

The last word on this sorry saga goes to *The Guardian*'s media editor Jim Waterson, talking to Emily Maitlis on another *Newsnight* programme. He said that different generations had different views of 'impartiality'; and that while it was a concept which was absolute and easily understood by an earlier BBC generation, younger cohorts who grew up on speaking out, rightly or wrongly, simply couldn't relate to David Jordan's judgement:

There's been a lot of anger within the BBC ... People you wouldn't expect have come forward privately ... And what we got hold of, at the Guardian, was the original complaint ... which showed the complaint had been about the two of them ... But what angered a lot of BBC journalists is that they feel that women and people of colour within the BBC get treated differently to older male presenters who are given more free rein to do what they want. It's gone way beyond the original complaint, the microscopic amount that breached the editorial guidelines ... There is a breakdown in the idea of what media should be, with older BBC executives who favour a patrician, authoritative, speaking-with-one-voice agenda, and younger audiences and journalists expecting to reflect on their own experiences and opinions. And that is a real clash of culture that is very hard to reconcile.[104]

A Disproportionate Fear of Failure?

Many of the mistakes we have described could have been avoided by the BBC with better oversight. For instance, many people knew or strongly suspected there was a dark side to Savile; the *Newsnight* episode on McAlpine should have been properly researched; the Sachsgate programme was recorded, not live, and should not have been broadcast with the presenters' lewd messages; and many of the issues in relation to the Digital Media Initiative were avoidable.

However, the danger is that, in trying to minimize the risk of future mistakes, the BBC ends up with a disproportionate fear of failure – the 'atmosphere of fear' described in Dame Janet Smith's report on the Savile case. There is a fear of failure in all organizations – and when a hospital, nuclear power station,

plane pilot or supertanker captain gets things wrong, the consequences are vastly worse than for the mistakes we've discussed
here. Nevertheless, there are several reasons why the fear of failure at the BBC seems to be so marked.

First, the relentless attacks upon it described in earlier chapters, and the government's ability to cut its funding over time,
are almost guaranteed to encourage something of a 'bunker
mentality'. Secondly, as we've seen, the extraordinary volume
and range of the BBC's original output and the vast scale of its
UK consumption give it unparalleled opportunities to make editorial mistakes – or, at least, to broadcast programmes or
segments that many viewers and listeners find offensive or objectionable. Thirdly, its exceptional level of transparency, including
to Freedom of Information requests, makes it unusually vulnerable to hostile players looking for information to use against it.

The fear of failure at the BBC is potentially very bad for viewers and listeners. The main dangers are that it may stop
programme makers from taking calculated risks, holding politicians and other powerful people and institutions to account in
its journalism, and reduce its creativity and ability to innovate in
other genres. There are potentially similar managerial and commercial costs to this fear of failure: it would certainly be against
licence payers' interest if the failure of the DMI and the Lonely
Planet acquisition made the BBC unduly cautious in its future
financial, technological and organizational development. Thus
far, the factors listed above do not seem to have inhibited the
BBC's general creativity, but they may have somewhat cowed
its journalism (as we discussed in Chapter 9).

A fear of speaking out, and the use of systems to manage risk,
also seem to have contributed to some of the problems we've
discussed earlier, notably to how Jimmy Savile was able to hide
in clear sight. In all organizations, people 'spin' and censor what
they say to their bosses, and bosses almost invariably underestimate the extent to which this is happening,[105] but – perhaps

because of the particular factors we've noted – this issue seems to be even worse at the BBC than in most organizations. To manage the risks, the BBC has to have elaborate systems in place. These are inevitably resented, especially by those producing programmes. The more the Corporation is pilloried for its mistakes, the more likely it is to respond by introducing more bureaucracy to reduce the risk of further mistakes – reducing creativity, productivity, competitiveness in the talent market and its willingness and ability to challenge people in power.

When responding to a listener's question, 'Why did you leave the BBC?' Virgin Radio's breakfast host Chris Evans replied, 'Because this would've taken three weeks of compliance meetings and then it wouldn't have happened!'[106] In actual fact, we think he probably went to the Murdoch organization mainly for the money *and* to get away from the endless criticisms about his (much lower) pay at the Beeb. But there's also probably some truth in his claimed desire to go somewhere with less bureaucracy and need for compliance. David Dimbleby has similarly described the BBC as over-managed and claimed that the management still speaks 'gobbledy-gook'.[107] Furthermore, as Tim Luckhurst argued after Sachsgate, over-elaborate risk management systems may end up *increasing* risk if everyone relies on the system – and on everyone else – rather than taking personal responsibility.[108]

The BBC is deeply embedded in British culture and society. It reflects, as well as influences, the nation's constantly changing social attitudes and concerns, while always seeking to strike a balance between the values and preferences of traditional – often older – viewers and listeners and those of, mostly younger, groups who see it as what we might summarize as too Auntieish – although they'd never use that term. Some of the cases we've described – Savile in particular – reflect a very different society from today's, not only in terms of its social attitudes but also a world before movements like Me Too, Black Lives Matter and Extinction Rebellion.

Given the number of opportunities the BBC has to offend and upset people, of course it sometimes gets things wrong. The public rightly holds it to a high standard – and it does the same itself, as it did in the October 2012 *Panorama* programme criticizing the cancellation of the planned *Newsnight* episode on Savile. As an organization, it is exceptionally transparent and under relentless, and often malicious, scrutiny. (It's far easier for companies and even government departments to bury their mistakes than it is for the BBC.) And, as we've seen, its enemies make the most of its missteps: recall how the *Mail on Sunday* and other newspapers managed to turn two genuine listener complaints on Sachsgate into 44,790!

In fact, it's surprising that the BBC doesn't make *more* mistakes. We've identified only one major commercial mistake (Lonely Planet) and one major managerial one (the DMI) during the last fifteen years. Over the same period, amid all the sound and fury about 'bias', we've also identified only one example of the BBC's reporting being inaccurate: in their *Newsnight* programme about Lord McAlpine (and even in that case, the programme didn't actually name the wrong person: as we've seen, a series of misunderstandings led to someone from *outside* the BBC doing so).

If there's a consistent theme running through these examples – and the Corporation's avoidance of sensitive political issues, discussed in Chapter 9 – it's that, if anything, people at the BBC tend to be too timid. That doubtless, at least partly, reflects the constant scrutiny under which it operates and the powerful forces often ranged against it. But it raises the question of whether the result is in the best interest of viewers and listeners. Reasonable people might disagree, but our own view is that, as a nation, we want a BBC that takes *more* risks – and therefore, inevitably, makes more mistakes. In our ideal world, this would have been a longer chapter.

13.   'Vox Populi, Vox Dei'[1]

Much of the war against the BBC involves its enemies saying it is not – or 'no longer' – trustworthy, and accusing it of various biases, invariably against their own positions. As we've seen, all kinds of right-wing players endlessly say that its news and current affairs coverage has a systematic left-wing and/or anti-Brexit bias, but, especially in recent years, it has also often been accused by those on the left of an anti-Labour and, especially, anti-Corbyn bias: its political editor Laura Kuenssberg even had to have a bodyguard during the 2017 general election campaign because of online threats from far-left Labour supporters.[2]

We've also seen how, recently, perhaps for the first time in its history, even some of the BBC's natural supporters in the political centre have also strongly criticized it, accusing it of a pro-Brexit bias. These new, centrist critics don't claim that its journalists themselves are biased in favour of Brexit, but rather that it has given too much airtime to pro-Brexit propagandists and failed to challenge their assertions sufficiently.

We've seen how academic content analyses have shown that many of the accusations against the BBC's news and current affairs coverage are just plain wrong – and, in some cases, even the opposite of the truth. In its reporting, the BBC strives for 'due impartiality' (as all UK broadcasters do, because they are all required to deliver the news without bias). However, the issues aren't straightforward, partly because bias will always be partly in the eye of the beholder, but also because 'due impartiality' is a tricky, nuanced concept. In particular, it is not the same as the 'false balance', of giving equal airtime to people with opposing views, especially on issues like climate change

231

and the likely economic consequences of Brexit, where there is a near-consensus among experts.[3] And people care more, and talk about it more, if the BBC (as opposed to any other media organization) gets things wrong – or can plausibly be accused of doing so – because it's the UK's most important and, as we'll see, most trusted news source. And, in politics, perceptions are what matter. So what has been the impact of decades of Beeb-bashing on the public's perceptions of the BBC and its programmes?

We first look at its perceived impartiality and trustworthiness – the central issues in the attacks on its news coverage – and how they compare with the same measures for other news sources. We then turn to how well the public thinks the BBC delivers its wider public purposes, such as 'helping [people] understand and engage with the world around them' and 'creating high quality content and services', and how this compares with their perceptions of other media brands. Finally, we consider the trends over time. How have the BBC's perceived trustworthiness, and the public's general perceptions of it, varied over the last fifteen years – including in response to the mistakes and scandals we discussed in the last chapter?

Turning to the specifics, how well does the BBC score on perceived impartiality after its enemies' relentless claims that it is biased? In particular, does the public as a whole think it is systematically biased to either the left or the right? And how does the public's view of the BBC's impartiality compare with its perceptions of other media? We have plenty of evidence.

What Is the Public's Perception of the BBC's Impartiality?

Figure 13.1 shows responses, among UK adults aged fifteen-plus who say they 'follow the news', to the question as to which single source they would go to if they were looking for an impartial

Of all the news sources (TV broadcaster, radio, newspaper, magazine or website), which ONE source are you most likely to turn to for impartial news?

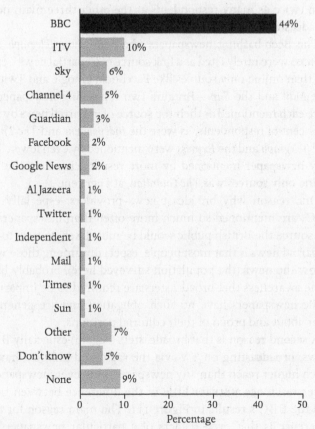

Figure 13.1
Top News Sources for IMPARTIAL News Coverage

Source: Ipsos MORI for the BBC, UK adults aged fifteen-plus who follow the news (1,829), April–May 2019. Newspaper titles include the Sunday edition. (All the percentages above do not add up to exactly 100% due to rounding errors)

account of the news. The BBC and the other three main TV news broadcasters (ITV, Sky and Channel 4)[4] occupy the top four slots. But the BBC, at 44 per cent, was mentioned by more than twice as many respondents as the other three main news broadcasters combined (21 per cent).

The Beeb-bashing newspapers (the *Mail*, *Sun*, *Telegraph* and *Express*) were rarely cited as a first source of impartial news – even less than online-only sources like Facebook, Google and Twitter. The *Mail* and the *Sun* – Britain's two top-selling newspapers – were each mentioned as their top source of impartial news by just 1 per cent of respondents, as were the *Independent* and *The Times*. The *Telegraph* and the *Express* were mentioned by even fewer. The only newspaper mentioned by more respondents than the top online-only sources was *The Guardian*, at 3 per cent.

One reason why broadcast news providers, especially the BBC, are mentioned so much more often than newspapers as the source the British public would be most likely to turn to for impartial news is that most people, especially among those who follow the news (the population surveyed here), probably have some awareness that broadcasters are required to be impartial, while newspapers have no such obligation and are generally clear about and proud of their editorial positions.

A second reason is that broadcasters – again, especially BBC News, broadcasting on TV, via the radio and online – have a much higher reach than any newspaper. However, newspapers' lower reach accounts for little of the difference between their and the BBC's results in Figure 13.1. The main reason for this difference is that even readers of a particular newspaper are more likely to mention the BBC than that newspaper as their top source for impartial news coverage.[5]

It's interesting and somewhat worrying to note that as many as 9 per cent of respondents said 'None' – presumably meaning that, in their view, there are *no* impartial news sources in the UK.[6] If this 9 per cent and the 5 per cent who responded 'Don't know' (making a total of 14 per cent) are excluded from the total figure, then more than half of those who did mention a specific source gave the BBC as the one they would be most likely to turn to for impartial news – and three-quarters gave one of the four main broadcasters. Fewer than one in four would first turn to either an online-only source or a newspaper for impartial news.

What can we say about the views of those who follow the news, but mentioned a source other than the BBC as the one they would be most likely to turn to for impartial news? We can gain some clues from another recent study.

Those Saying the BBC Is Biased Disagree About Which Way

In May 2018, BMG Research, an independent market research agency, published the results of a survey of British viewers' perceptions of whether the BBC and other TV news broadcasters in the UK were politically biased, and, if so, whether they were ('[s]omewhat' or 'strongly') biased towards the left or the right.[7] We would expect to see a high correlation between perceiving a news source to be politically biased (as measured in this survey) and *not* mentioning it as the source one is most likely to turn to for impartial news (as in Figure 13.1).

In this survey, 40 per cent of respondents felt that the BBC was politically biased – significantly more than the equivalent figures for Channel Four (22 per cent), Sky News (26 per cent), ITV (22 per cent) or even RT, formerly Russia Today (29 per cent). However, as in other studies, those who said the BBC was biased disagreed about the direction: 18 per cent said it was '[s]omewhat' (11 per cent) or 'strongly' (7 per cent) biased towards the right; 22 per cent said it was '[s]omewhat' (15 per cent) or 'strongly' (7 per cent) biased towards the left (see Figure 13.2). In line with the football referee analogy we introduced in Chapter

9, these perceptions were markedly influenced by respondents' own political positions. Forty-one per cent of those describing themselves as left wing said the BBC was biased towards the right, while as many as 52 per cent of those with self-described right-wing views saw it as biased towards the left. These results suggest that the endless efforts of right-wing think tanks, newspapers and politicians over many years to persuade the British public that the BBC's news coverage is systematically and strongly biased to the left have had remarkably little effect.

The BMG study found that the remaining 60 per cent of respondents either explicitly said that the BBC was politically neutral or balanced (37 per cent) or that they didn't know, meaning that they were unaware of any systematic BBC bias either way (24 per cent).[8] Furthermore, among the 40 per cent who *did* say the BBC was biased, the difference between the proportion saying it had a left-wing bias (total 22 per cent) and those saying it had a right-wing bias (total 18 per cent) was only 4 percentage points.[9]

The Corporation's right-wing critics might argue that, on balance, this – admittedly very small – difference shows that the public, at least marginally, agrees with them that the BBC is biased towards the left. But even that suggestion breaks down when we compare the 4 per cent figure for the BBC's purported left-wing bias with the equivalent figures for Channel 4 (12 per cent), ITV (6 per cent) and RT (11 per cent), all suggesting a somewhat greater left-wing bias than that of the BBC.[10] (The outlier was Sky News, which was seen as having a right-wing bias by slightly more respondents (16 per cent) than those who saw it as having a left-wing bias (10 per cent) – a difference of 6 percentage points in the opposite direction.)

The key point is that these differences in respondents' perceptions of the political biases of the four main news broadcasters (BBC, Channel 4, Sky News and ITV) were all small. There are further insights to be had from two polls conducted in late 2019 which were summarized in two articles in the *Daily Telegraph*

In your view, do you feel that the BBC is politically neutral or biased?

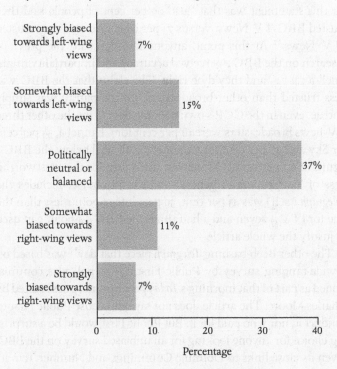

Figure 13.2

Public Perceptions of the Bias or Impartiality of BBC News

Source: BMG, May 2018. Excludes those who answered 'Don't know' (24 per cent)

on 28 December 2019. The first article reported a new poll commissioned by the evangelical Christian Communications Partnership (CCP).[11] (It's fascinating that the CCP, which runs Christian radio stations in the UK, should commission research on trust in the BBC and give it to the *Telegraph*. We're familiar with evangelical Christian bodies in the USA being politicized, but less so here.) The article began, 'The BBC is less trusted than other broadcasters, lagging 4 points behind ITV News over the perceived impartiality and accuracy of its news coverage'. The justification for this statement was that 'just' 69 per cent of people said they trusted BBC TV News, versus 73 per cent who said they trusted ITV News.[12] At this point, anyone familiar with the previous research on the BBC's perceived accuracy and impartiality might smell a rat ... and they'd be right. The claim that the BBC was 'less trusted than other broadcasters' (in the plural) was simply untrue, even in the CCP's own poll: the figures for the other three TV news broadcasters were 61 per cent for Channel 4, 55 per cent for Sky and 48 per cent for Channel 5 – all well below the BBC's figure of 69 per cent.[13] Moreover, the figure for the trustworthiness of 'newspapers in general' (which, of course, includes the *Telegraph* itself) was 43 per cent, 30 percentage points less than the one for ITV – seven-and-a-half times the BBC's 4-point gap used to justify the whole article.

The other Beeb-bashing *Telegraph* piece that day[14] was based on a wide-ranging survey by Public First.[15] The poll was commissioned as part of that morning's *Today* programme, guest-edited by Charles Moore. The article does not say who chose Public First to conduct it, nor who paid for it. But Public First would be a surprising choice for anyone looking for an unbiased survey on the BBC, given its close links to Dominic Cummings and Number Ten: its co-founders are James Frayne, a long-term associate of Cummings (including as his partner in the New Frontiers think tank in 2004, when Cummings wrote his infamous anti-BBC blog posts) and Rachel Wolf, co-author of the 2019 Conservative manifesto.[16] Only 27 per cent of respondents agreed that 'The BBC is neutral'. Thirty-six per cent disagreed – but, as in other studies, they also disagreed about the direction of the bias. Among the whole sample, 25 per cent saw the BBC as biased towards Labour, versus 28 per cent who disagreed; similarly, 24 per cent saw it as biased towards the Conservatives, against 30 per cent who disagreed. These figures again imply a remarkable degree of perceived impartiality, despite strident accusations of bias by both main parties.[17]

In summary, on the question of whether the public as a whole sees the BBC as systematically biased to either the left or the right, the answer is a clear no. The results on this are very consistent:

1. The BBC is, by far, the UK public's first choice for impartial news. The Ipsos MORI study found this even among those who read particular newspapers: they may get many good things from their newspaper, but for impartial news, they turn to the BBC.

2. A majority of the public does *not* perceive the BBC as biased to either the left or the right. In the BMG study, 60 per cent either explicitly said BBC News was neutral or balanced in its reporting or replied 'Don't know' (meaning they were unaware of any bias). In the Public First poll, 64 per cent gave similar responses to these or said 'Neither agree nor disagree'.

3. Those saying the BBC is biased disagree which way: among the large minority who do think the BBC is biased – 40 per cent in the BMG study, 36 per cent in the Public First one – they disagree about the direction of the perceived bias.

4. Across the wider public, roughly equal numbers see the BBC as biased to the left and the right. In the BMG research, slightly more respondents saw the BBC as biased to the left than saw it as biased to the right, but the difference (just 4 percentage points) was smaller than for any other broadcaster.

Other Perceived BBC Biases

However, there were bigger imbalances on some other questions in the Public First survey. In particular, 52 per cent saw the BBC as having a 'London' bias, versus only 11 per cent who disagreed. Thirty-five per cent said it had a 'pro-Establishment' bias, with 14 per cent disagreeing.

On Brexit, 33 per cent thought the BBC was biased towards *remaining* in the EU, versus 21 per cent disagreeing, while 20 per cent said it was biased towards *leaving* the EU, with 31 per cent not in agreement.[18] This relatively small, but consistent imbalance may have partly reflected the idea that the BBC was largely controlled from London and unquestionably part of the Establishment (however defined), both of which were seen as 'pro-EU' proxies.

As well as being the British public's top source for *impartial* news, the BBC is also by far the *most trusted* news source in Britain. In fact, it is if anything even more dominant on this measure than on perceived impartiality (see Figure 13.3).

Impartiality and trust are closely related but not the same. *The Guardian* and the *Telegraph* make no claim to be impartial in their selection of news stories and commentary on their implications, but they do claim that their reporting is accurate. In the famous words of the *Manchester Guardian*'s C. P. Scott, in his May 1921 centenary editorial, 'Comment is free, but facts are sacred'.[19] Even the Corporation's greatest enemies have been unable to find any material examples of *inaccurate* BBC news reporting.

How Well, in the Public's View, Does the BBC Deliver Its Wider Public Purposes?

The impartiality and trustworthiness of the BBC's news and current affairs are hugely important in their own right and also the main issue on which its programme content is attacked by its enemies. But they are only part of the BBC's mission. The BBC Charter spells out five wider public purposes. News and current affairs are at the heart of the first purpose, although even this can be interpreted more broadly. Here's the full list:

Of all the news sources (TV broadcaster, radio, newspaper, magazine or website), which ONE source are you most likely to turn to for news you trust the most?

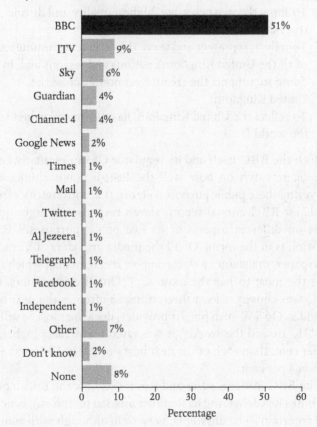

Figure 13.3
Top News Sources for TRUSTED News Coverage

Source: Ipsos MORI for the BBC, UK adults aged fifteen-plus who follow the news (1,829), April–May 2019. Newspaper titles include the Sunday edition

1. To provide impartial news and information to help people understand and engage with the world around them.
2. To support learning for people of all ages.
3. To show the most creative, highest quality and distinctive output and services.
4. To reflect, represent and serve the diverse communities of all the United Kingdom's nations and regions and, in doing so, support the creative economy across the United Kingdom.
5. To reflect the United Kingdom, its culture and values to the world.[20]

Both the BBC itself and its regulator Ofcom regularly commission research on how well the British public thinks it is delivering these public purposes. Figure 13.4, with statistics from the latest BBC annual report, shows responses to eight questions on different aspects of its five public purposes.[21] Each question is in the form, 'Of all the media providers (TV, radio, newspaper, magazine, website, app or social media), which one does the most to/has the most . . . ?' On all eight counts, the BBC was chosen at least three times as often as the next best provider. On '[W]hich [media provider] does the most to reflect the UK around the world?', it was rated *twelve times* higher, at 60 per cent, than each of the next best providers, ITV and Sky, both at 5 per cent.

The BBC also measures and reports on how the British public thinks it is delivering its Reithian mission to 'inform, educate and entertain'. The answer is, very well, although with some – very slight – recent slippage from the previous year. The figures from the 2018–19 BBC annual report[22] show the following percentage responses among UK adults in March–May 2019:

- The BBC is effective at *informing* people in the UK: 74 per cent agree (only 10 per cent say it is 'ineffective').

Of all the media providers (TV, radio, newspaper, magazine, website, app or social media), which ONE does the most to / has the most . . . ?

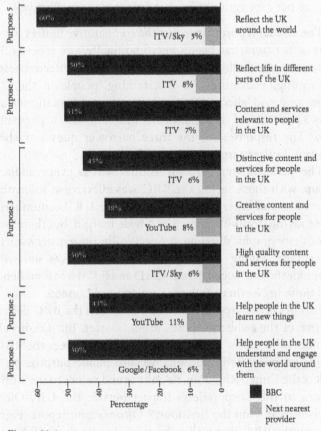

Figure 13.4
Perceived Delivery of the BBC's Public Purposes

Source: Ipsos MORI for the BBC, 3,551 adults aged sixteen-plus, March–May 2019

- The BBC is effective at *educating* people in the UK:
  71 per cent agree (only 10 per cent say it is 'ineffective').
- The BBC is effective at *entertaining* people in the UK:
  76 per cent agree (only 9 per cent say it is 'ineffective').

The annual report shows that the comparative figures from a year earlier (2018) had been – very marginally – even better. For instance, for a combined question on the BBC's effectiveness at 'informing, educating and entertaining' people in the UK, 75 per cent said 'effective' in 2018, versus 74 per cent in 2019, and only 8 per cent had said 'ineffective' in 2018, versus 10 per cent in 2019. The responses for the three narrower questions above showed similar marginal slippage.[23]

The patterns were broadly similar across every audience group, with those saying the BBC was effective at informing, educating and entertaining people in the UK outnumbering those saying it was ineffective by a wide margin, but there were some demographic differences. Specifically, the gap between the percentages saying 'effective' and 'ineffective' was somewhat lower for those in social classes C2, D and E,[24] BAME audiences and those in Northern Ireland, Scotland and London.

Part of Ofcom's role is to monitor how well the BBC delivers all five of the public purposes in its Charter. But Ofcom also monitors the extent to which the British public sees the BBC's public purposes as important. Because public purpose 5 ('To reflect the United Kingdom, its culture and values to the world') relates to the Corporation's impact outside the UK, Ofcom focuses mainly on the first four.[25] Ofcom's 2019 report (Figure 13.5.) on the BBC shows that the public considers all of these as important, and increasingly so.[26]

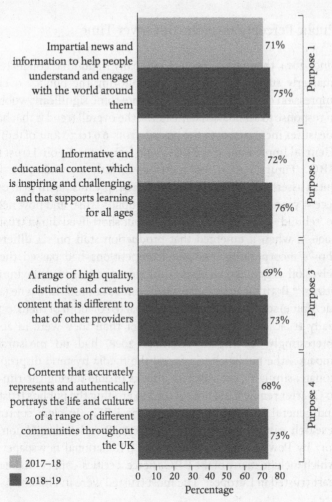

Figure 13.5
Perceived Importance to Society of the BBC's Public Purposes 1–4
Source: Ofcom's second performance report on the BBC, 24 October 2019

Public Perceptions of the BBC over Time

Since 2004, the market research company Kantar has conducted a quarterly survey for the BBC, monitoring the public's overall impression of it and trust in it.[27] Despite some significant wobbles in response to scandals and mistakes, the overall trend is that both measures increased over the period, from 6.6 to 7.0 (out of ten) on 'General Impression of the BBC' and from 5.9 to 6.3 on 'I trust the BBC' (Figure 13.6). These increases directly contradict the frequent assertion (whether malicious or simply mistaken) that, over recent years, the BBC has 'lost the public's trust' and now needs to 'rebuild' it. There was a marked, but short-lived dip in trust in 2006–7, when it emerged that production staff on six different shows incorporating phone-in competitions had passed themselves off as genuine viewers or listeners phoning in and winning prizes.[28] Both measures increased from 2004 until the Savile (and McAlpine) scandal in 2012, which impacted on both of them, especially trust. But now both are higher than they were in 2004. Interestingly, 'Sachsgate' (October 2008) had no measurable impact – the public clearly found the media hysteria disproportionate; similarly, the constant attacks in 2016 during the run-up to Charter renewal did not succeed in eroding the public's trust in and general favourability towards the BBC. (In clear contrast, research carried out for the European Broadcasting Union in 2017 by Pew Research showed that UK national newspapers – which include many of the BBCs fiercest critics – appear to be the least trusted in Europe.[29] The most trusted were in Holland.)

Some Recent Erosion of Public Trust: A Brexit Effect?

As we saw earlier (Figure 13.3), the BBC is by far the most trusted news source in Britain. But Figure 13.6 suggests that there may

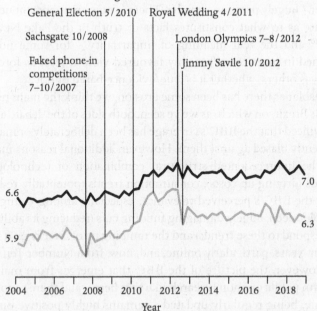

Average score out of 10

General Election 5/2010   Royal Wedding 4/2011

Sachsgate 10/2008   London Olympics 7–8/2012

Faked phone-in   Jimmy Savile 10/2012
competitions
7–10/2007

— General impression of the BBC – average score out of 10
   1 = extremely unfavourable; 10 = extremely favourable

— I trust the BBC – average score out of 10
   1 = extremely unfavourable; 10 = extremely favourable

Figure 13.6
Trust and Favourability of the BBC over a Fifteen-Year Period
Source: BBC

have been some erosion of public trust in, and the public's general impression of, the BBC over the most recently reported period, 2017–19. What might have caused this? The first consideration is that public perceptions of truth and reliability in media of all kinds has been affected by a widespread cynicism driven by Brexit frustrations and perceived media bias generally, underwritten by a barrage of focused criticism of the BBC from other – hugely partisan – media. There is now an important new debate as to what constitutes facts or truth in the Fake News era,[30] and the real meaning of impartiality – for some now defined in practice as 'puts my favoured view at least as forcefully as others, whether it is true/evidence-based or not'.

Insofar as there has been some erosion, we think the main reason is Brexit, on which, as we've seen, both sides of the debate are convinced that the BBC's coverage has been deliberately or inadvertently biased against them. However, additional reasons may be the unprecedented structural combination of technology trends (driving up costs), consumption trends (potentially reducing the BBC's perceived relevance, especially among younger people), deep, hugely damaging funding cuts (reducing its ability to respond to these trends) and the ramping up of attacks on it in recent years, particularly online, and, now, from Number Ten.

However, the picture of the BBC that emerges from mainstream public opinion research like that here – and there's more online, being regularly updated – remains highly positive on a number of levels, first of all on a historical level. Continuous research like Kantar's tends to show short-term downturns in public approval of the BBC following one or other 'fire and fury' negative incidents such as the Savile disclosures, but, overall, it displays remarkable continuity year on year. Moreover, compared to other news providers, the BBC continues to dominate key ratings such as those for 'trust' and 'first choice', by very considerable margins, and to be endorsed across the age groups too. No other sources – on- or offline, print or broadcast – come close. It is worth emphasizing here that although new online sources started the century with high expectations about their reliability and transparency and, although they have taken their 'share' as news platforms away from all the longer-established media, there is now increasing public criticism and cynicism about them.[31]

But news and current affairs reliability is not the only, or even the main, criterion for most audiences. The question of the *scope* of the BBC's output reveals a gulf between the British public and the BBC's enemies in government, free-market think tanks and some commercial media. In particular, the public clearly sees entertainment as a central and highly valued part of what the BBC offers. As we saw in the context of the green-paper consultation in 2015, their resounding answer to the question as to whether the BBC should go on providing entertainment was 'Yes'. And they rate its entertainment output highly: in the 2019 Ipsos MORI research reported earlier in this chapter, 76 per cent said that it was 'effective at entertaining people in the UK'.[32] This response is in line with that of participants in focus groups in 2015 during Charter renewal, who simply *assumed* that the BBC should provide programmes that entertained as well as those that informed and educated. This continuing public support is especially striking given the tsunami of anti-BBC propaganda described in this book, which has increased with the growth of social media. And it has been further ramped up as political pressures have combined to polarize existing social divides.

Although the overall picture of public trust in and support for the BBC is extremely positive, some groups are – somewhat predictably – less enthusiastic. There is, for instance, the class divide (there always has been; the BBC audience has always been skewed towards the middle classes), and the age divide, in which younger audiences are neither as positive about the BBC, nor, more importantly, as involved as other viewers because they have a wider variety of platforms from which to access media of all kinds and are increasingly less tied to 'linear' broadcasting of all varieties (just as they are still less tied to 'legacy' newspaper brands).[33]

But anyone who has been down the raucous cyber rabbit-holes we have explored in this book cannot help but wonder how and when and at what scale the hostile attitudes to the BBC expressed there will surface above the ground. Recent history has shown that there is a gestation period for new worldviews that develop unobserved online. In fact, we're starting to live with an earlier group of them now, in what's widely described as the 'coarsening of the political dialogue' (undoubtedly influenced by constant trolling from anonymous sources online), and in the expression of extreme views and conspiracy theories that until recently had been seen as 'marginal' in the prosperous West. These have been given wide distribution and credence online, as Cambridge professor John Naughton and his colleagues have shown in their research into conspiracy theories.[34]

How will the British public's perceptions of the BBC evolve in the future? Its big challenge is to remain valued and relevant in a world of increasing competition, rising content and distribution costs and fast-changing consumption patterns, but with 30 per cent less public funding than ten years ago. At the same time, politically, the realignment and polarization of UK politics around Brexit – very different from the more familiar left–right divide – also bears on possible future changes in public perceptions of the BBC. Although, as we saw in Chapter 9, the reality is that the BBC's news and current affairs coverage was *not* anti-Brexit, the perception among Brexiteers – especially the most ardent ones – was that it constantly slanted the debate against them in all sorts of ways. This charge, supported by an endless stream of hostile think-tank reports, newspaper articles and blog posts, might potentially undermine the public's trust in the BBC. The reality of Brexit over the next few years will doubtless fall somewhere between the sunny upland predicted by some and the disaster predicted by others; as always, the BBC will have to navigate its way through the various conflicting claims and counter-claims.

However, the public has relied on the BBC even more than usual during the Covid-19 pandemic, and the burgeoning of misinformation and conspiracy theories has reinforced the importance of reliable news and information. Maybe the remarkable level of public support – higher today than fifteen years ago – will continue.

In the next chapter we turn to the major, international *cultural* changes that influence how people see the world. These wider 'culture wars' are part of the context of the war against the BBC – itself a significant player in them.

14. *Culture Wars*

Politics is downstream from culture.
    Attributed to Andrew Breitbart

Nation shall speak peace unto nation.
    The BBC's motto, created by John Reith, 1927

Things fall apart; the centre cannot hold . . .
The best lack all conviction, while the worst
Are full of passionate intensity.
    W.B. Yeats, 'The Second Coming', 1920

To overseas supporters of beleaguered liberal democracy around the world, the BBC 'shines [like] a good deed in a naughty world'[1] through the breadth, accuracy and impartiality of its international news,[2] and the quality of its exported programmes. Within the UK itself, its fifth public purpose is to 'offer a range and depth of analysis and content . . . so that all audiences can engage fully with major local, regional, national, United Kingdom and global issues and participate in the democratic process, at all levels, as active and informed citizens'.[3] However, as in the 1930s, liberal democracy is being challenged by militant nationalism, populism, intolerance, division and disinformation, much of it enabled by social media.[4] The BBC's values are part of the old order – and firmly at odds with these new trends.

Although this book is about the domestic UK war against the BBC, the broader context includes both the global technology and media market trends, already discussed, and these international socio-political trends, often called the global culture war. 'Culture' is used here in the sociological or anthropological sense. It refers to the shared attitudes, beliefs, identities, historic and mythical references and patterns of behaviour that are seen as 'normal' and largely taken for granted within a given group or society. The twenty-first-century global culture war is an increasingly important part of the climate in which the BBC and the rest of us all find ourselves.

In modern usage, 'culture war' is an American term.[5] In 1992, in a pioneering book, James Davison Hunter described it, in the US context, as the polarization between groups with opposing views on abortion, gun laws, immigration and multiculturalism, the separation of church and state, climate change, drugs, feminism and LGBTQ rights. It's about 'progressive' against 'conservative', and urban against small-town and rural.[6] That same year, the conservative US commentator Pat Buchanan made these disagreements central to his pitch for the presidency, saying that the Clintons' liberal agenda was 'not the kind of change America needs'.[7]

In the 1990s and the first decade of the twenty-first century the social liberals appeared to have won. But now the culture war is back with a vengeance – and we use that term advisedly – transformed by younger, tougher, more anarchic protagonists with new issues, languages and platforms. These contemporary culture warriors look different and they've changed the way they operate too. The Conservative old guard might not even recognize themselves in this new breed. It's all cooler, faster and much, much nastier.

In this chapter, we sketch just a few aspects of this new, rather opaque, fast-changing international culture war. One constant theme is populist attacks on liberal media, of which the BBC is the pre-eminent global example. There are certainly some indications that nationalist and authoritarian regimes around the world would, like its UK enemies, be delighted to see the BBC weakened. These attacks aren't all part of a single, vast, seamless worldwide conspiracy – but they're not completely uncoordinated either.

The BBC's International Enemies

The BBC's news coverage cuts across every fault-line in global politics, and its enemies now seem to include both the Kremlin and President Trump's White House. Trump's dislike of international institutions, almost on principle, is widely recognized,[8] alongside his disdain for the 'liberal' US mainstream media (MSM) – which apparently, by extension, includes the BBC: when questioned by its US editor Jon Sopel at a press conference in 2017 (before he stopped giving traditional press conferences in early 2019),[9] Trump started by saying, with a sneer, 'The BBC – here's another beauty'.[10] And a BBC cameraman, Ron Skeans, was attacked by Trump supporters at a rally in El Paso, Texas, in February 2019.[11] Trump and Steve Bannon are closely linked to BBC-hating right-wing, British politicians such as Nigel Farage,[12] which may partly explain this antipathy.

Trump regularly exhorts his mass rallies against the mainstream media, as producers of 'fake news'. In July 2018, he told the Veterans of Foreign Wars Convention, 'Just stick with us; don't believe the crap you see from these people, the Fake News . . . Just remember what you're seeing and what you're reading is *not* what's happening'.[13] He has admitted that these constant attacks on the mainstream media are a deliberate ploy. In 2018, the veteran US journalist Lesley Stahl reported that she and her boss had met him immediately after his 2016 election victory, in advance of a recorded interview for the CBS News *60 Minutes* programme. 'At one point, he started to attack the press. There were no cameras there. I said, "You know, this is getting tired . . . You've won . . . why do you keep hammering at this?" And he said, "You know why I do it? I do it to discredit you all and demean you all so that when you write negative stories about me no one will believe you".'[14] The question of whether a story is true or false isn't the issue. In Trump's world, if it's negative and about him, it's 'fake news'. That's the *only* issue.

Russia, too, like the USSR throughout the Cold War, clearly sees the BBC as an enemy.[15] Russian enmity to the BBC has, if anything, increased under Putin, who, notably, has said that the 'liberal hour' in world politics is over.[16] In 2007, the BBC World Service was forced to abandon its FM radio Russian-language broadcasts (FM being its main way of reaching its audience) after it broadcast an interview in November 2006 with the defector Alexander Litvinenko shortly before he died, in which he had alleged that the Kremlin had had a role in his polonium poisoning in London.[17] (Litvinenko was a former FSB officer specializing in tackling Russian organized crime, including its links with the Kremlin (he coined the term 'mafia state' to describe Russia under Putin).)[18] In 2015, news broadcaster RT, formerly Russia Today, accused the Corporation of faking a Syrian air attack in an edition of *Panorama*.[19] And when Ofcom withdrew RT's licence for repeated breaches of the UK's impartiality rules, most recently on the Salisbury poisonings, Russia, in an explicit tat-for-tat action, banned all the BBC's Russian-language services from its airwaves (the FM service having already been banned twelve years earlier).[20] The world is now so interconnected the BBC is always on a global stage, often in the political firing line.

At the time of writing, what is unclear is the extent to which the overt attacks on the BBC in the UK (by the newspapers, think tanks and others we discussed in chapters 7 and 8 – and now by Number Ten too) and overseas (such as those we've just discussed by President Trump and Putin's Russia) are coordinated and/or supplemented by covert activities, especially in the digital space. At this point, all we can confidently say is the following. First, there are numerous connections between Putin's Russia, Donald Trump's 2016 election campaign (and subsequent actions – and inactions) and at least some leading Brexiteers and the 2016 EU referendum campaign. Secondly, all of these people are hostile to the BBC. And thirdly, some of their hostility appears to be part of the broader twenty-first-century global culture war discussed in this chapter.

The connections between Putin's Russia and Donald Trump's 2016 election campaign are well established, although whether the impact of Russian interference was enough to change the outcome is still – and perhaps always will be – unclear. The key official documentation of this is the March 2019 Mueller Report. Mueller says unequivocally that Russia sought to influence the US election and that links existed between the parties.[21] Other people have uncovered extensive evidence supporting these conclusions, most recently the Republican-led Senate intelligence committee.[22] In stark contrast with the open dialogue about Russian interference in the US, in the UK both the government and the intelligence and security services have – presumably, deliberately – avoided this 'hot potato' issue, as revealed in the Intelligence and Security Committee report finally published in July 2020 – despite continuing attempts to suppress it by Number Ten (of which more later). The UK government's reticence about Russian interference, especially in the 2016 EU referendum, has been paralleled by a similar silence in most mainstream British media – including the BBC, which appears to have sat on any detailed coverage that might be seen as delegitimizing the referendum result and further infuriating the Tories. The honourable exceptions have been *The Guardian/Observer*, especially Carole Cadwalladr, and Channel 4.[23] There has been no attempt to hide Trump's enthusiasm for Brexit and his links with leading Brexiteers – Nigel Farage even featured on his campaign platforms. The same people clustered around Cambridge Analytica (discussed shortly) were seen in both the Brexit and Trump campaigns – Farage, Arron Banks, Andy Wigmore, Steve Bannon and the Mercers.

In early 2020, Bannon told Open Democracy journalist Peter

Geoghegan, author of *Democracy for Sale*, that Cummings was a 'brilliant guy', Britain should go for a hard, no-deal Brexit ('It won't be disruptive') and Johnson would move ever further to the right and become 'more . . . nationalistic [and] populist over time'.[24] (This was some months before Bannon's arrest for an allegedly fraudulent crowdfunding scheme to build a wall between Mexico and the USA, described by Donald Trump Jnr as 'private enterprise at its finest'.)[25] Before 2016, few had seen this coming; the ideology and much of the power, of the protagonists in this war was created, almost unseen, in a different arena: the new digital space. And it affects us all.

The Origins of the Twenty-First-Century Culture War

Unbeknown to many, and away from the mainstream media limelight, during the late 1990s and early 2000s, a culture war was developing across the Western capitalist world. The conflict between social conservatives and progressives was supplemented by tensions between the economic beneficiaries and the casualties – the 'left behinds' – of new technology and business globalization. Increasingly, the battle lines were between the emerging populist right and centrist liberals,[26] especially those scornfully labelled by their critics as 'the metropolitan liberal elite' – a key phrase in the new culture war rhetoric. Back in the 1960s and 1970s, when Nixon's conservative 'silent majority' had pitched themselves against (mostly) young progressives on campus and in the media, the main battle lines were about personal behaviour – sex, drugs and rock'n'roll – and a familiar roster of international issues, especially the Vietnam War. But these areas are only part of the twenty-first-century culture war.

The impact of technology and globalization on Western societies goes well beyond economics. It is also about status and identity. The old inner checklist of personal status plus-points – being white, US-born, male, straight – that had compensated traditional blue-collar Americans for a modest education and limited career achievements was already under threat by the 1980s. Reaganomics (lower taxes, smaller government and less regulation) and the new globalizing world order of the 1980s and 1990s, with the replacement of US manufacturing with Chinese imports and offshore outsourcing, were starting to change many working-class lives and communities, undercutting those comforting certainties and pulling people apart.

In *What's the Matter with Kansas?*, published in 2004, the American political writer Thomas Frank speculated about why traditional blue-collar Democrats in his home state were increasingly voting Republican against, as he saw it, their own obvious economic interests. He thought they were turkeys voting for Christmas: tax cuts for the rich and a reduction in welfare – especially, European-style free healthcare. His explanation was that they were responding to emotional red-button issues to oppose liberal causes like feminism and LGBTQ rights, which – together with the Democrats' economic policies – had been framed as un-American, unchristian and socialistic.[27]

By the 1990s, small-town and middle America was also seeing a new world on TV, where very different people – high-achieving women, immigrants, people from ethnic minorities and gays – were apparently doing very well in the big East- and West-coast cities. These people – increasingly visible, partly because the liberal media liked to present them – appealed to the younger, better-educated audiences valued by advertisers and pay-TV companies. Many were 'intersectional' – not just black, female or gay, but more than one of these – *and* college-educated, articulate and middle-class. Even before the explosion of online fake news, Republicans campaigned on all these issues. Their political advertising majored, increasingly, on attacking liberal ideas. 'Liberal' was already a hate-word to many Americans.[28]

In Britain, David Goodhart, the founding editor of *Prospect* magazine, gave a detailed account of traditional white working-class people's increasing resentment in his 2017 book *The Road to Somewhere*.[29] He identified a growing gulf between two stereotypical groups he described as the 'Somewhere' people and the 'Anywhere' types. The Anywheres were highly educated and widely travelled, with 'achieved' identities forged through education and career success. They had valuable portable professional skills and qualifications and they could relate to similar people across the world. The Somewheres were less educated and less well travelled, and had 'ascribed' identities defined by place, community, family and local institutions. They were stuck. Goodhart portrays the Anywheres as smug meritocrats who, because of their achievements, think they know best. For everybody. They see themselves as benign because they're often socially liberal, but they're also economically neo-liberal and naturally globalist. In Goodhart's narrative, the Somewheres – at least half the population – were losing out to the sharp-elbowed Anywheres.[30]

In *Authentocrats*, Joe Kennedy describes how a variety of political commentators across the spectrum, but particularly from the centre–left, now fetishize white working-class opinions on race, immigration and the EU as somehow more 'real' or 'authentic' than everyone else's. He argues that this has enabled some commentators on the right to redirect and exploit genuine working-class grievances through tabloid editorials and shared Facebook posts, using arguments of a kind that these smart commentators would *never* use in their own dialogues.[31]

In Britain, the growth of identity politics after the 1960s – '[t]he personal is political'[32] – made the emerging 'rainbow coalition' on the left ever more fragmented and hard to keep together. Feminist activism, the growth of the LGBTQ lobby and the politics of race and class led to difficult competing priorities for 'progressive' parties like the UK Labour Party. This divide was particularly marked between Labour's older, poorer and more socially conservative voters, often in smaller-town northern and coastal constituencies, and the socially liberal, middle-class, big-city converts of the Blair years – the 1990s and pre-crash 2000s.

'We're Not in Kansas Anymore'

The new angry politics is aimed at people's deeply held – and sometimes unacknowledged – cultural assumptions, status anxieties and feelings of victimhood: the key idea – eternally promoted by demagogues – is that, if things are tough, it must be because someone else is benefiting at your expense. Many of its protagonists are shadowy, using closed online channels and aliases.

Everything looked different online. Earlier this century, Millennials[33] were confidently creating spaces and personal brands as bloggers and vloggers; inventing new niche positions in a world with low barriers to entry and what looked like a new democracy, a parity of voices, in line with the famous cartoon of a dog with a PC, saying 'On the Internet, nobody knows you're a dog'.[34] The first cohort of these new voices mostly came from the left (in America the 'progressive' left; the US political continuum is different from the UK's). The reference points of identity and lifestyle were more exciting and emotive than traditional social policies and economic facts and figures, the stuff of established media like the BBC. The advertising-funded economic model for bloggers and vloggers was largely based on simply generating as much traffic as possible ('clickbait'). This compounded their other motives for creating a more aggressive online politics offering shock value and entertainment.

Conspiracy Worlds

The Bradford-born half-Iranian playwright Javaad Alipoor premiered his play 'The Believers Are But Brothers' at the Bush

Theatre in west London during late January and early February 2018. It dramatized, to great effect, the striking parallels between two groups of screen-addicted alienated young men who'd joined new communities as online recruits. One group consisted of Muslims signed up to various extreme Islamic cults. The other comprised young Americans who had been recruited online to far-right white supremacist groups.

They were brothers under the skin, subject to similar feelings and insecurities and vulnerable to the same kinds of simple dramatic explanations for complicated problems – and to the excitement of the cause. At its most extreme, one rhetoric is behind the Christchurch and El Paso shootings, while the other is behind the Westminster and Manchester atrocities in Britain. Both groups believe that mainstream media have been lying to them about practically everything. Both see the BBC as a sort of 'deep state' conspiracy against their interests.

In December 2016, Carole Cadwalladr (the investigative journalist we met in Chapter 9), described in two articles how she first came across this whole new underground political universe on the internet, one inhabited by extremists peddling both new and ancient lies. Initially, the particular lie she happened upon was that of Holocaust denial. She writes:

Type this into your Google search bar: 'did the hol'. And Google suggests you search for this: 'Did the Holocaust happen?'

And this is the answer: no. The top result is a link to stormfront. org, a neo-Nazi site, and an article entitled: 'Top 10 reasons why the Holocaust didn't happen'. The third result is the article 'The Holocaust Hoax; IT NEVER HAPPENED'. The fifth is '50 reasons why the Holocaust didn't happen.' The seventh is a YouTube video, 'Did the Holocaust really happen?' The ninth is 'Holocaust Against Jews is a Total Lie – Proof.'[35]

Cadwalladr found that there was a *huge* amount more of the same: right-wing extremists had successfully colonized the digital space around subjects such as Muslims, black people, Jews and women, so that any search results on these topics were directly linked to hate sites. Like most people, Cadwalladr found it deeply shocking. She had had no idea that all this was there on the internet, 'just a few keystrokes away . . . on our laptops, our tablets, our phones'.[36] And almost entirely below the radar of mainstream media – including the BBC. How had all of this come about? The new alt-right warriors had managed to weaponize the internet while no one was watching.

'Steve Bannon's Psychological Warfare Mindfuck Tool'

One of Cadwalladr's December 2016 articles also introduced the reader to Cambridge Analytica (CA),[37] a small, still little-known, London-based data mining and influencing company, owned by the ultra-right-wing hedge-fund billionaire Robert Mercer.[38] But the biggest revelations of all about CA were yet to emerge: how, without their knowledge, thousands of people's social networking data had been used to manipulate the feelings of a large, but unknown number of US voters to try and win the 2016 election for Donald Trump. Six months later, Callwalladr published evidence that Cambridge Analytica had been at the heart of an extensive Brexit campaign network too: one connecting Robert Mercer and Steve Bannon (who was to become President Trump's adviser in 2016) in the US, and Arron Banks (who co-founded and chiefly funded Leave.EU) and Nigel Farage in the UK.[39]

In March 2018, Cadwalladr reported an incendiary series of interviews with Christopher Wylie, the Cambridge Analytica whistleblower, in an *Observer Review* article, in which he ruefully described himself as 'the gay Canadian vegan who somehow ended up creating Steve Bannon's psychological warfare mindfuck tool'. A brilliant young Canadian computer scientist, fascinated by the overlaps between data, politics and culture, Wylie first worked as a data analyst for the Canadian Liberal Party. In 2010, aged twenty, he moved to the UK with the aid of a British Tier 1 visa for exceptional talent to study law at the LSE. During his time there he also worked for the Liberal Democrats as a digital campaign strategist. By 2013 he had dropped law and started a PhD on fashion-trend forecasting at the University of the Arts London (which he was later to abandon after apparently finding his dream job). But his mind was still running on questions about the possible – and potentially profitable – connections between data science and politics:

> I wanted to know why the Lib Dems sucked at winning elections when they used to run the country for most of the 19th century . . . And I began looking at consumer and demographic data to see what united Lib Dem voters . . . And what I found is there were no strong correlations. There was no signal in the data . . . And then I came across a paper about how personality traits could be a precursor to political behaviour, and it suddenly made sense . . . when you think of Lib Dems, they're absent-minded professors and hippies. They're the early adopters . . . they're highly open to new ideas. And it just clicked all of a sudden.

What Wylie had learned was that you could deduce many of people's probable personality traits from their Facebook 'Likes'. And then you could predict their social and political values and beliefs – and work on them.

'Trump Is Like a Pair of Uggs, or Crocs'

At around the same time, another Liberal Democrat connection had made a very important introduction for Wylie: it was to a company called the SCL Group (and also to the CEO of one of its subsidiary companies, SCL Elections), and his new boss-to-be Alexander Nix. The SCL Group was a private contractor with operations in both elections and defence (with a particular speciality in psychological operations, or psyops), and Wylie became its research director. He relates how, in autumn 2013, he met Steve Bannon, then chairman of the alt-right Breitbart News, which Bannon had recently brought to Britain to support his friend Nigel Farage in his mission to take the UK out of the EU. They discussed not only SCL's use of data, but culture as well. Wylie's recent foray into trend-forecasting had set him thinking about the introduction of new political ideas. He told Bannon that politics was like fashion:

> [Bannon] got it immediately. He believes in the whole Andrew Breitbart doctrine that politics is downstream from culture, so to change politics you need to change culture. And fashion trends are a useful proxy for that. Trump is like a pair of Uggs, or Crocs, basically. So how do you get from people thinking 'Ugh. Totally ugly' to the moment when everyone is wearing them? That was the inflection point he was looking for.

Bannon pitched the idea of using SCL to Robert Mercer and his daughter Rebekah. Next, Wylie and Nix flew to New York to meet the Mercers. Rebekah Mercer, in particular, enthusiastically latched on to Wylie's pitch: 'She was like, "Oh we need more of your type [i.e. gays] on our side!" . . . She loved the gays. So did Steve. He saw us as early adopters. He figured, if you can get the gays on board, everyone else will follow.'

Cadwalladr's article also tells the broader Cambridge Analytica story. How two Cambridge University psychology researchers, Michal Kosinski and David Stillwell, had devised a free Facebook app called myPersonality, a self-assessment quiz enabling users to see where they fell on each of the 'big five' personality traits: openness, conscientiousness, extroversion, agreeableness and neuroticism. How myPersonality went viral, and 40 per cent of its users agreed to give the researchers access to their full Facebook profiles. How, from the correlations in this set of data (personality traits and Facebook 'Likes'), Kosinski and Stillwell were able to predict the personalities and many of the political attitudes of *other* Facebook users, based solely on their 'Likes'.[40] This pioneering research was published by a top, peer-reviewed academic journal.[41] It was this four-page paper which had inspired Wylie. Kosinki and Stillwell's work was then replicated by another Cambridge University psychologist, Aleksandr Kogan,[42] who sold it to SCL,[43] which was then reconfigured to commercialize it. SCL had political clients around the world. At first, it was mostly used to hijack elections in developing countries. It was then taken up by the US military and then (rebranded as Cambridge Analytica) by the Republicans. It offered 'information services' – a euphemism for changing people's minds, not through overt rational persuasion, but covertly, by tapping into their emotions using false conspiracy theories, hints, rumours and other disinformation. For Cambridge Analytica's campaigns to be effective, their true source – and funding – had to be concealed. Above all, target voters had to be misled into believing that the messages – carefully designed to resonate with their views, values and emotions – came from like-minded private individuals within their own communities. For example, during the 2016 US presidential election campaign, as a voter identified from your profile as, say, a white evangelical Christian (a key segment of voters whose support it was important to win, which, overwhelmingly, Trump did),[44] you might receive a message that – crucially – appeared to come from another evangelical, showing a very white Jesus (with no hint of his Jewishness) and a red devil with Hillary Clinton's face, both gloved up in a boxing ring, and the instruction, 'If you want Jesus to win, press Like and share with your friends'.[45] What Cambridge Analytica did, with great success, was to discover how to deploy this kind of approach, combining data-analytic targeting, deception (about the source) and visceral messaging.

However, almost everything else about the Cambridge Analytica story is confusing. (It's presumably meant to be.) Much of it is also contested.[46] Did Cambridge Analytica actually work on the UK referendum? Having appeared as part of the team at the launch of Leave.EU (and despite Andy Wigmore – Arron Banks' co-organizer – having told Carole Cadwalladr that they had done so), Banks and Wigmore later denied it when it looked as if their involvement might be illegal under British electoral law. But what is clear is that Cadwalladr's exploration also uncovered Cambridge Analytica's many connections to other, hidden bases of power, stretching from the UK to the USA to Russia. She describes that story as a kind of nexus, 'one point of focus through which we can see all these relationships in play': 'Because what is happening in America and what is happening in Britain are entwined. Brexit and Trump are entwined. The Trump administration's links to Russia and Britain are entwined'.[47]

There is a curious triangulation between Putin, Trump and Conservative Brexiteers. Trump's links to Russian business interests (which, under Putin, are inseparable from the Russian state) go back to the 1980s. By the time of the 2016 US presidential election, he and his associates had an extensive Russian network.[48] The British investigative journalist Luke Harding, Kathleen Hall Jamieson (director of the Annenberg Public Policy Center at the University of Pennsylvania), *The New York Times* and others, including the Mueller Enquiry, have uncovered clear evidence of large-scale covert Russian interference in the 2016 US election and multiple contacts between Trump's campaign team and Russian officials, including intelligence officials.[49]

Number Ten's Suppression of the ISC Report on Russian Interference in the UK

These connections may explain Boris Johnson's suppression of the parliamentary Intelligence and Security Commission (ISC)'s report on Russian interference in the UK (for a full *nine months* after it was cleared for publication by the intelligence and security agencies in October 2019). Prior to that, the ISC, then chaired by the Conservative MP Dominic Grieve, had spent eight months preparing the report, which was completed by March 2019 and fully cleared (suitably redacted) in October, well before the December 2019 election. But Boris Johnson halted it in a Trump-like act of prime ministerial fiat.

After the election, a new Parliament would normally mean the appointment of a new ISC as quickly as possible, to minimize the amount of time during which there was no parliamentary oversight of the Intelligence and Security services. So the fact that until July 2020 the ISC remained the only major parliamentary committee not to have been appointed was widely remarked on in Westminster.[50] To add insult to injury, with the new ISC still not in place – and the March 2019 Russia report still unpublished – Johnson appointed as National Security Adviser (a key, highly sensitive role) David Frost, a political appointee with no national security experience and whose day job was as the UK's chief Brexit negotiator – hardly a part-time role.[51] Finally, in July 2020, Number Ten sought to appoint as the new ISC chairman Chris Grayling, a former minister known for a string of failures – most famously, the award of a multimillion-pound government contract to a ferry company with no ferries – and, again, with no previous intelligence experience. This was almost universally seen as an attempt by Johnson and Cummings to weaken the committee and reduce its ability to hold the government to account.[52] However, the new committee members staged a coup, electing as their chairman the highly respected (right-wing and Brexit-supporting, but independent-minded) Conservative MP Julian Lewis – who, unlike Grayling, did have relevant experience – and then unanimously deciding to publish the report before the summer parliamentary recess. (To punish Lewis, the PM immediately banished him from the Conservative MPs in Parliament, just as he also had done to the previous ISC chairman, Dominic Grieve.)[53]

The report, heavily redacted throughout, was remarkable not so much for its juicy revelations as for its very robust conclusions, namely that successive Conservative prime ministers and the UK intelligence and security services had all studiously avoided looking into Russian interference of all kinds and failed to carry out any initiatives either to defend UK elections and the Scottish and EU referendums from such interference or even to investigate them after the event. The government therefore appears to have had no idea of the Russian impacts on the Scottish Referendum, the European Referendum, the 2017 election – or the 2019 one.[54] It was therefore able to say that no evidence of Russian meddling had been found, precisely because no one had looked for it! The report strongly recommended that there should be an urgent government investigation into these issues (a recommendation which the government immediately rejected).[55]

The BBC: Missing in Action?

There was an unspoken question hanging in the air at the press conference to launch the ISC report on 21 July 2020 – where was the BBC? Carole Cadwalladr had uncovered multiple connections between Putin's Russia, the Trump election campaign and the 2016 Brexit campaign, and others had reported evidence supporting her claims. But the BBC had been part of what appeared to be a wider conspiracy of silence about the Brexit part of this network. As the *Guardian* columnist Nick Cohen wrote in the *New European* on 19 July 2018, 'What is the point of the BBC if it is frightened of journalism?'[56]

Perhaps the last word on this should go to Cadwalladr herself. In her articles from late 2016 to early 2018, she always emphasized the importance of what had *also* been exposed alongside those shadowy networks which reach between Russia, the UK and the USA: the manipulation of the minds of so many, via internet search engines infiltrated by the hate sites of the alt-right; and social media messages directly targeted at people's sensibilities with the intention of changing their minds –'a critical and gaping hole in the political debate in Britain'.[57]

Social media really do foster fake news. To bad actors, they offer an unprecedented combination of scale, speed, targeting, the ability to adopt false identities and – if the messages go viral – outstanding value for money. False conspiracy theories and other emotive lies are often widely shared and are much harder to spot, fact-check and challenge on social media than in traditional media.[58] Large-scale online disinformation, much of it from or on behalf of state actors, is a massive challenge to liberal democracies – and to the BBC and other media that value accuracy and impartiality.[59] The new fragmenting, polarizing media ecology means that 'holding the centre' is becoming harder, as is providing an adequate response to false narratives – rebuttal of which, in any case, won't convince those most likely to have been taken in. Nevertheless, as the UK's most trusted news source, the BBC should always be in the forefront in the battle for the truth.

The Great Replacement Theory – Not a Joke

In 2018, Professor John Naughton and his colleagues at Cambridge University's Centre for Research in the Arts, Social

Sciences and Humanities (CRASSH) described the growing belief in conspiracy theories across the Western world. He argued that the internet had turned many (formerly mocked) marginal conspiracy fringe ideas into mainstream concerns, 'weaponizing' them and making them far more toxic.[60]

An important example is the 'great replacement plan' conspiracy theory which claims that white populations in the West are being deliberately replaced by Muslim immigrants in a long-term process of 'genocide by substitution' whose end point, in some versions, includes the imposition of Sharia law. This is supposedly happening under the direction of a shadowy liberal, globalist elite which is sometimes identified as Jewish. In 2018, 31 per cent of Brexit voters and 41 per cent of Trump voters believed in the great replacement theory, while only 6 per cent of Remainers and 3 per cent of Clinton voters believed it.[61]

The great replacement theory sounds mad to most people. It would be laughable if belief in it were not so widespread and it had no practical consequences. However, the CRASSH research suggests it may have had a significant, and possibly decisive, influence on both the Brexit referendum and the 2016 US presidential election. It also formed the basis of the Christchurch and El Paso shooters' 'manifestos' and the motivation of other alt-right killers, including Anders Breivik in Norway.[62] It is a staple of hard-right chatrooms.

This single example shows that the festering online, underground culture war seemed to have surfaced at scale as a sharp divide in British politics, as well as in many other countries. It is the kind of issue the BBC finds hard to address – or even to acknowledge. Instead, in response to constant claims from the right that it is censoring 'conservative voices', it routinely invites some of the more house-trained ones – younger think-tankers and political website types such as Kate Andrews (Institute of Economic Affairs), Dia Chakravarty (TaxPayers' Alliance and Brexit editor of the *Daily Telegraph*) and the ubiquitous Brexiteer

Isabel Oakeshott – to appear in its programmes, especially *Question Time* and *Newsnight*.[63] This is all very liberal and broad-minded, but more dangerous than it appears, because even the most house-trained right-wing spokespeople often – wittingly or unwittingly – promulgate disinformation from the anti-democratic far right.

Angela Nagle described something similar in her 2017 book about the online US culture war, *Kill All Normies*:

> Before the overtly racist alt-right were widely known, the more mainstream alt-light largely flattered it, gave it glowing write-ups in Breitbart and elsewhere, had its spokespeople on their YouTube shows and promoted them on social media. Nevertheless, when Milo's[64] sudden career implosion happened later,[65] they didn't return the favor, which I think may be setting a precedent for a future in which the playfully transgressive alt-light unwittingly play the useful idiots for those with much more serious political aims. If this dark, anti-Semitic, race segregationist ideology grows in the coming years, with their vision of the future that would necessitate violence, those who made the right attractive will have to take responsibility for having played their role.[66]

The BBC has an excruciatingly difficult balancing act to achieve: not only maintaining its unbiased stance, but also investigating and exposing conspiracy theories and hate speech, while not being seen to give them extra publicity. And, of course, it's not protected from disinformation campaigns itself either.

#DefundTheBBC: Genuine 'Grassroots' – or US-Style Astroturf?

On the evening of Sunday 7 June 2020, James Yucel, an eighteen-year-old student from Glasgow University, launched a new

Twitter campaign[67] from his bedroom in Ipswich. He tweeted, 'I'm just a student that's fed up so I've founded this movement to #DefundTheBBC.' The claim was that #DefundTheBBC was a spontaneous grassroots campaign for ordinary people who'd had enough of the BBC's general awfulness. Amazingly, an alert journalist at the *Daily Express* picked up the story first thing on the Monday morning. By 10:02, he'd already managed to interview Yucel and write and file his copy – later revised to report that, by 17:05, #DefundTheBBC had already attracted 30,000 followers. Yucel was quoted as saying, 'And yeah, I think the people have had enough really . . . Because, let's be honest, they can't ignore us forever.'[68]

Meanwhile, Dan Wootton, executive editor of the *Sun*, had also found time in his busy schedule that day to promote the campaign on Twitter, interview Yucel on talkRADIO *and* add 'No wonder a new campaign to Defund the BBC has gained such momentum over the past 48 hours' to a standard-issue *Sun* article, one misleadingly claiming that the Corporation had 'virtually ignored' violence by some Black Lives Matter protesters.[69]

By the Thursday, #DefundTheBBC, launched 'completely on a whim', had attracted a remarkable 62,000 followers. Yucel 'didn't really expect it to go big . . . I'm just a kid with a laptop frustrated at the way the BBC conducts themselves.'[70] However, #DefundTheBBC may have been a bit less spontaneous than Yucel's protestations suggested. Several commentators soon noted that the chorus of right-wing voices promoting it within its first few hours had all the hallmarks of a coordinated US-style astroturf campaign.[71] An analysis of the campaign's online 'epidemiology' by Steven Barnett and Doug Specht (Westminster University) suggested that these suspicions were well justified. Many of #DefundTheBBC's followers were anonymous – including one who tagged it nearly 150 times – making it hard to tell who they really were, and some apparently showed 'bot' characteristics. Many were Tommy Robinson

supporters or featured messages such as 'Enoch Powell was
right!' and 'African gangs of violent young men are terrorising
our communities with impunity'. The main common theme
was, naturally, hostility to the BBC, based on most of the criticisms we've discussed in this book – its alleged bias, wastefulness
and remoteness from ordinary people – and the supposed evils
of the licence fee, which supporters were urged not to pay. The
other common theme was support for Brexit, mostly from
accounts linked to the official Leave.EU site. Based on their
analysis, Barnett and Specht concluded that 'the campaign
wanted to look like a spontaneous eruption of popular anger. In
practice it looks like a suspiciously coordinated operation.'[72]

By mid-July, Yucel had raised £30,000 in donations from
125 people, an average of £240 per person – 50 per cent more
than the TV licence fee and implausibly high for a genuine
grassroots campaign without some big backers.[73] With this
funding, #DefundTheBBC 'had an official launch after morph-
ing into a full-blown campaign operation', according to a
sponsored story on the conservative website Guido Fawkes.[74]
Yucel hired staff, booked some large poster sites and had posters
designed, printed and displayed, all in record time. There was a
clever, jokey new 'DEFUND THE BBC' logo in which the
BBC's own logo was in mirror writing, making it look a bit Russian and distinctly dodgy. All this was enthusiastically reported
in right-leaning sources – especially the *Daily* and *Sunday Express*,
with *seven* articles between 8 June and 19 July.[75] One of Yucel's
main criticisms of the BBC was that it platformed 'left-wing'
people without explaining their political background to the
viewers and listeners. Yet his own, endlessly repeated, claim to
be 'just a student in his room' was itself highly misleading. In
reality, he was already a seasoned, media-savvy, well-connected
Conservative activist, both at home in Ipswich and at university.[76] In January 2020, unhappy at Tory infighting after their
huge election victory, he had created the *Tory Hunger Games*. The

plan was for twelve pairs of Twitter-active Tories, each with a witty factional label based on his analysis of their tweets ('the hacks', 'Northerners', 'Blukips', 'villains', etc.) to compete in a virtual *Hunger Games* – a death match, based on the dystopian 2012 science fiction movie, that picks off people (represented by their avatars) until only the winning pair remains.[77] It's unclear if the *Tory Hunger Games*, scheduled for 6–9 February 2020, actually happened.

Just days before launching #DefundTheBBC, Yucel had been working as an intern for his local Conservative MP, Tom Hunt.[78] Hunt had just been elected for the first time in December 2019. His first act was to join the hard-Brexit-supporting ERG group of Conservative MPs.[79] It was doubtless thanks to Yucel's Brexit connections that, on the first morning of the #DefundTheBBC campaign, he was already able to publish a piece publicizing it on Arron Banks' hard-right Westmonster site.[80] Based on the evidence, #DefundTheBBC certainly *appears* to be a textbook US-style astroturf campaign, involving well-connected, media-savvy young people backed by political professionals and obscure funding – albeit on a much smaller scale than we might see in the US. Its attack on the BBC is exactly in line with what Dominic Cummings has been advocating.

Ignore It at Your Peril

The BBC's approach to news can look decidedly slow when compared with the 'moronic inferno'[81] of online and cable news. The BBC's main evening bulletins inevitably tend to lead with stories that have already been widely covered online, including by the BBC itself. It completely avoids the sugar rush of, say, *Fox News* or the progressive US YouTube channel *Young Turks*, with their informal presentation, stylish young presenters, clear positions and strong language. And a key element in the perfect storm in which it sits today is the increasing flight of younger audiences from its channels, and from 'linear' TV generally – to a media diet they've chosen for themselves, including Netflix and YouTube and a lot else besides. To keep them engaged, the BBC must address the changing technologies and lifestyles of the young, as Ofcom has noted.[82] And the Corporation acknowledges it – its own research says the same.

More important still, this new group has been looking and learning and changing over the last decade. These younger cohorts are also much more in tune than older generations with the global culture war discussed in this chapter. They are more familiar with the ideas and the language, although they are generally more socially liberal than older generations and less likely to believe in false conspiracy theories such as the great replacement one. Nevertheless, this type of disinformation – overwhelmingly driven online as most mainstream media won't touch it – has almost certainly encouraged extreme acts and affected political outcomes across the West. The culture war really matters.

The BBC has been accused of ignoring important emerging concerns around Brexit because of its 'metropolitan/Establishment' worldview. If it continues to ignore the culture wars, the outcome could be even more damaging. 'Gen Z' increasingly looks for different types of media content in different ways and relies less and less on the BBC, and because of the deep funding cuts since 2010, the Corporation has limited resources to deploy in response.

What happens if the BBC's online nemesis actually turns out to be a new situation where neither alt-right ideology nor direct commercial rivalry matter as much as changing lifestyles and technologies, reducing the BBC to growing irrelevance as younger age groups desert it? What if the BBC survives the cultural gang warfare only to run under a passing bus?

Conclusion: We Have a Choice

The BBC is at a crossroads. Down one path lies a BBC reduced in impact and reach in a world of global giants. Down the other path is a strong BBC helping to bind the country together at home and champion it abroad.

BBC Director-General Tony Hall, address to staff, March 2015.[1]

When we began work on this book in April 2018, there was already a strong case that the BBC was under long-term threat because of technology and consumption trends, cumulative funding cuts and endless attacks by left- and, especially, right-leaning critics and competitors. (The imbalance between left- and right-wing attacks has turned out to be even greater than we realized: the deliberate, systematic 'war against the BBC' is waged *overwhelmingly* by the right).

Two recent factors now make the case even stronger and more urgent. First, Boris Johnson is the most hostile prime minister the BBC has ever faced, and with much less respect for democratic checks and balances than the other famously critical PM, Margaret Thatcher.[2] Mrs Thatcher was almost as hostile to the BBC as Mr Johnson, but her gung-ho instincts were moderated by her deputy prime minister, Willie Whitelaw. In marked contrast, Mr Johnson's chief strategist and enforcer is Dominic Cummings, a very different kind of Conservative from Whitelaw (and, so far, *untouchable* – as the government's response to his breaches of its coronavirus lockdown rules showed)[3] Cummings wants to destroy the BBC by systematically discrediting, undermining and defunding it. He said so, several times over, in his 2004 blog.[4] No messing about, no subterfuge or euphemisms: he wanted an American-style media ecology, dominated by a Fox News-type of TV news channel, a chain of Rush Limbaugh-style shock-jock right-wing phone-in radio stations and an end to the ban on political TV advertising. And all explicitly for party political reasons. Cummings has never repudiated these arguments – and he has recently shown himself to be even more hostile to the BBC than the PM.[5]

The second new factor is that the Voice of the Listener and Viewer has now shown that, by 2019, the 2010 and 2015 cuts imposed by George Osborne had already reduced the real (inflation-adjusted) public funding of the BBC's UK services by 30 per cent – more than even we had realized.[6]

As we go to press (August 2020), the BBC faces even more threats: new attacks such as #DefundTheBBC; the (largely confected) furore about free TV licences being restricted to households with a member aged seventy-five-plus and receiving Pension Credit (and the lies about what was agreed in 2015); the current government consultation on whether to decriminalize licence-fee evasion, only five years after this was rejected by a Conservative-appointed independent review; the imminent appointment of a new BBC chairman, chosen by the government; and the BBC Charter mid-term review, due in 2022, including a new five-year funding deal. Most people would now agree that the Corporation is in real, perhaps existential, peril. Where they disagree is on whether losing it (or having it reduced to a minor sideshow like PBS in America) – the eventual end point if the cuts and attacks continue as now – will be good or bad for the country. These issues come into sharp relief if we compare the BBC's situation with that of another great British institution, the NHS.

The BBC and the NHS: Two Great British Institutions under Pressure

Both the BBC and the NHS are widely seen as two of Britain's most important institutions – and both are now under severe, and growing, financial pressure. If we want future generations to enjoy free, universal access to their services, and for those services to be funded at a level that maintains their quality, we need to take urgent action to ensure their long-term sustainability. Everyone sort-of knows that, although they're much clearer about it in the case of the NHS. But there are two big differences between the challenges they face. The first is to do with what is driving the pressure.

The demand on the NHS reflects factors largely beyond anyone's control.[7] Very little of it comes from deliberate attacks or misinformation. The NHS doesn't face deep funding cuts, or regulations intentionally designed to reduce its ability to innovate and compete, to limit its impact on commercial suppliers.[8] But the Corporation faces all of these, on top of rapidly rising costs. And the BBC has many (and powerful) enemies. The NHS has not. Moreover, when people do explicitly criticize the NHS, they are also far more likely to be challenged than if they attack the BBC. For instance, when the right-wing Conservative MEP Daniel Hannan castigated the NHS in a series of interviews on US television in 2009, his party leader David Cameron immediately reaffirmed the Tories' support for it, branding his comments as 'eccentric'.[9] In contrast, when Hannan gleefully – and somewhat misleadingly – wrote in October 2019 that 'even' Nicky Morgan, the centre–right Conservative Culture Secretary, had said the TV licence fee was unsustainable – throwing in a few standard complaints about the BBC's supposed left–liberal bias at the same time – no one batted an eyelid.[10]

Again, after the December 2019 election (but before Covid-19 hit the NHS), the Johnson government, with an eighty-seat majority, immediately announced a large, and legally binding, increase in NHS spending aimed especially at appealing to first-time Conservative voters who had traditionally voted Labour.[11] Concurrently, as we have seen, it unleashed a new wave of attacks on the BBC and its (already much reduced) funding.

'You're Far Too Wet'

It isn't surprising that years of relentless attacks have given the BBC something of a bunker mentality, but it should sometimes be more assertive in its response. Sir Alan Moses, former chairman of the press regulator IPSO, put it perfectly on the *Today* programme in January 2020: 'Well, what a strange irony it is that there's a Prime Minister as a journalist who conceives of it as reasonable to criticise what the BBC has done. My view is that you're far too wet about it. I think you ought to be far more stringent in striking back at the attacks.'[12]

The headline figure in the government's announced increase in NHS funding was £33.9 billion by 2023–24.[13] This is serious money. It brings us to the second big difference between the NHS and the BBC: their vastly different scale. The NHS spent over £150 billion of central government money in 2018–19,[14] almost fifty times the £3.2 billion net public funding of the BBC.[15] In terms of headcount, the difference is even greater: the NHS' 1.4 million (full-time-equivalent) figure is *sixty-two times* more than the BBC's 22,400 full-time-equivalent headcount (see Figure 15.1).[16]

Because the challenges facing the NHS are largely beyond anyone's control and because of its vast scale and complexity, ensuring its long-term sustainability while maintaining its quality of service (and, now, increasing its resilience to future pandemics too) will be a hugely expensive, difficult and – realistically – neverending task. In comparison, ensuring the sustainability and service quality of the BBC is relatively easy and straightforward, and the cost will be minimal – if we can make it clear that's what we want. *We have a choice.*

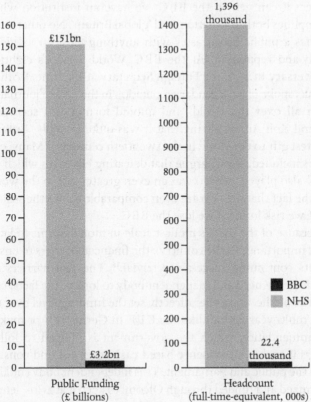

Figure 15.1
NHS versus BBC: Public Funding and Headcount 2017–18

Sources: House of Commons Library, Full Fact and 'BBC annual report and accounts 2018–19'.

Safeguarding Britain's Political Health and Place in the World

As Brexit becomes reality, the UK will not only need to pull together and rebuild the public's mutual tolerance and its trust in facts and institutions, it will also need all the international respect it can get. In the BBC we have an institution which exemplifies both 'one nation' and 'global Britain'. No other country has a public broadcaster with anything close to its global reach and reputation. At the BBC World Service's eightieth anniversary in 2012, the Foreign Secretary at the time, William Hague, spoke of its 'legendary reputation in the eyes of journalists from all over the world' and quoted former UN secretary-general Kofi Annan saying that it was quite possibly 'Britain's greatest gift to the world in the twentieth century'.[17] Many, ourselves included, would argue that defeating Hitler (in which the BBC also played its part) was an even greater gift to the world. But the fact that the two are even comparable shows the scale of what we risk losing if we lose the BBC.

Because of the BBC's modest scale in money terms (relative to its importance to the country), the financial barriers to ensuring its continuing success are trivial.[18] The real barriers are political. We need an independent body to look at the facts, consult the public, and either directly set the funding level over the next multi-year period, like the KEF in Germany,[19] or make a recommendation which the government is obliged to follow unless it makes an evidence-based case against it and consults both the public and Parliament. This independent body could be organized and funded through Ofcom, to keep it at arms' length from the government.

Although the main threat to the BBC's long-term sustainability is the deep funding cuts since 2010, the constraints placed on it to reduce its market impact are a further challenge to its ability to innovate and deliver its remit over the long term. The lessons of Project Kangaroo and, less well known, the earlier halting of the online service for children and schools BBC Jam in 2007, both discussed in Chapter 11, still appear not to have been fully learned. The whole nation loses if we hamstring the BBC's, and other PSBs', ability to innovate and develop.

This is not an imaginary problem. In 2018, nine years after

Project Kangaroo, the BBC planned to bring the iPlayer into line with the rest of the market, the expectations of younger viewers, and what audiences were asking for, mainly by changing it from a thirty-day catch-up service to one where downloaded programmes would be available for a year, and by increasing the number of box sets and making other improvements. Ofcom, understandably, decided that this package of proposals was 'material'. As the BBC's regulator, it was therefore *required* to put it through the full process of public interest tests, stakeholder consultation and analysis, and then to decide if the public value it would create justified any possible adverse impact on the BBC's competitors. It eventually gave the proposals the go-ahead – but the whole regulatory process delayed the improvements by *twelve months*. This is a market where the US tech companies, with no such regulation, are able to update their platforms every *week*.[20] Imposing this disproportionate level of bureaucracy on the BBC's ability to innovate is an extraordinary interpretation of the public interest, which appears either to prioritize (mainly US-owned) commercial interests over the UK public or simply to reflect free-market dogma. The BBC has asked for three changes to bring its regulation into line with the realities of today's market: (i) Define the TV market to cover *all* broadcast and online TV and video, including SVoD, (ii) Require Ofcom to intervene only when there is actual evidence of harm, rather than just a hypothetical possibility and (iii) Find ways to make the regulatory process much faster.[21] We agree with all three.

The relationship between politicians and the BBC is a fractious one at best, and always has been. In general, expecting politicians, of any stripe, to start admitting that the BBC's coverage is accurate and largely impartial – or accepting its political coverage without complaining or even threatening it – is about as realistic as expecting your cat or dog to ignore birds and squirrels. Nonetheless, everyone across the (remotely respectable) political spectrum now sees online lies and conspiracy theories as a threat to the cohesiveness and security of our democracy and society. For instance, if and when we finally have a safe, effective, widely available Covid-19 vaccine, how many people will refuse it – putting themselves and everyone else at risk – because they believe long-discredited anti-vaccination conspiracy theories – or perhaps even think that the pandemic is itself a hoax or conspiracy?

The BBC – with its universality and inclusiveness, its professionalism, its unrivalled global journalist network and its high public trust – despite all the efforts to undermine it – is an obvious safeguard against these challenges. It is widely accepted that it is in the UK's own interest that, as far as possible, people living under authoritarian regimes around the world should have access to accurate and impartial news and, despite cuts and the best efforts of hostile regimes, the BBC still manages to provide this more successfully than anyone else – it now reaches over 400 million people outside Britain each week.[22]

Confirmation of the BBC's success in bolstering democracy comes from a recent Zurich University study comparing eighteen countries' resilience to online disinformation. The scale and status of their PSBs was one of five key factors associated with greater resilience: 'in countries with wide-reaching public service media, citizens' knowledge about public affairs is higher compared to countries with marginalised public service media'. The most resilient countries were in northern and western Europe, led by the Nordics – closely followed by the UK, thanks to the strength of its PSBs. Southern European countries such as Spain, Italy and Greece were markedly more credulous. And the USA was in a category of its own, with a population 'particularly susceptible to disinformation campaigns – and its peculiar contextual conditions make it a unique case'.[23] These conditions include, of course, weak, badly funded PSBs, a dominant TV news broadcaster (namely Fox News) with no commitment to impartiality and a plethora of populist right-wing radio shock-jocks: *precisely* the divisive mix Dominic Cummings advocated for Britain in his notorious 2004 blog posts.[24]

'It's the Money, Stupid'

Everyone knows the BBC is in peril. Ask them why, and they'll give you a list: they may say it's too big and does too many things; it wastes money on celebrity pay and mink-lined offices for senior managers; it's lost the public's trust after decades of left-wing – or right-wing (or, more recently, pro- or anti-Brexit) – bias; it's too London-centric; its licence-fee funding is no longer fit for purpose when people can subscribe to whichever TV services they want; it's at war with the government, Rupert Murdoch and most of the newspapers; or it's doomed anyway because of technology and consumption trends, as young people now only watch Netflix and YouTube. As we've seen, this mish-mash is a mixture of truths, exaggerations, half-truths, myths and lies.

Well-informed people *may* also mention money: the combination of rising content and distribution costs and the funding cuts imposed (with no published analysis, no public consultation and no parliamentary scrutiny) by George Osborne in 2010 and 2015. They may also now mention the additional financial impact of Covid-19, the government's latest attempt to decriminalize licence-fee evasion and the financial and reputational nightmare of free TV licences.

But they almost certainly won't mention the *depth* of the funding cuts. The BBC is indeed facing a wide range of challenges. It will always be accused of bias and it will always face difficult trade-offs. But now – for the first time ever – it is in existential peril from the depth of the funding cuts, at a time of increasing competition and constantly rising content and distribution costs. Even worse, this is not widely understood: everyone knows about Netflix, but no one knows that George Osborne's cuts are a much bigger threat.

Without the huge cuts in its real public funding since 2010, the BBC's annual income would be *almost £1.4 billion* higher, enabling it to do pretty much everything that's demanded of it. Above all, it would be able to invest in new content, services and technologies for younger viewers and listeners. The main way for it to engage with younger audiences is to provide *content* they enjoy and know about – although of course this also needs to be available in ways that fit their new consumption habits (i.e., as far as possible, any time, any place and personalized). This is difficult for all established media, not just the Corporation, but perfectly doable. The BBC has a strong history of innovation: if it's given the financial freedom to do so, it will respond creatively to the challenges of the new digital age. And it's already starting to make progress in its approach to younger viewers: David Clementi reported at the VLV annual conference in November 2019 that he was 'pleased that we can now point to an iPlayer strategy that is starting to deliver: in the space of the last year, iPlayer's reach to young audiences is up by around 20%'. That's clearly progress.[25]

If the BBC is properly funded and its ability to compete is not unduly hampered by excessive red tape designed to protect its competitors from its (greatly overstated) market impact, the chances are that it will successfully deal with the other threats itself – the continuing accusations of bias and the rising technology, consumption and cost trends – as it has consistently done for nearly a century. Ensuring its sustainability will be relatively cheap and straightforward because the financial stakes are so low – a rounding error in the national budget. The trouble is that, right now, the political will isn't there – if anything, the opposite. But maybe you can help change that. Here's how.

'Your BBC Needs YOU': Recommendations to the Reader

Our first recommendation is simply to get as fully informed about the BBC as you can: its role, its funding, its strengths – and its weaknesses too. The issues are more urgent and important than ever. We've done our best to give you the facts, challenging a lot of widely held myths about the BBC. Some are *pretty much complete* myths. Others are *mostly* myths – about issues, like bias, that are inherently more subjective. Having read this book, you should be well equipped to challenge these myths. So let's recap, starting with the 'pretty much complete' myths.

Six Pretty Much Complete Myths about the BBC

1. 'Lots of people don't use the BBC but are still forced to pay the licence fee or go to prison.' In reality, only a tiny (although unknown) number of households pay for the BBC but use none of its services – unlike with many other public services that cost much more. The £157.50 licence fee (equivalent to just 43 pence per day) gives every household member unlimited access to all the BBC's services for a whole year. The only time the BBC's total household reach has been measured, in 2015, it was found that 99 per cent of households used it in just a single week (see Chapter 3). No one goes to prison for licence-fee evasion. A few are sent down each year for not paying the resulting fine, although no one knows how many of them, if any, are jailed *only* for this offence (as opposed to several, such as failure to pay council tax – which is much higher – at the same time). The Conservative-commissioned 2015 Perry Review recommended against decriminalizing licence-fee

287

evasion, describing the current system as 'broadly fair and proportionate'.[26] The (much exaggerated) problems created by licence-fee evasion being a criminal offence may, in any case, be only a short-term problem, i.e. until we switch to an alternative funding method.

2. 'It's bloated, wasteful and inefficient.' It often seems like that on the inside, as portrayed in the BBC's own spoof fly-on-the-wall documentary *W1A*. But the data say otherwise. As we showed in Chapter 4, the BBC actually puts most of its income into content – mainly original UK content (in which it's by far the biggest investor) and distribution. Its overheads are below the average for media and telecommunications companies. In fact, the way it's maintained the range and quality of its services after the deep funding cuts since 2010 is pretty remarkable.

3. 'It's the best-funded public broadcaster in the world.' No, it isn't: both Japan's NHK and Germany's ARD receive more public funding – see Chapter 5.

4. 'It does things that should be left to the market – crowding out competitors and actually *reducing* choice.' The idea that programmes can be tidily split into 'public service' and 'commercial' is badly flawed both in principle and in practice – remember the dire initial reviews of *The Great British Bake Off*, soon to be the UK's most popular TV programme. And studies of the BBC's market impact have consistently found it to be minimal. The claim that the BBC actually *reduces* choice by 'crowding out' content investment by commercial broadcasters is nonsense.

5. 'In 2015, it agreed to fund free TV licences for all over-seventy-fives but has now reneged on that agreement.' This is simply untrue – see Chapter 5.

6. 'If it didn't overpay its senior managers and star presenters, it could pay much or most of the cost of free TV
licences for all over-seventy-fives.' This, too, is untrue.
The BBC generally pays its managers and presenters
less than the market rate. If, nevertheless, it cut to
£150,000 per annum the pay of everyone currently paid
more than that, the annual saving would be only £20
million – less than 3 per cent of the £750 million annual
cost of free TV licences for all over-seventy-fives (see
Chapter 12).

And here are three widely held beliefs that are *mostly* mythical
though inherently more subjective.

Three Widely Held Beliefs about the BBC That Are Mostly Mythical

1. 'Its news and current affairs coverage is systematically
left-wing.' The evidence from independent academic
research is that the BBC constantly strives to be
impartial in its political coverage and, when it departs
from this, it tends towards *over*-representing the
Establishment, right-leaning view – increasingly so
over the last ten years. Its coverage tends to be biased in
favour of the government of the day, but more so when
the Conservatives are in power.
2. 'It's anti-Brexit.' The only evidence – as opposed to
evidence-free assertions – of anti-Brexit BBC bias
comes from the opaquely funded monitoring organization News-watch. As far as we know, News-watch *never*
publishes its methods and results in peer-reviewed
journals and never debates them. Research by university academics (who *do* publish in peer-reviewed
journals) reaches very different conclusions, suggesting
that the BBC's coverage was largely impartial both

before and after the 2016 EU referendum – and when it was not, it marginally favoured Leave rather than Remain. As with its slight, but systematic, bias to the right, the pro-Brexit bias of the BBC's EU coverage partly reflects the agenda-setting role of the (over-whelmingly right-leaning and pro-Brexit) national press.

3. 'People no longer trust it.' Despite decades of constant attack from right-wing media, politicians and think tanks, the BBC remains by far the nation's most trusted news source. People certainly trust it far more than they trust the politicians and newspapers telling them not to.[27]

The End of the TV Licence?

'Always keep a-hold of Nurse / For fear of finding something worse.'[28] We suggest you don't join those who want to 'keep a-hold of Nurse' and would fight to the last ditch to defend the TV licence. Linking the BBC's core funding to the ownership of a TV set is, increasingly, an anachronism when there are now so many other devices people can use for viewing. Fortunately, there are several better alternatives such as a household levy, as in Germany and Ireland, or a supplement to council tax or electricity bills.

But there are also a couple of potential lions. One of these – advertising – is now more like an old moggy sleeping in the shade. It's no longer a serious threat because its disadvantages are so clear and, mostly, well understood.[29] However, the other potential lion, subscription funding, is still alive and well and widely promoted by the likes of the IEA and #DefundTheBBC. But, because the motivation of those promoting it appears to be a combination of hostility to the BBC and free-market ideology, none of them has ever bothered to think through the practicalities and likely outcomes. Once one does so (see Chapter 10 and Appendix D), the rational case against it is just as strong as the case against advertising. Like advertising, it would fundamentally change the BBC – not only by distorting its incentives but, more importantly, by making it no longer universal. It would also damage the pay-TV companies. However, the biggest disadvantage of replacing the licence fee with subscriptions is that, to maintain the BBC's income (and original UK content investment), the subscription price would need to be much higher than the licence fee – partly to make up for the lost revenue from households choosing not to subscribe, but also because the BBC's overheads would be much higher to cover marketing, billing and customer service costs. Running a subscription business is expensive. Ask Sky.

Although the licence fee (although not its level) is guaranteed until the end of the current BBC Charter in 2027, we think it could and should be replaced sooner – but only by mutual agreement between the government and the BBC, based on rational analysis and evidence. Specifically, the government should commission a genuinely independent review of the range of options for replacing it and their likely outcomes – similar to the Peacock Committee, but explicitly looking across the full range of alternatives, including advertising, subscriptions (for the whole BBC or only a premium package), general taxation and the various options for a universal levy.

Tell People

If you agree with us that the BBC is worth saving, tell your family, friends and colleagues. Join the Voice of the Listener and Viewer,[30] which is non-party-political and does exactly what its title suggests, using rational analysis and evidence. Don't let the myths and lies pass unchallenged from the man or woman in the pub (unless they're really large and belligerent). And tell them why it's worth saving too. Above all, the clue's in the name: it's the *British* Broadcasting Corporation. In reality, it couldn't be more British in both its strengths and its weaknesses. It's owned and directly funded by the British public and it's extremely patriotic. But it's not nationalistic: *The Last Night of the Proms* – recently in the news – includes 'Rule, Britannia', 'Land of Hope and Glory' and a lot of flag-waving, but flags of every nation are welcome. And you, your family, friends and colleagues – and the person in the pub – can be its best allies and supporters: all of you. If we create enough noise and nuisance, then the government will have to listen.

In this book, we've done our best to *inform, educate* and, where possible, *entertain* you. But we hope we've also managed to *enrage* you a bit as well. Despite its faults, the BBC is incalcul-ably valuable to Britain and the world, and we think the war against it, mainly driven by powerful commercial and political vested interests (in many cases, foreign-owned or opaquely funded), is monstrous. We hope you agree – and that you'll do whatever you can to help it not just survive, but thrive, so that future generations in Britain and around the world can still enjoy the priceless benefits of a strong, independent and prop-erly funded BBC.

Appendix A: The 'BBC Deprivation' Study

No one likes paying taxes, but the BBC licence fee is a partial exception: *most* people see it as providing good value for money – despite endless hostile stories over the years about the Corporation's alleged profligacy and inefficiency.

Although surveys suggest more public support for the licence fee than for most taxes, the underlying reality is, if anything, even more positive. Some previous research has suggested that if people were either (i) allowed to reflect overnight on their initial survey responses[1] or (ii) shown the range of practical policy options and given enough time and information to discuss them and give a more considered response,[2] their views of the BBC – and the perceived value for money of the licence fee – became even more positive (or, for some, less negative). It was therefore decided to put this to a stronger test.

In 2014, the BBC commissioned market research agency MTM to explore how people's views of the value for money offered by the licence fee might change if they were 'forced' to spend some time without the BBC.[3] The study took several months and the results were reported in August 2015. It focused especially on the 28 per cent of households who, in an initial survey, said that the licence fee (then £145.50, equivalent to 40p per day) did *not* offer good value for money. Specifically, the researchers talked to seventy households from locations across the UK, split into three sub-groups:

1. Twenty-four households representing the 12 per cent who, in the initial survey, said they'd prefer to *pay nothing and receive no BBC services.*

2. Twenty-four households representing the 16 per cent who initially said they would *willingly only pay less than the current licence fee to receive the BBC's services.*

3. Twenty-two households representing the 69 per cent who initially said they would be *willing to pay at least the current level of the licence fee to continue receiving the BBC's services.*[4]

After nine days with no BBC, having received a cash payment of £3.60 (i.e. 9 x 40p) in return, thirty-three of the forty-eight households in the first two groups changed their minds and decided that the licence fee *did* represent good value for money after all. Conversely, just one of the twenty-two households in the third group, who initially said it was good value for money, went the other way, saying that, having lived without the BBC for the nine days, they'd prefer to continue doing so and save the cost of the licence fee.

It would be useful if the MTM study could be repeated in today's market, with more households and perhaps over a longer time period. But the result in 2015 was completely clear-cut: *more than two-thirds* (33/48 = 69 per cent) of the *minority* of households (28 per cent) who, in the well-conducted initial survey, had said that they saw the licence fee as either slightly or very poor value for money changed their minds after just nine days living without the BBC. The reasons they gave were that they:

- missed the BBC much more in their daily routines than they had expected;
- felt it had unique content and services that they could not get elsewhere;
- realized it provided a high level of quality versus the alternatives, which they had not previously appreciated;
- became frustrated at the amount of advertising on other services;

- were surprised by the range of BBC services (not all had known that BBC Radio and Online were included in the cost of the licence fee); and
- felt the BBC played a more important role in UK life and the national conversation than they had originally realized.

For instance, in the initial survey, one participant in the group who had responded initially that they would prefer to pay nothing and receive no BBC services had said at the same time: 'I think it's awful because the way I look at it is that I pay for Sky already. I think it's unfair. Everybody is moving with the times, and the BBC still . . . expects us to pay £145, £149 yearly . . . for what?' However, this participant was one of the two-thirds of initially anti-BBC respondents who changed their minds during the study, commenting at the end: 'That's for nine days? That's kind of cheap, isn't it? Surprisingly! £3.60 for nine days? That's peanuts really. That's affordable . . . In all honesty we do get a wealth of good programmes. We might be selective in what we watch but it is an integral part of our everyday existence . . . It would be weird if there was [*sic*] no BBC channels.'[5]

Appendix B: The Academic Research on BBC Bias

'In God we trust. All others must bring data.'

    Attributed to quality management guru W. Edwards Deming

There are two key questions on whether the BBC's news and current affairs coverage is biased. First, is it systematically biased to the left or the right and, if so, in which direction and to what extent (the main question for many years)? Secondly, is it systematically biased for or against Brexit and, if so, in which direction and to what extent (a significant issue in recent years)?

As we've seen, most of the BBC's critics and enemies are right-leaning and pro-Brexit. To them, the answers to both questions are self-evident: the BBC's news coverage is obviously biased to the left and anti-Brexit (and, therefore, it needs to be 'sorted out'). But, beyond anecdotes and general impressions, what is the evidence based on rigorous research?

The most reliable evidence – mainly on the first question, but also on the second and several others[1] – is from academic research in UK university departments of communication or journalism. However, this research is highly fragmented. Academics do sometimes write review articles and books which pull together and evaluate the scholarly research on a particular topic. These are extremely useful and often highly cited (albeit mainly by other academics). But, unfortunately, we have been unable to find anything close to a comprehensive academic review on the impartiality/bias of the BBC.

To illustrate the issues, we therefore focus here on just some of the research, mainly at Cardiff University's School of Journalism, Media and Culture, the largest academic group working on impartiality in UK broadcast news.[2]

Measuring Bias/Impartiality

As we've noted, the consistent and reliable accuracy of the BBC's news and current affairs coverage has never been seriously questioned by anyone with evidence to support the allegation. In fact, the *only* material case we know where the BBC got its facts wrong, at least in recent years, was the November 2012 *Newsnight* programme falsely accusing Lord McAlpine of having been a paedophile (albeit without naming him) which triggered George Entwistle's resignation as DG.

The contested issue isn't the Corporation's accuracy, but rather its impartiality – specifically its choice of which topics to cover, how its journalists frame and discuss those topics, the selection of commentators (politicians, experts, the general public, etc.) representing different views, and how they are introduced and questioned. All these involve editorial judgements that can be open to challenge. The BBC's TV, radio and online journalists make literally thousands of these judgements every day.

Some aspects of impartiality, such as an interviewer's tone of voice, are almost impossible to measure and categorize objectively, especially at scale. So research tends to focus on more tangible and quantifiable indicators such as the number of appearances by interviewees or panellists representing different political positions, parties or views of an issue and how much airtime they are given to argue their case.

Clearly, a challenge for this type of research is how to categorize interviewees and panellists as objectively as possible. In 2013, the Centre for Policy Studies (CPS), a right-wing think tank

founded in 1974 by Margaret Thatcher and her intellectual men-
tor Sir Keith Joseph, based at 57 Tufton Street, attempted to
develop an objective measure of where different UK think tanks
sit on the left-to-right political spectrum. However, its results
illustrate the inherent hazards of this approach, to such an
extent that a more rigorous analysis by Cardiff University led to
exactly opposite conclusions.

The 'Bias at the Beeb?' Study

The CPS study, by economist Dr Oliver Latham, starts with the
apparent puzzle that the UK public still had much higher trust
in the BBC than in other news sources,[3] despite numerous
studies by the CPS itself and other right-wing think tanks
accusing it of left-wing bias on issues ranging from business,
markets, and America[4] to the Euro,[5] and from immigration[6] to
whether its entertainment programmes also betrayed a left-
wing bias.[7]

Latham's explanation of this puzzle is that the reports accusing
the BBC of bias tend to be based on case studies; and that, for
these to be persuasive, the reader needs to trust the researcher
neither to 'cherry-pick' nor to editorialize the cases in a biased
way. He claims that, 'Given that the public holds more trust in the
BBC than it does [in] politicians, print journalists and, one can
only presume, think-tank researchers, these two requirements
are unlikely to hold'.[8] Latham then argues that a partial solution
to this problem is to use a quantitative methodology, singling out
News-watch as the supposed 'pioneer' of such an approach. However, as he rightly says, 'even these studies still rely on subjective
judgments as to which periods to study and deciding what constitutes, for example, a pro-EU or anti-EU voice'.[9]

His solution is to use an ingenious quantitative measure of
media bias developed by US economists Tim Groseclose and

Jeffrey Milyo to minimize the degree of subjective judgement involved.[10] A further benefit of using this approach is that, because much of the analysis is automated, Latham was able to cover every news article on the BBC's website over the three years since the 2010 election (1 June 2010 to 31 May 2013).[11]

Left- and Right-Leaning Think Tanks Cited on BBC Online News

The issue the CPS study addressed is the extent to which BBC Online News referred to left- versus right-leaning think tanks over these three years, using a statistical measure of each think tank's political leaning. The original Groseclose and Milyo study counted mentions by left- and right-leaning members of the American Congress. Latham's equivalent UK measure was mentions in *The Guardian* and the *Telegraph* over the same three years: with those in *The Guardian* assumed to be probably left-leaning and those in the *Telegraph* more likely to be right-leaning. The problem is that this does not distinguish between articles that mention a think tank to praise and publicize its work and those designed to attack it and discredit it.[12]

The resulting list of forty-one think tanks (for which there were sufficient data) ranks them on a continuum from Demos (the most left-leaning, using Latham's measure) to Migration Watch (the most right-leaning). Dr Latham describes this ranking as 'remarkably consistent with conventional wisdom',[13] but with three significant outliers: the largely apolitical National Institute of Economic and Social Research (NIESR) and the Institute for Fiscal Studies (IFS) were both ranked well to the right of centre – further to the right than the Henry Jackson Society, the Adam Smith Institute and several other staunchly right-wing think tanks; and the clearly left-leaning Institute for Public Policy Research (IPPR) was listed even further to the right than these – in fact, just to the right of the CPS itself.

However, there are several other clear anomalies in his

ranking. Chatham House (the Royal Institute of International Affairs) is strictly non-aligned, but he lists it as the third most left-wing of the forty-one think tanks he cites, while the Royal Society of Arts is listed as the ninth most left-wing. The short-lived Centre for Social Cohesion had impeccable right-wing credentials,[14] but sits in the very centre of Latham's list – while both the IEA and the Global Warming Policy Foundation are listed as left-leaning.

The main result in the CPS paper is a slightly higher correlation between think-tank citations on the BBC website and in *The Guardian* (a correlation coefficient of 0.53) than between the BBC and *Telegraph* citations (a correlation coefficient of 0.41).[15] On the basis of this small difference, Latham concludes that 'In a statistical sense, the BBC cites … think tanks "more similarly" [*sic*] to … The Guardian than [to] The Telegraph'.[16] Dr Latham also reported evidence that five left-leaning think tanks[17] were more likely to be described by the BBC as 'independent' and less likely to come with what he called a 'health warning' (describing its position on the issue in question, its general ideology or its party political affiliation) than five right-leaning ones, including the IEA, which his earlier analysis had ranked as left-leaning.[18] However, he does not explain how he selected these ten think tanks from the full list of forty-one, nor whether his five chosen left-leaning ones *really were* more likely to be politically independent than his five chosen right-leaning ones.[19] Nonetheless, the CPS study's conclusions were enthusiastically picked up and disseminated – with no questions about their validity – by the *Mail* and the *Telegraph*.[20]

The 'Think Tanks, Television News and Impartiality' Study

In 2017, Cardiff University professors Justin Lewis and Stephen Cushion addressed almost exactly the same issue in "Think

Tanks, Television News and Impartiality', published in the academic journal *Journalism Studies*.[21] Their paper explores the BBC's impartiality by establishing which think tanks were cited in its news and current affairs TV programmes in 2009, under a Labour government, and in 2015, under the Conservatives, and categorizing them into three groups: left, right and neutral (centrist or non-partisan). Using the BBC's comprehensive Redux archive,[22] Lewis and Cushion searched all the BBC's TV news and current affairs programmes during 2009 and 2015 – a total of over 30,000 programmes. Over 92 per cent were on the BBC News channel (74.9 per cent) or BBC One (17.6 per cent). A total of sixty-seven think tanks were mentioned in one or both of the two years. To categorize them, the authors used an approach developed by Andrew Rich in the US,[23] combining evidence from four sources:

1. The think tank's self-description as left- or right-leaning, where available, e.g. Compass on the left and the Bow Group on the right.
2. Key words or phrases, e.g. 'fairness', 'equality' and 'progressive' tend to be used by left-leaning think tanks, 'free markets' by right-leaning ones.
3. Key ideas, e.g. the think tank's position on tax, immigration or climate change.
4. The party political background of employees, advisory board members and trustees. This includes both politicians and others with clear left- or right-leaning backgrounds.

On this basis, they classified twenty of the sixty-seven think tanks as left-leaning, twenty-seven as neutral (centrist or non-partisan) and twenty as right-leaning. Unlike in the CPS ranking, there were no clear outliers, i.e. left-leaning think tanks categorized as right-leaning or vice versa. But, inevitably, there were some borderline cases. For instance, some on the right would disagree with the Royal United Services Institute (RUSI) being classified as right-leaning and the Social Market Foundation as neutral; while some on the left would see the Electoral Reform Society and the Institute for Government as neutral rather than left-leaning. By far the most important contestable case is the widely cited Institute for Fiscal Studies (IFS) which, using the above criteria, the authors classified as neutral. We agree, but many on the left would, with some justification, describe it as right-leaning because of its position on both corporate and personal taxation and its caution about public investment.[24] As we've seen, it was also ranked as strongly right-leaning in the CPS analysis.[25]

For the great majority of the sixty-seven think tanks, however, the Cardiff academics' classification is clear-cut and certainly much more reliable than the CPS ranking.

What Do the Cardiff Data Say about BBC Bias?

At first glance, the Cardiff classification suggests a remarkable degree of even-handedness by the BBC, with twenty-seven of the sixty think tanks referred to on BBC TV in the neutral category and twenty in each of the others. However, a slightly different picture emerges once the authors add in how many times each think tank was mentioned in each of the two years.

In 2009, there were 926 mentions of a think tank on the list: 16.5 per cent of left-leaning ones, 18.3 per cent of right-leaning ones, and 65.2 per cent of those classified as neutral. This direct measure of selection bias[26] using a much more reliable classification than the CPS's ranking, suggests a very marginal bias towards right-leaning sources on the BBC's news and current affairs programmes in 2009. However, the difference is so small (16.5 per cent left-leaning versus 18.3 per cent right-leaning, a difference of only 1.8 percentage points) as to be immaterial.[27]

In 2015, the total number of times one of the sixty-seven think tanks was mentioned on BBC TV news and current affairs programmes more than doubled from 926 in 2009 to 2,100. This increase is not surprising in an election year, as informing the public is a key part of the Corporation's remit.

However, the percentage distribution of mentions between the three categories had also shifted by 2015. Mentions of the 27 neutral think tanks increased from 65.2 per cent in 2009 to 75.3 per cent (perhaps reflecting the BBC's even greater preference for neutral sources in an election year). But virtually all this increase in the neutrals' share of mentions was at the expense of the left-leaning think tanks, which received only 8.5 per cent of the mentions in 2015, versus 16.2 per cent for the right-leaning ones – a difference of 7.7 percentage points (Figure B.1).

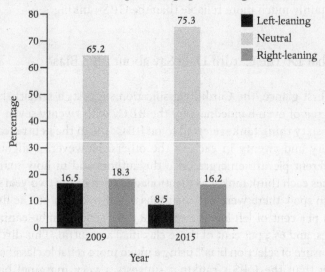

Figure B.1

Percentage Distribution of Mentions of Left-Leaning, Neutral and Right-Leaning Think Tanks on BBC TV in 2009 and 2015

Sources: Justin Lewis and Stephen Cushion, 'Think tanks, television news and impartiality', *Journalism Studies*, 20, October 2017

The BBC: Balanced in 2009, Biased to the Right in 2015

These percentage differences may sound rather trivial to those outside the Westminster bubble but they are important for two reasons. First, insofar as the BBC showed any bias in its mentions of think tanks in the 2015 election year, it unambiguously favoured the right-leaning ones. This is the exact opposite of the constant claims by these very same think tanks – and the BBC's other right-wing enemies – of a persistent left-wing bias.[28] Secondly, there was a clear shift to the right in between the two years. In the Cardiff authors' words, 'In 2009, there was a broad balance between left and right think tanks . . . In 2015, references to right-leaning think tanks remain at a similar level (16.2 per cent) while references to left-leaning think tanks are halved [from 16.5 per cent] to just 8.5 per cent. To put it in a broad political context, when Labour was in power, the BBC's use of think tanks was relatively even-handed, but when a Conservative-led coalition was in power,[29] the centre of gravity [in BBC coverage] shifted to the political right'.[30]

Two thousand and fifteen was also the final year of the Charter renewal process discussed in Chapter 5, when the BBC was under sustained attack and may have been particularly vulnerable to pressure from the ruling Conservatives. However, the BBC's apparent shift to the right between 2009 and 2015 does not seem to have been a one-off 'blip' due to Charter renewal. It is consistent with the results of an earlier review by the Cardiff team comparing BBC news coverage in 2007 and 2012. The background to this study was a 2007 report for the BBC Trust[31] by the author and independent documentary-maker John Bridcut, a former BBC employee, on how the Corporation's approach to impartiality should evolve in a world of blogs, social media, multiple channels and weakening party loyalties.[32]

John Bridcut: 'From Seesaw to Wagon Wheel'

Bridcut commissioned qualitative and quantitative audience research, interviewed BBC and other broadcasting executives and programme-makers, and organized a wide-ranging seminar with eighty broadcasters and commentators. His review was overseen by a steering group comprising four BBC governors/trustees, three BBC editorial leaders and five external experts. His report, 'From seesaw to wagon wheel: safeguarding impartiality in the 21st century', summarized the new challenges as follows:

> Impartiality in broadcasting has long been assumed to apply mainly to party politics and industrial disputes. It involved keeping a balance to ensure the seesaw did not tip too far to one side or the other. Those days are over. In today's multi-polar Britain, with its range of cultures, beliefs and identities, impartiality involves many more than two sides to an argument. Party politics is in decline, and industrial disputes are only rarely central to national debate. The seesaw has been replaced by the wagon wheel – the modern version used in the television coverage of cricket, where the wheel is not circular and has a shifting centre with spokes that go in all directions.[33]

'From seesaw to wagon wheel' ranges widely. The main text is over eighty pages and there are seven appendices. It proposed twelve 'guiding principles' and a list of specific recommendations to help BBC News remain duly impartial in a more complex world, without becoming 'insipid' or always anchored to the centre ground. It stated that the overriding aim, in line with the report's title, should be to report the full range of views on political issues, while also not shying away from reaching conclusions. The BBC incorporated many of these recommendations into its 2010 editorial guidelines.

In the summer of 2012, the Trust commissioned former ITV chief Stuart Prebble to lead an independent review into the BBC's progress in implementing Bridcut's recommendations, focusing on three areas: immigration, the UK's relationship with the EU and religion.[34] As an input to this review, it commissioned a content analysis by the Cardiff group comparing the BBC's coverage of these topics in 2007 (the date of the Bridcut review) and 2012 and an in-depth qualitative research study of the audience's perceptions of its coverage of religion.[35]

Cardiff Breadth of Opinion Studies

The main Cardiff content analysis focused on the BBC's TV, radio and online coverage of the three chosen topics (immigration, the UK and EU, and religion) in 2007 and 2012.[36] It found that party political voices dominated on all three topics in both years, but especially on the UK and EU in 2012, where the debate was mainly around the two main parties' political positions. In both years, the ruling party had the largest share of the voice, but the Conservative dominance in 2012 was much greater than the Labour dominance in 2007. The Liberal Democrats received limited coverage – even in 2012, when they were a (minority) partner in the coalition government. And whereas appearances by Gordon Brown outnumbered those by David Cameron by two to one in 2007, in 2012 Cameron outnumbered Ed Miliband by nearly four to one.

In addition, these findings confirmed what people outside the Westminster bubble constantly complained of: the dominance of party political sources – politicians and official party spokespeople – in the BBC's political coverage. In 2007 nearly half – 49.4 per cent of interviewees on these subjects – came from party-political sources. By 2012 that had increased to 54.8 per cent. (In coverage of the EU it was 65 per cent in 2007 and

79.2 per cent in 2012.) These results are very consistent with those for BBC TV's coverage of right- and left-leaning think tanks in 2009 and 2015, discussed above.

In summary: the BBC consistently gave the most coverage to voices from the two main political parties, but especially the governing party. However, there was some asymmetry. Under a Labour government, Labour voices had only slightly more air-time than the Conservatives and coverage of left- and right-leaning think tanks was almost balanced. But under the Conservatives, government voices dominated by a wide margin and right-leaning think tanks were mentioned almost twice as often as left-leaning ones.

Other Academic Studies

Other academic studies commissioned by the BBC Trust – then responsible for the BBC's regulation as well as its governance[37] – examined the Corporation's coverage of the 2008 banking crisis,[38] science (especially climate change),[39] rural issues and concerns[40] and other topics such as regional news, the Israel–Palestine conflict, the Arab Spring, the EU and business.[41]

On a number of issues where the BBC had consistently been accused of bias over the decades – for example, of being pro-EU and anti-business – the findings were counter-intuitive for many readers familiar with the charges. For instance, analysis of the *Today* programme's coverage of the banking crisis found that it had been dominated by City sources, closely followed by politicians. The other well-represented groups were, in order, non-BBC journalists (from the *Financial Times*, *Wall Street Journal*, *Newsweek*, *The Guardian*, etc.), general business representatives (from the Confederation of British Industry, the Institute of Directors, corporate businesses), academics – mainly neoclassical economists – and regulators/officials (from the Financial

Services Authority, the Treasury, etc.). Union leaders and other voices critical of the City hardly figured at all.[42]

In line with these results, the self-described democratic socialist Tom Mills, reviewing the BBC's political coverage – and politicians' endless attempts to influence it – over its whole history, strongly rejects the claim that the Corporation is left-wing and anti-business, believing it instead to be deeply embedded in what he sees as the right-leaning and pro-business British Establishment:

> [The] BBC, whatever liberals would like to imagine, does not stand apart from the world of politics and power and the corporate interests which predominate there . . . [I]nsofar as the BBC can be said to exhibit any political bias, it is not based in political partisanship, but rather in an orientation towards those networks of power and their shared interests.[43]

Reporting the Newspapers

These conclusions are further supported by a study by Professor Adrian Renton (University of East London) and Dr Justin Schlosberg (Birkbeck, University of London) of the BBC's coverage of front-page national newspaper stories in the run-up to the 2017 general election.[44]

As we discuss in Chapter 9, the UK's national papers are strongly skewed to the right, especially when weighted by readership (and even more so by print readership). This raises a question about how a politically impartial broadcaster should allocate its coverage of them: to what extent should it aim to reflect the distribution of political views among voters or in the (predominantly right-leaning) newspapers themselves? Renton and Schlosberg analysed the daily editions of the BBC's news programme *The Papers* on both the BBC News Channel (a twenty-minute studio discussion with a host and two guests, usually journalists)[45] and

BBC News Online (a brief, largely factual, written summary) from the date of the announcement of the election on 18 April 2017 until 21 May 2017 (the latter date being just two weeks before the election was due to take place on 8 June 2017).

The newspapers were categorized by the party endorsements they had given in the previous (May 2015) election, as either Conservative, Labour, 'Other' or 'No party'.[46] The studio guests were categorized into the same four groups based on the news source they represented, if any, and, for non-journalists, if there was any clear evidence of particular party support.

The Dominance of Conservative Sources on The Papers

On the daily broadcast show, there was an average of 720 seconds of discussion of the front-page stories of newspapers which had endorsed specific parties in 2015. Conservative-supporting papers represented 69 per cent of this, Labour-supporting papers 23 per cent, and those supporting other parties (UKIP or Liberal Democrat) just 8 per cent. For the sake of comparison, the authors noted that the UK's voting pattern in 2015 had been: Conservative, 37 per cent; Labour, 30 per cent; and other parties, 33 per cent. Using this as a benchmark, they argue that the Conservative papers received vastly more discussion time than would have been 'balanced' (at 69 per cent versus their 37-per-cent share of the vote in 2015) while Labour received less than its fair share (23 per cent versus its 30-per-cent share of the vote in 2015) and other parties were even more under-represented (at just 8 per cent versus a combined share of the vote of 33 per cent in 2015).

The Conservatives were similarly overrepresented in terms of the invited guests. Of the sixty-two guests over the study period with a clear party affiliation, 68 per cent were Conservative supporters, 15 per cent Labour supporters and 18 per cent supporters of other parties. There were no guests from trade unions or charities.

Turning to the BBC's online coverage of newspaper front-page stories, Renton and Schlosberg found an even greater skew towards Conservative-supporting papers. Of the 341 specific mentions of a front-page story, 72 per cent referred to Conservative-supporting papers, 19 per cent to Labour-supporting papers and only 9 per cent to papers supporting other parties.

Across all three measures (TV discussion time, guests on the broadcast show and online mentions) Conservative-supporting voices accounted for more than two-thirds of the total – double the combined exposure of those supporting other parties or none. The authors concluded that the BBC was:

> violating its Charter and Sections 5 and 6 of the Amended Broadcasting Code[47] . . . [It was] failing to give due weight to the coverage of parties during the election period by not taking account of evidence of past and current electoral support, as prescribed by Ofcom's amended guidelines. Finally, through the selection of guest discussants of newspaper coverage the BBC is failing to represent proportionate and diverse political perspectives, taking due account of the particular funding sources and editorial stance of organisations represented.[48]

Was the BBC Biased or Simply Reflecting the Pro-Conservative Imbalance in UK Newspapers?

In the BBC's defence, one might argue that the dominance of Conservative voices on *The Papers* was merely a reflection of the Conservative papers' market dominance. There are two reasons why this argument is hard to sustain, though. First, as noted by Renton and Schlosberg, broadcasters have a duty to take at least some account of past and current electoral support. Secondly, the imbalance was, arguably, even greater in the news programmes in question than within the newspaper market.

What is beyond dispute is that, in 2017, *The Papers* gave vastly more exposure to Conservative voices than to those supporting either Labour or another party. Although this was for only one programme during one election, it is hard to see how it could have happened if the BBC had the kind of constant left-wing bias endlessly claimed by its right-leaning enemies. More important, it is consistent with the results of a large-scale Cardiff study of how newspapers drove the TV news agenda during the previous election in May 2015.

How Newspapers Drove the TV News Agenda

As newspapers' circulation, revenue and resources decline under pressure from online media, especially Google and Facebook, it is tempting to assume that their political influence is being proportionately reduced. However, this ignores their huge role as agenda-setters,[49] including for broadcast news. In 2015, members of the Cardiff University group conducted a study of how the five UK television news broadcasters (BBC, ITV, Sky News, Channel 4 and Channel 5) decided which election-related issues and stories to cover during the general election campaign. The study comprised a content analysis of TV and newspaper coverage, supplemented by semi-structured interviews with senior broadcast news editors. The detailed results and theoretical implications were published in scholarly papers,[50] but the key findings were summarized in a *Guardian* article:

> Our analysis of the major evening TV bulletins shows issues where the Conservatives were seen as strong, such as the economy and a potential SNP–Labour coalition, were among the dominant themes. And while the broadcasters are required to seek balance, the rightwing press was responsible for pushing Tory-friendly issues to the forefront of TV news.

In over 2,000 news items between 20 March and 6 May, the main topics addressed by broadcasters were 'horse-race' coverage – notably in how close a contest it was meant to be between Labour and the Conservatives – a possible [Labour–SNP] coalition government, the handling of the economy and levels of taxation. Between them, they made up 43% of the entire TV news agenda.

In contrast, Labour's campaign issues – the NHS or housing for instance – were covered far less. While there was some variation between the broadcasters, social policy issues were not widely reported anywhere . . .

[The coverage] consolidated the dominant narrative of the campaign as a close contest between the two main parties and drew attention to the SNP's potential coalition power. And it meant most policy issues, with the exception of the handling of the economy, were marginalised.

The article went on to say that the broadcasters' pro-Conservative bias was also reflected in the contrasting coverage given to four letters to the press from different representative groups. The most TV airtime went to a *Daily Telegraph* letter from 102 Conservative-supporting business leaders. There was also extensive TV airtime for another *Telegraph* letter from 5,000 small business leaders, timed to coincide with the launch of the party's small business manifesto. There was much less for one from 140 health professionals to *The Guardian*, attacking the government's record on the NHS and for one to the *Independent* on a poll of leading economists criticizing the austerity measures.[51]

The BBC versus Other TV News Broadcasters

Despite the constant singling out of the BBC as a target for right-wing (as well as some left-wing) criticism, there was very little difference between its coverage of the 2015 election and that of the other TV news broadcasters. And, insofar as there was any difference, the BBC's was very marginally more in line with the agenda set by the Conservative-supporting newspapers.

For instance, for TV coverage of election-related policy items published by newspapers prior to being broadcast, 61 per cent of the items covered by ITV, Sky, Channel 4 and Channel 5 had been published in the five Conservative-supporting papers analysed[52] and only 39 per cent in the three Labour or LibDem-supporting papers.[53] But, on the BBC, the imbalance favouring the Conservatives was – very slightly – even higher: 64 per cent versus 36 per cent.[54]

These results suggest that one reason why the BBC's – and other broadcasters' – news coverage is, if anything, skewed to the right is that their agenda tends to be driven by the newspapers which, in both number and, especially, combined readership are strongly skewed to the right.

They also suggest that the UK newspapers' predominant bias to the right still matters because, even with falling circulations, they continue to drive the news agenda on television, which remains most people's main news source.[55]

What about the accusation that the BBC is systematically pro-EU and anti-Brexit? Because the EU has usually been of little interest to most people, but divisive and hugely emotive at other times and/or to some other people, covering it has long been a challenge for the BBC.

The Wilson Review

In 2004, the BBC Governors commissioned a five-person panel chaired by the former cabinet secretary Lord Wilson of Dinton – Master of Emmanuel College, Cambridge, and a non-executive director of Sky – to review the BBC's EU coverage, especially in response to claims that:

(i) the BBC is systematically europhile; (ii) anti-EU, pro-withdrawal voices [had] been excluded from BBC coverage; (iii) BBC coverage of the EU [was] seen too much through a Westminster prism with the result that significant EU developments [went] unreported; and (iv) BBC reporting [had] failed to increase public understanding of EU issues and institutions and their impact on British life, thereby contributing to public apathy.[56]

The panel commissioned research on public perceptions, received written submissions from a wide range of groups, and interviewed representatives from a sample of them. In January 2005, it reported as follows:

> We were asked whether the BBC is systematically Europhile. If systematic means deliberate, conscious bias with a directive from the top, an internal system or a conspiracy, we have not found a systematic bias. But we do think there is a serious problem. Although the BBC wishes to be impartial in its news coverage of the EU it is not succeeding. Whatever the intention, nobody thinks the outcome is impartial. There is strong disagreement about the net balance but all parties show remarkable unity in identifying the elements of the problem. Sometimes being attacked from all sides is a sign that an organisation is getting it right. That is not so here. It is a sign that the BBC is getting it wrong, and our main conclusion is that urgent action is required to put this right.[57]

The panel identified five reasons why, in its view, the BBC was failing to be impartial in its EU coverage: (i) an 'institutional mindset' leading to what 'one panel member' felt was an 'endemic ... reluctance to question pro-EU assumptions'; (ii) 'over-simplified polarisation of the issues and stereotyping' – a failure to reflect the full range of opinion, including the views of those who favoured continuing EU membership but disagreed with specific EU policies and/or further integration;[58] (iii) the

'Westminster prism', overemphasizing the main UK parties' perspectives; (iv) 'ignorance': BBC journalists being insufficiently on top of the details, for instance, 'The difference between the adversarial nature of British politics and the consensual nature of European politics is rarely explained or explored';[59] and (v) 'omission': 'All external witnesses pointed out that the BBC News agenda understates the importance and relevance of the EU in the political and daily life of the UK'.[60]

These conclusions inevitably reflect the panel members' relatively high engagement in EU-related issues, compared with most people's relative indifference. They should perhaps have made more allowance for the BBC's dilemma in trying to interest audiences in these issues without dumbing them down, when most viewers and listeners still saw the EU as remote, irrelevant and deadly dull. At the same time, the 'importance and relevance of the EU in the political and daily life of the UK' may in reality have been rather less than the panel was suggesting.[61]

Nevertheless, this hard-hitting but thoughtful review raised genuine issues which remain challenging. The BBC vowed to do better and set up a committee under its new Head of News, Helen Boaden, to develop new policies and guidelines.

The Cardiff Content Analysis of the BBC's EU Coverage in 2007 and 2012

There has been little academic research of the extent to which the BBC's *actual* coverage of the EU (as opposed to stakeholders' *perceptions* of its coverage, the basis of the Wilson Review) is as Europhile as often suggested, including by the review.

However, we do have some evidence from the same Cardiff content analysis for the 2013 Prebble Review we discussed earlier in the context of the airtime given to Labour and Conservative voices in 2007 and 2012, because the study also measured the BBC's coverage of Britain's relationship with the EU in the same two years. In each sample period, a single story dominated the BBC's EU coverage which, again, was largely monopolized by the two main parties – in fact, even more than on the other topics. In 2007 the big EU issue was the Lisbon Treaty, accounting for 70 per cent of coverage. Debate revolved around Conservative Eurosceptic claims that Britain hadn't secured its 'red lines' on British sovereignty; the treaty was a repackaged version of the EU constitution; and a referendum was needed to ratify it. Labour contested these claims. In 2012 the main focus was on negotiations over ratifying the EU budget. This accounted for 72 per cent of coverage, pitting the Conservative leadership (mainly David Cameron and George Osborne), who supported the budget settlement, against both Labour and the Eurosceptic wing of the Conservative party, who opposed it. In both years, the EU was framed narrowly, and in almost entirely negative terms, as a threat to British interests.

The BBC's coverage saw Europe largely through the prism of political conflict between Labour and the Conservatives and infighting within the Conservatives. In line with the conclusions of the Wilson Review, there was virtually no rounded debate about the multiplicity of ways the relationship between the EU and UK affects Britain. Also, although UKIP received little airtime, Euroscepticism was very well represented through Conservative politicians. Conversely, there were few voices arguing for the benefits of EU membership. Labour politicians were unwilling to make the positive case for Europe because of its perceived unpopularity amongst voters, so business representatives provided much of what little pro-EU opinion was available.[62]

TV Coverage of the 2016 EU referendum

In 2016, Cardiff's Stephen Cushion and Justin Lewis did a content analysis of the five TV news broadcasters' main evening bulletins over the 10-week EU referendum campaign (15 April to 22 June 2016).[63] Their conclusions were a strong indictment of the broadcasters:

It is now widely acknowledged that a binary notion of balance can distort coverage when the weight of evidence clearly falls on one side . . . most famously in the coverage of climate change or the reporting of the Measles, Mumps and Rubella (MMR) vaccine.[64]

And yet, our study . . . found that while broadcasters understandably balanced the airtime granted to official Leave and Remain actors, they did not consider or scrutinise the veracity or weight of opposing arguments . . . [W]e also found broadcasters did not reflect the full range of party political opinions and left little space for analysis beyond politicians and campaigners . . . the UK Conservative Party – who were split on leaving or remaining in the EU – made up by far the largest share of party political sources. Labour – or, indeed, any left of centre party voices, who represented a more left-wing perspective on EU membership – were marginalized . . .

In short, while the Conservative case for Remain was featured prominently, a more left-wing case for EU membership – despite intense campaigning by many senior Labour, Liberal Democrat, SNP, Plaid Cymru and trade union figures – was side-lined. The striking failure of the Remain campaign in many traditional Labour heartlands raises the plausible possibility that the lack of political balance in broadcast coverage – notably the absence of a left-wing case for Remain – may have been significant . . .

[C]overage was dominated by statistical tit-for-tats, with rival camps trading numerical claims with little journalistic arbitration or attempt to consult or interpret expert opinion . . . Strikingly absent . . . was coverage that explained how the EU worked, the nature of international trade, or the economic role of EU immigration and its impact on public services.[65]

Once again, there was no material difference between the BBC's and the other broadcasters' coverage.

Conclusions

At the start of this appendix, we noted that the two key questions on BBC bias were: 'Is it systematically biased to the left or right and, if so, in which direction and to what extent?' and 'Is it systematically biased for or against Brexit and, if so, in which direction and to what extent?' We can now answer both questions with some confidence. The BBC is clearly concerned to achieve balance and impartiality in its news and current affairs output and has put in place measures and oversight for this. Under the Governors and then the Trust, it has repeatedly sought evidence and guidance from academic studies and other independent sources to help it achieve impartiality on difficult subjects. Nevertheless:

1. Inasmuch as its coverage exhibits any bias on the left-to-right spectrum, the consistent evidence is that it leans somewhat to the right, and that this bias has increased in recent years.
2. Similarly, insofar as it shows any bias on its coverage of the EU, the limited evidence from academic research is that it tends to frame the issues in anti-EU terms. Arguments hostile to the EU received more exposure in the BBC than those supportive of the EU. In other words, the evidence suggests the opposite of the claim by News-watch and many others that its coverage is systematically pro-EU.

In the words of Cardiff's Mike Berry, 'The evidence from the research is clear. The BBC tends to reproduce a Conservative, Eurosceptic, pro-business version of the world, not a left-wing, anti-business agenda'.[66] One reason for this bias is that the BBC has tended to follow the agenda set by the (overwhelmingly right-leaning and Eurosceptic/pro-Brexit) newspapers. Another is surely that Conservative governments have almost always been more hostile to the BBC than Labour ones, both ideologically and – as shown to a marked degree by the current Johnson administration – in other ways too. As we've seen throughout this book, the war against the BBC is waged largely from the right.

Another weakness exposed by the research is that the range of voices tends to be narrow and 'Westminster-centric', with an over-emphasis on the main two political parties, especially the party in government, together with other Establishment voices, including business voices. In other words what 'surprised centrists' suspected from their own experience of recent BBC coverage (see Chapter 9) appears to be confirmed by these reports. However, we should stress that judgements about perceived bias/impartiality are, and will always be, to a degree, subjective.

Finally, we note that, in the research reviewed here (by the largest UK academic group conducting such research), there are no material differences between the BBC's news and current affairs coverage and that of the other TV broadcasters. The singling out of the BBC by those accusing it of left-wing and/or pro-EU bias presumably reflects its prominence in the public's news consumption, the high trust in which it is still held by the UK public, a feeling that – because of its public funding – it may be easier to cow than the other broadcasters, and perhaps its critics' other commercial, political and ideological agendas.

Appendix C: The Peacock Committee and Its Wider Legacy

In 1985, Margaret Thatcher appointed a committee under Professor Alan Peacock, a leading free-market economist, to investigate whether – and, if so, how – the BBC's UK services should be funded by advertising as an alternative or supplement to the licence fee. The committee's brief also asked it 'to consider any proposals for securing income from the consumer other than through the licence fee'.[1] At the time, there was strong lobbying by the Incorporated Society of British Advertisers (ISBA), the chief trade association, and the influential advertising agency Saatchi & Saatchi – the Conservatives' own ad agency – for the BBC to carry advertising. Mrs Thatcher was widely believed to support the idea,[2] perhaps encouraged by cabinet hawks such as Trade and Industry Secretary Norman Tebbit, whose special adviser was a twenty-five-year-old John Whittingdale.

Professor Peacock himself, the committee's chair, started with the same view, announcing at one of its early meetings, 'We are all agreed, aren't we, that we are going to have advertising on the BBC?'[3] However, that was before he began looking at the evidence and arguments. The committee sat for over a year and its report runs to 223 pages. Despite the chairman's initial view, its answer to the main question – should the BBC be wholly or partly funded by advertising? – was a firm no, for two reasons:

1. First, although there is wide uncertainty about how advertisers would fund their investment in BBC television and/or radio advertising, the evidence is that most of

> the money would be diverted from advertising in other (mainly broadcast and print) media, severely damaging them and reducing their ability to invest in content.
> 2. Secondly, advertising is a 'two-sided market' and the two sides – advertisers and audiences – have different priorities. If the BBC's income came wholly or partly from advertisers, it would have a financial incentive to prioritize their needs[4] above those of *all* viewers and listeners.[5]

As far as we know, everyone with the relevant knowledge agrees that the Peacock Committee gave the right answer to the main question in its brief: should the BBC be wholly or partly funded by advertising?[6] However, it then, controversially, went much further than this. In fact, less than a quarter of the main text of its report was about whether the BBC should be funded by advertising. We are still living with some of its wider legacy beyond its answer to this question.

The Peacock Committee's Wider Legacy

In line with Professor Peacock's intellectual background, the general thrust of the recommendations was to introduce direct consumer sovereignty and/or market competition into as many aspects of broadcasting as possible, including several that had nothing to do with BBC funding. Some recommendations were never implemented, such as privatizing BBC Radio 1 and Radio 2, extending payment of the licence fee to those with car radios and phasing out broadcasting content standards ('censorship'). However, the recommendation that pensioners dependent on benefits should be exempt from the licence fee, although rejected by the Thatcher government, is close to where we are in 2020.

Among the recommendations that were implemented, the

proposal that at least 40 per cent of BBC TV and ITV programming should be made by independent producers, despite being somewhat watered down, gave a significant additional boost to the emerging independent sector (reinforcing the initial impetus from Channel 4, launched less than four years earlier, in 1982, as a publisher–broadcaster which would buy most of its programmes from UK independent producers). This and the recommendation that Channel 4 should sell its own airtime – both well outside the committee's brief – nonetheless helped the evolution towards today's flourishing UK broadcasting ecosystem. However, not all of the Peacock Committee's straying beyond its brief was so beneficial.

The ITV Franchise Auction

The recommendation with the greatest short-term impact was that ITV franchises should be auctioned to the highest bidder. This four-to-three majority recommendation[7] was incorporated into the 1990 Broadcasting Act and implemented, with some programme quality and financial sustainability safeguards introduced by the regulator,[8] in 1991.

The outcome was that twelve of the sixteen ITV companies retained their franchises, either unopposed (three), or because the challengers failed the regulator's quality or business-plan tests (five), or the incumbent's bid was the highest (four). The Midlands and central Scotland franchisees both retained their lucrative areas unopposed for a derisory annual payment of £2,000.[9] To the delight – we suspect – of those on the left who hated Margaret Thatcher, right-wing Australian media tycoons and the franchise auctions, the by-now-ex-PM was said to have been astonished and devastated when, as a direct result of her 1990 Broadcasting Act, her friend and favourite broadcaster Bruce Gyngell, head of TV-am, lost the breakfast franchise to GMTV, which had bid almost two-and-a-half times as much.[10]

The 1991 ITV franchise auction is now ancient history and has never been repeated. It would be hard to find anyone today who regards it as a success. Our own view is that it was a triumph of textbook economic theory over real-world practicalities, as well as wrongly (despite the best efforts of the regulator) trying to treat broadcasting as little more than a commodity like oil or gas.

Direct responsibility for this fiasco goes to the Thatcher government and, before that, Peacock and the three other members of his committee who supported it. However, its roots may lie in a large but long-forgotten initiative of the Adam Smith Institute, the rather scarily titled Omega Project, which, appropriately enough, reported in 1984 (we're just saying!). This ambitious year-long project involved twenty working groups, each developing proposals in a particular policy area. The report on communications policy includes a range of radical free-market proposals for breaking up the BBC, deregulating tobacco advertising, etc. It recommends replacing the commercial broadcasting regulator, then the Independent Broadcasting Authority, with something 'more akin to the FCC [Federal Communications Commission] in the United States . . . [which] should license large numbers of new stations, both television and radio' and let the market decide what then emerged.[11] Several of Peacock's recommendations are in this spirit, including the one for the ITV franchise auctions.

Peacock's Longer-Term Vision: Direct Consumer Payments

In the long term, the Peacock Committee's greatest impact may turn out to be its vision of a broadcasting market funded by households paying directly for what they choose to watch and listen to and its recommendations to enable this:

British broadcasting should move towards a sophisticated market system based on consumer sovereignty. That is a system which recognises that viewers and listeners are the best ultimate judges of their own interests, which they can best satisfy if they have the option of purchasing the broadcasting services they require from as many alternative sources of supply as possible.[12]

Unlike many of the Committee's recommendations, such as auctioning ITV franchises, these could at least be justified as within its brief, the last part of which was 'to consider any proposals for securing income from the consumer other than through the licence fee'.[13] Peacock's vision of a broadcasting market based on direct consumer payments has been extremely influential – at least in terms of policy discussion, as opposed to specific policy proposals – especially among right-wing think tanks. Although there are many potential options, including those under which consumers (individuals or households) pay for individual programmes,[14] the general assumption has been that the free-market alternative to the compulsory TV licence fee would be voluntary monthly subscriptions.

As we discuss in Chapter 10 and Appendix D, the arguments against this are so strong that we think it is unlikely to happen if policy-makers look at the practical options and their likely consequences, as Peacock did with advertising. If the government were to switch to subscriptions without such a review, we think it would face a huge public backlash once the consequences became clear.

Appendix D: The Trouble with Subscriptions

Replacing the BBC's licence-fee funding with subscriptions would, as a prerequisite, require every device able to show BBC TV to have conditional access (CA) technology and every user or household to register, so that only those who had paid could watch it. Achieving this would take time and cost money – and the shorter the time, the greater the cost. But even with universal CA technology and all users registered, switching to subscriptions would permanently reduce value for money for most UK households and also reduce both short- and long-term UK content investment – in addition to the risk that it might fundamentally change the nature of the BBC and the certainty that it would make the BBC no longer a universal service, equally available to all.

The reasons for this damning conclusion are that switching to subscriptions would (i) significantly reduce the BBC's funding base, (ii) significantly increase its overheads and (iii) also reduce pay-TV companies' revenue and content investment. In this appendix, we look at each of these three factors (figures correct at the time of writing).

Factor 1: Reducing the BBC's Revenue Base

Suppose, for example, the licence fee were simply replaced by a voluntary subscription to BBC TV at exactly the same price, currently £154.50 a year – £12.88 per month. Assume the resulting revenue is used to (i) provide BBC TV to subscribing households[1] and (ii) as now, also fund BBC Radio and BBC Online for *all* UK households, plus the BBC World Service and the various non-BBC activities currently funded by the licence fee. Twelve pounds and eighty-eight pence per month is less than 60 per cent of the £22-per-month price of the basic, entry-level Sky Entertainment package. In 2016, 58 per cent of homes subscribed to basic or – at a much higher monthly price – premium pay TV.[2] Given the popularity of BBC TV even in pay-TV homes, at £12.88 per month the great majority of households would see it as excellent value for money and probably subscribe. But a few – perhaps younger ones happy to rely on Netflix and Amazon, or older, poorer ones happy to rely on the free-to-air commercial PSBs – would not.

Let's assume (we think, optimistically) the initial take-up rate was as high as 90 per cent of homes, with 10 per cent choosing not to subscribe. Even this would perceptibly reduce the range, quality and value for money of TV and radio for most households. The BBC's revenue would be reduced by 10 per cent for starters. And because many of its costs are fixed – not only distribution, technology and most administration, but also its funding of the World Service and other activities like S4C – its content budgets (TV, radio and online) would be cut by slightly more, proportionately, than this first reduction of 10 per cent. These initial cuts of slightly more than 10 per cent in its content budgets would reduce the value of a BBC subscription, leading to a small second round of cancellations, which would lead in turn to some further content budget cuts, and so on, until the market reached an equilibrium with – again optimistically – perhaps 12 or 13 per cent of homes choosing not to subscribe, and the BBC's content budgets (across the board – TV, radio and online) reduced by, say, 15 per cent.

These numbers are for illustration only: to show how, even with optimistic assumptions, subscriptions at the same level as the licence fee would materially reduce the BBC's revenue base and content investment. Who would be the winners and losers under this optimistic scenario? For the 10 per cent of homes for whom the current BBC TV offer is worth less than £12.88 per month, it is unclear whether they would, on average, be marginal winners or marginal losers. The outcome would depend on their usage of other BBC services (radio and online) and the value they placed on the BBC's public service benefits, the BBC World Service and the other government activities funded by BBC subscriptions. But the great majority – 90 per cent – would be unambiguously worse off: they would be getting at least 15 per cent less content – on TV, radio and online – for exactly the same money. (However, the outcome would actually be significantly worse than this, because of the two other factors we'll discuss below.

Of course, there are many alternative pricing options, including charging a *higher* price for BBC TV than the current licence fee. For instance, £18 per month would be about 40 per cent higher than the current licence fee – but still 18 per cent below Sky's entry-level price. In this case, the revenue base would shrink more – maybe down to 75 or 80 per cent of homes – who would each be paying 40 per cent more than now. On the plus side, the BBC's revenue would be, on these numbers, between 5 and 12 per cent higher than with the current licence fee.[3] However, it's unlikely that even this 40-per-cent price increase would lead to higher BBC content budgets because of another negative factor: the impact of subscriptions on its overheads.

Factor 2: The Impact on the BBC's Overheads

Collection costs for the licence fee were 2.8 per cent of revenue in 2018–19.[4] Subscriptions involve *much* higher overheads than this, to cover marketing, billing and customer service costs. Consider Sky, the leading UK pay-TV service, well managed, and not seen as having excessive overheads. But in 2017–18, its Sales, General and Administration (SG&A) expenses in the UK and Ireland were £2,696 million, 30 per cent of its £8,931 million total revenue from external customers, 35 per cent of its £7,611 million direct consumer revenue[5] – and a gob-smacking *80 per cent* of the BBC's total licence-fee revenue after top-slicing.

We repeat: during 2017–18, Sky's sales, general and administrative expenses in the UK and Ireland were 80 per cent of the BBC's total licence-fee revenue after top-slicing. If the BBC were funded by subscriptions, its overheads would need to increase by at least 10 to 15 per cent of its revenue from UK households to cover these additional marketing, billing and customer service costs.[6] Relating this to the first scenario above – with the subscription set at the same level as the current licence fee – the combination of the reduced revenue base *and* an increase in overheads equivalent to 10 to 15 per cent of revenue would further reinforce the vicious circle of reductions in content budgets, leading to reduced value, further reductions in the revenue base and so on. We have no idea where this would end – and nor do any of those calling for the licence fee to be replaced with subscriptions (or, if they do, they've kept very quiet about it).

But it's clear that, under this scenario, with the subscription priced at the same level as the licence fee, virtually every UK household would be significantly worse off, getting much less value (on TV, radio and online) for the same money. UK producers would also be getting significantly fewer and/or smaller commissions from the BBC.

Under the more realistic pricing of the second scenario, with a single-tier subscription of £18 per month (40 per cent higher than the current licence fee), the increase in overheads would almost certainly more than wipe out the likely increase in gross revenue (in the order of 5 to 12 per cent), so the income available for content investment would actually be lower than with the licence fee. The great majority of households would, again, be unambiguously worse off, paying 40 per cent more for slightly lower-quality BBC TV, radio and online services.

Obviously, the exact outcome depends on the assumptions one makes. For instance, if the subscription were set lower than £18 per month, the increase in cost for subscribing homes would be less and the take-up might be a bit more than the 80 per cent we've assumed – but the BBC's income and content investment would be lower. The opposite is true if the price were higher than £18 per month. There is an almost infinite number of other options involving different BBC service packages at different prices. But, because of the two factors above (a smaller revenue base and much higher overheads), we think there are *no* good options.

Factor 3: The Impact on Pay-TV Companies' Revenue and Content Investment

Finally, a subscription-funded BBC would, in practice, almost certainly be priced below pay-TV companies' current entry-level subscriptions while – judging by the continuing popularity of BBC TV in pay-TV homes – offering what most viewers would see as more valuable content than the pay-TV companies' basic package. This would impact upon their revenue still further (which has already been diminished by the growth of SVoD). To cover this impact, they would presumably be forced to reduce their content investment, including in the origination of UK programmes, besides reducing value to subscribers and UK production companies' revenue.

Appendix E: Research on the BBC's Market Impact

The BBC's market impact was raised as a potentially important policy issue in the late 1990s when, in line with its 1997 Charter, the Corporation was developing its new digital TV, radio and online services.[1] As discussed in Chapter 11, during 2002–4, as an input to Charter renewal in 2006, Culture Secretary Tessa Jowell commissioned performance reviews of these new digital services. Part of the reviews' remit was to evaluate, with additional input from Ofcom, the new services' market impact. None of the 2002–4 reviews found evidence that the new BBC services were significantly impacting their markets or crowding out content investment by commercial media. Instead, they reported a mixture of positive and negative market impacts, but nothing suggesting that the services were, on balance, reducing content investment by commercial players.

The Big Issue in Whittingdale's Charter Renewal Green Paper

Ten years later, in the run-up to Charter renewal in 2016 and with John Whittingdale as Culture Secretary, the BBC's market impact was seen as a much bigger issue, accounting for eleven of the nineteen questions in the July 2015 green paper consultation. The question was no longer whether a particular new service would unfairly impact, or pre-empt, commercial services in a specific market area, but whether the BBC as a whole was too big and broad, and even whether it should show popular entertainment programmes – at all or, at least, perhaps not when viewers most wanted to watch them. John Whittingdale, James Murdoch and others wanted the 2016 Charter review to explore significantly reducing the funding, scope and scale of the BBC, justified – at least implicitly – by the assumption that the huge resulting increase in provision by the rest of the market would be more than enough to replace the lost provision by the BBC. In rational policy terms, the challenge was to assess the probable outcome of this policy, based on estimating the extent to which the Corporation was actually crowding out commercial provision.

Assessing the BBC's Market Impact and 'Crowding Out' of Commercial Provision

There is no direct way to observe the extent to which, if the BBC's funding, scope and scale were significantly reduced, commercial media revenue and content investment would be higher or lower.[2] However, there are three indirect ways to reach an educated view on this.

First, we can make international comparisons of the strength of commercial broadcasting in countries with larger or smaller public broadcasters. In particular, if PSB funding really does significantly crowd out commercial broadcaster revenue, there should be a negative correlation between them across different countries.

Secondly, we can apply econometric methods to the long-term trends and short-term variations in the relevant UK data.

Thirdly, we can use the available evidence to create internally consistent 'What if?' scenarios under a range of reasonable best- and worst-case assumptions which are broad enough to reflect the considerable uncertainty about what the UK market might be like if there were no, or – as suggested by James Murdoch – a 'much, much smaller' BBC.

None of these methods is perfect but their strengths and weaknesses are complementary:

- International comparisons use real data from countries with large differences in PSB funding, scope and scale; but they exclude the many other potentially relevant differences between the countries.
- Econometric studies avoid this problem by focusing on only one market and they, too, use real data. But they involve a number of simplifying assumptions and their results are mainly based on marginal, short-term variations in the data. They are unsuitable for exploring radical policies, large long-term changes or markets undergoing major structural shifts such as the growth of SVoD.
- Scenario studies also focus on only one market and are good at addressing the probable implications of more radical policies, long-term structural market changes and uncertainty. The assumptions they make are explicit and open to debate. But, of course, their results are only as good as these assumptions, most of which cannot be directly tested.

In the run-up to Charter renewal in 2016, there were four quantitative studies of the BBC's market impact: one based on international comparisons, two econometric studies and one using assumption-based 'What if?' scenarios.

The Inflection Point Study: International Comparisons

Richer countries have richer TV systems, so per capita revenue for both commercial and public television correlates with per capita GDP. To see if public TV crowds out private TV, the international comparisons relevant to the UK must therefore be limited to developed countries, to avoid a spurious positive correlation (i.e. because richer countries tend to have higher per capita revenue for both public and private TV).

In 2013, the BBC published a fourteen-country study by Dr Jonathan Simon of the consultancy Inflection Point on the relationship between the strength and per capita funding of public TV (defined as publicly owned and in receipt of public funds) and several measures of the 'health' of commercial TV in the same country.[3] The key analysis looked at per capita public- and commercial TV revenue. The US was an outlier, by far the biggest market in absolute terms and with very high per capita commercial-TV revenue but virtually zero per capita public-TV revenue. Excluding the US, there was a strong positive relationship between the two variables, suggesting that public TV does not crowd out private TV.[4]

There were also strong positive relationships between the per capita investment in original content by the biggest PSB channel (e.g. BBC One) and the biggest commercial channel (e.g. ITV);[5] the proportion of key public service content[6] in the schedules of these channels; and the perceived quality of all the main public and commercial TV channels.[7]

These positive correlations between all four measures of the strength and health of public and commercial TV are inconsistent with the claim that the former crowds out the latter. Instead, they suggest the exact opposite: a 'competition for quality', in which well-funded PSBs create diverse, high-quality, original programmes which raise audience expectations, leading commercial broadcasters to match the PSBs' standards by also investing in diverse, high-quality, original programmes.

Based on the consistent evidence of these correlations, and also the UK's top ranking on all the measures of PSB strength *except* per capita funding, Jonathan Simon saw this country as exemplifying what he described as a 'race to the top': 'The UK broadcast market works as a "virtuous circle" with the public and private sectors competing for audiences but not for funding sources. The result has been better programmes for audiences, creative innovation and growth of the overall economic pie'.[8]

The KPMG Economic Review of Potential 'Crowding Out'

In response to the July 2015 green paper, the BBC Trust commissioned the financial consultancy KPMG to conduct an economic review of the extent to which the Corporation crowded out private-sector activity. The results were published in October 2015.[9] The KPMG study specifically looked at the extent to which (i) BBC TV entertainment programmes crowd out commercial TV entertainment programmes, (ii) BBC TV news programmes crowd out commercial TV news programmes and (iii) BBC Online News crowds out local newspapers. In each case, it used econometric methods to investigate 'what happens to the level of activity in commercial [TV] broadcasting, and to local newspaper readership and revenues, when the BBC's activity increases or decreases by amounts observed in recent history'.[10]

For instance, for entertainment TV, KPMG developed a large number of statistical models[11] in which the dependent variable was the total number of minutes of viewing of commercial TV entertainment programmes in each quarter over the thirteen-year-period (2002–14) of the study (thus fifty-two 'quarters' in all), and the independent variables included measures of the BBC's entertainment TV activity in the same quarter.

In the 'baseline' model (i.e. the one excluding the BBC activity), the independent variables were the number of commercial TV entertainment minutes broadcast during the quarter, the real GDP per capita,[12] a time trend and some seasonality variables.[13]

A number of models incorporating the BBC's entertainment TV activity in each quarter were tested against this baseline model.[14] There was no statistically reliable indication that the viewing of commercial TV entertainment was crowded out by the level of BBC activity. The study concluded that it was therefore 'difficult to conclude that there is any statistically significant relationship between BBC activity in entertainment broadcasting and commercial broadcasters' entertainment viewer hours'.[15]

The econometric analyses similarly found no evidence that BBC TV news crowds out commercial TV news or that BBC Online News crowds out local newspapers: 'The general finding from our analysis is that there is no clear evidence, from the available data, that any increase (decrease) in the level of BBC activity has resulted in a decline (increase) in commercial broadcasters' viewer hours or revenues, or local newspapers' readership or revenues'.[16]

The study also reviewed the few previous attempts to quantify the extent of crowding out by PSBs. In addition to those discussed here, these included only one other study, an econometric analysis of US radio markets. This, too, found no evidence of public radio crowding out commercial radio news and only limited evidence of it crowding out commercial classical music and jazz stations.[17] Despite this (very limited) crowding out, without public radio over 80 per cent of US markets would have no classical music or jazz radio.[18]

The Oliver & Ohlbaum and Oxera Report on the BBC's Market Impact and Distinctiveness

As discussed in Chapter 5, in July 2015, John Whittingdale, as Culture Secretary, commissioned the media, sport and entertainment consultancy Oliver & Ohlbaum (O&O), supported by the economic consultancy Oxera, to evaluate the market impact and 'distinctiveness' of the BBC's television, radio and online services. The Oliver & Ohlbaum and Oxera report was published in February 2016.[19] The O&O and Oxera study was a major project personally led by Mark Oliver, chairman and co-founder of O&O. The report is 243 pages long, including three detailed annexes and an eight-page bibliography. Like Whittingdale's green paper, it described the BBC as 'the best funded public service broadcasting organization in the world', again ignoring NHK in Japan (which receives more public funding but earns much less from its commercial activities). But, unlike the green paper, it added that 'the German PSB system as a whole receives more public monies'.

More importantly – and in marked contrast to the green paper – it noted that 'the BBC is a smaller player in the UK media market overall than it was 10 years ago, at the start of the last Charter period'. It also highlighted the growth of the FAANGs and the consolidation of traditional US media companies to create giants such as Sky Europe, Liberty Global, Comcast/NBC Universal and Disney – all much bigger than the BBC – adding that, 'In the next decade these trends are likely to continue, potentially leaving the BBC smaller again in 2026 in terms of its share of overall media consumption and revenue in the UK, and in its main overseas markets, and facing formidable global platform and content groups as both competitors and suppliers/distributors'.[20]

This is a perfect summary of the BBC's market predicament apart, perhaps, from the word 'potentially': in our view, under almost any plausible scenario, the BBC's revenue share *will* be even lower in 2026 (the last year of the current Charter) than in 2016 and it will be very surprising if its share of consumption is not lower too. O&O and Oxera focused mainly on the extent to which the BBC's commercial rivals' advertising revenue would be higher if the Corporation's main TV, radio and online services were made more 'distinctive' – and therefore less popular – by reducing the proportion of entertainment content (and also through less competitive scheduling, i.e., showing its top entertainment programmes at less popular times). In summary, they concluded that, if BBC One and the BBC's national radio stations and online news services were made more 'distinctive' and, therefore, less popular:

- commercial TV broadcasters' advertising revenue could increase by £33 million–£40 million a year, with a positive net market impact;
- commercial radio stations' advertising revenue could increase by £22 million–£38 million a year, with a positive net market impact; and
- commercial online services' advertising revenue would be likely to increase by £3.2 million–£8.2 million a year with, potentially, a positive net market impact.

They also concluded that, in addition to the potential increase in advertising revenue, a more differentiated BBC could also increase consumer revenue (subscriptions and one-off payments) across pay TV and online news and information and, possibly, music and speech audio on demand. These conclusions are inevitably hedged with a lot of 'coulds' and other qualifiers. We agree with the need for such caution and believe that the ranges quoted, if anything, understate the full level of uncertainty.

But the response has to be: 'So what?' Specifically, who would benefit, and how much, if the BBC's services were made more 'distinctive' and, therefore, less popular? The O&O and Oxera study suggests that the likely benefit to the BBC's rivals of making its most popular services more 'distinctive' is, at best, marginal: a maximum total increase in advertising revenue of only £86 million a year in the short term, rising to a maximum of £115 million a year by the end of the current Charter period, spread across all TV, radio and online services; plus any add-itional increase in consumer revenue. Eighty-six million pounds is equivalent to just 0.6 per cent of the £14.5 billion total TV, radio and online advertising in 2015[21] – hardly enough to justify the idea that the BBC had a 'chilling' effect on its commercial competitors, as claimed by James Murdoch and implied by John Whittingdale's obsession with its market impact.[22]

The area where the relative impact on advertising would be greatest, according to O&O and Oxera, is radio: an increase of £22 million–£38 million would be equivalent to 3.7–6.4 per cent of the total £592 million radio advertising revenue in 2015.[23] But even in this case, there is no evidence that the extra funds would be invested in more content for the benefit of listeners – and, for obvi-ous reasons, claims by the companies themselves can hardly be seen as reliable.[24] Meanwhile, UK commercial radio is booming, with record listening figures and advertising revenue in 2019.[25]

Other Considerations

For a complete assessment of whether reducing the funding, scope and scale of the BBC would be in the public interest, we need to take account of three important, but widely ignored, other considerations, beyond whether it crowds out its commer-cial competitors. O&O and Oxera were careful to acknowledge the first two of these, but did not mention the third.

First, they noted that, even if the BBC's market impact slightly reduces its commercial rivals' revenue, the overall effect on consumer choice might still be positive for several reasons: the BBC's role in developing new platforms; its own content investment, especially in original UK content (which not only has direct value to UK consumers but can also encourage rivals to invest more of their income on UK content); and various indirect benefits along the supply chain and in adjacent markets, such as the BBC's commissioning of UK independent producers and its promotion of new UK music.[26] In particular, as noted in Chapter 11 in the context of *The Great British Bake Off*, to evaluate the overall consumer impact of cutting the BBC's funding, we need to allow for the significant direct consumer detriment of losing BBC programmes – especially if the cuts were mainly concentrated on popular entertainment shows – which the great majority of consumers would consider only partly compensated for by the lower licence fee.

Secondly, O&O and Oxera explicitly noted that they had not looked at the BBC's total public value impact (i.e. including 'citizenship'/public service issues: 'the broader benefits to society from BBC activities'), nor its significant direct and indirect contribution to the wider economy (see Chapter 3). These issues fell outside the scope of the study.

The third important additional consideration, neither analysed nor mentioned by O&O and Oxera – is that any increase in commercial broadcasters' revenue resulting from cutting the funding, scope and scale of the BBC would itself not be costless to UK consumers: they would be paying for most or all of any incremental revenue either directly (through subscriptions) or indirectly (via advertising).[27]

The final major study of the BBC's market impact, which we now discuss, is, as far as we know, the only one to date to have incorporated this last consideration, as well as explicitly looking at the probable loss of BBC programmes and the impact on UK producers, if the funding, scope and scale of the BBC were reduced.

Scenarios Under Different Assumptions: The Reuters Institute Study

In February 2014, the Reuters Institute published a scenario-based study, by Patrick and Professor Robert Picard, of the total extent to which BBC television might be crowding out commercial TV, and the implications for UK consumers and producers.

This Reuters Institute study modelled what the 2012 UK television market might have been like if – beyond James Murdoch's wildest dreams when he ran Sky – there had been no BBC television and therefore no market impact on commercial TV broadcasters' revenue and no potential crowding out of their content investment.

A possible objection to this approach is that even the BBC's worst enemies are not – yet – proposing that it should be completely abolished, although that may be the eventual result of the cumulative funding cuts and some of the more radical proposals. However, the authors of the study concluded that: 'This objection is invalid for two reasons. First, those arguing that the BBC crowds out commercial provision assume that, if there were no BBC, commercial broadcasters would increase their content investment and consumers would, on balance, benefit. That is what we are testing. Secondly . . . the black-and-white no-BBC scenario provides a strong basis for evaluating less extreme proposals such as that the BBC should be scaled back'.[28]

To allow for the very wide range of uncertainty, the study explored both optimistic and pessimistic scenarios, where the 'optimistic' ones assumed relatively large increases in commercial broadcasters' revenue and content investment if there were no BBC TV and the 'pessimistic' ones assumed much smaller increases. This approach is broadly similar to the way companies evaluate alternative strategies and strategic investment decisions.

There are a lot of variables and scenarios in the study but the central 'base case', halfway between the main optimistic and pessimistic ones, serves to illustrate the analysis and results. Although the evidence, as already discussed, is that competition from public broadcasters does not, in reality, reduce commercial broadcasters' revenue and content investment, the Reuters Institute 'base case' optimistically assumed that, if there had been no

BBC TV in 2012, the commercial players' revenue would have been significantly, although not dramatically, higher: +6 per cent for the commercial PSBs (ITV, Channel 4 and Channel 5, mainly funded by advertising) and +22 per cent for the non-PSBs (all other commercial channels and platforms, mainly funded by subscriptions). The base-case scenario also assumed – again optimistically – that the commercial players' investment in both total and original UK content would have been higher by the same proportions (+6 per cent and +22 per cent, respectively).[29]

These rather modest increases would be even lower today because BBC TV's revenue share (and, therefore, potential market impact) has been sharply reduced by the 2010 and 2015 funding cuts and the rapid growth of pay TV and now SVoD since 2012.

Despite optimistic assumptions about how much higher commercial broadcasters' revenue and content investment would have been if there had been no BBC TV, the central base case projected that total UK TV industry revenue would have been 9 per cent lower without BBC TV's share of licence-fee revenue.

Even more important is the fact that the commercial players, especially the non-PSBs, invest a significantly lower proportion of their revenue in content, especially original British content, than the very high proportion invested by the BBC. The increase in their content investment if there had been no BBC TV would therefore have been far less than the lost BBC investment, especially in original British TV programmes. Specifically, in the base case with no BBC TV, the projected increase in commercial TV content investment would have been less than half of the lost investment by BBC TV. The net effect would have been a 15 per cent (£0.94 billion) reduction in total UK content investment.

For original British programmes, the impact would have been even worse: a projected increase of only £190 million invested by the commercial broadcasters – just one-eighth of the £1.52 billion actually invested in UK originations by BBC TV – leading to a massive 40 per cent (£1.33 billion) net reduction in first-run UK content investment.[30]

We repeat: the central base-case scenario in the Reuters Institute study is that, if there had been no BBC television, the total investment in original British TV programmes would have been 40 per cent lower – even after allowing for an increase in revenue and content investment by commercial broadcasters. Recall that this dire scenario is, if anything, optimistic: it assumes that, if there had been no BBC TV, commercial broadcasters' revenue would have been materially higher, despite extensive evidence to the contrary, and that this revenue increase would have fed through to a proportionate increase in their total and UK content investment.

Based on the results from the full range of scenarios, the study concluded that, if there had been no BBC TV, total TV content investment would have been 5 to 25 per cent lower and investment in original UK TV content 25 to 50 per cent lower – bad for viewers and a huge blow to independent British TV producers. There was *no* plausible scenario in which losing BBC TV would lead to a net increase in content investment.

What Drives These Results?

These results are driven by three factors.

First, as discussed in Chapter 4, in reality – if not in Paul Dacre's *Daily Mail* – the BBC's content investment represents a very high proportion of the licence-fee revenue it receives after top-slicing – and over 90 per cent of this investment is in original UK programmes. That's why eliminating BBC TV would reduce total content investment, especially in UK originations, so much.

Secondly, although they also invest a high proportion of their revenue in programmes, including UK originations – less than the BBC but much more than the non-PSBs – the commercial PSBs' revenue would increase only slightly if there were no BBC TV (+6 per cent in the base case). The reason is that most of their revenue as broadcasters[31] comes from advertising. The increase in the viewing of advertising-funded TV if there were no BBC would translate into a much smaller percentage increase in their revenue, because the price of TV advertising (the 'cost per thousand' viewers, or CPT) would be lower.[32] So the increase in their content investment would be small, even if they maintained it as a percentage of revenue.

Thirdly, pay-TV subscriptions might, conversely, be quite a lot higher[33] if there were no BBC TV (+22 per cent in the base case). But the pay-TV companies invest a much lower proportion of their revenue in content, especially first-run UK content (excluding sport), than the BBC and the commercial PSBs. So the increase in their content investment, although potentially significant in percentage terms, would still be small in absolute financial terms.

It is the combination of these three factors that explains why eliminating BBC TV would have such a negative impact on content investment – especially in first-run UK content – even after allowing for the BBC's market impact and the resulting 'crowding out' of commercial broadcasters' content investment.

All the Scenarios Are Bad, But the Reasons Differ

The key result of the Reuters Institute study is that, under all the scenarios explored (a very wide range), UK consumers and producers would be worse off overall if there were no BBC TV.[34] However, the reasons differ somewhat between the scenarios.

The optimistic scenarios assume that there would be no

significant net reduction in total UK content investment, because the increase in investment by commercial broadcasters would roughly – depending on the specific scenario – be enough to replace the lost investment by the BBC. However, these scenarios have two downsides. First, the assumed increase in commercial broadcasters' revenue would directly (subscriptions) or indirectly (advertising) come from consumers, and this increased cost would be much more than they would be saving on the licence fee. Secondly, even in the most optimistic scenario, total investment in UK originations would still be much lower without the BBC. In other words, even in these optimistic scenarios, if there were no BBC Television, viewers would on average be paying significantly more for their TV services but getting little, if any, increase in total TV content and much less original British TV content.

The pessimistic scenarios are, on balance, even worse, with much less choice for most households (a large reduction in total TV content investment and even bigger cuts in UK originations). The evidence is that very few households would consider this reduction in the available content to be compensated for by the lower licence fee and the slightly lower indirect cost of TV advertising.

On this basis, the Reuters Institute study suggested that, whatever the precise outcome might be if there were no BBC TV, (i) the range, quality and perceived value for money of television would be reduced for the great majority of British households, and (ii) independent producers would lose a large proportion of their UK revenue.

What About a 'Much, Much Smaller' BBC?

The damage would, of course, be less if, instead of no BBC TV, there was a 'much, much smaller' BBC, as advocated by Rupert and James Murdoch and some others. The study discussed a range of such intermediate options but found no reason to believe that any of them would be better for UK households than the status quo.[35] Crucially, neither the Murdochs, nor Paul Dacre, nor John Whittingdale, nor anyone else advocating a reduction in the funding, scope and scale of the BBC has ever, to our knowledge, provided any evidence suggesting that it would, on balance, benefit UK consumers.

Finally, note that the Reuters Institute study is only about the impact of no BBC TV, or a much smaller BBC, on the UK public as consumers. Like the econometric studies, it excludes the loss of all the additional 'citizenship' benefits of the BBC we discussed in Chapter 3.

The Reuters Institute study was published in February 2014. As far as we know, no one has published anything that seriously challenges either its analysis or its qualitative conclusions.[36]

Notes

Introduction: 'You Don't Know What You've Got 'Till It's Gone'

1 'Big Yellow Taxi', from *Ladies of the Canyon*, Joni Mitchell, 1970.

2 See https://www.youtube.com/watch?v=p3q2iZuU5WM.

3 For the lyrics, see https://genius.com/Mitch-benn-im-proud-of-the-bbc-lyrics.

4 BBC News, 'Emmy Awards 2019: the winners and the nominees', https://www.bbc.co.uk/news/entertainment-arts-49791351.

5 'Auntie' is a British nickname for the BBC, now rarely used.

6 For more information about BBC Radio 4's *Saturday Live* programme, see http://downloads.bbc.co.uk/radio/commissioning/Radio_4_Saturday_Live_Sat_0900-1030.pdf.

7 Although the BBC *was* used, very successfully, as a propaganda – and deception – weapon during the Second World War.

8 BBC News, 'BBC News to close 450 posts as part of 8m savings drive', 29 January 2020, https://www.bbc.co.uk/news/entertainment-arts-51271168.

9 Steven Barnett and Andrew Curry, *The Battle for the BBC*, Aurum Press, 1994.

10 'Why the BBC matters: memo to the new parliament about a unique British institution', *Political Quarterly*, 81, 3, July–September 2010, https://www.academia.edu/22625199/Why_the_BBC_matters_memo_to_the_new_parliament_about_a_unique_British_institution.

11 From Armando Iannucci's MacTaggart Lecture, 'We're All in This Together', 26 August 2015, https://www.thetvfestival.com/website/wp-content/uploads/2015/08/Armando-Iannucci-MacTaggart-Lecture-2015.pdf.

12 These attacks came to a head under Margaret Thatcher's premiership in the 1980s: see Jean Seaton, *Pinkoes and Traitors: The BBC and the Nation, 1974–1987*, Profile, 2015, and Steven Barnett and Andrew Curry, *The Battle for the BBC*, Aurum Press, 1994, which covers the decade 1984–94. Charlotte Higgins briefly covers the BBC's history since its foundation in *This New Noise: The Extraordinary Birth and Troubled Life of the BBC*, Faber & Faber in association with *The Guardian*, 2015. All three of these books are by authors largely supportive of the BBC. For a left-wing critique covering its whole history, see Tom Mills, *The BBC: Myth of a Public Service*, Verso, 2016. There are also many right-leaning critiques, such as Robin Aitken, *The Noble Liar: How and Why the BBC Distorts the News to Promote a Liberal Agenda*, Biteback, 2018, and, on a more hysterical note, David Sedgwick, *BBC: Brainwashing Britain? How and Why the BBC Controls Your Mind*, Sandgrounder, 2018.

13 Strictly speaking, YouTube is not a subscription video-on-demand service, because it is largely funded by advertising.

14 That is, apart from the Welsh-language TV channel S4C, which gets almost all of its funding from the licence fee.

15 For a growing proportion of consumers, but by no means all. In 2019, 48 per cent of UK households subscribed to one or more SVoD services, and that trend is increasing at a rate equivalent to 6–7 per cent of homes each year. SVoD take-up was significantly *higher* among those with pay TV. Tom Harrington, 'SVoD subscriber trends: who is buying and how many subs', Enders Analysis, 23 October 2019 [2019-084].

16 House of Lords, Select Committee on Communications and Digital, 'Public service broadcasting: as vital as ever', 5 November 2019, https://publications.parliament.uk/pa/ld201920/ldselect/ldcomuni/16/16.pdf.

17 Voice of the Listener and Viewer, 'VLV research shows a 30% decline in BBC public funding since 2010', 4 March 2020, https://www.vlv.org.uk/news/vlv-research-shows-a-30-decline-in-bbc-public-funding-since-2010/. The BBC's real net public funding refers to

licence-fee income plus government grants (to cover part of the cost of the BBC World Service), minus licence-fee income 'top-sliced' to fund other government activities, all adjusted for cumulative inflation using the Consumer Price Index.

18 Using VLV's figures, the net public funding of the BBC's UK services in 2019–20 was £3,203 million. In 2010–11 it was £4,580 million (£3,545 million x 1.292 cumulative inflation factor) in the same (2019–20) money. The difference (£4,580 million minus £3,203 million) was £1,377 million – 43 per cent of the £3,203 million net public funding of the BBC's UK services in 2019–20.

19 Chris Barrie, 'Free TV licence for over-75s', *The Guardian*, 10 November 1999, https://www.theguardian.com/business/1999/nov/10/4.

20 For instance, Jocelyn Hay, founder of the pressure group Voice of the Listener and Viewer, in conversation with Patrick Barwise. (See https://www.vlv.org.uk/.)

21 The annual cost of a colour TV licence was £101 and it was estimated that about 3 million households would be eligible.

22 Patrick Forster, 'Former BBC boss says government wrong to force corporation to pay for over-75 licences', *Daily Telegraph*, 23 December 2015, https://www.telegraph.co.uk/news/bbc/12067582/Former-BBC-boss-says-government-wrong-to-force-corporation-to-pay-for-over-75-licences.html.

23 For the Age UK campaign, see https://www.ageuk.org.uk/our-impact/campaigning/save-free-tv-for-older-people/.

24 The Market Research Society, at https://www.mrs.org.uk/.

25 Heather Stewart, 'Boris Johnson says BBC should "cough up" for TV licences for over-75s', *The Guardian*, 26 August 2019, https://www.theguardian.com/media/2019/aug/26/boris-johnson-bbc-cough-up-tv-licences-over-75s.

26 Jim Waterson, 'BBC licence fee: proposals to decriminalise non-payment', *The Guardian*, 5 February 2020, https://www.theguardian.com/media/2020/feb/05/bbc-facing-funding-cut-as-licence-fee-consultation-launched.

27 Yes, we know: Marie-Antoinette almost certainly *didn't* say 'Let them eat cake'. This *might* have been said about a hundred years earlier by Louis XIV's wife Marie-Therese. It was first attributed to Marie-Antoinette in a satirical left-wing journal, in 1843, fifty years after her death, by Alphonse Karr, editor of *Le Figaro*. See https://www.lievabout.com/let-them-eat-cake-er-brioche-oh-never-mind-3299161.

28 James Tapsfield, Jack Maidment, Claire Ellicott, Jason Groves and Paul Revoir, 'BBC goes to war with Boris Johnson after Prime Minister hints the TV licence fee could be SCRAPPED as he says it doesn't "make sense in the long term" ', *Daily Mail*, 9 December 2019, https://www.dailymail.co.uk/news/article-7771341/PM-woos-voters-Grimsby-saying-Jeremy-Corbyn-betrayed-Brexit.html. This article triggered 6,000 comments from *Daily Mail* readers.

29 Rowena Mason, 'Dominic Cummings think tank called for "end of BBC in current form" ', *The Guardian*, 21 January 2020, https://www.theguardian.com/politics/2020/jan/21/dominic-cummings-thinktank-called-for-end-of-bbc-in-current-form.

30 It's worth looking at *exactly* what Cummings wrote about the BBC in his short-lived 'New Frontiers Foundation' blog of 2004 (there is a link to it in Rowena Mason's article cited above). He described it as the 'mortal enemy of the Right' and called for 'the end of the BBC in its current form.' He then set out a four-point plan to achieve that. First, the BBC must be *discredited* – and it's clear he meant Trump-style pre-emptive discrediting, with front-organization 'monitors' and constant online attacks to make people distrust the BBC's reporting. Second, he called for a *Fox News-style ultra-right-wing TV broadcaster* over here. The third front would be *phone-in-based, shock-jock British radio stations* (think Rush Limbaugh and Glenn Beck). Finally, he suggests *lifting the UK ban on political TV advertising*. That means, say, Lord Ashcroft, and others, less openly, using their millions to talk politics to the nation in the *Coronation Street* ad breaks. All of this is straight out of the US right-wing playbook. It would give us a

media and political ecology similar to the American one, which underpins the divisions we're now seeing there.

31 Jemma Carr, 'Nicky Morgan and Andrew Neil are in the running to be the BBC's next chairman as Boris Johnson seeks candidates who do not want to "blow up" the broadcaster', *Mail on Sunday*, 9 August 2020, https://www.dailymail.co.uk/news/article-8609191/Nicky-Morgan-Andrew-Neil-running-BBCs-chairman.html.

Chapter 1: What, Exactly, Is the BBC?

1 General Post Office, the UK's postal, telephone and telegraph (PTT) service, a government agency, later split into three parts was privatized as British Telecom (BT), the Royal Mail Group and the Post Office Ltd.

2 He was secretary to the London Conservative and Unionist candidates in the November 1922 general election.

3 About a thousand UK public and private bodies operate under Royal Charters, a system going back to the thirteenth century. They include towns and cities, universities and colleges (including London Business School, awarded its Charter in 1986), city guilds and livery companies, charities and other institutions that work in the public interest and can demonstrate 'pre-eminence, stability and permanence in their particular field'. The Royal Charter defines the Corporation's purpose and privileges. It is granted by the monarch on the advice of the Privy Council, a committee of senior politicians, see https://privycouncil.independent.gov.uk/royal-charters/#.

4 There are fourteen BBC board members. The chairman and the non-executive members for England, Scotland, Wales and Northern Ireland are appointed by the government; five other non-executive members and four executive members, including the Director-General, are appointed by the board itself: see https://www.bbc.com/aboutthebbc/whoweare/bbcboard.

5 Sarah Cook, 'China Central Television: A long-standing weapon in Beijing's arsenal of repression', *Diplomat*, 25 September 2019, https://thediplomat.com/2019/09/china-central-television-a-long-standing-weapon-in-beijings-arsenal-of-repression/.

6 See CBS News, Bob Bicknall, 'Russian news, English accent', 11 December 2015, https://www.cbsnews.com/news/russian-news-english-accent-11-12-2005/; Luke Harding, 'Russia Today launches first UK ad blitz', *The Guardian*, 18 December 2009, https://www.theguardian.com/world/2009/dec/18/russia-today-propaganda-ad-blitz; Brett LoGiurato, 'Russia's propaganda channel just got a journalism lesson from the US state', *Business Insider*, 29 April 2014, https://www.businessinsider.com/state-department-responds-rt-russia-today-john-kerry-2014-4?r=US&IR=T#!HDahV; Michael Crowley, 'Tit-for-tat: Putin's maddening propaganda trick', *Time Magazine*, 1 May 2014, https://time.com/84843/vladimir-putin-russia-propaganda/; Neil MacFarquhar, 'A powerful Russian weapon: the spread of false stories', *The New York Times*, 28 August 2016, https://www.nytimes.com/2016/08/29/world/europe/russia-sweden-disinformation.html; BBC News, Stephen Ennis, 'Ukraine hits back at Russian TV onslaught', 12 March 2014, https://www.bbc.co.uk/news/world-europe-26546083; RT, 'Salisbury poisoning: one year on, still no evidence of Novichok nerve agent use disclosed to public', 4 March 2019, https://www.rt.com/news/452946-skripal-anniversary-truth-novichok/; and Solape Alatise and David Bond, 'Russia spread "disinformation" on Skripal attack', *Financial Times*, 1 March 2019, https://www.ft.com/content/c655aa4a-3b82-11e9-b856-5404d3811663.

7 The USAGM, formerly the Broadcasting Board of Governors, broadcasts in one hundred countries and sixty-one languages. It operates five networks: Voice of America (VOA), Radio Free Europe/Radio Liberty, the Office of Cuba Broadcasting (*Radio y Television Marti*), Radio Free Asia and the Middle East Broadcasting Networks (MBN).

8 FP/The Cable, John Hudson, 'U.S. repeals propaganda ban, spreads government-made news to Americans', 14 July 2013, https://foreignpolicy.com/2013/07/14/u-s-repeals-propaganda-ban-spreads-government-made-news-to-americans/.

9 John Bonazzo, '"Most worthless" US government agency may become Trump TV', *Observer*, 23 August 2018, https://observer.com/2018/08/broadcasting-board-of-governors-us-agency-for-global-media-michael-pack-trump/; Arwa Mahdawi, 'Michael Pack: the Bannon ally critics fear will become Trump's global propagandist', *The Guardian*, 6 June 2018, https://www.theguardian.com/media/2018/jun/06/michael-pack-steve-bannon-ally-broadcasting-board-of-governors; Michael Hastings, 'Congressmen seek to lift propaganda ban', Buzzfeed News, 18 May 2012, https://www.buzzfeednews.com/article/mhastings/congressmen-seek-to-lift-propaganda-ban.

10 His real name was Eric Blair, but he is best known as George Orwell, the name we use here.

11 Maev Kennedy, 'George Orwell returns to loom over the BBC', *The Guardian*, 7 November 2017, https://www.theguardian.com/books/2017/nov/07/george-orwell-returns-to-loom-over-bbc.

12 From an unused preface to *Animal Farm*.

13 Something rather similar happens with Churchill and Brexit.

14 Kennedy, 'George Orwell returns to loom over the BBC'.

15 Telegraph reporters, 'Andrew Marr: George Orwell would have "sneered and spat" on his statue unveiled by the BBC', *Daily Telegraph*, 7 November 2017, https://www.telegraph.co.uk/news/2017/11/07/andrew-marr-george-orwell-would-have-sneered-spat-statue-unveiled/.

16 Michael Shelden, *Orwell: The Authorised Biography*, Heinemann, 1991, p. 274.

17 Antony Beevor, *The Battle for Spain: The Spanish Civil War 1936–1939*, Weidenfeld & Nicholson, 2007, Chapter 23, 'The Civil War within the Civil War'.

18 George Orwell, *Homage to Catalonia*, Secker and Warburg, 1938.

19 See William Dalrymple, 'Novel explosives of the Cold War', *Spectator*, 24 August 2019.

20 It is now thought that he picked up TB in a Spanish hospital as he was recovering from his war wound, although he suffered from respiratory problems all his life. See Jason Daley, 'Did George Orwell pick up TB during the Spanish Civil War?', *Smithsonian*, 2 August 2018, https://www.smithsonianmag.com/smart-news/george-orwell-may-have-picked-tb-during-spanish-civil-war-180969807/.

21 On 23 August 1939, Germany and the Soviet Union signed a secret non-aggression pact ('the 'Treaty of Non-Aggression between Germany and the Union of Soviet Socialist Republics', usually referred to as the Hitler–Stalin Pact or the Molotov–Ribbentrop Pact). They agreed to carve up Eastern Europe (Finland, the Baltic States, Poland and Romania) between them without interfering with each other. Nine days later (on 1 September 1939) Germany invaded Poland, triggering the Second World War. For a brief summary of the pact, see https://www.history.com/this-day-in-history/the-hitler-stalin-pact.

22 In June 1940 this was followed by Italy becoming Germany's ally too, further increasing the military imbalance. Japan and the USA joined the Axis and the Allies, respectively, in December 1941.

23 Edward Stourton, *Auntie's War: The BBC during the Second World War*, Doubleday, 2017, pp. 161 and 357.

24 He had been struck by the success of Arthur Koestler's 1940 novel *Darkness at Noon*, also triggered by the author's experience fighting for the Republicans in Spain, in contrast to the failure of Orwell's factual *Homage to Catalonia*. See Dalrymple, 'Novel explosives'.

25 George Orwell, *Nineteen Eighty-Four*, Secker and Warburg, 1949.

26 *The Real Room 101*, BBC Four, 10 July 2003, https://web.archive.org/web/20070105132434/http://www.bbc.co.uk/bbcfour/documentaries/features/room-101.shtml. The programme suggested that another

inspiration may have been the headmaster's study at Orwell's prep school, St Cyprian's in Eastbourne.

27 There is a large literature on the General Strike. For the BBC's role, we draw on Tom Mills, *The BBC: Myth of a Public Service*, Verso, 2016, especially pp. 11–19, and Charlotte Higgins, *This New Noise: The Extraordinary Birth and Troubled Life of the BBC*, Faber & Faber in association with *The Guardian*, 2015, pp. 140–44.

28 In summary, the facts of the strike are as follows: in response to falling coal prices in the 1920s, the mine owners tried to impose wage cuts. The miners' union refused, supported by the Trades Union Congress (TUC), which threatened a general strike. Attempts to negotiate a settlement failed. According to one authority (Keith Laybourne, *The General Strike of 1926*, Manchester University Press, 1993, p. 43) the breakdown was triggered by the refusal by printers at the *Daily Mail* to print an editorial ('For King and Country') condemning the threatened strike as 'not an industrial dispute [but] a revolutionary move which can only succeed by destroying the government and subverting the rights and liberties of the people'. Whatever the exact causes, the mine owners locked out the miners and the TUC called a general strike on 3 May 1926. The aim was to force the government, under Stanley Baldwin, to intervene, thus preventing the cuts to miners' wages. In addition to the 1.2 million miners already locked out by their employers, the TUC called out 500,000 other workers in strategic industries, such as steelworkers, dockers, railwaymen and printers. It avoided calling an all-out general strike because it wanted to avoid the risk of a Communist revolution. The strike ended after nine days, having achieved no concessions for the miners.

29 Andrew Boyle, *Only the Wind Will Listen: Reith of the BBC*, Hutchinson, 1972, p. 195.

30 Mills, *The BBC: Myth of a Public Service*, p. 12.

31 Ibid., p. 4.

32 There were certainly those in Britain and elsewhere who *had* hoped the strike would lead to a Communist revolution – and

there were many more who had feared it: in the words of Virginia Woolf's dentist on 7 May, 'It is red rag versus Union Jack, Mrs Woolf', Higgins, *This New Noise*, p. 141. The Tsar and Kaiser, first cousins of the king, had both been overthrown and the former machine-gunned to death in a basement with his family. The dangers to the British state may have been less than Woolf's dentist thought, but his fears were not baseless.

33 Lord Moran, *Churchill: The Struggle for Survival, 1940–1965*, Constable, 1966, p. 390.

34 Higgins, *This New Noise*, p. 144.

35 Strictly speaking, the first regular BBC TV service ran from 1936 until September 1939, but the number of households able to watch was tiny. The service restarted after the war, in June 1946. TV penetration grew steadily and then took off for the Queen's Coronation in June 1953 and thereafter. The initial launch of ITV was in London in September 1955. The ITV network covered most homes by 1959, and the whole of the UK, including remote rural areas and the Channel Islands, by 1962.

36 This figure includes the commercial PSBs ITV, Channel 4 and Channel 5.

37 The first regular US television services started on a very limited scale in 1928: 'WRNY [a short-lived radio station in New York] has extended television schedule', says *The New York Times*, 30 September 1928, p. 155. The 1941 broadcast was the first one with a paid advertisement, as reported by R. W. Stewart, 'Imagery for Profit', *The New York Times*, 6 July 1941.

38 The first non-profit broadcaster in the US was the Educational Television and Radio Center (ETRC) funded by the Ford Foundation. Since 1970, the main US public service broadcasters have been the Public Broadcasting Service (PBS) and National Public Radio (NPR).

39 George Orwell's 'Notes on Nationalism' was first published in *Polemic*, in October 1945. It's also at https://www.orwellfoundation. com/the-orwell-foundation/orwell/essays-and-other-works/ notes-on-nationalism/.

Chapter 2: The Media Landscape Today: A Netflix Universe?

1 Steven Glover, *Daily Mail*, 1 March 2018, 'I say this in sadness, but unless the B B C gets its act together it may not be here in 15 years', http://www.dailymail.co.uk/news/article-5447965/The-BBC-not-15-years.html.

2 The *Independent* is described as 'left–center' (by U S standards) according to the Media Bias/Fact Check website: https://mediabiasfactcheck.com/the-independent/.

3 Stephen Glover, 'We all know the B B C is Leftie. But making a Labour henchman head of radio would be beyond satire', *Daily Mail*, 26 August 2016, https://www.dailymail.co.uk/debate/article-3760771/STEPHEN-GLOVER-know-BBC-Leftie-making-Labour-henchman-head-radio-satire.html.

4 Stephen Glover, 'Why did the all-powerful BBC refuse to tell the truth about Mr Corbyn?', *Daily Mail*, 10 June 2017.

5 Unlike most serial Beeb-bashers, Glover also occasionally criticizes the other PSBs, both Channel 4 ('Tawdry, banal and tediously Left-wing. Will someone tell me why we don't just sell off Channel 4?', *Daily Mail*, 30 March 2017, https://www.dailymail.co.uk/debate/article-4362756/Will-tell-don-t-just-sell-Channel-4.html) and I T V – although, in this case, with a side swipe at the B B C as well ('Replacing News at Ten with this tripe gives yet more power to the B B C and damages democracy', *Daily Mail*, 2 March 2017, https://www.dailymail.co.uk/debate/article-4273586/STEPHEN-GLOVER-Replacing-News-Ten-gives-power-BBC.html).

6 Glover, 'I say this in sadness'.

7 Ibid.

8 See Jeremy Tunstall, *The Media Are American: Anglo-American Media in the World*, Constable, 1977, and Jean K. Chalaby, *The Format Age: Television's Entertainment Revolution*, Polity, 2015.

9 In Channel 4's case, only just: despite repeated denials, the government was accidentally revealed in September 2015 to be actively considering privatizing it, a pet project of Culture

Secretary John Whittingdale; see also Jane Martinson, 'Government may privatise Channel 4, document reveals', *The Guardian*, 24 September 2015, https://www.theguardian.com/media/2015/sep/24/government-considering-channel-4-privatisation-document-slip-up-reveals. Had it been privatized, the buyer would most likely have been one of the large US media companies: see Patrick Barwise and Gillian Brooks, 'The consequences of privatizing Channel 4', report commissioned by Channel Four, 4 May 2016.

10 Although the proprietors of the *Telegraph* and *Mail* are based offshore for tax purposes.

11 Other foreign-owned UK media include Bauer Radio, the Number Two commercial radio group (Bauer Media), the *Sun*, *The Times*, the *Sunday Times* and Wireless Group stations, mainly Talksport and Virgin Radio UK (News Corp); and the *Financial Times* (Nikkei).

12 Bauer is German, Nikkei Japanese.

13 The main exception is the hugely popular *Peppa Pig* on Channel 5 and Nick Jr. Its UK producer, Astley Baker Davies, is now owned by Toronto-based Entertainment One, but the spirit of the programme and the characters' language and accents (an important issue for many parents) remain resolutely British.

14 On Sky's electronic programme guide, CBBC and CBeebies are listed below *twelve* US cartoon networks: see James Purnell, 'British TV is being hidden away by global digital giants. They should be forced to play fair', *Sunday Telegraph*, 19 March 2017, https://www.telegraph.co.uk/tv/2017/03/19/british-tv-hidden-away-global-digital-giants-should-forced-play/.

15 BBC, 'BBC annual report and accounts 2018–19', p. 68, https://downloads.bbc.co.uk/aboutthebbc/reports/annualreport/2018-19.pdf.

16 Patrick Barwise and Leo Watkins, 'The Evolution of Digital Dominance: How and Why We Got to GAFA', in Martin Moore and Damian Tambini, eds., *Digital Dominance: The Power of Google, Amazon, Facebook and Apple*, Oxford University Press, 2018, pp. 21–49, https://lbsresearch.london.edu/914/.

17 Josef Adalian, 'Inside the binge factory', *New York Magazine*, 11 June 2018, https://www.vulture.com/2018/06/how-netflix-swallowed-tv-industry.html?_ga=2.178490400.546117194.1546439346-1890554006.1542129545.

18 Thanks to the opaque financial reporting of Google's parent company, Alphabet, it is unclear whether YouTube, with its high content costs and overheads, is profitable: https://www.theregister.co.uk/2018/02/28/sec_google_youtube/.

19 In January 2020, Disney announced that, to avoid any association with Fox News, it would drop the Fox name from this business, rebranding the 20th Century Fox film studio as 20th Century Studios, https://variety.com/2020/film/news/disney-dropping-fox-20th-century-studios-1203470349/.

20 See James Brumley, 'Netflix cash burn likely to get worse . . . much worse', *Seeking Alpha*, 31 July 2019, https://seekingalpha.com/article/4279764-netflix-cash-burn-likely-get-worse-much-much-worse.

21 See Anna Nicolaou, 'Netflix to lift prices for US customers by up to 18%', *Financial Times*, 15 January 2019, https://www.ft.com/content/9f060f18-18d5-11e9-9e64-d150b3105d21.

22 See James Dean, 'European projects are Netflix's latest billion-dollar baby', *The Times*, 19 April 2018, https://www.thetimes.co.uk/article/european-projects-are-netflix-s-latest-billion-dollar-baby-nwkn57vh3.

23 Video on demand is extremely bandwidth-heavy, especially with high-definition TV (during the peak evening hours, when networks are under the most stress, Netflix alone already often accounts for 40 per cent of all download traffic in the US). See Jane Wakefield, 'Netflix viewing eats up the world's data', BBC News, 4 October 2018, https://www.bbc.co.uk/news/technology-45745362.

24 Ofcom, 'Media nations: UK 2019', 18 July 2018, p. 11, https://www.ofcom.org.uk/__data/assets/pdf_file/0019/160714/media-nations-2019-uk-report.pdf.

25 See Dean, 'European projects'.

26 For instance, in the heyday of mainframe computers, IBM enjoyed not only market-leading economies of scale in research, production, systems software development and customer support, but also the advantage that programmers, operators and application developers all had an incentive to focus on working within its huge customer base of installed systems (using its dominant System/360 and 370 standard) rather than the much smaller customer base of any of its competitors using different standards – and anything developed within that framework would have a large and immediate uptake. When most computing shifted to PCs, Microsoft (the main supplier of PC software) enjoyed similar advantages. Patrick Barwise, 'Why tech markets are winner-take-all', LSE Media Policy Project, http://blogs.lse.ac.uk/mediapolicyproject/2018/06/14/why-tech-markets-are-winner-take-all/.

27 Much of the data available is per household, though, which is why parents may receive recommendations based on their children's viewing, and vice versa. Viewing data are also used to inform content investment decisions, although these are still largely based on judgements about the expected value to subscribers, relative to the cost of the programme, rather than by using automatic algorithms. Adalian, 'Inside the binge factory'.

28 Jo Ellison, 'Is Netflix's global dominance a force for good or bad?', *Financial Times*, 28 December 2018, https://www.ft.com/content/13078a02-0465-11e9-99df-6183d3002ee1.

29 Sarah Hughes, 'The BBC's Bodyguard is becoming a "Netflix Original". So who gets the credit?', *The Guardian*, 20 September 2018, https://www.theguardian.com/commentisfree/2018/sep/20/bbc-bodyguard-netflix-original-streaming.

30 Ellison, 'Netflix's global dominance'.

31 See BBC, 'The BBC's distribution strategy', 12 February 2018, http://downloads.bbc.co.uk/aboutthebbc/insidethebbc/howwework/accountability/consultations/bbc_distribution_strategy.pdf. See also the House of Lords, Select Committee on Communications

and Digital, 'Public service broadcasting: as vital as ever', 5 November 2019, https://publications.parliament.uk/pa/ld201920/ldselect/ldcomuni/16/16.pdf.

32 Global competitors in the commercial sector can usually get out of paying corporation tax on their earnings. However, UK-based broadcasters in the commercial sector are obliged to pay corporation tax on their earnings, which gives them a major disadvantage. But, in actual fact, the publicly owned BBC and Channel 4 have to pay very little corporation tax as they aim to run on a break-even basis over the medium term. The pay-TV companies, ITV and Channel 5, pay more tax.

33 Another competitive disadvantage for PSBs has to do with rules on intellectual property (IP). If a programme is commissioned by a PSB from an independent producer, that PSB will carry most of the financial risk, but, under the current terms of trade, the independent producer retains the IP for subsequent exploitation and therefore the profit if the show becomes a big success. This separation of risk (mostly carried by the PSB) and potential reward (mostly going to the producer) has undoubtedly contributed to the success of the UK's flourishing independent production sector, but it places the PSBs at a disadvantage in competing against US-based SVoD services, which have no such constraints on them.

34 House of Lords, Select Committee on Communications and Digital, 'Public service broadcasting', p. 44.

35 David Clementi, speech to the annual conference of Voice of the Listener and Viewer, 20 November 2019, see https://www.bbc.co.uk/mediacentre/speeches/2019/clementi-vlv.

36 Peter Thiel, 'Competition is for losers', *Wall Street Journal*, 12 September 2014, https://www.wsj.com/articles/peter-thiel-competition-is-for-losers-1410535536.

37 See Bharat Ganesh, 'The Silicon Valley mantra of "Move fast and break things" has fallen miserably short', *New Statesman*, 26 April 2018, https://tech.newstatesman.com/guest-opinion/move-fast-break-things-mantra.

38 This is a serious threat. Mainly because of lower-priced SVoD services, the proportion of UK broadband households with pay TV saying they were likely to cancel in the next year doubled from 12 per cent in late 2015 to 24 per cent in late 2018, see the article from noted media research company Parks Associates: http://www.parksassociates.com/blog/article/pr-05012019.

39 Including the pay-TV companies: although they get most of their revenue from subscriptions, their advertising revenue is high-margin and makes a significant profit contribution.

40 'BARB Establishment Survey', April 2011–March 2012 and April–June 2019, Broadcasters' Audience Research Board, https://www.barb.co.uk/resources/establishment-survey/.

41 Anna Nicolaou, 'Disney unveils streaming service aimed at undercutting Netflix', *Financial Times*, 12 April 2019, https://www.ft.com/content/44d2cc30-5cbd-11e9-9dde-7aedca0a081a.

42 By competing for viewers, especially younger viewers, with low-priced or 'free' (i.e. advertising-funded) online TV and video services, global SVoD competitors may also, over the long term, reduce the perceived value of BBC Television. It is not that large numbers of viewers no longer watch broadcast TV. Instead, most people now watch a mixture of broadcast and online TV and video, from multiple services, and with a steadily increasing proportion of their viewing time allocated to YouTube and SVoD, especially among younger viewers.

43 From 1965–9, BBC Two's channel controller was David Attenborough, although he preferred making nature programmes to being a senior manager.

44 The BBC first introduced FM in 1955, but it was not fully deployed until the 1980s: https://en.wikipedia.org/wiki/FM_broadcasting_in_the_UK.

45 The Competition Commission, now the Competition and Markets Authority, was the UK government agency tasked with regulating markets and company mergers and acquisitions to ensure healthy competition.

46 Mark Sweeney, 'Broadcasters to launch joint VoD service', *The Guardian*, 27 November 2007, https://www.theguardian.com/media/2007/nov/27/bbc.itv.

47 The OFT was a non-ministerial UK government department from 1973–2014 which was responsible for consumer protection.

48 For instance, if an already large company was allowed to acquire a particular competitor.

49 Unilever's UK 'umbrella brand' for ice cream is Wall's. Magnum is a specific product brand (or sub-brand) under the Wall's brand, with several varieties, such as Magnum Classic.

50 That is, recorded by a member of the household on a video-cassette recorder (VCR) or digital (or personal) video recorder (DVR/PVR).

51 The Competition Commission has now been closed, so it's not possible to access their reports, but WiredGov, a government and public-sector news alerting service, issued this press release on 4 February 2009, 'Project Kangaroo: final report', https://www.wired-gov.net/wg/wg-news-1.nsf/0/64CCF126521FB2B38025755300321E08?OpenDocument.

52 There was one exception: Sky's Now TV, a relatively marginal player, launched in 2012. By 2019, it was available in 10 per cent of homes, but in almost all cases (about nineteen out of twenty) as a supplement to Netflix and/or Amazon Prime Video, see Ofcom, 'Media nations: UK 2019', p. 60, at https://www.ofcom.org.uk/__data/assets/pdf_file/0019/160714/media-nations-2019-uk-report.pdf.

53 BBC News, 'BritBox: UK broadcasters enter the streaming wars as new service launches', 7 November 2019, https://www.bbc.co.uk/news/entertainment-arts-50320731.

54 YouTube launched in 2005 and was bought by Google in 2006. It is advertising-funded and has always been available worldwide, except where it is blocked by individual governments. Netflix launched in the UK in 2012. Amazon acquired the UK DVD rental and SVoD company LoveFilm in 2011 and turned it into Amazon Prime Video in the UK in 2014.

55   Tony Hall, in a speech at the 2018 Royal Television Society London Conference, 18 September 2018, https://www.bbc.co.uk/mediacentre/speeches/2018/tony-hall-rts.

Chapter 3: 'What Have the Romans Ever Done for Us?'

1   From the 1979 film, *Monty Python's Life of Brian*, http://montypython.50webs.com/scripts/Life_of_Brian/10.htm.

2   See https://www.similarweb.com/top-websites/united-kingdom.

3   BBC, 'BBC group annual report and accounts 2018–19', https://downloads.bbc.co.uk/aboutthebbc/reports/annualreport/2018-19.pdf.

4   Kantar Media undertook a survey for the BBC to ascertain this (across 1,038 UK households during July–August 2015). Note that this is the lowest time of the year for BBC consumption even among those not away on holiday. Source: BBC, 'BBC's response to the Department of Culture, Media and Sport's green paper: BBC charter review', Audience appendix, 2015, http://downloads.bbc.co.uk/aboutthebbc/insidethebbc/reports/pdf/bbc_charter_review_audiences_appendix.pdf.

5   BBC, 'BBC group annual report and accounts 2018–19', p. 56.

6   For the hours watching television and listening to the radio, see, ibid. p. 27; however, the online figure is for 2017–18, see the 'BBC group annual report and accounts 2017–18', p. 2, http://downloads.bbc.co.uk/aboutthebbc/insidethebbc/reports/pdf/bbc_annualreport_201718.pdf. (BBC Online reach was slightly higher in 2018–19, but the BBC did not publish the 2018–19 figures for average hours.)

7   Source: Office of National Statistics.

8   MTM, 'Life without the BBC: household study', August 2015, https://downloads.bbc.co.uk/aboutthebbc/reports/pdf/lifewithoutthebbc.pdf. Previous research had suggested that if people were either (i) allowed to reflect overnight on their initial

survey responses (Andrew Ehrenberg and Pam Mills, 'Viewers' willingness to pay for the BBC', London Business School, 1990), or (ii) shown the range of practical policy options and given enough time and information to discuss them and think about them (Opinion Leader Research, report prepared for the BBC Governance Unit, 'BBC governors' licence-fee-bid forum', March 2006, http://downloads.bbc.co.uk/bbctrust/assets/files/pdf/our_ work/govs/olr_citizensforum.pdf), their views of the BBC and the value for money of the licence fee became even more positive – or, for some, less negative. It was therefore decided to put this to a stronger test.

9 Specifically, the researchers talked to seventy households from across the UK, split into three sub-groups: (i) Twenty-four households representing the 12 per cent who, in the initial survey, said they'd prefer to *pay nothing and receive no BBC services*, (ii) Twenty-four households representing the 16 per cent who initially said they would *willingly only pay less than the current licence fee to receive the BBC's services*, and (iii) Twenty-two households representing the 69-per-cent majority, who initially said they would be *willing to pay at least the current level of the licence fee to continue receiving the BBC's services*.

10 Thirty-three out of a total of forty-eight households tested, making 69 per cent. Conversely, just one in twenty-two households who initially claimed the licence fee was good value for money went the other way, saying that, having lived without the BBC for nine days, they'd prefer to continue doing so and save the cost.

11 MTM, 'Life without the BBC: household study', August 2015.

12 BBC, About the BBC, Governance and regulation, Charter and agreement, https://www.bbc.com/aboutthebbc/governance/charter.

13 See p. 3 of the Federation of Entertainment Unions' booklet, 'BBC cuts: there is an alternative', 12 November 2012, at the National Union of Journalists' weblink address following : https://www.nuj.org.uk/documents/bbc-cuts-there-is-an-alternative/.

14 See Dominic Sandbrook, *The Great British Dream Factory*, Allen Lane, 2015; Jean K. Chalaby, *The Format Age: Television's Entertainment Revolution*, Polity, 2015.

15 Oscar A. H. Schmitz, *Das Land ohne Musik: Englische Gesellschaftsprobleme*, Munich, Georg Mueller, 1914. For an English translation, see Schmitz, *The Land without Music*, trans. H. Herzl, Jarrold, 1926.

16 Deloitte, 'The economic impact of the BBC: 2008–9', 2010. This and subsequent studies used standard economic methodology under which the GVA includes three elements: (i) direct value added (revenue minus purchases from other organizations), (ii) the indirect impact on the GVA of firms in the supply chain and (iii) the 'induced' impact on the GVA of firms outside the supply chain.

17 Estimated by the BBC itself, using Deloitte's 2010 methodology with updated figures: BBC, 'The economic value of the BBC: 2011–12', January 2013, http://downloads.bbc.co.uk/aboutthebbc/insidethebbc/howwework/reports/pdf/bbc_economic_impact_2013.pdf.

18 This is due to a so-called 'multiplier effect': the money the BBC spends on its suppliers increases how much they spend with their suppliers, and so on, and so on.

19 The PwC study focused on the effect of a 25-per-cent cut in the TV licence fee. According to PwC, the net impact would be a reduction of £630 million per year in UK GDP. See PwC, 'BBC: the impact of a change in the BBC's licence fee revenue', 26 August 2015, http://downloads.bbc.co.uk/aboutthebbc/reports/pdf/bbclfpwc2015.pdf.

20 'Electromagnetic spectrum' refers to a range of radiation frequencies that can be used by wireless communication services, mainly broadcasters and mobile communications operators. To avoid interference, each frequency band can normally be used by only one service. Spectrum within a country is therefore a scarce national asset, which the country's rulers can choose to give or sell to companies wishing to use particular frequency bands.

Nowadays, at least in democratic countries, it is usually auctioned to maximize the financial return and, at least in theory, ensure that it goes to the company most likely to maximize its commercial value. However, there are various ways in which this can go wrong, even in theory (e.g. from companies overbidding). The theory also assumes no collusion or corruption and completely ignores the differing *social* value of different types of service, notably public service broadcasters versus mobile telecoms. Allocating spectrum between different *types* of service therefore comes down to a political decision: Patrick Barwise, Martin Cave, Peter Culham, Tony Lavender, Neil Pratt and Damian Tambini, 'Incorporating social value into spectrum allocation decisions', for the DCMS, November 2015, https://assets.publishing.service.gov.uk/government/uploads/system/uploads/attachment_data/file/480112/SVOS_REPORT_-_FINAL_18112015REV26112015.pdf.

21 From a presentation to a UK Competition Network consumer remedies workshop: Alex Pumfrey, 'The UK's switch to digital TV', 22 June 2017, https://assets.publishing.service.gov.uk/government/uploads/system/uploads/attachment_data/file/630712/alex-pumfrey-the-uks-switch-to-digital-tv.pdf.

22 House of Commons, DCMS, 'BBC licence fee settlement and annual report', 19 May 2011, pp. 28–9, https://publications.parliament.uk/pa/cm201012/cmselect/cmcumeds/454/454.pdf.

23 BBC, 'BBC annual plan 2019–20', March 2019, p. 33, http://downloads.bbc.co.uk/aboutthebbc/reports/annualplan/annualplan_2019-20.pdf.

24 That is, between 2018 and 2019, see the BBC Media Centre report, 'BBC international audience soars to record high of 426m', 18 June 2019, https://www.bbc.co.uk/mediacentre/latestnews/2019/bbc-international-audience-record-high.

25 Portland Communications, '2018: the soft power 30', https://softpower30.com/country/united-kingdom/.

26 That is, apart from the income S4C earns from airtime sales and other commercial activities, which is only about 3 per cent of its

total revenue: 'S4C annual report 2017–18', p. 147, https://dlo6cycw1kmbs.cloudfront.net/media/media_assets/s4c-annual-report-and-accounts-spreads.pdf.

27 Set up in 1939, BBC Monitoring reports and analyses broadcast, print and online media news in seventy languages from 150 countries, especially those where foreign journalists are banned or their activities severely restricted. It aims to show 'not only what the media are reporting but also how they are telling the story' (see https://www.bbc.co.uk/programmes/p024nq1g). Its reports are used by the UK government, other governments and agencies and commercial clients. Since April 2013, it has been fully funded out of TV licence-fee revenue: see House of Commons, Defence Committee, 'Open source stupidity: the threat to the BBC Monitoring Service', 13 December 2016, https://publications.parliament.uk/pa/cm201617/cmselect/cmdfence/748/748.pdf. Following recent cuts, the annual cost is £25 million. The cuts to BBC Monitoring were also criticized by the House of Commons' Foreign Affairs Committee in their report, 'The future operations of BBC Monitoring', https://publications.parliament.uk/pa/cm201617/cmselect/cmfaff/732/732.pdf.

28 The local news partnerships comprise 150 local democracy reporters covering councils and other public bodies on behalf of the BBC and local news media; a news hub giving local news partners access to BBC video and audio material for use online; and a shared Data Unit training reporters on secondment from local media in data journalism skills. The annual cost is £8 million, see BBC, 'Local news partnerships: annual review 2017–18', 2018, http://downloads.bbc.co.uk/aboutthebbc/insidethebbc/howwework/reports/pdf/local_news_partnerships_annual_review_2018.pdf. The scheme has been criticized on the grounds that, as of February 2018, 130 of the 144 Local Democracy Reporter contracts had been allocated to Trinity Mirror, Newsquest or Johnston Press – 'those very publishers that have been consolidating operations and closing papers while protecting their profit

base' – rather than supporting independent local and hyperlocal publishers: Steven Barnett, 'Why Theresa May's plan to save local journalism could end up benefiting media moguls', *The Conversation*, 9 February 2018, https://theconversation.com/why-theresa-mays-plan-to-save-local-journalism-could-end-up-benefiting-media-moguls-91581. It is unclear to what extent the scheme is increasing the number of local reporters rather than simply boosting the profits of the big publishing groups. The initial contracts end in January 2021 and, at that point, it will be possible to take stock and adjust the scheme if need be.

29 Kevin Rawlinson, 'BBC says Amazon and Netflix may get surplus rural broadband funds', *The Guardian*, 19 October 2018, https://www.theguardian.com/media/2018/oct/19/bbc-says-amazon-and-netflix-may-get-rural-broadband-surplus-funds.

Chapter 4: '£230,000 . . . on TEA'

1 Katherine Rushton and Daniel Martin, 'BBC spends less than half its cash on programmes: Critics demand inquiry into "staggering" waste', *Daily Mail*, 15 June 2015, https://www.dailymail.co.uk/news/article-3123867/BBC-spends-half-cash-programmes-Critics-demand-inquiry-staggering-waste.html.

2 Daily Mail Comment, 'BBC behemoth must be cut down to size', *Daily Mail*, 15 June 2015, https://www.dailymail.co.uk/debate/article-3123951/DAILY-MAIL-COMMENT-BBC-behemoth-cut-size.html.

3 Max Hastings, 'Decent TV shows? No, the BBC prefers splurging your cash on a bloated army of jobsworths', *Daily Mail*, 16 June 2015, https://www.dailymail.co.uk/debate/article-3125632/MAX-HASTINGS-Decent-TV-shows-No-BBC-prefers-splurging-cash-bloated-army-jobsworths.html.

4 HuffPost, Ian Haythornthwaite, BBC Director of Finance, 'The facts about our income and expenditure', 16 June 2015, https://

www.huffingtonpost.co.uk/ian-haythornthwaite/bbc-facts-about-our-income-and-expenditure_b_7592892.html?utm_hp_ref=uk.

5   *W1A* (2014–17) posed an interesting dilemma for right-wing Beeb-bashing media like the *Telegraph* and the *Spectator*. They had to admit its quality but, because it portrayed the BBC as highly dysfunctional – as they had always claimed – they tried to have it both ways, describing it as 'so pitch perfect as to be profoundly depressing' (James Walton, 'Target practice', *Spectator*, 23 April 2015, https://www.spectator.co.uk/2015/04/w1a-reviewed-so-pitch-perfect-as-to-be-profoundly-depressing/) or – even more revealingly – 'Like the BBC . . . easier to admire than to love' (Michael Hogan, *Telegraph*, 18 September 2017, https://www.telegraph.co.uk/tv/2017/09/18/like-bbc-w1a-series-three-easier-admire-love-episode-one-review/).

6   We're assuming the errors in this article were honest mistakes rather than deliberate ones, although Rushton had been the *Telegraph*'s US Business Editor from May 2013 to February 2015, and was presumably financially literate, even if Martin, the *Mail*'s chief political correspondent, was not.

7   Rushton and Martin, 'BBC spends less than half its cash on programmes'.

8   An approximate analogy would be to divide a company's cost of manufacturing products for the UK consumer market by its total UK *and international* sales revenue at retail prices – and then claim that the difference between these two numbers was all waste and inefficiency, ignoring not only that the international revenue was from outside the UK (and had its own associated costs), but also unavoidable distribution costs (the company's own logistics costs and the wholesalers' and retailers' margins). In reality, the ratio of the two numbers would tell us nothing whatsoever about the company's efficiency.

9   For the BBC World Service, 2013–14 was the last year of government funding prior to it becoming licence-fee funded.

10 Including £91 million 'other [PSB group] direct content spend', see BBC, 'BBC: full financial statements, 2013–14', p. 3, http://downloads.bbc.co.uk/annualreport/pdf/2013-14/BBC_Financial_statements_201314.pdf.

11 BBC, 'BBC: full financial statements 2013–14'.

12 The other expenditures *excluded* from this analysis were the costs of pension-deficit reduction (£60 million), orchestras and performing groups (£28 million) and taxation (£35 million), giving a total of £123 million (3.7 per cent of the licence-fee revenue actually received by the BBC).

13 The National Audit Office (NAO) is an independent body which scrutinizes public spending on behalf of Parliament. Its main role is to help Parliament hold government and public services to account, but it also provides information to facilitate improvements. For more information about the National Audit Office, see https://www.nao.org.uk/about-us/.

14 National Audit Office, 'The BBC's commercial activities: a landscape review', 7 March 2018, p. 7.

15 BBC, 'BBC: full financial statements 2013–14'.

16 Strictly speaking, the BBC's *controllable* costs. These exclude the cost of government activities funded by 'top-sliced' licence-fee revenue.

17 EY, 'Benchmarking the BBC's overhead rate', July 2018.

18 BBC, 'A simpler BBC: more efficient, more open, more creative', 10 October 2018, http://downloads.bbc.co.uk/aboutthebbc/reports/pdf/efficiency_review_2018.pdf.

19 Jemma Buckley, 'Fury after BBC splashes out £63,000 on cabs that went unused – and another £170,000 paying for waiting times', *Daily Mail*, 23 February 2015, https://www.dailymail.co.uk/news/article-2964568/BBC-splashes-63-000-cabs-went-unused-170-000-paying-waiting-times.html; 'Arrogant, smug and sneering: JANET STREET-PORTER, who spent years as a senior BBC boss, excoriates the incestuous luvvie clique who

run it', *Daily Mail*, 27 March 2015, https://www.dailymail.co.uk/news/*article*-3013946/Arrogant-smug-sneering-JANET-STREET-PORTER-spent-years-senior-BBC-boss-excoriates-incestuous-luvvie-clique-run-it.html.

20 Clarkson had been offered soup and a cold meat platter, rather than the steak he wanted, after the hotel chef had gone home (Heather Saul, 'Jeremy Clarkson: David Cameron backs "friend" and "huge talent" after witnesses claim Top Gear "fracas" was over steak', *Independent*, 13 March 2015, https://www.independent.co.uk/news/people/jeremy-clarkson-david-cameron-backs-friend-and-huge-talent-after-witnesses-claim-top-gear-fracas-was-10102585.html). He later apologized to the producer and paid him over £100,000 to settle a racial discrimination and personal injury claim ('Tara Conlan, 'Jeremy Clarkson apologises to former Top Gear producer Oisin Tymon', *The Guardian*, 24 February 2016, https://www.theguardian.com/media/2016/feb/24/jeremy-clarkson-top-gear-producer-bbc-oisin-tymon).

21 Sam Marsden and Arthur Martin, 'Does BBC boss really need bodyguards after Top Gear death threat? £1,000-a-day security bill over single email from overseas', *Daily Mail*, 30 March 2015, https://www.dailymail.co.uk/news/article-3017316/Does-BBC-boss-really-need-bodyguards-Gear-death-threat-1-000-day-security-bill-single-email-overseas.html.

22 Alan Cowell, 'Fans petition BBC to reinstate "Top Gear" host Jeremy Clarkson', *The New York Times*, 11 March 2015, https://www.nytimes.com/2015/03/12/world/europe/thousands-of-fans-of-suspended-top-gear-host-seek-his-return.html?_r=0; 'Petition backing Jeremy Clarkson hits one million signatures', *Daily Telegraph*, 20 March 2015, https://www.telegraph.co.uk/news/bbc/11485289/The-Stig-delivers-Jeremy-Clarkson-petition-to-BBC.html.

23 Strictly speaking, an Abbot self-propelled gun rather than a tank.

24 Jonathan Prynn, 'Amazon Prime sign Top Gear's Jeremy Clarkson, Richard Hammond and James May for exclusive new show', *Evening Standard*, https://www.standard.co.uk/news/celebritynews/

amazon-sign-top-gears-jeremy-clarkson-richard-hammond-and-james-may-for-new-show-10426102.html; Lucy Clarke-Billings, 'Jeremy Clarkson "to become highest-paid T V host in Britain" on post-Top Gear Amazon Prime show', *Daily Telegraph*, 28 August 2015, https://www.telegraph.co.uk/news/celebritynews/11829887/Jeremy-Clarkson-set-to-become-highest-paid-TV-host-in-Britain-on-post-Top-Gear-Amazon-Prime-show.html.

25 Katherine Rushton, 'BBC news presenters' portraits – taken by £20,000-a-DAY photographer: Rankin was hired for marketing campaign as director-general was complaining about cuts', *Daily Mail*, 22 July 2015, https://www.dailymail.co.uk/news/article-3171465/BBC-news-presenters-portraits-taken-20-000-DAY-photographer-Rankin-hired-marketing-campaign-director-general-complaining-cuts.html.

Chapter 5: Under Sustained Attack – Towards the Current Charter and Funding Deal

1 The BBC's first major organization-wide efficiency programme was started in the early 1990s by Michael Checkland as DG and John Birt as Deputy DG. Checkland, a former accountant, was nicknamed 'Michael Chequebook' by BBC producers, who resented his cost savings and, in their view, excessive editorial caution. In 2007, the BBC Trust set the Executive a tough target – to make 3 per cent per annum additional efficiency savings, building up to a £487 million reduction in annual expenditure by the end of 2012–13, compared to the expenditure for 2007–8, which they were using as a baseline. In 2011, the Trust commissioned the National Audit Office, which reports to Parliament, to review its progress. The National Audit Office reported that the programme was ahead of schedule, with a forecast of £560 million of annual savings in 2012–13, 15 per cent above the target, while maintaining the BBC's overall performance in terms of

audience measures: https://www.nao.org.uk/wp-content/uploads/2011/11/1012_BBC_Efficiency.pdf.

2 Katherine Rushton, 'Mark Thompson in line for up to $10.5m at The New York Times', *Daily Telegraph*, 17 August 2012, https://www.telegraph.co.uk/finance/newsbysector/mediatechnologyandtelecoms/9483767/Mark-Thompson-in-line-for-up-to-10.5m-at-The-New-York-Times.html. The $10.5 million included a joining bonus ('golden hello') of $3.0–4.5 million. The rest – up to $6 million – comprised Thompson's salary and annual bonus and share awards based on the company's performance. In February 2019 Thompson's annual salary and bonus was $5.2 million (£4.0 million) and he also held, or had sold in the previous two years, *New York Times* stock worth $18.5 million (£14.3 million): see https://gb.wallmine.com/people/39072/mark-thompson.

3 For most of the BBC's history, it was governed and regulated by the Board of Governors, but under the 2007–16 Charter this was replaced by the BBC Trust and a strengthened Executive Board.

4 Ben Fenton, 'George Entwistle faces questions on Jimmy Savile scandal', *Financial Times*, 23 October 2012, https://www.ft.com/content/b256237b-f023-3d13-b6db-5fdf93858ddf. The House of Commons select committees are cross-party committees of backbench MPs, usually overseeing the work of a particular central government department. At the time, the DCMS was still the Department for Culture, Media and Sport. Its responsibility for digital policy was added in 2017, but it is still known by the same acronym. Its select committee is called the DCMS Committee.

5 Brian Brady, 'John Humphrys vs George Entwistle: A humiliating interview, and a career was at an end', *Independent on Sunday*, 11 November 2012, https://www.independent.co.uk/news/media/tv-radio/john-humphrys-vs-george-entwistle-a-humiliating-interview-and-a-career-was-at-an-end-8303900.html.

6 Greg Dyke, 'The BBC can get out of this hole', *Daily Telegraph*, 23 November 2012, https://www.telegraph.co.uk/culture/tvandradio/

bbc/9699031/The-BBC-can-get-out-of-this-hole.html; Victoria Ward, 'George Entwistle "toppled after taking on warring BBC tribes"', *Daily Telegraph*, 26 November 2012, https://www.telegraph.co.uk/ culture/tvandradio/bbc/9704063/George-Entwistle-toppled-after-taking-on-warring-BBC-tribes.html; Lisa O'Carroll and Maggie Brown, 'BBC in crisis as George Entwistle quits over Newsnight fiasco', *The Guardian*, 10 November 2012, https://www.theguardian.com/media/2012/nov/10/bbc-crisis-george-entwistle-resigns; and Steve Hewlett, 'George Entwistle was a prisoner of BBC bureaucracy', *The Guardian*, 19 November 2012, https://www.theguardian.com/media/2012/nov/18/george-entwistle-bbc-bureaucracy.

7 As discussed in Chapter 1, the BBC is a public corporation operating under a renewable Royal Charter which is formally granted by the monarch on the advice of the Privy Council. In practice, the Charter is issued by the Culture Secretary, based on a previous white paper. The proposals are debated in Parliament, which can lead to some amendments, but the Charter is not voted on by MPs or peers, since it is not government legislation.

8 The full membership was John Whittingdale (Con), Ben Bradshaw (Lab), Angie Bray (Con), Conor Burns (Con), Tracey Crouch (Con), Philip Davies (Con), Paul Farrelly (Lab), John Leech (Lib Dem), Steve Rotheram (Lab), Jim Sheridan (Lab) and Gerry Sutcliffe (Lab). For TFA's 'Axe the TV Tax', see http://www.tfa.net/ axe_the_tv_tax. TFA also 'opposes the BBC on what it perceives as bias' – especially on its other main policy issue, Brexit. We have seen no evidence that Whittingdale and Davies declared their membership of the TFA Council as a conflict of interest in the context of this major inquiry into the future of the BBC, although it's possible that they did so and we have failed to find it. TFA also runs other campaigns from time to time: in the 1970s, its main focus was on trade union reform and in the 1980s it campaigned against sporting sanctions on apartheid-era South Africa. More recent campaigns include opposition to identity cards; libel reform; a 2015 book for schoolchildren on *Magna Carta in the 21st*

Century; and a 'Freedom to Vape' campaign launched in August 2016 to oppose EU restrictions on the sale and advertising of e-cigarettes.

9 Under the Freedom of Information Act 2000 and the Freedom of Information (Scotland) Act 2002, individuals have a statutory right to information about UK public bodies, with certain exemptions. One exemption is that the BBC is not subject to the act in relation to information held for editorial purposes.

10 Tim Ross, 'BBC could lose right to licence fee over "culture of waste and secrecy", minister warns', *Sunday Telegraph*, 27 October 2013, https://www.telegraph.co.uk/culture/tvandradio/bbc/10406971/BBC-could-lose-right-to-licence-fee-over-culture-of-waste-and-secrecy-minister-warns.html.

11 Remember that it was Entwistle's interview with John Humphrys on the BBC Radio 4 *Today* programme that triggered his resignation as director-general.

12 BBC News, 'TV licence "faces cut unless BBC rebuilds trust" – Shapps', 27 October 2013, https://www.bbc.co.uk/news/uk-24690002.

13 What he was selling was a 'toolkit' which cost $497, but promised to earn the buyer $20,000 in twenty days if they followed the instructions to recruit one hundred 'Joint Venture Partners' who would agree to sell the buyer's online guide for a share of the profits. In the words of *The Guardian*, 'We have no evidence that this amounted to a pyramid scheme. It just sounds like one'; Leo Benedictus, 'The Grant Shapps guide to making money', *The Guardian*, 16 March 2015, https://www.theguardian.com/politics/shortcuts/2015/mar/16/grant-shapps-business-mp-conservative-chairman-michael-green.

14 That undeniable evidence consisted of a forty-minute recording of a 'Michael Green' sales pitch over a year after his election: Randeep Ramesh, 'Grant Shapps admits he had a second job as "millionaire web marketer" while MP', *The Guardian*, 15 March 2015, https://www.theguardian.com/politics/2015/mar/15/

grant-shapps-admits-he-had-second-job-as-millioniare-web-marketer-while-mp.

15 Wikipedia banned the 'sock-puppet' account (called 'Contribsx') after it made numerous flattering changes to Shapps' page (including deleting references to payments from firms linked to his portfolio as a shadow minister) and many unflattering ones to those of several Conservative colleagues (with whom he was presumably rivalrous); Randeep Ramesh, 'Grant Shapps accused of editing pages of Tory rivals', *The Guardian*, 21 April 2015, https://www.theguardian.com/politics/2015/apr/21/grant-shapps-accused-of-editing-wikipedia-pages-of-tory-rivals.

16 A 'blockchain' is a list of records ('blocks') linked using cryptography. Multiple copies of the blockchain are held and updated in parallel to prevent tampering, hence its alternative name: 'distributed ledger' technology. See https://medium.com/the-mission/a-simple-explanation-on-how-blockchain-works-e52f75da6e9a.

17 Jemima Kelly, 'Grant Shapps resigns from blockchain positions after FTAV discovers secret pay deal', *Financial Times*, 1 August 2018, https://ftalphaville.ft.com/2018/08/01/1533116572000/Grant-Shapps-resigns-from-blockchain-positions-after-FTAV-discovers-secret-pay-deal-/.

18 Kate Allen, 'Grant Shapps resigns over bullying row in Conservative Party youth wing', *Financial Times*, 28 November 2015, https://www.ft.com/content/03e6b9e2-95de-11e5-95c7-d47aa298f769; Jamie Grierson and Caroline Davies, 'Grant Shapps resigned within hours of Guardian allegations', *The Guardian*, 29 November 2015.

19 Telegraph view, 'The great BBC rip-off', *Daily Telegraph*, 5 November 2013, https://www.telegraph.co.uk/comment/telegraph-view/10427984/The-great-BBC-rip-off.html.

20 Rob Wilson, 'Rob Wilson, MP: Time to scrap unfair poll tax on television', *Sunday Telegraph*, 2 November 2013, https://www.telegraph.co.uk/culture/tvandradio/bbc/10423021/Rob-Wilson-MP-Time-to-scrap-unfair-poll-tax-on-television.html.

21 Tim Ross, 'BBC licence fee should be cut or scrapped, poll finds', *Sunday Telegraph*, 2 November 2013, https://www.telegraph.co.uk/culture/tvandradio/bbc/10423117/BBC-licence-fee-should-be-cut-or-scrapped-poll-finds.html.

22 Tim Ross, 'BBC faces new bias row over charity given millions by EU', *Sunday Telegraph*, 2 November 2013, https://www.telegraph.co.uk/news/politics/10423013/BBC-faces-new-bias-row-over-charity-given-millions-by-EU.html.

23 Jasper Copping, 'Lord Patten attacks Tory chairman', *Daily Telegraph*, 13 November 2013, https://www.telegraph.co.uk/culture/tvandradio/bbc/10447464/Lord-Patten-attacks-Tory-chairman.html.

24 House of Commons, DCMS Committee, 'Future of the BBC: fourth report of session 2014–15', 10 February 2015, https://publications.parliament.uk/pa/cm201415/cmselect/cmcumeds/315/315.pdf.

25 The PSBC would also set the level and manage the allocation (via competitive bids) of 'contestable' funding for public service content provided by commercial broadcasters.

26 Up until 2017, external auditing had been done by an auditor hired by the Trust, as a commercial company would do. In April 2017 the NAO took over.

27 House of Commons, DCMS Committee, 'Future of the BBC', summary, pp. 3–5.

28 House of Commons, DCMS Committee, 'Future of the BBC', p. 4.

29 Strictly speaking, the belief is that the market will supply all the entertainment whose audience will pay enough to justify the cost of providing it. The assumption is not that the market provides a *perfect* set of products and services (in terms of range, quality and value for money, from the consumers' point of view), but that *any intervention by government will lead to a worse one.*

30 We say 'market failure' within quotation marks because this viewpoint assumes that the BBC's only role is to compensate for the market's failure to supply sufficient informational and educational content.

31 Tara Conlan, 'How the BBC licence fee deal was done', *The Guardian*, 20 October 2010, https://www.theguardian.com/media/2010/oct/20/bbc-licence-fee-negotiations.

32 House of Commons, DCMS Committee, 'Future of the BBC', p. 123.

33 Frontier Economics, 'Review of over-75s funding: a report prepared for the BBC', November 2018, https://downloads.bbc.co.uk/mediacentre/frontier-economics-review-of-over-75s-funding.pdf.

34 Frontier Economics, 'Review of over-75s funding'.

35 The funding deal did, however, include some aspects which would very slightly ameliorate the effect of this body blow to the BBC's funding. The change would be phased in from April 2018, with the full cost falling on the BBC from April 2020 onwards, and the licence fee (for the households that still had to pay it (i.e. those with no members aged seventy-five-plus)) would rise in line with inflation (the Consumer Price Index) over the next Charter period. The government also specified that the BBC was allowed to close the 'iPlayer loophole' and to charge non-TV-owning households which watched live BBC TV online – if it could find a practical way of doing this. (Previously, households using only online TV services had not been required to pay the TV licence fee). Finally, BBC funding of the government's broadband roll-out would be ended by April 2020: see BBC News, 'BBC to fund over-75s' TV licences', 6 July 2015, https://www.bbc.co.uk/news/uk-politics-33414693.

36 This was before Carrie Symonds' relationship with Boris Johnson started.

37 House of Commons, DCMS Committee, 'BBC charter review: public consultation 16 July–8 October 2015' (the 'green paper'), 2015, https://assets.publishing.service.gov.uk/government/uploads/system/uploads/attachment_data/file/449830/DCMS_BBC_Consultation_A4__1_.pdf.

38 Whittingdale commissioned the media, sport and entertainment consultancy Oliver & Ohlbaum (O&O), supported by the economic

consultancy Oxera, to assess the market impact and distinctiveness of the BBC's UK television, radio and online services, and Sir David Clementi, a business executive and a former deputy governor of the Bank of England, to review its governance and regulation. DCMS commissioned the market research firm GfK to explore public views about the BBC.

39 Questions 1, 2, 4, 5, 6, 8, 9, 10, 14, 15 and 16.

40 This was, of course, not the first time the BBC's actual or potential market impact had been raised. Going back to its launch in the 1920s, the main reason why it had not carried radio advertising (perhaps in addition to its Calvinist founder John Reith's feeling that commercials would lower the tone of its broadcasts) was the newspapers' justifiable concern about the potential impact on their advertising revenue. But this was the first time the BBC's market impact was treated as *the single most important issue* in Charter renewal.

41 John Whittingdale, DCMS Committee, press release, 'Future of the BBC', 26 February 2015.

42 Rajeev Syal, 'Osborne accuses BBC of "imperial ambitions" and calls for savings', *The Guardian*, 5 July 2015, https://www.theguardian.com/uk-news/2015/jul/05/osborne-accuses-bbc-of-imperial-ambitions-and-calls-for-savings.

43 Two panel members – Ashley Highfield, chief executive of the local newspaper group Johnston Press, and Dawn Airey, former chief executive of Channel 5 – were 'outspoken critics of the corporation', according to *The Guardian*: see Jasper Jackson, 'John Whittingdale defends BBC charter panel secrecy', *The Guardian*, 17 November 2015, https://www.theguardian.com/media/2015/nov/17/john-whittingdale-defends-bbc-charter-panel-secrecy.

44 John Whittingdale, DCMS Committee, press release, 'Future of the BBC'.

45 House of Commons, DCMS Committee, 'BBC charter review: public consultation', pp. 48–9.

46 Ibid., Question 4, p. 57.

47 Toby Syfret, 'The plight of the BBC post-intervention', Enders Analysis, 13 July 2015 [2015-058].

48 House of Commons, DCMS Committee, 'BBC charter review: public consultation', p. 44.

49 Voice of China, which now combines all China's state-owned domestic and (fast-growing) international TV and radio services, is almost certainly even larger, but it is a state broadcaster under tight political control, not a PSB.

50 NHK's *licence-fee* revenue has been consistently higher over the last ten years than the BBC's after top-slicing, although the relative numbers vary from year to year with the fluctuating sterling/yen exchange rate. However, because the BBC generates much more commercial income than NHK (six times as much during 2017–18), mainly from international sales, its *total* revenue has been fractionally higher than theirs in recent years (sources: NHK and BBC annual reports).

51 House of Commons, DCMS Committee, 'BBC charter review: public consultation', p. 45.

52 Previously from TV licences, now from a universal household levy; for the latter, see Chapter 10.

53 However, the comparison is not straightforward. The nine regional German broadcasters and Deutsche Welle (equivalent to the BBC World Service but still government-funded) are all part of the ARD consortium (motto *'Wir sind eins'* – 'We are one'). The ARD partners pool resources for their national TV channels, including their flagship network Das Erste, and for a wide range of other activities such as their main online offerings, catch-up TV, film production and acquisition, children's TV, coverage of national and international politics, and participation in international partnerships such as the pan-European cultural channel Association relative à la télévision européenne (ARTE). ARD's annual *licence-fee* income for the current four-year period, 2017–20, is 5.59 billion Euros after collection costs, over 40 per cent higher than the BBC's after parts of the latter were

top-sliced for other uses. Its *total* income in 2017 was 6.495 billion euros, over 15 per cent more than the total revenue of the BBC Group in 2018–19 after top-slicing – despite ARD's commercial revenue being much less than the BBC's. Eighty-six per cent of ARD's 2017 income came from the licence fee. The rest was equally split between (i) a small amount of advertising and sponsorship (7 per cent) and (ii) a combination of other commercial revenue and the government grant for Deutsche Welle (also 7 per cent). The figures are from ARD and the '21st Report of the KEF' (Kommission zur Ermittlung des Finanzbedarfs, the independent commission that evaluates the funding needs of the three German PSB – ARD, the second-largest public TV broadcaster, Zweites Deutsches Fernsehen (ZDF) and the much smaller Deutschlandradio (DLR) – over each four-year period), February 2018, https://kef-online.de/fileadmin/KEF/Dateien/Berichte/21._Bericht.pdf. The total annual licence-fee funding for *all* the German PSBs – at 7.8 billion Euros for 2017–20 – is *double* the BBC's licence-fee income after top-slicing.

54 Jackson, 'John Whittingdale defends BBC charter panel secrecy'.
55 House of Commons, DCMS Committee, 'BBC charter review public consultation: summary of responses', March 2016, https://assets.publishing.service.gov.uk/government/uploads/system/uploads/attachment_data/file/504099/BBC_Charter_Review_Public_Consultation_Summary_of_Responses.pdf.
56 The percentage figures quoted are from Annex 7 of the white paper of May 2016 ('A BBC for the future? A broadcaster of distinction', https://assets.publishing.service.gov.uk/government/uploads/system/uploads/attachment_data/file/524863/DCMS_A_BBC_for_the_future_linked_rev1.pdf) and were based upon the DCMS Committee's 'BBC charter review public consultation: summary of responses' of March 2016.
57 In addition to these, there were also positive reports from the devolved administrations in Scotland, Wales and Northern Ireland.

58 House of Commons, DCMS Committee, 'BBC charter review: first report of session 2015–16', 11 February 2016, p. 3, https://publications.parliament.uk/pa/cm201516/cmselect/cmcumeds/398/398.pdf.

59 House of Lords, Select Committee on Communications, 'BBC charter review: Reith not revolution', 24 February 2016, https://publications.parliament.uk/pa/ld201516/ldselect/ldcomuni/96/96.pdf.

60 Ibid., p. 3.

61 Ibid., p. 3.

62 GfK, for the DCMS, 'Research to explore public views about the BBC', 12 May 2016, https://assets.publishing.service.gov.uk/government/uploads/system/uploads/attachment_data/file/522509/Research_to_explore_public_views_about_the_BBC.pdf.

63 Oliver & Ohlbaum Associates Ltd and Oxera Consulting LLP, for the DCMS: 'BBC television, radio and online services: an assessment of market impact and distinctiveness', February 2016, https://assets.publishing.service.gov.uk/government/uploads/system/uploads/attachment_data/file/504012/FINAL_-_BBC_market_impact_assessment.pdf.

64 David Clementi, for the DCMS, 'A review of the governance and regulation of the BBC', March 2016, https://assets.publishing.service.gov.uk/government/uploads/system/uploads/attachment_data/file/504003/PDF_FINAL_20160224_AM_Clementi_Review.pdf.

65 As already discussed in Chapter 3, 'contestable' in this context is economists' jargon for money for which interested parties can compete. Free-market economists generally favour public funding to be allocated through some kind of competitive bidding process.

66 Alan Peacock, 'Public service broadcasting without the BBC?', Institute of Economic Affairs, 2004, https://iea.org.uk/wp-content/uploads/2016/07/upldbook254pdf.pdf.

67 House of Commons, DCMS Committee, 'A BBC for the future? A broadcaster of distinction', May 2016, p. 98. The mid-term review of

the funding deal would 'enable the government to assess whether the revenue generated from the licence fee has been as expected over the first five years of the Charter and what the [subsequent] level of the licence fee should be', depending on household growth, the BBC's commercial revenues, evasion rates and industry costs.

68 This – mistakenly, in the event – assumed two full-term five-year parliaments (under the Fixed Term Parliaments Act 2011): 2015–20 and 2020–25. It established the important principle of separating Charter renewal from the political cycle.

69 Laura Hughes and Barney Henderson, 'Theresa May wields the axe on Cameron's Notting Hill set', *Daily Telegraph*, 14 July 2016, https://www.telegraph.co.uk/news/2016/07/14/theresa-mays-cabinet-reshuffle-who-will-join-boris-johnson-and/.

70 These included the threat of decriminalizing licence-fee evasion (and the likely resulting damage to the BBC's funding), which was removed by the Perry Review, which had exposed the exaggeration and misinformation behind the decriminalization campaign; and also the idea that the government might appoint a majority of the members of the BBC Board (Mark Tran, 'Government will choose most members of BBC board, says Whittingdale', *The Guardian*, 13 March 2016, https://www.theguardian.com/media/2016/mar/13/government-choose-bbc-board-john-whittingdale).

Chapter 6: 'The Addams Family of World Media'

1 Matthew Gwyther and Andrew Saunders, 'Management Today interview – James Murdoch', *Management Today*, 25 April 2007, updated 31 August 2010, https://www.managementtoday.co.uk/world-exclusive-mt-interview-james-murdoch/article/653028.

2 James Murdoch's MacTaggart Lecture, 'The Absence of Trust', Edinburgh International Television Festival, 28 August 2009, http://image.guardian.co.uk/sys-files/Media/documents/2009/08/28/JamesMurdochMacTaggartLecture.pdf.

3 James Robinson and Maggie Brown, 'A chill wind', *The Guardian*, 31 August 2009, https://www.theguardian.com/media/2009/aug/31/james-murdoch-attacking-bbc-ofcom.

4 The internet uses a set of rules for putting digital data into standardized 'packets', enabling different types of information – including different media content – to be stored, transmitted and processed using the same networks and routines. It's a bit like shipping containers carrying completely different types of product being stored and transported together. (The main internet rules, usually referred to as TCP/IP, are the 'Transmission Control Protocol' and the 'Internet Protocol'.) See Katie Hafner and Matthew Lyon, *Where Wizards Stay Up Late: The Origins of the Internet*, Simon & Schuster, 1998.

5 James Murdoch's MacTaggart Lecture, 'The Absence of Trust'.

6 TV net advertising revenue (i.e. excluding agency fees and commercial production costs) fell from £3.58 billion in 2007 to £3.14 billion in 2009. Cumulative inflation during 2007–9 was 3.8 per cent. Source: www.statista.com.

7 Robinson and Brown, 'A chill wind'.

8 Sky, 'Sky annual report and accounts: 2009', p. 8, https://static.skyassets.com/contentstack/assets/bltdc2476c7b6b194dd/blt230d d51dc1bbbb6b/598067c47d0a754f343f83b2/report_09.pdf.

9 Ofcom, 'Communications market report: 2010', p. 99, https://www.ofcom.org.uk/research-and-data/multi-sector-research/cmr/cmr10.

10 Patrick Barwise and Leo Watkins, 'The evolution of digital dominance: how and why we got to GAFA', in Martin Moore and Damian Tambini, eds, *Digital Dominance: The Power of Google, Amazon, Facebook, and Apple*, Oxford University Press, 2018, pp. 21–49, https://lbsresearch.london.edu/914/.

11 News UK's submission to the Cairncross Review on the financial sustainability of UK public interest journalism argued that 'the BBC's online coverage should be severely reduced, because its wide range, and the fact that it appears to be free [*sic*], make it a

serious threat to the success of commercial providers'. However, Dame Frances was not convinced by this argument, writing that 'there are several studies that do not support this conclusion' and that 'It would . . . make little sense to curtail the BBC without strong evidence that this would lead to something better', 'The Cairncross review: a sustainable future for journalism', for the DCMS, 12 February 2019, p. 54, https://assets.publishing.service. gov.uk/government/uploads/system/uploads/attachment_data/ file/779882/021919_DCMS_Cairncross_Review_.pdf.

12 James Murdoch's MacTaggart Lecture, 'The Absence of Trust'. Darwin's ideas on natural selection were, in reality, strongly influenced by his knowledge of the 'managed process' of selectively breeding plants and animals, including his extensive personal experience as a pigeon breeder (see his *The Variation of Animals and Plants Under Domestication*, 1868). Darwin was unaware of the underlying mechanisms of genetic inheritance – Mendel's seminal 1864 paper on this was largely ignored for over thirty years – but had a good understanding of the practicalities (see Katrina van Grouw, *Unnatural Selection*, Princeton University Press, 2018). Above all, he was quite clear that his theory of evolution was an *explanation* of the way things were, not a *prescription* for the way they ought to be. To be fair to James Murdoch, he is certainly not the only person to have believed Darwin made the category error of confusing the two.

13 Emily Bell, 'The evolution of a feud', *The Guardian*, 28 August 2009, https://www.theguardian.com/media/2009/aug/28/james-murdoch-mactaggart-lecture-bbc.

14 The main reason for this is that advertisers pay much less per thousand readers for online display advertising than for print display advertising. A second reason is that the percentage of display advertising expenditure reaching the publisher is also much lower online because of a complex, costly and opaque trading system (the online advertising 'value chain'). Meanwhile, print

classified advertising, especially important for local newspapers but also a source of revenue for the nationals, has been largely replaced by more flexible and cost-effective online search.

15 However, News International's attempt to encourage competitors to charge for their online content was somewhat at odds with its wider view of pricing. Just three months before James Murdoch's MacTaggart speech, News International had been found guilty by the Office of Fair Trading of deliberately harming competition in the national newspaper market by cutting the cover price of *The Times* to 10p on Mondays, deliberately selling at a loss: Michael Harrison, 'Murdoch guilty in "Times" price war', *Independent*, 22 May 1999, https://www.independent.co.uk/news/murdoch-guilty-in-times-price-war-1094999.html.

16 The rules are complicated. For each of the three commercial PSBs (ITV, Channel 4 and Channel 5) only its main flagship channel is deemed to be a 'PSB channel', with less commercial airtime allowed per hour than for other commercial channels, including its own 'portfolio' channels (ITV2, More4, etc.). Despite these complexities, the net effect, compared with a level playing field, is to increase the share of TV advertising revenue of Sky and the other non-PSBs at the expense of the commercial PSBs. (The impact on total TV advertising revenue depends on the 'price elasticity' of TV advertising, discussed in Chapter 10 and Appendix E). These rules are a rare example of a non-tariff barrier that systematically benefits foreign companies at the expense of domestic ones. We see them as well past their sell-by date, but they fall outside the focus of this book. See also Gill Hind and Alice Enders, 'Time to liberalise UK TV advertising minutage', Enders Analysis, 24 September 2019 [2019-080].

17 George Monbiot, 'The most potent weapon wielded by the empires of Murdoch and China', *The Guardian*, 22 April 2008, https://www.theguardian.com/commentisfree/2008/apr/22/chinathemedia.rupertmurdoch. See also Bruce Dover, *Rupert's*

Adventures in China: How Murdoch Lost a Fortune and Found a Wife, Penguin (Australia), 2008, p. 152.

18 Nick Davies, 'Murdoch papers paid £1m to gag phone-hacking victims', *The Guardian*, 8 July 2009, https://www.theguardian.com/media/2009/jul/08/murdoch-papers-phone-hacking; see also his *Hack Attack: How the Truth Caught Up with Rupert Murdoch*, Vintage, 2015.

19 Roy Greenslade, 'Their master's voice', *The Guardian*, 17 February 2003, https://www.theguardian.com/media/2003/feb/17/mondaymediasection.iraq.

20 These rights are embodied in the First Amendment of the US Constitution, the first of the ten amendments in the 1791 US Bill of Rights.

21 Guardian staff, 'Fox News drops "fair and balanced" slogan', *The Guardian*, 15 June 2017, https://www.theguardian.com/media/2017/jun/15/fox-news-drops-fair-and-balanced-slogan.

22 Lucia Graves, 'Donald Trump and Rupert Murdoch: inside the billionaire bromance', *The Guardian*, 16 June 2017, https://www.theguardian.com/us-news/2017/jun/16/donald-trump-rupert-murdoch-friendship-fox-news.

23 Brian Fung, 'FCC relaxes rule limiting foreign ownership of media stations', *Washington Post*, 14 November 2013, https://www.washingtonpost.com/news/the-switch/wp/2013/11/14/the-next-rupert-murdoch-wont-have-to-change-his-citizenship-to-rule-the-tv-biz/?utm_term=.e396dd5f7680.

24 See the *Observer* article 'Murdoch becomes American', 24 August 2003, https://www.theguardian.com/media/2003/aug/24/rupertmurdoch.business and also Bruce Page's *The Murdoch Archipelago*, Simon & Schuster, 2011.

Chapter 7: Rupert, Paul and the Gang

1 Most are British, although some of the most jingoistic are not quite as British as they seem.

2 Robin Aitken, *'Can We Trust the BBC?'*, Continuum, 2007; *'Can We Still Trust the BBC?'*, Bloomsbury Continuum, 2013; and *'The Noble Liar'*, Biteback, 2018.

3 Dacre was editor of the *Daily Mail* from July 1992 to November 2018. See Adrian Addison, *Mail Men: The Unauthorized Story of the Daily Mail*, Part IV: King of Middle England, Atlantic Books, 2017. Dacre is still editor-in-chief of DMG Media at the time of writing.

4 Did his fellow students make fun of his accent? That could explain a lot.

5 Bill Johnstone, 'News International buys 65% of satellite group', *The Times*, 29 June 1983.

6 'Freedom in Broadcasting', Rupert Murdoch, MacTaggart Lecture, Edinburgh Television Festival, 25 August 1989, http://www.thetvfestival.com/wp-content/uploads/2018/03/MacTaggart_1989_Rupert_Murdoch.pdf. Peter York was there – and also at the third Murdoch MacTaggart Lecture by Elisabeth Murdoch in August 2012.

7 See the YouTube video featuring John Ford himself, https://www.youtube.com/watch?v=Ao_TwvDG8bY&feature=youtube, and the website Guestlist's interview with Bylines Investigates' lead investigator, Graham Johnson, about a series of exposés detailing John Ford's actions: https://guestlist.net/article/93921/organised-crimes-of-the-sunday-times-interview-with-byline-s-graham-johnson.

8 A judicial public inquiry into the culture, practices and ethics of the British press. Chaired by Lord Justice Leveson, it was set up by Conservative Prime Minister David Cameron in July 2011 in response to the News International phone-hacking scandal and reported in November 2012: https://www.gov.uk/government/publications/leveson-inquiry-report-into-the-culture-practices-and-ethics-of-the-press.

9 Nicholas Hellen, 'Birt tells the BBC: "We're boring, biased and bourgeois"', *Sunday Times*, 12 February 1995.

10 Nicholas Hellen and Nicholas Fox, 'BBC to move into pay TV channel', *Sunday Times*, 4 February 1996.

11 Jim Waterson, 'Rupert Murdoch's Sky reign to end as Fox sells all shares to Comcast', *The Guardian*, 26 September 2018, https://www.theguardian.com/media/2018/sep/26/rupert-murdochs-sky-reign-to-end-as-fox-sells-all-shares-to-comcast.

12 Previously, complaints had been handled internally by the BBC. It had been regulated by its governors and then, from 2007 until 2017, the BBC Trust.

13 Tim Luckhurst, Ben Cocking, Ian Reeves and Rob Bailey, 'Assessing the delivery of BBC Radio 5 Live's public service commitments', Abramis Academic Publishing, 2019, also available on open access at https://kar.kent.ac.uk/71586/1/Radio5Live_03%20%28002%29.pdf.

14 Matthew Moore, 'BBC 5 Live is "all talk and little news"', *The Times*, 29 January 2019, https://www.thetimes.co.uk/article/bbc-5-live-is-all-talk-and-little-news-t25k3lnq5.

15 James Walker, 'Academics defend News UK-funded research into Radio 5 Live news output after BBC dubs it "shameless paid-for lobbying"', *Press Gazette*, 29 January 2019, https://www.pressgazette.co.uk/academics-defend-news-uk-funded-research-into-radio-5-live-news-output-after-bbc-dubs-it-shameless-paid-for-lobbying/.

16 Luckhurst, Cocking, Reeves and Bailey, 'Assessing the delivery of BBC Radio 5 Live's public service commitments'.

17 Academic research in the natural and social sciences is usually published in journals that use anonymous academic reviewers selected by the journals' editors for expertise relevant to the particular study. Scholarly peer review is usually 'double blind': that is to say, the reviewers and authors do not know each other's identities. The process is managed by the journal's editor (or an associate editor) who knows the identities of all the parties. Based on the reviewers' comments and recommendations, the editor decides whether to accept the paper for publication, reject it, or

invite the authors to revise it and resubmit it for another round of reviews. Papers typically go through several rounds and the overall acceptance rate is low.

18 All-party parliamentary groups (APPGs) are informal cross-party groups that have no official status within Parliament. They are run for and by Members of the Commons and the Lords, though many choose to involve individuals and organizations from outside Parliament in their activities.

19 *Private Eye* (issue no. 1486, 22 December 2018, p. 15) was characteristically perceptive and droll on the subject of the invitations to the event: 'Members of the all-party parliamentary media group were surprised to receive an invitation from their chair, Rosie Cooper MP, to a working breakfast in January to discuss a "new report on BBC radio" – specifically an assessment of "the delivery of BBC Radio 5 Live's public service commitments" . . . While the Murdoch press has long railed against any BBC service that might interfere with its commercial interests, exploiting an APPG to promote its private war is a new development. It has infuriated some MPs.' After the event, a source told us that few members of the APPG attended the working breakfast.

20 Matthew Garrahan, 'Rupert Murdoch's News UK takes a potshot at BBC radio', *Financial Times*, 1 February 2019, https://www.ft.com/content/aceefb52-262d-11e9-8ce6-5db4543da632.

21 Max Goldbart, 'Ofcom rejects call for BBC sports rights review', *Broadcast*, 18 December 2018, https://www.broadcastnow.co.uk/broadcasting/ofcom-rejects-call-for-bbc-sports-rights-review/5135398.article.

22 Roy Greenslade, 'BBC licence fee deal – the FT vs the Times, Sun and Daily Mail', *The Guardian*, 7 July 2015, https://www.theguardian.com/media/greenslade/2015/jul/07/bbc-licence-fee-deal-the-ft-versus-the-times-sun-and-daily-mail.

23 However, at least one Murdoch *doesn't* hate the BBC. James' sister Elisabeth's 2012 MacTaggart Lecture explicitly supported

both the Corporation and the universal licence fee. She praised her father's vision and courage in setting up Sky, but was sharply critical of the values revealed in the News International (later, News UK) phone-hacking scandal and of several aspects of James' MacTaggart Lecture three years earlier. Dan Sabbagh, 'Elisabeth Murdoch rounds on brother in MacTaggart Lecture', *The Guardian*, 23 August 2012, https://www.theguardian.com/media/2012/aug/23/elisabeth-murdoch-mactaggart-lecture.

24 Bruce Page, *The Murdoch Archipelago*, Simon and Schuster, 2003.

25 Brittany Vonow and Tara Evans, 'Fury as millions of over-75s to lose free TV licence as perk is axed by BBC', *Sun*, 10 June 2019, https://www.thesun.co.uk/money/9261451/free-tv-licences-bbc/; Steve Hawkes, 'Boris Johnson slams BBC and demands they "cough up" to fund free TV licences for over-75s', *Sun*, 25 August 2019, https://www.thesun.co.uk/news/9797379/boris-johnson-blast-bbc-free-tv-licences-oaps/; Matt Dathan, 'BBC bosses told they will share the blame when pensioners are jailed over licence fees', *Sun*, 30 August 2019, https://www.thesun.co.uk/news/9825395/bbc-share-blame-pensioners-jailed/; and Miles Goslett and Chris Pollard, 'BBC blows more than £745m on presenter pay hikes and buildings while axing free TV licences for millions of OAPs', *Sun*, 8 September 2019, https://www.thescottishsun.co.uk/news/4695912/bbc-blows-more-than-745m-on-presenter-pay-hikes-and-buildings-while-axing-free-tv-licences-for-millions-of-oaps/.

26 Goslett and Pollard, 'BBC blows more than £745m'.

27 Simon Jack, 'Papers' phone-hacking bill "could reach £1bn"', BBC News, 4 May 2019, https://www.bbc.co.uk/news/business-48146162.

28 Adrian Addison, *Mail Men: The Unauthorized Story of the Daily Mail*, Atlantic Books, 2017, Chapter 15.

29 Geoffrey Levy, 'The Man who Hated Britain', *Daily Mail*, 27 September 2013, https://www.dailymail.co.uk/news/article-2435751/

Red-Eds-pledge-bring-socialism-homage-Marxist-father-Ralph-Miliband-says-GEOFFREY-LEVY.html.

30 James Slack, 'Enemies of the people', *Daily Mail,* 4 November 2016, https://www.dailymail.co.uk/news/article-3903436/Enemies-people-Fury-touch-judges-defied-17-4m-Brexit-voters-trigger-constitutional-crisis.html.

31 Liz Gerard, private research.

32 The median pay gap is the difference between the midpoints in the ranges of hourly earnings of men and women. It takes all the salaries in a given sample, lines them up in order from lowest to highest, and picks the middle salary.

33 See the BBC's 'Statutory gender pay gap report' of 2018, http://downloads.bbc.co.uk/aboutthebbc/insidethebbc/reports/gender_pay_report_2018.pdf and Adam McCulloch's article in *Personnel Today* (in relation to the *Daily Mail*): 'Media organisations vow to narrow gender pay gap', 12 April 2018, https://www.personneltoday.com/hr/media-companies-gender-pay-gap/.

34 Charlotte Tobitt, 'Gender pay gap figures in full: Conde Nast, Telegraph and Economist groups among worst offenders for pay disparity in UK media', *Press Gazette,* 5 April 2018, https://www.pressgazette.co.uk/gender-pay-gap-figures-in-full-conde-nast-telegraph-and-economist-groups-among-worst-offenders-for-pay-disparity-in-uk-media/.

35 The only one we could find is from 2002 (although there may be others): Bill Hagerty, 'Mail man: Interview with Paul Dacre', *The Guardian,* 9 September 2002, https://www.theguardian.com/media/2002/sep/09/dailymail.pressandpublishing.

36 To watch Paul Dacre giving evidence at the Leveson Inquiry, see https://www.theguardian.com/media/video/2012/feb/09/dacre-leveson-inquiry-video.

37 See https://hoydenabouttown.com/2010/03/30/the-daily-mail-song/.

38 Addison, *Mail Men*, p. 44.

39 With considerable justification: he and the *Mail*'s owners very successfully invested in both talent and the paper itself to produce a most impressive profit.

40 Hugh Cudlipp was a Welsh journalist and newspaper editor noted for his work on the *Daily Mirror* in the 1950s and 1960s. After his death, his widow, Jodi, joined up with some of his former colleagues to found the Cudlipp Trust with the intention of 'education and furthering the interests and standing of journalism'. The trust organizes the annual Hugh Cudlipp Memorial Lecture and student journalism prize.

41 Paul Dacre, 'Society of Editors: Paul Dacre's speech in full', *Press Gazette*, 9 November 2008, https://www.pressgazette.co.uk/society-of-editors-paul-dacres-speech-in-full/. Dacre is also said to be a strong supporter of the BBC World Service.

42 Mark Sweney, 'Paul Dacre paid almost £2.7m in final year as Daily Mail editor', *The Guardian*, 7 December 2018, https://www.theguardian.com/media/2018/dec/07/paul-dacre-was-paid-almost-3m-in-final-year-as-daily-mail-editor.

43 Alastair Campbell, 'Alastair Campbell vs The Daily Mail', *GQ*, 7 June 2018, https://www.gq-magazine.co.uk/article/daily-mail-paul-dacre.

44 Henry Mance, 'Geordie Greig: "Provocation is a good thing"', *Financial Times*, 4 October 2019, https://www.ft.com/content/16b7c032-de20-11e9-9743-db5a370481bc, and Alex Barker and Henry Mance, 'Mail's Paul Dacre delivers biting riposte to Geordie Greig', *Financial Times*, 11 October 2019, https://www.ft.com/content/ee82201e-ec3c-11e9-a240-3b065ef5fc55.

45 Matthew Garrahan and George Parker, 'Daily Mail change of guard puts journalists and politicians on edge', *Financial Times*, 8 June 2018, https://www.ft.com/content/5682dd7c-6b3b-11e8-b6eb-4acfcfb08c11.

46 Henry Mance, 'A Damascene conversion for the Daily Mail raises heart rates', *Financial Times*, 15 September 2018, https://www.ft.com/content/654eaf90-b689-11e8-b3ef-799c8613f4a1.

47 Dan Sabbagh, 'Richard Desmond: a crude, ruthless proprietor who squeezed profits', *The Guardian*, 9 February 2018, https://www.theguardian.com/media/2018/feb/09/richard-desmond-crude-ruthless-proprietor-express-newspapers.

48 Giles Sheldrick, 'Songs of Praise in Calais EXPOSED – this is how the BBC is spending YOUR cash', *Daily Express*, 11 August 2015, https://www.express.co.uk/news/uk/597444/Songs-of-Praise-Calais-BBC.

49 David Bond, 'Trinity Mirror in talks to acquire Express', *Financial Times*, 8 September 2017, https://www.ft.com/content/2f9710c2-945c-11e7-a9e6-11d2foebb7fo. Bond wrote that this deal, if completed, would 'raise political questions over how the Labour Party-supporting Mirror titles will coexist in the same parent group as the right-wing Express newspapers'.

50 In the letter which Age UK suggested interested people could send to their MPs, it said: 'We believe it's the government's responsibility to look after older people, not the BBC's', https://campaigns.ageuk.org.uk/page/46081/action/1?chain.

51 The Barclays are strongly committed to Brexit and the UK's sovereignty outside the EU. However, this patriotic commitment to Britain's sovereignty does not stretch to actually living here for tax purposes. See also Jane Martinson's article, 'The break-up: Barclay v Barclay', 2 March 2020, on news website Tortoise, https://members.tortoisemedia.com/2020/03/02/barclays-1-end-of-empire/content.html.

Chapter 8: In Which We Meet . . .

1 Jane Mayer, *Dark Money: How a Secretive Group of Billionaires is Trying to Buy Political Control in the US*, Scribe, 2016, p. 79.

2 An 'astroturf' organization is one that conceals its powerful sponsors and masquerades as an independent grassroots movement driven and funded by ordinary, concerned citizens – 'Mothers for this' and 'Americans for that'.

3 Tom Bawden, 'The address where Eurosceptics and climate change sceptics rub shoulders', *Independent*, 10 February 2016, https://www.independent.co.uk/news/uk/politics/eu-referendum-eurosceptics-climate-change-sceptics-55-tufton-street-westminster-a6866021.html; Brexit Shambles, 'Brexit Scam: We Need to Talk About Tufton Street', 4 September 2018, http://www.brexitshambles.com/brexit-scam-we-need-to-talk-about-tufton-street/.

4 See the business news website Quartz for Marie Le Conte's article, 'Boris Johnson's cabinet shows us exactly what kind of leader he will be', 25 July 2019, https://qz.com/1675056/boris-johnsons-cabinet-shows-us-what-kind-of-leader-he-will-be/; and Robert Booth, 'Who is behind the Taxpayers' Alliance?', *The Guardian*, 9 October 2019, https://www.theguardian.com/politics/2009/oct/09/taxpayers-alliance-conservative-pressure-group.

5 See the investigative media news outlet DeSmog UK for an article by Mat Hope, ' "Opaque" and "deceptive" think tanks spend millions pushing Brexit and climate science misinformation', 8 February 2017, https://www.desmog.co.uk/2017/02/08/opaque-and-deceptive-think-tanks-spend-millions-pushing-brexit-and-climate-science-misinformation.

6 Rob Evans, Felicity Lawrence and David Pegg, 'US groups raise millions to support right-wing UK think tanks', *The Guardian*, 28 September 2018, https://www.theguardian.com/politics/2018/sep/28/us-groups-raise-millions-to-support-rightwing-uk-thinktanks.

7 Felicity Lawrence, Rob Evans, David Pegg, Caelainn Barr and Pamela Duncan, 'How the right's radical thinktanks reshaped the Conservative party', *The Guardian*, 29 November 2019, https://www.theguardian.com/politics/2019/nov/29/rightwing-thinktank-conservative-boris-johnson-brexit-atlas-network.

8 Desmog UK, Mat Hope and Chloe Farand, 'Matthew and Sarah Elliot: how a UK power couple links US libertarians and fossil fuel lobbyists to Brexit', 19 November 2018, https://www.desmog.

co.uk/2018/11/18/matthew-sarah-elliott-uk-power-couple-linking-us-libertarians-and-fossil-fuel-lobbyists-brexit.

9 Jamie Doward, 'Liam Fox's Atlantic Bridge linked top Tories and Tea Party activists', *The Guardian,* 15 October 2011, https://www.theguardian.com/politics/2011/oct/15/liam-fox-atlantic-bridge. The sincerity of Johnson's support for Brexit is unclear, but that question falls outside the scope of this book.

10 Carole Cadwalladr, 'TaxPayers' Alliance concedes it launched smears against Brexit whistleblower', *Observer,* 11 November 2018, https://www.theguardian.com/politics/2018/nov/11/brexit-whistleblower-shahmir-sanni-taxpayers-alliance-concedes-it-launched-smears.

11 Emma Graham-Harrison, 'Vote Leave whistleblower sues Tax-Payers' Alliance for unfair dismissal', *The Guardian,* 18 July 2018, https://www.theguardian.com/politics/2018/jul/18/vote-leave-whistleblower-sues-taxpayers-alliance-for-unfair-dismissal.

12 There were two interviews: one in January 2019, see: 'How BBC bias works', 7 January 2019 at https://www.youtube.com/watch?v=aucDmK5E4bU, and one in March 2020, see 'BBC insider exposes BBC bias and lack of diversity of opinion', 1 March 2020, https://www.youtube.com/watch?v=bSy8bWuuWQU.

13 See Joshua Funnell's article on left-wing news website The Canary: 'A think tank is finally challenged over its funding on Question Time but why was it ever given a platform?', 4 November 2018, https://www.thecanary.co/discovery/analysis-discovery/2018/11/04/a-thinktank-is-finally-challenged-over-its-funding-on-question-time-but-why-was-it-ever-given-a-platform/.

14 Mayer, *Dark Money.* As far as we know, no one has yet done a comparably detailed study of the equivalent influence of networks in Britain, nor of the connections between the US and UK networks.

15 Fisher moved to the US in 1977 where he met Charles Koch and contributed to the early development of right-wing think tanks in America.

16 The Charity Commission rules state that an organization cannot be a charity if its purposes are political: see their online publication, 'Guidance: What makes a "charity"', https://assets.publishing. service.gov.uk/government/uploads/system/uploads/attachment_ data/file/637648/CC4.pdf, p. 3.

17 Mayer, *Dark Money*, p. 80.

18 Jamie Doward, 'Health groups dismayed by news that "big tobacco" funded rightwing thinktanks', *The Guardian*, 1 June 2013, https://www.theguardian.com/society/2013/jun/01/thinktanks-big-tobacco-funds-smoking.

19 Robert Booth, 'Rightwing UK thinktank "offered ministerial access" to potential US donors', *The Guardian*, 30 July 2018, https:// www.theguardian.com/politics/2018/jul/29/rightwing-thinktank-ministerial-access-potential-us-donors-insitute-of-economic-affairs-brexit.

20 Michael Gove, David Davis, Boris Johnson and Liam Fox would have been the four key cabinet members for a US agriculture business lobbying for looser post-Brexit food regulations: Gove was Environment, Food and Rural Affairs Secretary, Davies was Brexit Secretary, Johnson was Foreign Secretary and Fox was International Trade Secretary.

21 Booth, 'Rightwing UK thinkthank "offered ministerial access"'.

22 Mrs Thatcher was widely assumed at the time to regard the BBC as very left-wing and to disapprove of PSBs in general, and the BBC and the licence fee in particular, both on ideological grounds and because of her closeness to Rupert Murdoch. In 2014, government papers released under the thirty-year rule confirmed this, revealing that, in the early 1980s, she had led a covert war against the Corporation: like Dominic Cummings twenty years later, she had wanted to 'knock [it] down to size'; Edward Malnick, 'Margaret Thatcher conducted covert war against BBC', *Daily Telegraph*, 30 December 2014, https://www.telegraph. co.uk/news/politics/margaret-thatcher/11313380/Margaret-Thatcher-conducted-covert-war-against-BBC.html. (We discussed

Cummings's apocalyptic 2004 blog posts on the BBC in the Introduction.)

23 Philip Booth, ed., 'In focus: the case for privatising the BBC', Institute of Economic Affairs, 2016, https://iea.org.uk/publications/research/in-focus-the-case-for-privatising-the-bbc. Cento Veljanovski contributed Chapter 2: 'Public Service Broadcasting: Ownership, Funding and Provision'.

24 Apparently, it's pro-EU, too deferential to the royal family, anti-Scottish independence, anti-Israel, pro-immigration, hostile to NHS reform, unduly pro-Obama: see Booth, ed., 'In focus: the case for privatising the BBC', p. 67.

25 It does, however, argue that the BBC's licence-fee funding is another reason why its supposed bias is especially objectionable: 'Consumers are not able to punish the institution financially for perceived coverage bias', (ibid., p. 71). This is true, but it still fails to explain why, instead of exercising their freedom as viewers, listeners and online users to boycott BBC News, they voluntarily choose it day after day as their main, and most trusted, news source.

26 Chapter 4: 'Why Is the BBC Biased?' is written by Stephen Davies, the IEA's Head of Education. Davies asserts that the BBC's dominant culture is that of educated middle-class people – or more precisely, *privately educated upper-middle-class* people with backgrounds in the professions rather than 'trade'. How exactly this differs from, say, the class mix at the IEA itself, which boasts a range of highly educated contributors – albeit often with some American academic experience in places like George Mason University (a kind of right-wing seminary) – is unclear. Davies does not offer the IEA's own profile for comparison – nor does he compare the demographic mix at the BBC with that of *other* broadcasters (there is, unsurprisingly, considerable movement between the senior news and current affairs people at the BBC, Channel 4, ITN and Sky News). (Sam Friedman's *The Class Ceiling* – Policy Press, 2019 – is very funny about the class background of broadcasting employees, especially

at Channel 4.) Nor does Davies mention the profile of journalists at the Beeb-bashing *Times*, *Telegraph* and *Mail*. As with so many other issues, the class mix is, apparently, a problem only at the BBC.

27 See Ryan Bourne's Chapter 3: 'The Problem of Bias in the BBC'.

28 See their website at http://newcultureforum.org.uk/.

29 Ibid.

30 'Cultural Marxism' is a recurrent term of abuse in this kind of rhetoric, particularly in America. There does not seem to be a formal definition, but in practical terms it is used to suggest that progressive and/or liberal policies and politicians are evidence of some sort of covert communism. The fact that many of the people and policies that are attacked on this basis would be utterly unacceptable in any recognizably authoritarian communist state is irrelevant. For a grown-up review see Russell Blackford's blog post of 28 July 2015, 'Cultural Marxism and our current culture wars: Part 1', on the independent news website The Conversation: www.theconversation.com/cultural-marxism-and-our-current-culture-wars.part-1-45299.

31 Peter Whittle, *Being British: What's Wrong with It?*, Biteback, 2012.

32 See their website at http://news-watch.co.uk/about-us/.

33 The Media Research Centre website is at https://www.mrc.org/.

34 Similarly, the MRC's previous stated mission, 'To expose and neutralise the propaganda arm of the Left: the national news media', has now been replaced by 'To create a media culture in America where truth and liberty flourish'.

35 See the 'Contact Us' page of News-watch's website at http://news-watch.co.uk/contact-us/. Accessed 12 March 2020.

36 At https://conservativewoman.co.uk/.

37 See the Conservative Woman website Peter Smith, 'Coronavirus: is the cure worse than the disease?', 12 March 2020, https://conservativewoman.co.uk/coronavirus-is-the-cure-worse-than-the-disease/.

38 openDemocracy, Adam Ramsay and Peter Geoghegan, 'Who's paying for these "reports" on BBC Brexit coverage?', 23 October 2017,

https://www.opendemocracy.net/en/dark-money-investigations/whos-paying-for-these-reports-on-bbc-brexit-coverage/.

39 Powerbase is an encyclopaedia of people, issues and groups which shape the public agenda. Follow the weblink for the information they have about the Institute: https://powerbase.info/index.php/Institute_for_Policy_Research.

40 See https://traditionalbritain.org/.

41 Mark Townsend, 'Katie Hopkins to speak at far-right rally with Holocaust denier', *The Guardian*, 23 September 2018, https://www.theguardian.com/media/2018/sep/23/katie-hopkins-speak-far-right-for-britain-islamophobe-holocaust-denier.

42 See https://rationalwiki.org/wiki/Traditional_Britain_Group.

43 At https://www.youtube.com/watch?v=Pp5u_RQ6oLk.

44 See http://news-watch.co.uk/?s=ofcom.

45 Tamasin Cave and Andy Rowell, *A Quiet Word: Lobbying, Crony Capitalism and Broken Politics in Britain*, Bodley Head, 2014.

46 David Cameron's 'Rebuilding trust in politics' speech of 8 February 2010, https://conservative-speeches.sayit.mysociety.org/speech/601536.

47 See https://www.statista.com/statistics/257337/total-lobbying-spending-in-the-us $3.45.

48 Mayer, *Dark Money*.

49 No reporter name given, 'Rupert Murdoch's No 10 visits made through the back door', *Independent*, 20 July 2011, https://www.independent.co.uk/news/uk/politics/rupert-murdochs-no-10-visits-made-through-the-back-door-2317220.html.

50 Cave and Rowell, *A Quiet Word*.

51 For TV Licence Resistance, see https://www.youtube.com/channel/UC9DL8SBTvq6eezSLGCrfXoA.

52 For its YouTube channel, see https://www.youtube.com/channel/UCUoQx_r4KP7onC5jjtJ_tvg; and its blog, https://banthebbc.wordpress.com/.

53 At https://biasedbbc.org.

54 At http://tuv.org.uk/about-tuv/.

55 See this news and opinion portal for this story: https://sluggerotoole.com/2010/06/29/tuv-candidates-website-faces-closure-over-hate-speech/.

56 See https://www.altnewsmedia.net/.

57 On 14 January 2017, https://twitter.com/dvatw/status/820193329950363648?lang=en and 27 March 2019, https://twitter.com/DVATW/status/1110896500496891904.

58 At https://www.youtube.com/watch?v=xzJjoAispdY.

59 See https://mediabiasfactcheck.com/21st-century-wire/.

60 Kurt Andersen, *Fantasyland: How America Went Haywire: A 500-Year History*, Ebury Press, 2018.

61 Robert Ford, *Revolt on the Right: Explaining Support for the Radical Right in Britain*, Routledge, 2014.

62 A phrase used by the US counsellor to the President, Kellyanne Conway, during a 'Meet the Press' interview on 22 January 2017.

Chapter 9: 'Bolshevism', Brexit and Bias

1 Michael Deacon, 'The BBC's obsession with "balance" is driving me up the wall', *Daily Telegraph*, 28 July 2018, https://www.telegraph.co.uk/opinion/2018/07/28/bbcs-obsession-balance-driving-wall/.

2 However, the right arguably has more to gain, even politically, from reducing the scale and credibility of the BBC to increase the public's reliance on newspapers, most of which lean to the right.

3 A classic Conservative convert from the far left: https://www.city-journal.org/html/liberalism-12417.html.

4 Janet Daley, 'The BBC is panicking at the public's rejection of its arrogant Left-liberal worldview', *Sunday Telegraph*, 26 January 2020, https://www.telegraph.co.uk/news/2020/01/25/bbc-panicking-publics-rejection-arrogant-left-liberal-worldview/.

5 The *only* material case we know of where the BBC got its facts wrong, at least in recent years, was the 2 November 2012 *Newsnight*

programme falsely accusing Lord McAlpine of having been a paedophile (a case of mistaken identity), which triggered George Entwistle's resignation (see Chapter 5).

6 To our knowledge, the only major precedent for *any* centrist criticism was the centre–left Blair government's criticisms of a BBC report that the intelligence on Iraq's weapons of mass destruction (what came to be known as the 'Dodgy Dossier') had been knowingly 'sexed up' in September 2003. The government's retaliation for this (in most people's view, correct) claim led to the resignation of both the then BBC chairman (Gavyn Davies) and director-general (Greg Dyke) – the only time this has ever happened.

7 The description of the BBC as 'Pinkoes and traitors', sometimes attributed to Margaret Thatcher's husband, Dennis, actually came from the satirical 'Dear Bill' letters in *Private Eye* – ostensibly from Dennis Thatcher to Bill Deedes – which were written by Richard Ingrams and immortalized by Jean Seaton as the title of her official history of the BBC from 1974 to 1997.

8 Bryony Gordon, '"Wokeness" has been weaponised – and we're all caught in the crossfire', *Daily Telegraph*, 25 January 2020, https://www.telegraph.co.uk/women/life/wokeness-has-weaponised-war-left-right-aint-pretty/. In our experience, terms like 'politically correct' and now 'woke' are *only* used – always sneeringly – by commentators on the right, implying that they are speaking for the silent majority, perpetually assailed by the distorted ('PC' or 'woke') view of the world peddled by the BBC and *The Guardian*, in particular. Within this worldview, any prosocial action or comment by someone on the left is dismissed as 'wokeness' or 'virtue signalling'.

9 *Bodyguard* was commissioned by the BBC but *actually made* by World Productions, part of ITV Studios. But, to Delingpole, it was a BBC programme and therefore, almost by definition, full of 'PC bollocks'.

10 James Delingpole, 'High five: you don't get quite the same production values in things like C5's How the Victorians Built Britain, but

you don't get the PC bollocks of Bodyguard and King Arthur's Britain', *Spectator*, 29 September 2018, https://www.spectator.co.uk/2018/09/forget-the-bbc-only-channel-5-does-proper-documentaries-these-days/. As its title suggests, the article made the valid point that Channel 5, long seen as an also-ran, is now developing a reputation for showing good, low-budget documentaries. But Delingpole just *had* to turn it into a hyperbolic Beeb-bashing rant, including about the BBC's latest *drama* success.

11 Theresa May, Sajid Javid, Sadiq Khan and Amber Rudd.

12 Neil Basu is the Assistant Commissioner for Specialist Operations.

13 Damian Reilly, 'Forget the BBC – it's Netflix and Amazon that are "woke"', *Spectator*, 18 March 2020, https://life.spectator.co.uk/articles/forget-the-bbc-its-netflix-and-amazon-that-are-woke/. The article cites other examples of 'wokeness' from Netflix, Disney and, by implication, Amazon, which is controlled by Jeff Bezos, 'the proprietor of The Washington Post, the American wokerati's broadsheet of choice'.

14 Since the 1970s there has been a steady competition among some of the BBC's more plodding right-wing critics to create new acronyms to dramatize its supposed left-wing and pro-EU bias and other alleged crimes. Examples include: Bullshit Broadcasting Corporation, Buggering British Children, Big Brother Corporation, Brexit-Bashing Corporation, British Broadcasting Cover-up and Bloated Broadcasting Corporation, among others.

15 Alan Travis, 'Thatcher forced to intervene over Tebbit's "obsessive" criticism of BBC, papers reveal', *The Guardian*, 23 January 2017, https://www.theguardian.com/politics/2017/jan/23/thatcher-norman-tebbit-criticism-of-bbc-us-bombing-libya. Thatcher was responding to Tebbit's attacks on Kate Adie's BBC reporting of the US bombing of Libya in 1986.

16 Bill Gardner, 'BBC has been accused of bias throughout history', *Spectator*, 11 March 2014, https://www.telegraph.co.uk/culture/tvandradio/bbc/10690226/BBC-has-been-accused-of-bias-throughout-history.html.

17 The specific charge against the BBC, widely taken up by its right-wing enemies, such as the *Daily Mail*, was that its war reports always referred to 'British', rather than 'our', forces, troops, etc. The reports were always strictly accurate, but selective, to avoid revealing anything that might help the Argentines. Much the same policy had been successfully used during the Second World War. The wisdom of this approach became clearer as the Falklands War continued and the credibility gap between the British reports (by the BBC and the wonderfully understated MoD spokesman Ian McDonald) and the Argentine ones grew wider and wider. Truth is often the first casualty in war, but the BBC's reputation for accuracy was reinforced by its reporting of the conflict.

18 'For Brexit and Beyond', UKIP's manifesto of 2019.

19 The Brexit Party's 'Contract with the People' of 2019.

20 Robin Aitken, *Can We Trust the BBC?*, Continuum, 2007; *Can We (Still) Trust the BBC?*, Bloomsbury Continuum, 2013; and *The Noble Liar: How and Why the BBC Distorts the News to Promote a Liberal Agenda*, Biteback, 2018.

21 Robin Aitken, 'What is the loneliest job in Britain? Being a Tory at the BBC', *Daily Mail*, 17 February 2007, https://www.dailymail.co.uk/news/article-436794/What-loneliest-job-Britain-Being-Tory-BBC.html.

22 For instance, in the *Telegraph*, *Spectator*, *Conservative Home* and the *Catholic Herald*. In 2019, he also appeared on two extended YouTube videos, including one based on an interview with Peter Whittle, director of the New Culture Forum.

23 See https://www.youtube.com/watch?v=YuYYVRtZ1sM.

24 On 16 March 2018, https://twitter.com/johnclarke1960/status/976048145464545280.

25 PoliticsHome, John Johnston, 'BBC deny photoshopping Jeremy Corbyn's hat to make him appear more "Leninesque"', 18 March 2018, https://www.politicshome.com/news/article/bbc-deny-photoshopping-jeremy-corbyns-hat-to-make-him-appear-more-leninesque.

26 Donald Clarke, 'The great Jeremy Corbyn Russian hat conspiracy', *Irish Times*, 23 March 2018, https://www.irishtimes.com/culture/the-great-jeremy-corbyn-russian-hat-conspiracy-1.3435149.

27 Jack Mendel, 'Labour councillor in "appalling", "anti-Semitic" Rothschilds Twitter tirade', *Jewish News*, 7 February 2017, https://jewishnews.timesofisrael.com/labour-councillor-rothschilds/.

28 Published by Verso in 2016.

29 openDemocracy, Ian Sinclair, 'The BBC is neither independent or impartial: interview with Tom Mills', 25 January 2017, https://www.opendemocracy.net/en/ourbeeb/bbc-is-neither-independent-or-impartial-interview-with-tom-mills/.

30 openDemocracy, Sinclair, 'The BBC is neither independent or impartial'.

31 Mehdi Hasan, 'Bias and the BBC', *New Statesman*, 27 August 2009, https://www.newstatesman.com/uk-politics/2009/08/mehdi-hasan-bbc-wing-bias-corporation.

32 Andrew Neil, 'Europe and China: the fatal conceit', fourteenth annual Hayek Lecture, 28 November 2005, https://www.lancaster.ac.uk/staff/ecagrs/HL202005.

33 Friedrich Hayek (1899–1992) was a leading member of the 'Austrian' school of liberal, free-market economics. He was both eminent (a Nobel Prize winner in 1974) and highly influential, including on Margaret Thatcher.

34 Nick Robinson was also at Oxford University with Boris Johnson.

35 Owen Jones, 'It's the BBC's right-wing bias that is the threat to democracy and journalism', *The Guardian*, 17 March 2014, https://www.theguardian.com/commentisfree/2014/mar/17/bbc-leftwing-bias-non-existent-myth.

36 Owen Jones, 'If the BBC is politically neutral, how does it explain Andrew Neil?', *The Guardian*, 11 April 2018, https://www.theguardian.com/commentisfree/2018/apr/11/bbc-andrew-neil-media-politics.

37 The Canary, Alex Nunns, 'Author Alex Nunns dismantles the myth of BBC impartiality in a brutal number crunch', 19 June 2018, https://www.thecanary.co/trending/2018/06/21/author-alex-nunns-dismantles-the-myth-of-bbc-impartiality-in-a-brutal-number-crunch/. Nunns categorized the guests on *Sunday Politics* from 11 June 2017, immediately after the 8 June election, until 22 July 2018, when the show ended. Over this period, there were 126 guests: 54 per cent were from the right, 13 per cent from the political centre and 32 per cent from the left, suggesting a clear, although not overwhelming, imbalance to the right. Perhaps more tellingly, on 64 per cent of the shows, *two of the three guests* were from the right. And, of course, the skew to the right was potentially reinforced by the lead presenter/interviewer being Andrew Neil. (The other was Jo Coburn, with no obvious party-political affiliation.) Nunns added that only thirteen guests (10 per cent) were from the *Corbynite* left – despite Corbyn's leadership of the Labour Party at the time and his unexpectedly strong performance in the recent general election: from the perspective of a Corbyn supporter, *90 per cent* of the guests and both presenters were 'hostile'. Nunns kindly shared his analysis and data with us. Having seen them, we think there is little to challenge in his categorization of the guests: with only one exception, they were all politicos with clear party allegiances.

38 As are those working in most other news media, including those employed by right-leaning papers such as the *Telegraph* and *The Times*.

39 With correlation coefficients of 0.53 and 0.41, respectively.

40 Centre for Policy Studies, Oliver Latham, 'Bias at the Beeb? A quantitative study of slant in BBC Online reporting', 15 August 2013, https://www.cps.org.uk/research/bias-at-the-beeb/.

41 Oliver Latham, 'Careful, Auntie, here's real proof of your bias: a statistical analysis of BBC reports challenges its claim to fairness', *Sunday Times*, 11 August 2013, https://www.thetimes.co.uk/article/

careful-auntie-heres-real-proof-of-your-bias-j3xzkwphg2f; Hayley Dixon, 'BBC is biased towards the left, study finds', *Sunday Telegraph*, 11 August 2013, https://www.telegraph.co.uk/culture/ tvandradio/bbc/10235T967/BBC-is-biased-toward-the-left-study-finds. html; and Lucy Osborne, 'BBC is "twice as likely to cover Left-wing news stories as Right-wing ones" says study', *Daily Mail*, 12 August 2013, https://www.dailymail.co.uk/news/article-2389589/BBC-twice-likely-cover-Left-wing-news-stories-Right-wing-ones.html.

42   In a forum on the DCFCFANS website, 'David' started a thread entitled, 'My TV licence money goes towards this', on 26 February 2017, see https://dcfcfans.uk/topic/25414-my-tv-licence-money-goes-towards-this/page/3/.

43   Namely: the think tank's self-description; its use of key words or phrases; its position on key issues; and the political background of those associated with it.

44   The most important of these was the frequently cited Institute for Fiscal Studies (IFS), which was classified in the Cardiff study as neutral, although many – including the Centre for Policy Studies' Oliver Latham – would describe it as right of centre. The IFS is cautious about both taxation and public investment (making it right-leaning), but also cautious about the economic impact of Brexit (making it broadly centrist).

45   If the IFS were classified as right-leaning, then there was a material bias to the right, even in 2009, and the bias in 2015 was still more marked.

46   From 7 May 2015, the Conservatives had an absolute majority, rather than leading a coalition government.

47   Stephen Cushion and Justin Lewis, 'Think tanks, television news and impartiality', *Journalism Studies*, 20, 4, 26 October 2017, pp. 480–99, https://orca.cf.ac.uk/105302/1/Think%20Tanks%20 Television%20News%20and%20Impartialityb.pdf.

48   BBC, 'A BBC Trust review of the breadth of opinion reflected in the BBC's output', July 2013, http://downloads.bbc.co.uk/bbctrust/ assets/files/pdf/our_work/breadth_opinion/breadth_opinion.pdf.

49 It's usually presented at 10:40 p.m. on weeknights and between 10:30 p.m. and 11:30 p.m. at weekends on the BBC News Channel.

50 See Adrian Renton and Justin Schlosberg, 'Reporting the news-papers: evidence of bias skew in the BBC's selection of titles, stories and guest discussants of newspaper coverage, 18 April–21 May 2017', 5 June 2017, on the Media Reform Coalition website, https://www.mediareform.org.uk/wp-content/uploads/2017/06/BBC-NEWSPAPERS-REPORT-FINAL.pdf. The Media Reform Coalition, based at Goldsmiths, University of London, is a group of academics, partner organizations and individual supporters that campaigns for 'a media system that operates in the public interest'.

51 Sixty-nine per cent of the TV discussion was of stories in Conservative-supporting papers versus only 23 per cent for stor-ies in Labour-supporting papers and just 8 per cent for those in papers supporting other parties (UKIP or the Liberal Demo-crats). The distribution of TV guests showed a similar imbalance, with 68 per cent of those with a clear party affiliation being Conservative supporters. The show's online coverage was even more dominated by the Conservative-supporting papers, which accounted for 72 per cent of the stories mentioned.

52 Ofcom, 'Ofcom's rules on due impartiality, due accuracy, elec-tions and referendums', 9 March 2017, https://www.ofcom.org.uk/__data/assets/pdf_file/0030/98148/Due-impartiality-and-elections-statement.pdf. The voting pattern in the previous election, just two years earlier in 2015, had been 37 per cent for the Conservatives, 30 per cent for Labour and 33 per cent for all other parties.

53 Maxwell McCombs, *Setting the Agenda: Mass Media and Public Opinion*, Polity Press, 2004.

54 The BBC, ITV, Sky, Channel 4 and Channel 5.

55 Stephen Cushion and Richard Sambrook, 'How TV news let the Tories fight the election on their own terms', *The Guardian*, 15 May 2015, https://www.theguardian.com/media/2015/may/15/tv-news-let-the-tories-fight-the-election-coalition-economy-taxation.

56 Two thousand and forty British adults aged eighteen plus were
    included in the sample who responded to the questionnaire,
    excluding those who answered 'Don't know'. The results were
    published on 7 March 2017 by Matthew Smith, who asked the
    question: 'How left or right-wing are the UK's newspapers?', at
    https://yougov.co.uk/topics/politics/articles-reports/2017/03/07/
    how-left-or-right-wing-are-uks-newspapers. See the full survey
    results at: https://d25d2506sfb94s.cloudfront.net/cumulus_
    uploads/document/n34shyp79t/InternalResults_170215_Left-
    RightScale_ExtraCB_W.pdf.

57 The study did not cover the *Financial Times*, presumably on the
    grounds that many respondents may have been unfamiliar with
    its editorial coverage (probably assuming it to be pro-business
    and right-leaning). We would characterize it as socially liberal,
    economically centre–right (and pro-business), party politically
    neutral, internationalist and anti-Brexit.

58 The survey on YouGov asked: 'Some people talk about "left",
    "right" and "centre" to describe parties and politicians. With this
    in mind, where would you place yourself?'

59 For instance, as one might expect, most (65 per cent) of those who
    had voted Remain in 2016 saw the *Mail* as 'very right wing'. But,
    even among those who had voted Leave, 27 per cent said the
    same, as did 29 per cent of those who had voted Conservative
    in 2015. And clear majorities of both Leavers and Conserva-
    tives said it was 'fairly' or 'very' right wing (59 and 65 per cent,
    respectively).

60 Respondents were grouped by gender, age, socio-economic sta-
    tus and region.

61 British adults aged fifteen-plus, September 2019. Source: The Pub-
    lishers Audience Measurement Company (PAMCo): https://pamco.
    co.uk/pamco-data/data-archive/. 'Online' newspaper reading is
    done mostly on smartphones but also on tablets and desktops.

62 The *Independent* had stopped its print edition and was online-only
    by this point.

63 Initially, as Minotaur Media Tracking.

64 See http://news-watch.co.uk/about-us/.

65 See http://news-watch.co.uk/archive/.

66 News-watch, 'BBC bias against Brexit: News-watch surveys since the 2016 referendum', 2 July 2019, http://news-watch.co.uk/wp-content/uploads/2019/07/BBC-Bias-Against-Brexit-News-watch-Surveys-since-the-2016-referendum-.pdf.

67 'For instance, the BBC has not considered whether the ideas behind the "project" of European integration are still valid today', ibid.

68 At http://news-watch.co.uk/about-us/.

69 Combined with other categories, such as their professional or political roles/affiliations, e.g. a pro-Remain Confederation of British Industry spokesperson or Labour-supporting Leaver.

70 Academic journals are 'double-blind' peer-reviewed: the journal editor sends the manuscript to suitably qualified reviewers – other academics working in the same area – without revealing the authors' names; and then sends the reviewers' comments back to the authors without revealing the reviewers' names. Successful papers typically go through two or three rounds of revision and resubmission. It's a tough system, especially for the top journals, where most papers are rejected by the editor rather than accepted for publication, either straightway, or after one or more rounds of revision and resubmission.

71 See http://news-watch.co.uk/about-us/.

72 Centre for Policy Studies, Oliver Latham, 'Bias at the Beeb?', p. 3.

73 'Mortal enemy: what Cummings' think tank said about the BBC', *The Guardian*, 21 January 2020, https://www.theguardian.com/politics/2020/jan/21/mortal-enemy-what-cummings-thinktank-said-about-bbchttps://www.theguardian.com/politics/2020/jan/21/mortal-enemy-what-cummings-thinktank-said-about-bbc.

74 Tom Mills, *The BBC: Myth of a Public Service*, Verso, 2016, pp. 107–8.

75 Mills, *The BBC: Myth of a Public Service*, pp. 113–16.

76 In 2019, News-watch launched a request for a judicial review to 'stop BBC bias': David Keighley, 'Appeal: help us stop BBC bias!', 4 July 2019, http://news-watch.co.uk/2019/07/. The case was dismissed by the High Court and, on appeal, by the Court of Appeal, which ruled that there were no grounds on which it had any real prospect of success: Charlotte Tobitt, 'Judge rejects appeal for judicial review into alleged BBC "Brexit bias"', *Press Gazette*, 2 March 2020, https://www.pressgazette.co.uk/judges-reject-appeal-judicial-review-alleged-bbc-brexit-bias/. News-watch also submitted what it somewhat immodestly called a 'meticulously researched complaint' to Ofcom about the 'anti-Brexit bias' of BBC One's *Question Time*. It was outraged when this, too, was rejected: see News-watch, David Keighley, 'Ofcom BBC bias whitewash', 17 February 2020, http://news-watch.co.uk/ofcom-bbc-bias-whitewash/.

77 The other four panel members, in addition to Lord Richard Wilson, were Lucy Armstrong, chief executive of a business providing consultancy and venture capital in the north-east; Rodney Leach, a director of Jardine Matheson and chairman of Business for Sterling; Nigel Smith, former managing director of David Auld Valves, Ltd, Glasgow, and former chairman of the No-Euro campaign; and Sir Stephen Wall, former head of the Cabinet Office European Secretariat and a board member of Britain in Europe. Leach and Smith were committed Eurosceptics and Wall was a Europhile. Wilson, the chairman, was a non-executive director of Sky and Armstrong was from the highly Eurosceptic north-east, but we have no information on their views on Britain and the EU.

78 A report commissioned by the BBC Governors, 'BBC news coverage of the European Union: independent panel report', January 2005, p. 8, http://downloads.bbc.co.uk/bbctrust/assets/files/pdf/our_work/govs/independentpanelreport.pdf. These conclusions inevitably reflected the panel members' relatively high engagement in EU-related issues (in contrast with most people's relative indifference to them). They should perhaps have made

more allowance for the BBC's dilemma in trying to interest audiences in these issues, without over-simplifying them, at a time when most viewers and listeners still saw the EU as remote, irrelevant and deadly dull. At the same time, the 'importance and relevance of the EU in the political and daily life of the UK' may in reality have been rather less than the panel was suggesting.

79 Ibid, p. 4.

80 For Media Tenor, see http://us.mediatenor.com/en/about-us.

81 Jasper Jackson, 'BBC's EU reporting "more negative than its Putin coverage"', *The Guardian*, 21 April 2016, https://www.theguardian.com/media/2016/apr/21/bbc-eu-reporting-putin-coverage; Newsweek, Josh Lowe, 'BBC "treats Assad better than the EU": Analysis', 21 April 2016, https://www.newsweek.com/bbc-treats-assad-better-eu-450543; Politico, Florian Elder, 'Brussels playbook', 21 April 2016, https://www.politico.eu/newsletter/brussels-playbook/politico-brussels-playbook-presented-by-google-obama-mini-summit-how-media-cover-the-eu/. Typically, none of the rightwing, Brexit-boosting, BBC-bashing papers – frequent promoters of News-watch's research – even mentioned this study.

82 Similarly, Media Tenor's comparative study of the coverage of the EU and the three 'strongmen' on *News at Ten* and *Newsnight* in 2015 still had to make judgements about positive, negative and neutral reports.

83 *BBC News at Ten*, *ITV News at Ten*, *Sky News at Ten*, *Channel 4 News* at 7 p.m. and *Channel 5 News* at 6:30 p.m.

84 Stephen Cushion and Justin Lewis, 'Impartiality, statistical tit-for-tats and the construction of balance: UK television news reporting of the 2016 EU referendum campaign', *European Journal of Communication*, 32 (2017) 3, pp. 208–23.

85 Cushion and Lewis, 'Impartiality, statistical tit-for-tats and the construction of balance', pp. 220–21.

86 The Conversation, Mike Berry, 'How biased is the BBC?', August 2013, https://theconversation.com/hard-evidence-how-biased-is-the-bbc-17028.

87 James Harding, 'A truly balanced view from the BBC: don't blame us for Brexit', *The Guardian*, 24 September 2017, https://www.theguardian.com/commentisfree/2016/sep/24/dont-blame-bbc-for-brexit-false-balance.

88 Hugo Dixon, Letters page, *The Guardian*, 1 October 2016.

89 Ofcom, *Ofcom Broadcast and On Demand Bulletin*, Issue 351, 9 April 2018, pp. 12–23, https://www.ofcom.org.uk/__data/assets/pdf_file/0012/112701/issue-351-broadcast-on-demand-bulletin.pdf.

90 Carole Cadwalladr, Emma Graham-Harrison and Mark Townsend, 'Revealed: Brexit insider claims Vote Leave may have breached spending limits', *The Guardian*, 24 March 2018, https://www.theguardian.com/politics/2018/mar/24/brexit-whistleblower-cambridge-analytica-beleave-vote-leave-shahmir-sanni.

91 See https://twitter.com/shahmiruk/status/1156281060201828352.

92 At https://twitter.com/shahmiruk/status/1190293453873266690.

93 See the article by Peter Jukes in the Byline Times, a crowdfunded, independent news website, 'The BBC on the edge of the abyss', 21 November 2018, https://bylinetimes.com/2018/12/21/a-duty-to-inform-as-well-as-entertain-the-bbc-on-the-edge-of-an-abyss/.

94 Kathleen Hall Jamieson, *Cyberwar: How Russian Hackers and Trolls Helped Elect a President: What We Don't, Can't, and Do Know*, Oxford University Press, 2018.

95 See Carol Cadwalladr, 'Steve Bannon: "We went back and forth" on the themes of Johnson's big speech', *The Guardian*, 22 June 2019, https://www.theguardian.com/politics/2019/jun/22/boris-johnson-steve-bannon-texts-foreign-secretary-resignation-speech; Jim Pickard, 'Steve Bannon says he advised Johnson on speech attacking May', *Financial Times*, 23 June 2019, https://www.ft.com/content/68896b0a-959f-11e9-8cfb-30c211dcd229; and Matthew d'Ancona's article on news website Tortoise: 'Bannon's Britain: Boris Johnson, Nigel Farage and Tommy Robinson are enmeshed in the new network politics of the Right', 28 September 2019, https://members.tortoisemedia.com/2019/09/28/bannons-britain/content.html.

96 David Cay Johnson's book, *It's Even Worse Than You Think*, Simon & Schuster, 2018, describes these changes in detail.

97 Tim Shipman, 'BBC whistleblower: bosses suppressing Russia stories', *Sunday Times*, 23 November 2019, https://www.thetimes.co.uk/article/bbc-whistleblower-bosses-suppressing-russia-stories-lwzn2pm9x.

98 John Sweeney's letter is on a page of his website at https://www.johnsweeney.co.uk/?blog=blogs/archive/2019/11/24/john.sweeneys.letter.to.ofcom.aspx.

99 Andrew Adonis' letter, 9 April 2018, https://twitter.com/Andrew_Adonis/status/983318927672578048/photo/1.

100 Andrew Adonis, 'Andrew Marr's handling of Arron Banks was pathetic – and damaging', *The Guardian*, 5 November 2018, https://www.theguardian.com/commentisfree/2018/nov/05/andrew-marr-arron-banks-bbc-brexit.

101 Nick Cohen, 'Why isn't there greater outrage about Russia's involvement in Brexit?', *The Guardian*, 17 June 2018, https://www.theguardian.com/commentisfree/2018/jun/17/why-isnt-there-greater-outrage-about-russian-involvement-in-brexit.

102 Nick Cohen, 'How the BBC lost the plot on Brexit', *New York Review of Books*, 12 July 2018, https://www.nybooks.com/daily/2018/07/12/how-the-bbc-lost-the-plot-on-brexit/.

103 James Stephenson and Nick Cohen, 'The BBC and Brexit: an exchange', *New York Review of Books*, 17 July 2018, https://www.nybooks.com/daily/2018/07/17/the-bbc-and-brexit-an-exchange/.

104 Cohen, 'Why isn't there greater outrage'.

105 Jane Mayer, 'How Russia helped swing the election for Trump', *New Yorker*, 24 September 2018, https://www.newyorker.com/magazine/2018/10/01/how-russia-helped-to-swing-the-election-for-trump.

106 Jamieson, *Cyberwar: How Russian Hackers and Trolls Helped Elect a President*.

107 Jane Mayer, 'New evidence emerges of Steve Bannon and Cambridge Analytica's role in Brexit', *New Yorker*, 18 November 2018, https://www.newyorker.com/news/news-desk/new-evidence-emerges-of-steve-bannon-and-cambridge-analyticas-role-in-brexit.

Chapter 10: 'Worse Than Poll Tax'

1 The other right-wing targets, in addition to the BBC's alleged
  bias and the licence fee, include its supposed profligacy and inefficiency (already discussed in Chapter 4) and its market impact
  and 'distinctiveness' (discussed in the next chapter).

2 See the Adam Smith Institute's website for articles on the BBC,
  https://www.adamsmith.org/search?q=bbc.

3 A reference to Margaret Thatcher's failed attempt in 1989–90 to
  replace domestic rates (local taxes based on the theoretical rental
  value of the home) with a per capita 'community charge' based
  on the number of registered voters in the household. See also
  Hannah Furness, 'Licence fee "worse than poll tax", says John
  Whittingdale', *Daily Telegraph*, 28 October 2014, https://www.
  telegraph.co.uk/culture/tvandradio/bbc/11192145/BBC-licence-
  fee-worse-than-poll-tax-says-John-Whittingdale.html.

4 John Whittingdale has been MP for Maldon in Essex since 1992.
  He was Mrs Thatcher's Political Secretary from 1989 until his
  election in 1992, https://www.johnwhittingdale.org.uk/index.
  php/about/about-john.

5 Hannah Furness, 'Licence fee "worse than poll tax", says John
  Whittingdale'.

6 TV Licence Resistance, 'Fresh calls to decriminalise non-payment
  of BBC TV licence fee', https://www.tvlicenceresistance.info/
  forum/index.php?topic=13860.0, and Matt Dathan, 'Fresh calls to
  decriminalise non-payment of the BBC's TV licence as figures
  reveal a record 166,000 people pay more than £28m in fines in a
  year', *Daily Mail*, 30 December 2016, https://www.dailymail.co.uk/
  news/article-4075874/Fresh-calls-decriminalise-non-payment-TV-
  Licence-fee-figures-reveal-record-166-000-people-pay-greedy-BBC-
  28m-fines-just-one-year-seven-ten-women.html.

7 In 2016, see Russell Webster, 'Hidden criminal justice facts',
  blog post, 25 August 2017, http://www.russellwebster.com/
  hidden-criminal-justice-facts/. Thirty-eight people were jailed for

not paying a TV-licence-evasion fine in England and Wales in 2016.

8 TV Licence Resistance, 'Fresh calls to decriminalise non-payment'.

9 Tara Conlan, 'BBC licence fee: decriminalising non-payment a matter of time, says MP', *The Guardian*, 20 March 2014, https://www.theguardian.com/media/2014/mar/20/bbc-licence-fee-decriminalising-licence-fee-non-payment-andrew-bridgen.

10 Nicholas Watt, 'Nick Clegg cautious on plan to drop licence fee prosecutions', *The Guardian*, 20 March 2014, https://www.theguardian.com/media/2014/mar/20/nick-clegg-licence-fee-prosecutions.

11 Mark Sweney, 'BBC licence fee: top barrister to look into decriminalisation of evasion', *The Guardian*, 21 October 2014, https://www.theguardian.com/media/2014/oct/21/bbc-licence-fee-david-perry-sajid-javid.

12 'The Perry review: TV licence fee enforcement', for the DCMS, July 2015, https://assets.publishing.service.gov.uk/government/uploads/system/uploads/attachment_data/file/445212/166926_Perry_Review_Text-L-PB.pdf.

13 House of Commons, DCMS Committee, 'Consultation on decriminalizing TV licence evasion', 5 February 2020, https://www.gov.uk/government/consultations/consultation-on-decriminalising-tv-licence-evasion/consultation-on-decriminalising-tv-licence-evasion.

14 Steven Swinford, 'Boris Johnson at odds with Dominic Cummings over BBC licence fee', *The Times*, 18 February 2020, https://www.thetimes.co.uk/article/boris-johnson-at-odds-with-dominic-cummings-over-bbc-licence-fee-206nkjrqj.

15 House of Commons, DCMS Committee, 'Consultation on decriminalizing TV licence evasion', p. 3.

16 New Weather Institute, Lindsay Mackie, 'Let Them Eat Netflix', 28 February 2020, http://www.newweather.org/2020/02/28/let-them-eat-netflix/.

17 House of Commons, DCMS Committee, 'Consultation on decriminalizing TV licence evasion', p. 3.

18 House of Commons, Library, Commons research briefing, 'Winter fuel payments update', 5 November 2019, https://commonslibrary. parliament.uk/research-briefings/sn06019/.

19 House of Commons, DCMS Committee, 'Future of the BBC: fourth report of session 2014–15', 26 February 2015, p. 71, https:// publications.parliament.uk/pa/cm201415/cmselect/cmcumeds/ 315/315.pdf.

20 John Reith, *Broadcast over Britain*, quoted in Charlotte Higgins, *This New Noise: The Extraordinary Birth and Troubled Life of the BBC*, Faber & Faber in association with *The Guardian*, 2015, pp. 9 and 211.

21 And if a tiny handful of TV households (*possibly* a few dozen – we simply don't know) really are paying 43 pence per day for a public service they choose not to use, this is hardly as scandalous as it is routinely portrayed: almost every household pays much more than that for public services they never use, e.g. schools.

22 However, 'perception is reality', and this issue is fraught with *mis*perceptions. For instance, some people do not realize that the TV licence fee also funds BBC Radio and Online; a few may genuinely, although mistakenly, think their households 'never' watch BBC TV, listen to BBC Radio or use the BBC's online services; and some Sky and Virgin subscribers may think they are paying for the BBC twice because it's already included in their pay-TV package. Finally, many people seem to think there are lots of *other* people suffering the injustice of being forced to pay for the BBC despite never using its services.

23 BBC, 'BBC annual report and accounts 2018–19', pp. 61, 208, https://downloads.bbc.co.uk/aboutthebbc/reports/annualreport/ 2018-19.pdf.

24 House of Commons, DCMS Committee, 'Future of the BBC', p. 82.

25 In 2015, collection costs were only 2.8 per cent and the estimated evasion level 5.5 per cent, total 8.3 per cent.

26 The only people who can still legally free-ride are those in the very small (and unknown, but almost certainly growing)

number of households that most likely do consume the BBC's radio and/or online services but where – genuinely – no household member ever watches, records or streams live TV on any channel or online TV service or watches or downloads any BBC programmes on the iPlayer: https://www.tvlicensing.co.uk/check-if-you-need-one.

27 House of Commons, DCMS Committee, 'Future of the BBC', p.70. It also briefly considered a mixed funding model but there was and is little support for this. Different funding methods involve different fixed collection costs, reducing the efficiency of combining them.

28 The advantages of funding the BBC through general taxation are that it would be more progressive than the licence fee and eliminate (or, rather, pass on to HMRC) the collection and enforcement costs. The disadvantages are the threat to the BBC's editorial independence and the likelihood of progressive cuts, especially if the BBC exercised its independence by criticizing government policies or politicians.

29 We are using the term here to include sponsorship and product placement.

30 House of Commons, Home Office Committee, 'Report of the committee on financing the BBC [Peacock Report]', Cmnd. 9824, July 1986, p. 1, https://tvlicensingnews.com/TVLicensingNews/Home_files/Peacock%20Report.pdf.

31 These figures are from trade sources. Historically, combined creative and media agency commissions were 15 per cent of gross media spend, but agency fees are significantly lower than that now. (Clients are also taking more work in-house, which transfers the cost but does not materially reduce it without risking the quality of the campaign.) Controversially, there may also be hidden 'agency rebates' paid by media owners to the agency which are not being passed on to the client: Seb Joseph, ' "We're both playing the game": confessions of a procurement director on agency rebates', *Digiday*, 3 September 2019, https://digiday.com/

marketing/playing-game-confessions-procurement-director-agency-rebates/. On top of these agency fees (and, possibly, rebates), the chief executive of advertising agency WCRS recommends investing 12.5 per cent of TV advertising costs in commercial production: Matt Edwards, 'Why 12.5% is the magic number', *Campaign*, 23 May 2018, https://www.campaignlive.co.uk/article/why-125-magic-number/1465203. However, a more typical figure might be a production cost of 5–7 per cent.

32 The digital advertising value chain is notoriously complex and opaque. There are no reliable figures for the total proportion of advertisers' investment it absorbs, but we would expect it to be *at least* 30 per cent. At the time of writing, the Competition and Markets Authority (CMA) is conducting an investigation into this market which should shed more light on it, see 'Online platforms and digital advertising study: statement of scope', 3 July 2019, https://assets.publishing.service.gov.uk/media/5d1b297e40f0b609dba90d7a/Statement_of_Scope.pdf. See also, House of Lords, Select Committee on Communications and Digital, 'UK advertising in a digital age', 11 April 2018, https://publications.parliament.uk/pa/ld201719/ldselect/ldcomuni/116/116.pdf, and Alex Barker, 'Half of online ad spending goes to industry middlemen', *Financial Times*, 6 May 2020, https://www.ft.com/content/9ee0ebd3-346f-45b1-8b92-aa5c597d4389.

33 'Channel 4 annual report', 2018, https://annualreport.channel4.com/assets/downloads/203_30612_Channel4_AR2018-accessible-v2.pdf, p. 207.

34 These figures cover creative agency fees, media agency fees, commercial production costs and possibly some hidden agency rebates, plus the internal costs of the broadcaster's sales operation. The total will be even more if a high proportion of the campaign is digital.

35 House of Commons, DCMS Committee, 'Future of the BBC', p. 72. The DCMS Committee, like Peacock, seems not to have thought about consumers' preferences for avoiding advertising

or the hidden overhead costs, but rejected this funding option anyway.

36 Critics of the BBC sometimes point out – correctly – that the BBC already interrupts the breaks between programmes with trailers and promotions for its own programmes and services; and that its coverage of sporting events often gives exposure to advertising hoardings, sponsors' logos and so on as well. But it is hard to see how advertisers' collateral exposure at sporting events materially benefits the BBC, distorts its priorities or harms its competitors. However, if the BBC carried commercial advertising, the interruptions would be much more frequent and intrusive, especially mid-programme breaks, which are more valuable to advertisers.

37 However, with sufficiently biased question wording and 'framing', it is possible to nudge many survey respondents to support advertising on the BBC. In August 2015, the *Financial Times* ran a story claiming that 'A majority of Britons want the BBC to be financed by advertising rather than the licence fee, backing the option once favoured by Margaret Thatcher' (Henry Mance, 'Majority of Britons want BBC financed by advertising', *Financial Times*, 24 August 2015, https://www.ft.com/content/b113f782-4756-11e5-af2f-4d6e0e5eda22). This claim was based on a survey commissioned by the Whitehouse Consultancy, a public affairs communications agency, but who funded it was not revealed. The headline results claimed that 52 per cent of the UK public supported replacing the licence fee with advertising, while only 34 per cent opposed it, the rest being 'Don't knows'. As the *Financial Times* article pointed out: (i) 'Other opinion polls have given very different results ... In December 2014, Ipsos Mori found 53 per cent backed the licence fee ... with 26 per cent supporting advertising and 17 per cent subscription' and (ii) 'an advertising-funded BBC would also be opposed by commercial broadcasters, who would lose revenue'. A letter to the *Financial Times* by one of the authors of this book (Patrick Barwise, 'BBC funding survey

asked slanted questions', *Financial Times*, Letters page, 26 August 2015, https://www.ft.com/content/36bd3b3a-4b41-11e5-9b5d-89a026fda5c9) described the research as 'a great example of a biased survey', noting three sets of wording likely to skew the results against the licence fee ('priming'); one significantly misleading statement describing it as paid for by 'individuals' (not households); and also that, as the *Financial Times* said, advertising funding for the BBC was opposed by commercial broadcasters because of its probable impact on their revenue, which of course the survey had not pointed out to its respondents. Patrick Barwise's letter concluded: 'Despite most of the public not knowing [the likely impact on other advertising-funded media and programme budgets], surveys that ask a simple multiple-choice question (without priming) typically find that only 25–30 per cent choose advertising funding. The Whitehouse [Consultancy's] 52 per cent is, as far as I know, a record. They are to be commended for ingenuity, but not for validity'. There was no response to this letter.

38 The one with the biggest short-term impact was that ITV franchises should be auctioned to the highest bidder. This was implemented, with minor changes, in 1991, but seen by most commentators as something of a fiasco and never repeated (see Appendix C). The most sensible, in our view, were: (i) that at least 40 per cent of BBC TV and ITV programming should be made by independent producers and (ii) Channel 4 should sell its own commercial airtime. Both of these were implemented, with beneficial effects.

39 House of Commons, Home Office Committee, 'Report of the committee on financing the BBC [Peacock Report]'.

40 These include, 'pay per view', short-term rentals and 'download to own'.

41 Adam Smith Institute, David Graham, 'Global player or subsidy junkie? Decision time for the BBC', 2010, https://www.adamsmith.org/research/global-player-or-subsidy-junkie-

decision-time-for-the-bbc; Tim Congdon, 'Scrap the licence fee and privatise the BBC', *Standpoint*, 25 November 2013, https://standpointmag.co.uk/issues/december-2013/features-december-13-scrap-the-licence-fee-and-privatise-the-bbc-tim-congdon/; Philip Booth, ed., *In Focus: The Case for Privatising the BBC*, Institute for Economic Affairs, April 2016, https://iea.org.uk/wp-content/uploads/2016/07/Booth-BBC-Interactive.pdf; TaxPayers' Alliance blog post, 'Time to scrap the licence fee', 3 May 2016, https://www.taxpayersalliance.com/time_to_scrap_the_licence_fee.

42 House of Commons, DCMS Committee, 'Future of the BBC', pp. 73–5.

43 Ibid., p. 74.

44 Ibid.

45 Advocates of subscription funding almost invariably use the language of economics, but economists' views on the BBC and PSBs vary widely. Most accept that there is a degree of 'market failure' in broadcasting, meaning that the market on its own will undersupply some public-service content. But they differ greatly in the scale and nature of public intervention they recommend, although most would agree that the best approach is still a mixed economy that includes the BBC and commercial PSBs, each showing a wide range of programmes, in competition with more lightly regulated non-PSBs and SVoD service, e.g. see Andrew Graham and Gavyn Davies, *Broadcasting, Society and Policy in the Multimedia Age*, University of Luton Press, 1977; Helen Weeds, 'Is the television licence fee fit for purpose in the digital era?', *Economic Affairs*, 36, 1, February 2016, pp. 2–20, https://iea.org.uk/wp-content/uploads/2016/07/Introduction.pdf (*Economic Affairs* is the IEA's journal). In contrast, some free-market 'ultras' dismiss the whole idea of public intervention and public service broadcasting: Cento Veljanovski, 'Is the market-failure approach to the BBC licence fee fit for purpose? Comment', *Economic Affairs*, 36, 1, February 2016, pp. 369–72.

Professor Peacock's own position was somewhere between these two views. He accepted a limited degree of market failure, but not that we need PSBs to address it. Instead, as elsewhere, he favoured a market solution: a government-financed Public Service Broadcasting Fund (PSBF) would allocate resources to subsidize the production of public-service content in response to competitive bids from commercial broadcasters, see: Alan Peacock, 'Public Service Broadcasting without the BBC?', IEA, September 2004, https://onlinelibrary.wiley.com/doi/full/10.1111/ecaf.12197. How well this approach – sometimes referred to as an 'Arts Council of the Air' – would work in practice is unclear. The indirect evidence from some other countries' contestable funding of public service content for children (perhaps the strongest case for it, apart from minority language content) is that it is best suited to linear broadcast TV programmes with international market potential, especially animation. But even with substantial subsidies and tax breaks for such programmes, according to the Communications and Media Research Institute (CAMRI) report of May 2016, 'commercial broadcasters . . . are unlikely to invest significant sums in local children's content unless there is regulation in the form of output and investment quotas': 'Policy solutions and international perspectives on the funding of public service media content for children', CAMRI, University of Westminster, May 2016, p. 23, https://pdfs.semanticscholar.org/04c1/b2c1e8cfa102b9dcbe5e45ebe8dca859b819.pdf. We will soon have some direct UK evidence on this, at least on a small scale, from the recently launched three-year Young Audiences Content Fund administered by the British Film Institute, see https://www.bfi.org.uk/supporting-uk-film/production-development-funding/young-audiences-content-fund. Even then, however, the wider scope for such contestability for all 'public service' content, as advocated by Peacock, will still be unknown.

46 House of Commons, DCMS Committee, 'Future of the BBC', p. 74.

47 How the BBC's services would be packaged and priced; the percentage of homes that might subscribe to each package; the substantial additional costs of marketing, billing and customer service; the market impact on pay-TV companies; and the net effect of all this on the BBC's (and commercial players') content investment and value for money.

48 As critics of the licence fee sometimes point out, whenever the BBC invests in a service for a new platform like colour TV, digital TV or the iPlayer, that service is not universal until every home has access. This rather Jesuitical argument ignores several facts: (i) everyone agrees that the BBC has to adapt to new technologies and, indeed, it is often specifically tasked with helping to drive their adoption; (ii) 'universality' means being available to *every* household, regardless of which platforms they have; (iii) in most cases, the expectation is that the new platform will, over time, become universal or almost universal; and (iv) most of the BBC's resources are invested in services for established, universally available platforms.

49 Or, indeed, to consume *any* BBC content (on TV, radio or online), depending on the policy. Every user or household would also have to register. Provided the timescale is sufficiently long (fifteen years, say), this cost should not be prohibitive, as the technology could be adopted over time as part of users' normal equipment-replacement cycle, perhaps supplemented by a scheme to subsidize and support poorer households.

50 House of Commons, DCMS Committee, 'Future of the BBC', p. 76.

51 Ibid., 'Future of the BBC', pp. 81–2.

52 Mark Sweney, 'BBC backs replacing licence fee with universal levy', *The Guardian*, 7 September 2015, https://www.theguardian.com/media/2015/sep/07/bbc-licence-fee-universal-levy; John Plunkett and Jane Martinson, 'BBC licence fee replacement gets backing from culture secretary', *The Guardian*, 9 September 2015, https://www.theguardian.com/media/2015/sep/09/

bbc-licence-fee-replacement-gets-backing-from-culture-secretary; Weeds, 'Is the television licence fee fit for purpose in the digital era?'.

53 Adrian Weckler and Gabija Gataveckaite, 'TV licence fee to be replaced by charge on all households', *Irish Independent*, 2 August 2019, https://www.independent.ie/irish-news/tv-licence-fee-to-be-replaced-by-charge-on-all-households-38367892.html; Jack Horgan-Jones, 'TV licence fee to be replaced with charge for all household devices', 2 August 2019, https://www.irishtimes.com/news/ireland/irish-news/tv-licence-fee-to-be-replaced-with-charge-for-all-household-devices-1.3974617; Fiachra Ó Cionnaith, 'No way to avoid it: everything you need to know about the new broadcasting charge', *Irish Examiner*, 2 August 2019, https://www.irishexaminer.com/breakingnews/ireland/everything-you-need-to-know-about-the-new-broadcasting-charge-941563.html.

54 Cabinet Gregory, 'French property taxes', updated January 2020, https://www.cabinetgregory.com/html/frproptax.html.

55 Italian Solicitor, Giandomenico De Tullio, 'Italian supreme court approves adding TV licence to household electricity bills', 5 May 2016, http://italiansolicitor.co.uk/italian-supreme-court-approves-adding-tv-licence-to-household-electricity-bills/.

56 Paul Revoir, 'People with big houses could be forced to pay higher TV licence fee under "progressive" BBC proposals', *Daily Mail*, 4 May 2020, https://www.dailymail.co.uk/news/article-8286127/TV-Licence-cost-people-larger-homes-BBC-insider-reveals.html; Brian McGleenon, 'BBC licence fee shock: Bizarre new fee system could see YOU paying more', *Daily Express*, 5 May 2020, https://www.express.co.uk/news/uk/1277935/bbc-licence-fee-council-tax-band-cost-value-of-house-property. These were a response to a sixteen-page analysis by Matthew d'Ancona on Tortoise Media (founded by the BBC's former director of news James Harding) which quoted an anonymous source at the BBC: Matthew d'Ancona, 'The BBC is back', 4 May 2020, https://members.tortoisemedia.com/2020/05/04/the-bbc-is-back/content.html.

57 Earning extra revenue in this way outside the UK is non-controversial. But within the UK BritBox can be (maliciously or mistakenly) portrayed as forcing consumers to pay a second time for content they have already paid for through the licence fee. In reality, they are being *offered the opportunity* (and *not* forced) to pay a supplementary fee of just under 50 per cent on top of the standard licence fee for greater access to BBC (and ITV, Channel 4 and Channel 5) programmes, similar to buying a DVD box set (the £5.99 monthly fee for BritBox is equivalent to £71.88 per year, 46.5 per cent of the £154.50-per-year licence fee). But this may need to be more clearly communicated to the general public.

58 Ofcom, 'Review of prominence for public service broadcasting: recommendations to government for a new framework to keep PSB TV prominent in an online world', 4 July 2019, https://www.ofcom.org.uk/__data/assets/pdf_file/0021/154461/recommendations-for-new-legislative-framework-for-psb-prominence.pdf.

59 Ofcom, 'Code on sports and other listed and designated events', accessed 24 July 2019.

60 Live rights must be offered for sporting events on the A list, such as, currently, the Olympic Games, the Grand National and the FA Cup Final. Highlights packages must be offered for events on the B list, such as cricket test matches played in England, the Ryder Cup and Six Nations Rugby involving the home nations. See House of Lords, Select Committee on Communications and Digital, 'Public service broadcasting: As vital as ever', House of Lords, 5 November 2019, pp. 26–8, https://publications.parliament.uk/pa/ld201919/ldselect/ldcomuni/16/16.pdf.

61 Age UK, 'Age UK's licence fee campaign delivers', 19 July 2019, https://www.ageuk.org.uk/discover/2019/july/age-uks-tv-licence-campaign-delivers/.

62 House of Lords, Select Committee on Communications, 'BBC charter review: Reith not revolution', 24 February 2016, pp. 54–6, https://publications.parliament.uk/pa/ld201516/ldselect/ldcomuni/96/96.pdf.

63 House of Commons, DCMS Committee, 'BBC annual report and accounts 2018–19: TV licences for over 75s', 8 October 2019, p. 20, https://publications.parliament.uk/pa/cm201719/cmselect/cmcumeds/2432/2432.pdf.

Chapter 11: 'The Scope of Its Activities Is Chilling'

1 From James Murdoch's 2009 MacTaggart speech, 'The Absence of Trust', http://image.guardian.co.uk/sys-files/Media/documents/2009/08/28/JamesMurdochMacTaggartLecture.pdf.

2 Lucy Mangan, 'TV review: The Great British Bake-Off, the Making of King Arthur and Ideal', *The Guardian*, 18 August 2010, https://www.theguardian.com/tv-and-radio/2010/aug/18/lucy-mangan-tv-review.

3 Iain Hollingshead, 'The Great British Bake Off, BBC Two, review', *Daily Telegraph*, 18 August 2010 https://www.telegraph.co.uk/culture/tvandradio/7950624/The-Great-British-Bake-Off-BBC-Two-review.html.

4 Sarah Rainey, 'How the Great British Bake Off changed Britain', *Daily Telegraph*, 12 October 2013, https://www.telegraph.co.uk/foodanddrink/10370144/How-the-Great-British-Bake-Off-changed-Britain.html.

5 Patrick Foster, 'Great British Bake Off dominates list of most-watched shows of 2015', *Daily Telegraph*, 17 December 2015, https://www.telegraph.co.uk/news/media/12054696/Great-British-Bake-Off-dominates-list-of-most-watched-shows-of-2015.html.

6 Tara Conlan, 'Great British Bake Off recipe has proved a sweet success for BBC Worldwide', *The Guardian*, 4 August 2015, https://www.theguardian.com/tv-and-radio/2015/aug/04/great-british-bake-off-recipe-sweet-success-bbc-worldwide.

7 Hannah Ellis-Peterson, 'Sue Perkins and Mel Giedroyc to leave Great British Bake Off', *The Guardian*, 13 September 2016, https://www.theguardian.com/tv-and-radio/2016/sep/13/sue-perkins-and-mel-giedroyc-to-leave-great-british-bake-off.

8 Patrick Foster, 'BBC loses Great British Bake Off as Channel 4 swoops for Britain's biggest show', *Daily Telegraph*, 13 September 2016, https://www.telegraph.co.uk/news/2016/09/12/bbc-loses-great-british-bake-off/.

9 See Jason Deans and agencies, 'Great British Bake Off: Ofcom rules out investigation despite complaints', *The Guardian*, 29 August 2014, https://www.theguardian.com/media/2014/aug/29/great-british-bake-off-ofcom-complaints-bbc-diana-beard-iain-watters.

10 William Goldman, *Adventures in the Screen Trade: A Personal View of Hollywood and Screenwriting*, Grand Central Books, 1989. The full quotation is more nuanced: 'Nobody . . . knows for a certainty what's going to work. Every time out it's a guess and, if you're lucky, an educated one'.

11 Conlan, 'Great British Bake Off recipe'. Mel and Sue doubtless added a bit of humour and innuendo (another source of controversy) to the show in response to the hostile initial reviews.

12 Mel and Sue refused to stay with the programme when it switched to Channel 4, saying that the BBC had 'nurtured the show from its infancy . . . growing it from an audience of 2 million to nearly 15 [million] at its peak', Ellis-Peterson, 'Sue Perkins and Mel Giedroyc to leave Great British Bake Off'. Ten days later, Berry followed suit, also citing her loyalty to the BBC, which had nurtured the team and the show: Jane Martinson, 'Mary Berry to leave Great British Bake Off – but Paul Hollywood agrees to stay', *The Guardian*, 23 September 2016, https://www.theguardian.com/culture/2016/sep/22/mary-berry-leave-great-british-bake-off-paul-hollywood-bbc-mel-giedroyc-sue-perkins.

13 An alternative justification might be that, for some reason, we need to balance the interests of the British public (who pay for the BBC and naturally want as much value from it as possible, including popular entertainment shows) against the interests of its competitors. But none of those advocating a reduction in the BBC's scale says that the aim is to benefit the shareholders of ITV, Comcast (Sky), Viacom (Channel 5 and Nickelodeon),

Liberty Global (Virgin Media), Netflix, Amazon or Disney at the expense of the British public. That may be the *effect* of the current regulations, but it is not their stated *aim*.

14 However, even this is a significant oversimplification. It omits four other important considerations: (i) the BBC's *positive* market impacts (e.g. by driving new technology adoption and forcing its rivals to invest more in quality content in order to compete); (ii) the proportion of content investment that goes into original UK content for UK viewers and listeners (and of which the BBC is by far the biggest investor both in absolute terms and as a proportion of its income); (iii) the Corporation's numerous public service contributions; and (iv) the fact that, even if reducing the BBC's scale and scope did lead to a large increase in commercial media revenue, this would not be a 'free lunch' as far as viewers and listeners were concerned: most or all of it would come from consumers, either directly (in the form of subscriptions) or indirectly (in the form of advertising). These four considerations, including the indirect cost to consumers of TV advertising, are discussed more fully in Appendix E. On the advertising point, however, we are not saying that *advertising in general* is paid for by consumers: consumers benefit greatly from living in a competitive market economy, and advertising is an essential part of that. The question is whether *TV advertising* comes without hidden costs in a market economy with numerous other advertising media, price promotions and so on.

15 One of the authors of this book led the review of the BBC's digital TV services: Patrick Barwise, 'Independent review of the BBC's digital television services', for the DCMS, October 2004, which can be found on the same weblink as Tim Gardam's 'Independent review of the BBC's digital radio services', for the DCMS, October 2004, https://webarchive.nationalarchives.gov.uk/20060214111506/http://www.culture.gov.uk/global/publications/archive_2004/review_bbc_digital_radio_services.htm?properties=%2C%2C&month=. The other two reviews were: Richard Lambert, 'Independent review of BBC News 24', for the

DCMS, December 2002, https://webarchive.nationalarchives. gov.uk/20050302035852/http://www.culture.gov.uk/global/publications/archive_2002/review_bbcnews24.htm; and Philip Graf, 'Independent review of BBC Online', for the DCMS, October 2004, https://webarchive.nationalarchives.gov.uk/20050302002146/http://www.culture.gov.uk/global/publications/archive_2004/BBC_Online_Review.htm.

16 Ofcom, 'Assessment of the market impact of the BBC's new digital TV and radio services', 13 October 2004, https://www.ofcom.org.uk/__data/assets/pdf_file/0020/34139/bbc-news.pdf.

17 In the event, it has launched no new channels in the interim apart from BBC Scotland in February 2019; BBC Three was disbanded as a broadcast channel in 2016, to cut costs, continuing as an online-only service with a much-reduced budget (and audience). The BBC's more recent digital initiatives have focused on (i) the iPlayer, enabling viewers and listeners to consume BBC content more flexibly and conveniently and (ii) some distribution joint ventures, mainly with other PSBs (Freeview, Freesat, YouView, BritBox).

18 Most of the research to date has been on the market impact of, and potential crowding out by, BBC *television*. However, Gardam, 'Independent review of the BBC's digital radio services', Ofcom, 'Assessment of the market impact of the BBC's new digital TV and radio services', and Oliver & Ohlbaum and Oxera's report for the DCMS, 'BBC television, radio and online services: an assessment of market impact and distinctiveness', February 2016, https://assets.publishing.service.gov.uk/government/uploads/system/uploads/attachment_data/file/504012/FINAL_-_BBC_market_impact_assessment.pdf covered the market impact of BBC *radio*, and Graf, 'Independent review of BBC Online'; KPMG, 'An economic review of the extent to which the BBC crowds out private sector activity', for the BBC Trust, October 2015, https://assets.kpmg/content/dam/kpmg/uk/pdf/2017/02/bbccrowdingwebaccess.pdf; and Oliver & Ohlbaum Associates

and Oxera, 'BBC television, radio and online services: an assessment of market impact and distinctiveness', covered that of the BBC's *online* services.

19 The BBC's disproportionate investment in original UK content is especially important for UK producers but also benefits UK consumers, who – other things being equal – tend to prefer original British content.

20 Frances Cairncross, 'The Cairncross Review: a sustainable future for journalism', for the DCMS, 12 February 2019, p. 54, https://assets.publishing.service.gov.uk/government/uploads/system/uploads/attachment_data/file/779882/021919_DCMS_Cairncross_Review_.pdf.

21 See the Internet Advertising Bureau UK.

22 Oliver & Ohlbaum Associates and Oxera, 'BBC television, radio and online services: an assessment of market impact and distinctiveness'.

23 Greg Dyke, 'An education vision for the BBC': BBC *Spectator* Lecture, 2009.

24 BBC News, 'Blunkett welcomes Dyke's education commitment', 19 November 1999, http://news.bbc.co.uk/1/hi/education/525971.stm.

25 Margaret Scanlon and David Buckingham, 'Debating the Digital Curriculum: intersections of the public and private in educational and cultural policy', *London Review of Education*, 1, 3 (November 2003), pp. 191–205, https://www.ingentaconnect.com/contentone/ioep/clre/2003/00000001/00000003/art00003. BBC, 'BBC, a Digital Curriculum: have your say', 2000.

26 These non-core subjects are only marginally profitable for commercial educational publishers.

27 Scanlon and Buckingham, 'Debating the Digital Curriculum'; Maria Michalis, 'Balancing public and private interests in online media: the case of the BBC digital curriculum', *Media, Culture & Society*, vol. 34, no. 8, 9 November 2012, pp. 944–60, https://journals.sagepub.com/doi/10.1177/0163443712455557.

28 Maggie Brown, 'Switched off: BBC schools television is under serious threat', *The Guardian*, 14 May 2002, https://www.theguardian.com/media/2002/may/14/bbc.schools; Michalis, 'Balancing public and private interests in online media: the case of the BBC digital curriculum', p. 949. The probable impact on inequality is debatable: BBC Jam would have reduced the gap in opportunities between the majority and the most privileged schools and children, but increased the gap between the poorest and the rest, at least until IT access became almost universal.

29 The leading educational IT supplier, which was moving into content provision.

30 A total of eighteen conditions.

31 'BBC told to dump "anti-competitive" revision website', *Daily Mail*, 14 March 2007, https://www.dailymail.co.uk/news/article-442272/BBC-told-dump-anti-competitive-revision-website.html.

32 House of Commons, DCMS Committee, 'New media and the creative industries', 16 May 2007, p. 82, https://publications.parliament.uk/pa/cm200607/cmselect/cmcumeds/509/509i.pdf.

33 J. Kenny, 'Teachers slam BBC Jam pull-out', *The Guardian* Education supplement, 20 March 2007.

34 Maria Michalis, 'Balancing public and private interests in online media: the case of the BBC digital curriculum'.

35 FTI, 'Competitive impact assessment of Bitesize, Learning Zone Broadband and Learning Portal: a report for the BBC Trust', 2010, p. 53, https://downloads.bbc.co.uk/bbctrust/assets/files/pdf/appeals/fair_trading/cia_fti.pdf.

36 House of Commons, DCMS Committee, 'A BBC for the future? A broadcaster of distinction', May 2016, https://assets.publishing.service.gov.uk/government/uploads/system/uploads/attachment_data/file/524863/DCMS_A_BBC_for_the_future_linked_rev1.pdf.

37 David Mitchell, 'The trouble with getting the BBC to be less popular', *The Guardian*, 6 March 2016, https://www.theguardian.com/commentisfree/2016/mar/06/bbc-report-niche-distinctiveness-

david-mitchell?CMP=share_btn_tw. Mitchell may be being a tad unfair to the report's authors, who were merely answering the question they had been asked by their client, John Whittingdale.

38 George Orwell, *Animal Farm: A Fairy Story*, Penguin Books, 2000.

39 Unless there's *very* strong evidence of harm to customers (some risky and addictive products) and/or third parties (products that are dangerous to others or highly polluting).

40 John Whittingdale, DCMS Committee, press release, 'Future of the BBC', 26 February 2015.

41 The same 'four-legs-good-two-legs-bad' double standard also applied to the BBC's scheduling. When Whittingdale, as Culture Secretary, was preparing the 2016 white paper for the current BBC Charter, it was widely reported that, in response to lobbying by ITV, he planned to limit competition and choice by preventing the BBC from showing popular programmes such as *Strictly Come Dancing*, *Doctor Who* and *Sherlock* when people most wanted to watch them because this reduces the audiences for ITV's popular entertainment shows, which of course ITV likes to schedule at a time when people most want to watch them, notably on Saturday nights. There's a valid argument that viewers who prefer to watch these shows live, especially elimination shows like *Bake Off* and *Strictly*, would benefit if the top BBC and ITV entertainment programmes were not scheduled at the same time. Also, those who do have time-shift technology tend to record the ITV show at the same time as viewing the BBC one live, enabling them to watch both without commercials by skipping the advertising breaks in the ITV show when playing it back. Viewers prefer this, but it understandably infuriates ITV's sales team. But should it *always* be the BBC that is forced to 'give way' to the commercial competitor?

Chapter 12: 'To Err Is Human'

1 *'Errare humanum est'*, Latin proverb.

2 BBC One, BBC Two, BBC Four, CBBC, CBeebies and the BBC News Channel. This excludes BBC Three, no longer a broadcast channel, BBC Scotland and BBC Parliament – something of a special case, with very low viewing figures and the BBC unlikely to be blamed, even by the *Daily Mail*, for content that upsets or offends.

3 The figures for 2018 were: 7.6 hours of TV, 9.55 hours of radio and 0.9 hours spent online, making a total of 18 hours per week. Almost all of this (95 per cent) was spent watching television and listening to the radio so, for simplicity, we here refer to 'programme choices'. Strictly speaking, they also include other online choices which represent the remaining 5 per cent of consumption.

4 Source: Office of National Statistics.

5 The distinction between editorial, commercial and managerial mistakes is not clear-cut: ultimately, every mistake is, directly or indirectly, a management and/or leadership failure (the director-general of the BBC is also its CEO and editor-in-chief). The Savile case, in particular, reflects long-running, generic issues around the BBC's organizational culture as well as specific ones around the editorial decisions that were made – which is why it led to two independent reviews (and why, as we'll see, the one on organizational culture was much more extensive). Nevertheless, it's helpful to distinguish between mistakes which were *primarily* editorial and those that were largely or purely commercial or managerial.

6 Charles Moore, 'Treating every allegation against Jimmy Savile as a "fact" undermines justice', *Daily Telegraph*, 11 January 2013, https://www.telegraph.co.uk/news/uknews/crime/jimmy-savile/9795920/Treating-every-allegation-against-Jimmy-Savile-as-a-fact-undermines-justice.html.

7 BBC News, 'Sir Jimmy Savile's funeral takes place at Leeds Cathedral', 9 November 2011, https://www.bbc.co.uk/news/uk-england-leeds-15647363.

8 Neil Tweedie and Tom Rowley, 'A strange and sordid life unravels after death', *Daily Telegraph*, 26 October 2012, https://www.telegraph.co.uk/news/uknews/crime/jimmy-savile/9636035/Jimmy-Savile-a-strange-and-sordid-life-unravels-after-death.html.

9 National Society for the Prevention of Cruelty to Children, a leading UK child protection charity.

10 'Giving victims a voice', a joint MPS and NSPCC report into allegations of sexual abuse made against Jimmy Savile under Operation Yewtree, January 2013, https://www.nspcc.org.uk/globalassets/documents/research-reports/yewtree-report-giving-victims-voice-jimmy-savile.pdf.

11 BBC News, 'Police detective failed to report Jimmy Savile intelligence', 7 July 2015, https://www.bbc.co.uk/news/uk-england-york-north-yorkshire-33428170.

12 BBC News, 'Jimmy Savile groomed a nation, police say', 11 January 2013, https://www.bbc.co.uk/news/av/uk-20989568/jimmy-savile-groomed-a-nation-police-say.

13 Vanessa Allen, 'Revealed: Lady Thatcher's FIVE attempts to secure knighthood for Jimmy Savile while her aides warned of his "strange and complex" life', *Daily Mail*, 17 July 2013, https://www.dailymail.co.uk/news/article-2366576/Revealed-Lady-Thatchers-FIVE-attempts-secure-knighthood-Jimmy-Savile.html.

14 BBC News, 'Jimmy Savile's public persona', 22 October 2012, https://www.bbc.co.uk/news/uk-20027996.

15 Lloyd Evans, 'Savile exposed', *Spectator*, 27 June 2015, https://www.spectator.co.uk/2015/06/weve-forgotten-just-how-attractive-jimmy-savile-once-was/.

16 Robert Booth, 'Jimmy Savile caused concern with behaviour on visits to Prince Charles', *The Guardian*, 29 October 2012, https://www.theguardian.com/media/2012/oct/29/jimmy-savile-behaviour-prince-charles.

17 'Giving victims a voice', a joint MPS and NSPCC report.

18 The NHS completed reports at forty-four institutions, see GOV. UK, 'NHS and Department of Health investigations into Jimmy Savile', 26 June 2014 (updated 26 November 2015), https://www. gov.uk/government/collections/nhs-and-department-of-health-investigations-into-jimmy-savile. The BBC Trust reports, the 'Dame Janet Smith review' and the 'Dame Janet Smith review: opening statement' can both be found at http://www. damejanetsmithreview.com/.

19 Nick Pollard, 'The Pollard Review: report', ReedSmith, 18 December 2012, http://downloads.bbc.co.uk/bbctrust/assets/files/pdf/ our_work/pollard_review/pollard_review.pdf.

20 The ex-headmistress's comments posed something of a dilemma to Paul Dacre: fully accepting them would have been consistent with the *Mail*'s general approach on juvenile delinquents but would marginally weaken the case against Savile and, by implication, the BBC. He therefore chose, as usual, to have it both ways, describing the statement as a 'cruel dismissal of the girls abused by Jimmy Savile' and treating it with some scepticism, but also including plenty of lurid detail to shock or titillate his readers: Claire Ellicott and Sam Greenhill, 'They were no angels: Headmistress's cruel dismissal of the girls abused by Jimmy Savile (and she claims no-one told her what he was up to)', *Daily Mail*, 2 November 2012, https://www. dailymail.co.uk/news/article-2227086/They-angels-Headmistresss-cruel-dismissal-girls-abused-Jimmy-Savile-claims-told-to.html.

21 BBC News, 'Jimmy Savile accused of sexual abuse', 1 October 2012, https://www.bbc.co.uk/news/entertainment-arts-19776872.

22 BBC News, 'Sir Jimmy Savile: BBC "horrified" over rape allegations', 3 October 2012, https://www.bbc.co.uk/news/entertainment-arts-19801768.

23 John Plunkett, 'Jeremy Paxman: Newsnight's failure to tackle Jimmy Savile was "pathetic"', *The Guardian*, 22 February 2013, https://www.theguardian.com/media/2013/feb/22/jeremy-paxman-newsnight-jimmy-savile.

24 BBC Trust, 'Dame Janet Smith review'.

25 Pollard, 'The Pollard Review: report'.

26 Channel 4 News, Paraic O'Brien, 'Email reveals how editor "killed" Jimmy Savile story', 23 October 2012, https://www.channel4.com/news/jimmy-savile-newsnight-peter-rippon-email-kill-story.

27 Pollard, 'The Pollard Review: report'.

28 Liz MacKean died of a stroke, aged only fifty-two, in August 2017. David Grossman, 'Liz MacKean obituary', *The Guardian*, 20 August 2017, https://www.theguardian.com/media/2017/aug/20/liz-mackean-obituary.

29 BBC Trust, 'Dame Janet Smith review: opening statement'.

30 GOV.UK, 'NHS and Department of Health investigations into Jimmy Savile'.

31 BBC News, 'Panorama airs programme on Newsnight's Savile investigation', 23 October 2012, https://www.bbc.co.uk/news/uk-20037437.

32 Dominic Ponsford, 'Meirion Jones: "Everyone on the right side of the Savile argument has been forced out of the BBC"', *Press Gazette*, 29 July 2015, https://www.pressgazette.co.uk/meirion-jones-speaks-out-everyone-who-was-right-side-savile-argument-has-been-forced-out-bbc/.

33 The Bureau of Investigative Journalism is an independent organization which 'holds power to account'. It was founded in 2010 by David and Elaine Potter, and is funded by donations.

34 David Leigh, 'The Newsnight fiasco that toppled the BBC director general', *The Guardian*, 10 November 2012, https://www.theguardian.com/media/2012/nov/10/newsnight-mcalpine-scoop-rumour.

35 Roy Greenslade, 'Newsnight's McAlpine scandal: 13 days that brought down the BBC's chief', *The Guardian*, 19 February 2014, https://www.theguardian.com/media/greenslade/2014/feb/19/newsnight-lord-mcalpine.

36 Leigh, 'The Newsnight fiasco that toppled the BBC director general'. For Michael Crick's tweet of 2 November 2012, see https://twitter.com/michaelcrick/status/264352884320260096.

37 BBC Two, *Newsnight*, 2 November 2012.

38 Greenslade, 'Newsnight's McAlpine scandal'. However, the Radio 5 Live documentary in 2000 by the Bureau of Investigative Journalism's reporter Angus Stickler had highlighted what Stickler saw as serious flaws in this inquiry.

39 David Leigh, Steven Morris and Bibi van der Zee, 'Mistaken identity led to top Tory abuse claim', *The Guardian*, 8 November 2012, https://www.theguardian.com/uk/2012/nov/08/mistaken-identity-tory-abuse-claim.

40 'Jimmy Savile: "worst crisis" in 50 years, says John Simpson', *Daily Telegraph*, 22 October 2012, https://www.telegraph.co.uk/news/uknews/crime/jimmy-savile/9625257/Jimmy-Savile-worst-crisis-in-50-years-at-BBC-says-John-Simpson.html.

41 Dominic Cavendish, 'Russell Brand at the Hexagon Theatre, Reading: review', *Telegraph*, 19 January 2009, https://www.telegraph.co.uk/journalists/dominic-cavendish/4288130/Russell-Brand-at-the-Hexagon-Theatre-Reading-review.html.

42 Leigh Holmwood, 'BBC fined £150,000 over Russell Brand and Jonathan Ross phone prank scandal', *The Guardian*, 3 April 2009, https://www.theguardian.com/media/2009/apr/03/russell-brand-jonathan-ross-bbc-fine; Alice Vincent, 'Russell Brand, Jonathan Ross and the voicemails that "deeply hurt" Andrew Sachs; how Sachsgate unfolded', *Daily Telegraph*, 2 December 2016, https://www.telegraph.co.uk/tv/2016/12/02/russell-brand-jonathan-ross-voicemails-sachsgate-unfolded/; and Urmee Khan, 'Ofcom fines BBC £150,000 for Russell Brand and Jonathan Ross prank phone calls', *Daily Telegraph*, 3 April 2009, https://www.telegraph.co.uk/finance/newsbysector/mediatechnologyandtelecoms/media/5100256/Ofcom-fines-BBC-150000-for-Russell-Brand-and-Jonathan-Ross-prank-phone-calls.html.

43 Miles Goslett, 'Russell Brand and Jonathan Ross could face prosecution after obscene on air phone calls to Fawlty Towers actor, 78', *Mail on Sunday*, 26 October 2008, https://www.dailymail.co.uk/

news/article-1080621/Russell-Brand-Jonathan-Ross-face-prosecution-obscene-air-phone-calls-Fawlty-Towers-actor-78.html.

44 Vincent, 'Russell Brand, Jonathan Ross and the voicemails that "deeply hurt" Andrew Sachs'.

45 Holmwood, 'BBC fined £150,000 over Russell Brand and Jonathan Ross phone prank scandal'.

46 Khan, 'Ofcom fines BBC £150,000 for Russell Brand and Jonathan Ross prank phone calls'. Barber's main compliance role may have been about music copyright rather than the broadcast standards (offensiveness and the invasion of privacy) issues raised by the broadcast.

47 Vincent, 'Russell Brand, Jonathan Ross and the voicemails that "deeply hurt" Andrew Sachs'.

48 Tim Luckhurst, 'Get back to the basics', *The Guardian*, 30 October 2008, https://www.theguardian.com/commentisfree/2008/oct/30/bbc-russell-brand.

49 BBC News, ' "No justification" for Brand show', 21 November 2008, http://news.bbc.co.uk/1/hi/entertainment/7741322.stm.

50 House of Commons, Early day motions: 'Jonathan Ross and Russell Brand', 27 October 2008, https://edm.parliament.uk/early-day-motion/36723/jonathan-ross-and-russell-brand.

51 Vincent, 'Russell Brand, Jonathan Ross and the voicemails that "deeply hurt" Andrew Sachs'.

52 Jane Croft, 'BBC refused permission to appeal against Cliff Richard judgement', *Financial Times*, 26 July 2018, https://www.ft.com/content/97c4a270-90de-11e8-bb8f-a6a2f7bca546.

53 BBC News, 'Sir Cliff Richard: Reaction to the High Court ruling', 18 July 2018, https://www.bbc.co.uk/news/uk-44870190.

54 Roy Greenslade, 'The Cliff Richard ruling is a chilling blow to press freedom', *The Guardian*, 18 July 2018, https://www.theguardian.com/commentisfree/2018/jul/18/cliff-richard-bbc-press-freedom-privacy; BBC News, 'Cliff Richard: BBC would be "crazy" to appeal against ruling', 19 July 2018, https://www.bbc.co.uk/news/uk-44883331.

55 Emily Kent Smith, 'Sir Cliff Richard case could have "worrying consequences" for the free press, legal experts warn', *Daily Mail*, 19 July 2018, https://www.dailymail.co.uk/news/article-5968707/Sir-Cliff-Richard-case-worrying-consequences-free-press-legal-experts-warn.html.

56 BBC News, 'BBC One boss quits over Queen row', 5 October 2007, http://news.bbc.co.uk/1/hi/entertainment/7029940.stm.

57 Duncan Larcombe and Neil Millard, 'Diamond Jubilation', *Sun*, 1 June 2012, https://www.thesun.co.uk/archives/news/661767/diamond-jubilation/.

58 Nicole Martin, 'The BBC "fawns" over the Royal family, says Jeremy Paxman', *Daily Telegraph*, 6 October 2008, https://www.telegraph.co.uk/news/uknews/theroyalfamily/3145520/The-BBC-fawns-over-the-Royal-Family-says-Jeremy-Paxman.html.

59 Tom Utley, 'Red faces in the BBC newsroom as the corporation is caught on the hop', *Daily Telegraph*, 1 April 2002, https://www.telegraph.co.uk/news/uknews/1389446/Red-faces-in-BBC-news-rooms-as-corporation-is-caught-on-the-hop.html.

60 BBC News, 'Jubilee coverage; BBC receives more than 2,000 complaints', 6 June 2012, https://www.bbc.co.uk/news/entertainment-arts-18337851.

61 Caroline Davies, 'Michael Buerk savages BBC's coverage of the Queen's diamond jubilee', *The Guardian*, 30 December 2012, https://www.theguardian.com/media/2012/dec/30/michael-buerk-bbc-queens-jubilee. Buerk's sexist and snooty description of Cotton as a 'pneumatic bird brain' already looks like something from a different era.

62 Jo Usmar, 'Fearne Cotton: grown men who slag me off are huge bullies', *Daily Mirror*, 8 June 2012, https://www.mirror.co.uk/3am/celebrity-news/fearne-cotton-hits-back-at-twitter-867797.

63 Mark Sweney, 'BBC to buy out Lonely Planet', *The Guardian*, 18 February 2011, https://www.theguardian.com/media/2011/feb/18/bbc-worldwide-lonely-planet-travel-guides.

64 Mark Sweney, 'BBC plans digital boost for Lonely Planet', *The Guardian*, 1 October 2007, https://www.theguardian.com/media/2007/oct/01/business.bbc.

65 In 2018, Tony and Maureen Wheeler funded the Wheeler Institute for Business and Development at London Business School.

66 Richard Wray, 'Calling time out on the BBC', *The Guardian*, 1 September 2008, https://www.theguardian.com/media/2008/sep/01/bbc.pressandpublishing.

67 House of Commons, DCMS, 'BBC commercial operations', 25 March 2009, pp. 26–7, https://publications.parliament.uk/pa/cm200809/cmselect/cmcumeds/24/24.pdf.

68 We note that UK programme producers also benefit indirectly from the extra investment funded by the BBC's commercial activities.

69 House of Commons, DCMS, 'BBC commercial operations', pp. 29–30.

70 Mark Sweney and Tara Conlan, 'BBC Worldwide can keep Lonely Planet, says Trust, but no repeat of deal', *The Guardian*, 24 November 2009, https://www.theguardian.com/media/2009/nov/24/bbc-worldwide-lonely-planet-trust.

71 BBC News, 'BBC Worldwide sells Lonely Planet business at 80m loss', 19 March 2013, https://www.bbc.co.uk/news/entertainment-arts-21841479; Sweney and Conlan, 'BBC Worldwide can keep Lonely Planet, says Trust, but no repeat of deal'.

72 Friends Reunited and MySpace were social networking sites bought by ITV and News Corp, respectively, in 2005, but soon overtaken and flattened by Facebook. MySpace is still operating under new ownership. Jason Clampet, 'How and why the BBC messed up in its acquisition of Lonely Planet', *Skift*, 7 November 2013, https://skift.com/2013/11/07/how-and-why-the-bbc-messed-up-its-acquisition-of-lonely-planet/.

73 Business Matters, 'Project failure could be costing UK businesses £254.3 billion in turnover', 3 July 2017, https://www.bmmagazine.

co.uk/news/project-failure-costing-uk-businesses-254-3-billion-turnover/.

74 Brian Glick, 'The BBC DMI project – what went wrong?', *Computer Weekly*, 5 February 2014, https://www.computerweekly.com/news/2240213773/The-BBC-DMI-project-what-went-wrong.

75 House of Commons, Public Accounts Committee, 'BBC's Digital Media Initiative a complete failure', 10 April 2014, https://www.parliament.uk/business/committees/committees-a-z/commons-select/public-accounts-committee/news/bbc-dmi-report-substantive/.

76 John Plunkett, 'Sacked BBC technology chief wins unfair dismissal', *The Guardian*, 7 August 2014, https://www.theguardian.com/media/2014/aug/07/sacked-bbc-technology-chief-wins-unfair-dismissal-john-linwood.

77 Computing, Sooraj Shah, 'BBC has learnt from the failure of the digital media initiative says NAO', 10 May 2016, https://www.computing.co.uk/ctg/news/2457529/bbc-has-learnt-from-failure-of-the-digital-media-initiative-says-nao.

78 Those making this comparison never allow for the substantial market value of the Prime Minister's rent-free official residences (10 Downing Street and Chequers) and chauffeur-driven car, which greatly reduce living costs, nor the £115,000 per year post-retirement Public Duties Cost Allowance set up 'to assist former prime ministers with the costs of continuing to fulfil duties associated with their previous position in public life'. In September 2016, it was revealed that Sir John Major was still receiving the Public Duties Cost Allowance nearly twenty years after his retirement, see https://www.parliament.uk/business/publications/written-questions-answers-statements/written-question/Commons/2016-09-02/44051/. More to the point, the market for prime ministers is clearly a *very* unusual one. Most of us would see it as a ghastly job, but in June 2019 *eleven* Tory MPs put their names forward to replace Theresa May, and Jeremy Corbyn was equally keen to do so. There were doubtless many others. If this were a normal market, all this competition for the job

might even suggest that the PM's £150,000 annual salary and substantial perks are *above* the market rate.

79 Jasper Jackson, 'BBC should reveal pay of stars earning more than £143,000, say MPs', *The Guardian*, 2 August 2016, https://www.theguardian.com/media/2016/aug/02/bbc-reveal-pay-stars-earning-more-prime-minister.

80 'Amend Royal Charter to stop BBC paying more than twice the Prime Minister's salary', ended 12 June 2019, see https://petition.parliament.uk/petitions/233519.

81 National Audit Office, 'Managing the BBC's pay-bill', a report by the comptroller and auditor-general, 16 May 2019, https://ww.nao.org.uk/wp-content/uploads/2019/05/Managing-the-BBC%E2%80%99s-pay-bill.pdf.

82 John Plunkett and Helen Pidd, 'Jonathan Ross leaves the BBC', *The Guardian*, 7 January 2010, https://www.theguardian.com/media/2010/jan/07/jonathan-ross-bbc-moving-on.

83 Jason Deans, 'BBC spent £54m on top-earning stars', *The Guardian*, 9 February 2010, https://www.theguardian.com/media/2010/feb/09/bbc-bbc-expenses.

84 Oliver & Ohlbaum Associates Ltd, 'A review of the BBC's arrangements for managing on-screen and on-air talent', for the BBC Trust, 26 February 2015, http://downloads.bbc.co.uk/bbctrust/assets/files/pdf/review_report_research/managing_talent/managing_talent.pdf.

85 Andy Halls, 'British broadcasting cover-up: BBC "hiding top stars' sky-high salaries" after axing free licences for over-75s', *Sun*, 2 July 2019, https://www.thesun.co.uk/news/9423371/bbc-cover-up-pay-graham-norton-shirley-ballas-fiona-brnduce/.

86 Anne McElvoy, 'BBC chief pledges he is tackling the gender pay gap but admits: "Some salaries sound gargantuan"', *Evening Standard*, 20 July 2017, https://www.standard.co.uk/lifestyle/london-life/bbc-chief-tony-hall-opens-up-on-gender-pay-gap-a3592076.html.

87 'Enough is enough: Carrie Gracie's letter on pay inequality in full', *The Guardian*, 8 January 2018, https://www.theguardian.com/media/2018/jan/08/carrie-gracie-letter-in-full.

88 That is, the median full-time-equivalent pay for men was 9.3 per cent higher than the median full-time-equivalent pay for women.

89 Graham Ruddick, Matthew Weaver and Owen Bowcott, 'Equalities watchdog intervenes after Carrie Gracie's complaint about BBC pay', *The Guardian*, 8 January 2018, https://www.theguardian.com/media/2018/jan/08/bbc-journalists-who-backed-carrie-gracie-face-broadcast-ban.

90 Editorial, 'The Guardian view on BBC pay: Carrie Gracie tells the story', *The Guardian*, 8 January 2018, https://www.theguardian.com/commentisfree/2018/jan/08/the-guardian-view-on-bbc-pay-carrie-gracie-tells-the-story.

91 Patricia Nilsson, 'Ofcom drawn into BBC row over censure of presenter', *Financial Times*, 27 September 2019, https://www.ft.com/content/55c896ae-e125-11e9-b112-9624ec9edc59.

92 Ofcom, *Ofcom Broadcast and On Demand Bulletin*, Issue 388, 7 October 2019, p. 7, https://www.ofcom.org.uk/__data/assets/pdf_file/0026/170882/issue-388-broadcast-and-on-demand-bulletin.pdf.

93 Especially given Trump's own immigrant heritage, with a mother born in Scotland and paternal grandparents born in Germany. (Trump is now a rather unusual colour, but that's a separate story). See also David A. Graham, Adrienne Green, Cullen Murphy and Parker Richards, 'An oral history of Trump's bigotry', *Atlantic Magazine*, June 2019 issue, https://www.theatlantic.com/magazine/archive/2019/06/trump-racism-comments/588067/.

94 Jim Waterson, 'Naga Munchetty: BBC reverses decision to censure presenter', *The Guardian*, 30 September 2019, https://www.theguardian.com/media/2019/sep/30/naga-munchetty-bbc-reverses-decision-to-censure-presenter.

95 Jim Waterson, Caroline Davies and Heather Stewart, 'Growing backlash against BBC in Naga Munchetty race row', *The Guardian*, 27 September 2019, https://www.theguardian.com/media/2019/sep/27/growing-backlash-against-bbc-in-naga-munchetty-race-row.

96 Afua Hirsch, Lenny Henry, Adrian Lester, Krishnan Guru-Murthy and others, 'You can't be impartial about racism – an

open letter to the BBC about the Naga Munchetty ruling', *The Guardian*, 27 September 2019, https://www.theguardian.com/commentisfree/2019/sep/27/racism-no-such-thing-as-impartiality-open-letter-bbc.

97 Harry Howard, Darren Boyle and Joseph Curtis, 'BBC Director-General writes to all staff to say Breakfast host Naga Munchetty was "completely within her rights" to reprimand Donald Trump and Beeb is "not impartial on racism" after 150 BAME broadcasters demanded ruling was overturned', *Daily Mail*, 27 September 2019, https://www.dailymail.co.uk/news/article-7513255/BBC-say-theyre-not-impartial-racism-following-row-Naga-Munchetty-Donald-Trump-comments.html.

98 Nilsson, 'Ofcom drawn into BBC row over censure of presenter'.

99 BBC News, 'BBC reverses decision on Naga Munchetty complaint', 30 September 2019.

100 Roisin O'Conner, 'Piers Morgan attacks BBC for rebuking Naga Munchetty over Trump "racism" comment: shameful censorship', *Independent*, 26 September 2019, https://www.independent.co.uk/arts-entertainment/tv/news/naga-munchetty-bbc-trump-racism-comment-piers-morgan-latest-a9121316.html.

101 The Conservative Woman, David Keighley, 'BBC censures presenters, but not very much', 27 September 2019, https://conservativewoman.co.uk/bbc-censures-presenters-but-not-very-much/.

102 Ofcom, *Ofcom Broadcast and On Demand Bulletin*, pp. 6–15.

103 Patricia Nilsson, 'BBC should explain Naga Munchetty decision, says regulator', *Financial Times*, 7 October 2019, https://www.ft.com/content/04a73860-e8f6-11e9-a240-3b065ef5fc55.

104 BBC Two, *Newsnight*, 30 September 2019.

105 In the immortal words of Hollywood producer Sam Goldwyn, 'I don't want any yes-men around me. I want everybody to tell me the truth even if it costs them their job'. There is an extensive research literature on the corrosive influence of fear within organizations, see Patrick Barwise and Seán Meehan, *Beyond the*

Familiar: Long-Term Growth through Customer Focus and Innovation, Jossey-Bass, 2011, pp. 129–38, and especially note 152.

106 Rebecca Miller, 'Chris Evans news', *Daily Express*, 2 February 2019, https://www.express.co.uk/showbiz/tv-radio/1081131/Chris-Evans-Virgin-Radio-breakfast-host-bbc-2-jingle-blunder.

107 Reuters, Kate Holton, 'News chief steps aside as BBC crisis deepens', 12 November 2012, https://uk.reuters.com/article/uk-britain-bbc-news-idUKBRE8AB09020121112.

108 Luckhurst, 'Get back to the basics'.

Chapter 13: 'Vox Populi, Vox Dei'

1 'The voice of the people is the voice of God', Latin proverb. Not everyone agrees that this is always the case. One thousand and two hundred years ago, the great Yorkshireman Alcuin, the leading scholar and teacher at Charlemagne's court in Aachen, wrote: 'And don't listen to those who keep saying the voice of the people is the voice of God, since the tumult of the crowd is always close to madness'.

2 After the 2017 election, in which Labour had done better and the Tories worse than expected, Kuenssberg was subjected to online abuse from Conservatives, while the left-wing abuse subsided: Telegraph reporters, 'BBC's Laura Kuenssberg was "given a bodyguard" during general election campaign', *Daily Telegraph*, 14 July 2017, https://www.telegraph.co.uk/news/2017/07/14/laura-kuenssberg-given-bodyguard-general-election-campaign/.

3 Virtually all climate scientists, other than those funded by the fossil fuel industry, agree that long-term climate change is real and, to a large extent, driven by human activity, see Tom Bawden, 'MPs accuse BBC of creating "false balance" on climate change with unqualified sceptics', 2 April 2014, https://www.independent.co.uk/environment/mps-accuse-bbc-of-creating-false-balance-on-climate-change-with-unqualified-sceptics-9231176.html. On Brexit,

a May 2016 survey of over 600 members of the Royal Economic Society and the Society of Business Economists found that 72 per cent expected the long-term economic consequences of Brexit to be negative, 24 per cent were unsure, and just 4 per cent expected a positive long-term impact: Sonia Sodha, Toby Helm and Phillip Inman, 'Economists overwhelmingly reject Brexit in boost for Cameron', *The Guardian*, 28 May 2016, https://www.theguardian.com/politics/2016/may/28/economists-reject-brexit-boost-cameron.

4 Channel 5 News and Independent Radio News are also required to be impartial but were rarely mentioned in response to this question. They are presumably among the 'Other' sources mentioned by 7 per cent of respondents. These are also likely to have included smaller online and print media too.

5 For instance, the *Daily Mail* has a multi-platform daily reach of 6.56 million people (source: Newsworks, December 2019) – 12 per cent of UK adults aged fifteen-plus. (There were 54.5 million UK adults aged fifteen-plus in 2018: see https://www.statista.com/statistics/281174/uk-population-by-age/). But only 1 per cent of adults aged fifteen-plus who 'follow the news' (clearly, fewer than 1 per cent of *all* adults) mentioned the paper as the source they would be most likely to turn to for impartial news.

6 We have no evidence on what drove this response, e.g. how many of these were conspiracy theorists who think impartiality is attainable but that the 'mainstream media' are rigged, and how many considered impartiality an impossible ideal.

7 BMG Research, press release, '40% of adults believe the BBC to be politically biased, according to a new poll', 16 May 2018, http://www.bmgresearch.co.uk/wp-content/uploads/2018/05/BMG-Research-BBC-bias-press-release.pdf. The poll was of 1,005 British adults aged eighteen-plus.

8 These two figures do not add up to exactly 60 per cent because of rounding errors (and nor do all the percentages discussed in the BMG study add up to precisely 100 per cent for the same reason).

9   And there was *no* difference between the percentages saying the
     BBC was *strongly* biased to the left or right (it was 7 per cent in
     each case).

10 The percentage of respondents saying '[Broadcaster X]' is 'Some-
     what or strongly biased to the left' minus the percentage saying it
     is 'Somewhat or strongly biased to the right'.

11 As Premier Media, the CCP publishes two evangelical Christian
     magazines and owns Premier Christian Radio.

12 Amy Jones, 'New poll finds the BBC is less trusted than ITV
     amid concerns over bias', *Daily Telegraph*, 28 December 2019,
     https://www.telegraph.co.uk/politics/2019/12/28/new-poll-finds-
     bbc-less-trusted-itv-amid-concerns-bias/.

13 Christian Communications Partnership, press release, 'New
     Savanta ComRes/CCP survey suggests UK news broadcasting
     "may be ripe for a shake-up"', 28 December 2019.

14 Henry Bodkin, 'Three-quarters want BBC licence fee abolished,
     poll finds', *Daily Telegraph*, 28 December 2019, https://www.
     telegraph.co.uk/news/2019/12/28/three-quarters-want-bbc-licence-
     fee-abolished-poll-finds/.

15 Public First is a right-leaning 'public policy and research special-
     ist', conveniently based at 11 Tufton Street, and founded by James
     Frayne and his wife Rachel Wolf. Frayne was Dominic Cum-
     mings' partner at the New Frontiers Foundation in 2004, when
     Cummings wrote his infamous blog posts about the need to
     undermine the BBC. He also worked with Cummings at the
     Department for Education, under Michael Gove. Wolf co-wrote
     the 2019 Conservative manifesto with Munira Mirza, head of
     the Number Ten Policy Unit – and an alumna of the Revolution-
     ary Communist Party, alongside Claire Fox, now a Brexit Party
     MEP – and a baroness: see Bella Caledonia, Bob from Brockley,
     'The RCP's long march from anti-imperialist outsiders to the
     doors of Downing Street', 27 July 2019, https://bellacaledonia.org.
     uk/2019/07/27/the-rcps-long-march-from-anti-imperialist-
     outsiders-to-the-doors-of-downing-street/.

16 Bodkin, 'Three-quarters want BBC licence fee abolished, poll finds'.

17 Even more so, given that (in line with the election result), the sample had more Conservative voters (who tend to see the BBC as pro-Labour) than Labour voters (who tend to see it as pro-Conservative), which increased the proportion likely to see the BBC as biased to the left.

18 Bella Caledonia, Bob from Brockley, 'The RCP's long march from anti-imperialist outsiders to the doors of Downing Street'.

19 C. P. Scott, 'A hundred years', 5 May 1921, reprinted in 'C. P. Scott's centenary essay', *The Guardian*, 23 October 2017, https://www.theguardian.com/sustainability/cp-scott-centenary-essay.

20 BBC, About the BBC, Governance and regulation, Mission, values and public purposes, https://www.bbc.com/aboutthebbc/governance/mission.

21 One question corresponds to each of public purposes 1, 2 and 5, three correspond to different aspects of public purpose 3 and two to different aspects of public purpose 4.

22 BBC, 'BBC group annual report and accounts 2018–19', p. 3, https://downloads.bbc.co.uk/aboutthebbc/reports/annualreport/2018-19.

23 The figures in 2018 were: 'informing': 75 per cent 'effective', 9 per cent 'ineffective'; for 'educating', 72 per cent 'effective', 9 per cent 'ineffective'; for 'entertaining', 77 per cent 'effective', 7 per cent 'ineffective'. In all three cases, between 2018 and 2019, the percentage saying 'effective' went down by one percentage point and the percentage saying 'ineffective' went up by either one ('informing' and 'educating') or two ('entertaining') percentage points.

24 Broadly, those living in households where the main earner is a skilled manual worker (C2), an unskilled or semi-skilled manual worker (D) or on social security or a state pension (E).

25 This raises the question of who monitors how well the BBC delivers its public purpose 5. Our understanding is that this falls to the DCMS and the Foreign Office (and other government

departments covering international politics, trade, defence and security) and their respective parliamentary committees, all of which regularly report on the relevant BBC activities. Many of the select committee meetings at which the BBC's leaders give evidence relate to its international activities.

26 The source for the latest figures are the Ipsos MORI polls for the BBC, for March–April 2018 and March–May 2019, both published by Ofcom in their second annual report on the BBC, 24 October 2019, p. 30, https://www.ofcom.org.uk/__data/assets/pdf_file/0026/173735/second-bbc-annual-report.pdf.

27 From July 2017, the measurement method was slightly changed, but there is no evidence that the change had any systematic impact on the average scores.

28 BBC News, 'Faked BBC phone-in competitions', 18 July 2007, http://news.bbc.co.uk/1/hi/entertainment/6905095.stm.

29 Charlotte Tobitt, 'UK news media least trusted among eight European nations to "get the facts right" and "cover important stories of the day", report shows', *Press Gazette*, 15 May 2018, https://www.pressgazette.co.uk/uk-news-media-least-trusted-among-eight-european-nations-to-get-the-facts-right-and-cover-important-stories-of-the-day-report-shows/.

30 Matthew d'Ancona, *Post-Truth: The New War on Truth and How to Fight Back*, Ebury Publishing, 2017.

31 Campaign, John Harrington, 'Trust in traditional media grows, but UK now "a nation of news-avoiders"', 22 January 2018, https://www.campaignlive.co.uk/article/trust-traditional-media-grows-uk-a-nation-news-avoiders/1455095.

32 BBC, 'BBC group annual report and accounts 2018–19'.

33 Ibid., p. 39.

34 John Naughton, 'Populism and the internet – a toxic mix shaping the age of conspiracy theories', *The Guardian*, 25 November 2018, https://www.theguardian.com/commentisfree/2018/nov/25/populism-and-the-internet-a-toxic-mix-shaping-the-age-of-conspiracy-theories.

Chapter 14: Culture Wars

1 William Shakespeare, *The Merchant of Venice*, Act 5, Scene 1, l. 89.
2 The BBC World Service, BBC News and BBC Online.
3 BBC, About the BBC, Governance and regulation, Mission, values and public purposes, https://www.bbc.com/aboutthebbc/governance/mission.
4 We're not suggesting that this is a rerun of the 1930s: there are now many more sovereign democracies and they are much better placed to withstand these challenges.
5 The term 'culture war' ('*Kulturkampf*') was originally coined to describe the struggle in the 1870s between the values of the emerging German Empire under Bismarck and those of the Catholic Church. It now usually refers to the conflict between conservative and liberal values and attitudes in the US and, increasingly, elsewhere.
6 James Davison Hunter, *Culture Wars: The Struggle to Define America*, Basic Books, 1992.
7 The American Yawp Reader, Pat Buchanan, 'Pat Buchanan on the Culture War', 1992, https://www.americanyawp.com/reader/29-the-triumph-of-the-right/pat-buchanan-on-the-culture-war-1992/.
8 'Strop Trumps: How Donald Trump's war on NATO and EU has rattled the West as he cosies up to Putin and Kim', *Sun*, 9 June 2018, https://www.thesun.co.uk/news/6676982/how-donald-trumps-war-on-nato-and-eu-has-rattled-the-west-as-he-cosies-up-to-putin-and-kim/.
9 ABC News, Jordyn Phelps, 'Trump White House hasn't held a traditional press briefing in 6 months', 11 September 2019, https://abcnews.go.com/Politics/trump-white-house-held-traditional-press-briefing-months/story?id=65509975.
10 BBC News, 'Trump to BBC correspondent Jon Sopel: here's another beauty', 16 February 2017, https://www.bbc.co.uk/news/av/world-us-canada-38999996/trump-to-bbc-correspondent-jon-sopel-here-s-another-beauty.

11 Matthew Weaver and Erin Durkin, 'BBC cameraman shoved and abused at Trump rally in El Paso', *The Guardian*, 13 February 2019, https://www.theguardian.com/media/2019/feb/12/bbc-cameraman-shoved-and-abused-at-trump-rally-in-el-paso.

12 Oliver Wright, 'BBC is now the enemy, declares furious Farage after TV grilling', *The Times*, 13 May 2019, https://www.thetimes.co.uk/article/bbc-is-now-the-enemy-declares-furious-farage-after-tv-grilling-zrmfobdv5.

13 President Donald Trump delivers remarks to the one-hundred-and-nineteenth Veterans of Foreign Wars' national convention in Kansas City, Missouri, on 24 July 2018, see https://www.youtube.com/watch?v=1VjCMuqrDFE.

14 CNBC, Dan Mangan, 'President Trump told Lesley Stahl he bashes press "to demean you and discredit you so . . . no one will believe" negative stories about him', 22 May 2018, https://www.cnbc.com/2018/05/22/trump-told-lesley-stahl-he-bashes-press-to-discredit-negative-stories.html.

15 Gordon Johnston and Emma Robertson, *BBC World Service: Overseas Broadcasting 1932–2018*, Palgrave Macmillan, 2019, p. 188.

16 Lionel Barber, Henry Foy and Alex Barker, 'Vladimir Putin says Liberalism has "become obsolete"', *Financial Times*, 27 June 2019, https://www.ft.com/content/670039ec-98f3-11e9-9573-ee5cbb98ed36.

17 Luke Harding, 'Russia forces World Service off FM radio', *The Guardian*, 18 August 2007, https://www.theguardian.com/world/2007/aug/18/russia.media.

18 Luke Harding, 'Litvinenko inquest: newspapers launch challenge over withholding of evidence', *The Guardian*, 25 February 2013, https://www.theguardian.com/world/2013/feb/25/litvinenko-inquest-challenge-withholding-evidence.

19 Ian Burrell, 'RT breached broadcasting rules over claims BBC faked pictures of Syrian chemical attack, says Ofcom', *Independent*, 21 September 2015, https://www.independent.co.uk/news/media/rt-breached-broadcasting-rules-over-claims-bbc-faked-pictures-of-syrian-chemical-attack-says-ofcom-10511515.html.

20 Reuters and Julian Robinson, 'BBC faces potential restrictions in Russia over "tendentious, politically motivated reporting" in tit-for-tat response to Ofcom ruling that found TV station RT broke impartiality rules over Salisbury novichok attack', *Daily Mail*, 21 December 2018, https://www.dailymail.co.uk/news/article-6519665/BBC-faces-potential-restrictions-Russia-response-Ofcoms-RT-ruling.html.

21 Robert S. Mueller III, US Department of Justice, 'Report on the Investigation into Russian interference in the 2016 presidential election', March 2019, https://www.justice.gov/storage/report.pdf.

22 Luke Harding, *Collusion: How Russia Helped Trump Win the White House*, Faber & Faber in association with *The Guardian*, 2017; James Comey, *A Higher Loyalty: Truth, Lies, and Leadership*, Macmillan, 2018; Jack Bryan, *Active Measures* (film), 2018; Kathleen Hall Jamieson, *Cyberwar: How Russian Hackers and Trolls Helped Elect a President – What We Don't, Can't, and Do Know*, Oxford University Press, 2018; and Katrina Manson, 'Trump campaign manager dealt with Russian agent, report says', *Financial Times*, 18 August 2020, https://www.ft.com/content/a8f90300-e30f-45a3-a75e-0261384c60a7.

23 Channel 4 News, 'Brexit campaign was "totally illegal", claims whistleblower', 24 March 2018, https://www.channel4.com/news/brexit-campaign-was-totally-illegal-claims-whistleblower; Channel 4 News, 'The Banks files: How Brexit "bad boy" Arron Banks was eyeing a massive Russian gold deal', 5 March 2019, https://www.channel4.com/news/the-banks-files-how-brexit-bad-boy-arron-banks-was-eyeing-a-massive-russian-gold-deal; Channel 4 News, 'Nigel Farage's funding secrets revealed', 16 May 2019, https://www.channel4.com/news/nigel-farages-funding-secrets-revealed.

24 Mark Townsend, 'Steve Bannon hails Dominic Cummings and predicts lurch to right for No 10', *The Guardian*, 1 August 2020, https://

www.theguardian.com/politics/2020/aug/01/steve-bannon-hails-dominic-cummings-and-predicts-lurch-to-right-for-no-10.

25 Ben Riley-Smith, 'Ex-White House adviser Steve Bannon arrested in "Build the Wall" fraud scam', *Daily Telegraph*, 20 August 2020, https://www.telegraph.co.uk/news/2020/08/20/ex-white-house-adviser-steve-bannon-arrested-fraud-scam/; Rozina Sabur, 'Trump Jnr distances himself from Bannon's "Build the Wall" scheme after organisers charged with fraud', *Daily Telegraph*, 21 August 2020, https://www.telegraph.co.uk/news/2020/08/21/trump-jnr-distances-bannons-build-wall-scheme-organisers-charged/).

26 We here use the term 'liberal' in the British sense, meaning 'centrist'. In the US, liberal means left-leaning (relative to the US political centre of gravity). The use of 'liberal' in most other developed countries is similar to the British usage.

27 Thomas Frank, *What's the Matter with Kansas?*, Henry Holt, 2004.

28 Although not to the extent that ultra-right-wing commentators like Ann Coulter have now made it. Coulter's numerous book titles include *Slander: Liberal Lies about the American Right*, Crown, 2002; *How to Talk to a Liberal (If You Must): The World According to Ann Coulter*, Crown Forum, 2004; and the delightfully phrased *Adios, America: The Left's Plan to Turn our Country into a Third World Hell Hole*, Regnery, 2015.

29 David Goodhart, *The Road to Somewhere*, C. Hurst & Co, 2017.

30 Ibid.

31 Joe Kennedy, *Authentocrats*, Repeater Books, 2018.

32 The phrase was popularized by the publication of a 1969 essay by feminist Carol Hanisch under the title 'The Personal is Political' in 1970.

33 According to the *Cambridge Dictionary*, a Millennial is someone born in the 1980s, 1990s or early 2000s. Millennials have grown up with the internet and can't imagine a world without it.

34 The cartoon was originally published in the *New Yorker* in July 1993. See Michael Cavna, '"NOBODY KNOWS YOU'RE A

DOG": As iconic Internet cartoon turns 20, creator Peter Steiner knows the joke rings as relevant as ever', *Washington Post*, 31 July 2013, https://www.washingtonpost.com/blogs/comic-riffs/post/nobody-knows-youre-a-dog-as-iconic-internet-cartoon-turns-20-creator-peter-steiner-knows-the-joke-rings-as-relevant-as-ever/2013/07/31/73372600-f98d-11e2-8e84-c56731a202fb_blog.html.

35 Carole Cadwalladr, 'Google is not "just" a platform. It frames, shapes and distorts how we see the world', *Observer*, Sunday 11 December 2016, https://www.theguardian.com/commentisfree/2016/dec/11/google-frames-shapes-and-distorts-how-we-see-world.

36 Carole Cadwalladr, 'Google, democracy and the truth about internet search', *Observer*, Sunday 4 December 2016, https://www.theguardian.com/technology/2016/dec/04/google-democracy-truth-internet-search-facebook.

37 Cadwalladr, 'Google is not "just" a platform. It frames, shapes and distorts how we see the world'.

38 Carole Cadwalladr, 'Robert Mercer: the big data billionaire waging war on mainstream media', *Observer*, 26 February 2017, https://www.theguardian.com/politics/2017/feb/26/robert-mercer-breitbart-war-on-media-steve-bannon-donald-trump-nigel-farage.

39 Carole Cadwalladr, 'The great British Brexit robbery: how our democracy was hijacked', *Observer*, 7 May 2017, https://www.theguardian.com/technology/2017/may/07/the-great-british-brexit-robbery-hijacked-democracy.

40 Carole Cadwalladr, '"I made Steve Bannon's psychological warfare tool": meet the data war whistleblower', *Observer Review*, 18 March 2018, https://www.theguardian.com/news/2018/mar/17/data-war-whistleblower-christopher-wylie-faceook-nix-bannon-trump.

41 Michal Kosinski, David Stillwell and Thore Graepel, 'Private traits and attributes are predictable from digital records of human behavior', *Proceedings of the National Academy of Sciences*, 110 (15), 9 April 2013, 5802–5, https://www.pnas.org/content/pnas/110/15/5802.full.pdf.

42 Kogan also goes by his married name, Aleksandr Spectre.

43 Julia Carrie Wong, Paul Lewis and Harry Davies, 'How academic at centre of Facebook scandal tried – and failed – to spin personal data into gold', *The Guardian*, 24 April 2018, https://www.theguardian.com/news/2018/apr/24/aleksandr-kogan-cambridge-analytica-facebook-data-business-ventures.

44 Kate Shellnutt, 'Trump elected president, thanks to 4 in 5 white evangelicals', *Christianity Today*, 9 November 2016, https://www.christianitytoday.com/news/2016/november/trump-elected-president-thanks-to-4-in-5-white-evangelicals.html.

45 Jamieson, *Cyberwar*. See also Jane Mayer's detailed summary of Jamieson's research, 'How Russia Helped Swing the Election for Trump', *New Yorker*, 24 September 2018, https://www.newyorker.com/magazine/2018/10/01/how-russia-helped-to-swing-the-election-for-trump.

46 Alex Hearn, 'Academic at centre of Cambridge Analytica scandal sues Facebook', *The Guardian*, 18 March 2019, https://www.theguardian.com/uk-news/2019/mar/18/aleksandr-kogan-cambridge-analytica-scandal-sues-facebook. See also a statement from the University of Cambridge about Dr Aleksandr Kogan of 11 April 2018, https://www.cam.ac.uk/notices/news/statement-from-the-university-of-cambridge-about-dr-aleksandr-kogan.

47 Cadwalladr, 'The great British Brexit robbery: how our democracy was hijacked'.

48 Bonnie Berkowitz, Denise Lu and Julie Vitkovskaya, 'Here's what we learned about Team Trump's ties to Russian interests', *Washington Post*, 31 March 2017, https://www.washingtonpost.com/graphics/national/trump-russia/.

49 Michael S. Schmidt, Mark Mazzetti and Matt Apuzzo, 'Trump campaign aides had repeated contacts with Russian intelligence', *The New York Times*, 14 February 2017, https://www.nytimes.com/2017/02/14/us/politics/russia-intelligence-communications-trump.html; Harding, *Collusion*; Jamieson, *Cyberwar*; and Robert S. Mueller III, 'Report on the investigation into Russian interference in the 2016 presidential election'.

50 Andrew Defty, 'Where is the Intelligence and Security Committee and why does its absence matter?' Hansard Society blog, 9 June 2020, https://www.hansardsociety.org.uk/blog/where-is-the-intelligence-and-security-committee-and-why-does-its-absence.

51 Dominic Nicholls, 'Why David Frost as National Security Adviser risks repeating mistakes made ahead of Iraq war', *Daily Telegraph*, 3 July 2020, https://www.telegraph.co.uk/news/2020/07/03/david-frost-national-security-adviser-risks-repeating-mistakes/.

52 Sean O'Grady, 'Chris "Failing" Grayling as chair of the intelligence committee? Sounds like an oxymoron to me', *Independent*, 10 July 2020, https://www.independent.co.uk/voices/chris-grayling-intelligence-security-committee-boris-johnson-russian-interference-justice-transport-a9611831.html; Marina Hyde, 'Chris Grayling's track record? There is no track: just a stretch of scorched earth', *The Guardian*, 10 July 2020, https://www.theguardian.com/comment-isfree/2020/jul/10/chris-grayling-chair-intelligence-committee- and Eliot Wilson, 'Chris Grayling's appointment marks a new low in the Government's aversion to scrutiny', *Daily Telegraph*, 15 July 2020, https://www.telegraph.co.uk/politics/2020/07/15/chris-graylings-appointment-marks-new-low-governments-aversion/.

53 HuffPost, Paul Waugh, 'How Julian Lewis pulled off a very British coup to chair the Intelligence and Security Committee', 17 July 2020, https://www.huffingtonpost.co.uk/entry/julian-lewis-chris-grayling-committee_uk_5f0f753dc5b619afc3fcb59b.

54 House of Commons, Intelligence and Security Committee, 'Russia', 21 July 2020, https://docs.google.com/a/independent.gov.uk/viewer?a=v&pid=sites&srcid=aW5kZXBlbmRlbnQuQuZ292LnVrfGlzY3xneD01Y2RhMGEyN2Y3NjM0OWFl.

55 Government response to the House of Commons, Intelligence and Security Committee 'Russia' report, 21 July 2020, https://www.gov.uk/government/publications/government-response-to-intelligence-and-security-committee-russia-report.

56 Nick Cohen, 'What is the point of the BBC if it is frightened of journalism?', *New European*, 19 July 2018, https://www.theneweuropean.

co.uk/top-stories/nick-cohen-what-is-the-point-of-the-bbc-if-it-is-frightened-of-journalism-1-5614097.

57 Cadwalladr, 'The great British Brexit robbery: how our democracy was hijacked'.

58 Facebook's role in the 2016 US presidential election is the obvious example. Any reader sceptical of the charge that Russian interference was sufficiently well planned and executed, and on a sufficient scale, to have won the election for Donald Trump should read the Mueller Report, Kathleen Hall Jamieson's *Cyberwar*, Luke Harding's *Collusion* and Jane Mayer's *Dark Money*.

59 Polly Toynbee, 'Paul Dacre, Daily Mail poisoner-in-chief, is quitting: good riddance', *The Guardian*, 7 June 2018, https://www.theguardian.com/commentisfree/2018/jun/07/paul-dacre-gone-daily-mail-next-associated-newspapers.

60 John Naughton, 'Populism and the internet: a toxic mix shaping the age of conspiracy theories', *The Guardian*, 25 November 2018, https://www.theguardian.com/commentisfree/2018/nov/25/populism-and-the-internet-a-toxic-mix-shaping-the-age-of-conspiracy-theories.

61 The great replacement theory was first proposed in France by Renaud Camus in 2011 in his best-selling *Le Grand Remplacement* (4th edn, Lulu Books, 2017; see also his *You Will Not Replace Us*, Chez l'auteur, 2018). It is both Islamophobic *and* antiSemitic because it typically claims that there is a Jewish plan to replace the white population with foreign Muslims. See Jonathan Freedland and Mehdi Hasan, 'Muslims and Jews face a common threat from white supremacists. We must fight it together', *The Guardian*, 3 April 2019, https://www.theguardian.com/commentisfree/2019/apr/03/muslims-jews-white-supremacists.

62 Rosa Schwartzburg, 'The "white replacement theory" motivates alt-right killers the world over', *The Guardian*, 5 August 2019, https://www.theguardian.com/commentisfree/2019/aug/05/great-replacement-theory-alt-right-killers-el-paso.

63 Kate Andrews is the former political editor of the *Sunday Times* and political editor-at-large of the *Daily Mail*. Oakeshott co-authored, with Michael Ashcroft, the unauthorized biography of David Cameron, *Call Me Dave*, ghost-wrote Arron Banks' *The Bad Boys of Brexit* and, at the time of writing, is in a relationship with the Brexit Party chairman Richard Tice (Andrew Gilligan and Tim Shipman, 'Trump leak scandal engulfs Brexit Party', *Sunday Times*, 14 July 2019, https://www.thetimes.co.uk/article/trump-leak-scandal-engulfs-brexit-party-2w7dn3hrm). The latter story relates to Oakeshott's article a week earlier in the *Mail on Sunday* which leaked confidential cables critical of President Trump by Sir Kim Darroch, British Ambassador to the US, and that led to Sir Kim's resignation (Isabel Oakeshott, 'Britain's man in the US says Trump is "inept": leaked secret cables from ambassador say the President is "uniquely dysfunctional and his career could end in disgrace"', *Mail on Sunday*, 7 July 2019, https://www.dailymail.co.uk/news/article-7220335/Britains-man-says-Trump-inept-Cables-ambassador-say-dysfunctional.html). Six years earlier, Oakeshott persuaded the economist Vicky Pryce to implicate her estranged husband, former Liberal Democrat cabinet minister Chris Huhne, in perverting the course of justice, in a *Sunday Times* article by Oakeshott that led to both Pryce and Huhne going to prison (Dominic Ponsford, 'Sunday Times journalist Isabel Oakeshott says she fulfilled her moral obligation to Vicky Pryce', *Press Gazette*, 11 March 2013, https://www.pressgazette.co.uk/sunday-times-journalist-isabel-oakeshott-says-she-fulfilled-her-moral-obligation-vicky-pryce/). However, Oakeshott's commitment to the public's right to know does not, apparently, extend to the links between Arron Banks and Russian officials and businessmen (Daily Beast, Nico Hynes, 'How a journalist kept Russia's secret links to Brexit under wraps', 10 June 2018, https://www.thedailybeast.com/how-a-journalist-kept-russias-secret-links-to-brexit-under-wraps; Jim Waterson, 'Profile: Isabel Oakeshott and the Bad Boys of Brexit', *The Guardian*, 11 June 2018, https://www.theguardian.

com/uk-news/2018/jun/11/profile-isabel-oakeshott-and-the-bad-boys-of-brexit).

64 Milo Yiannopoulos is a right-wing writer and notorious troll who was barred from using Twitter in 2016.

65 Elle Hunt, 'Milo Yiannopoulos, rightwing writer, permanently banned from Twitter', *The Guardian*, 20 July 2016, https://www.theguardian.com/technology/2016/jul/20/milo-yiannopoulos-nero-permanently-banned-twitter.

66 Andrea Nagle, *Kill All Normies*, Zero Books, 2017, p. 99.

67 See https://twitter.com/defundbbc?lang=en-gb.

68 Brian McGleenon, 'BBC crisis: 30,000 sign up to Twitter campaign to "DEFUND THE BBC" – "It's time!"', *Daily Express*, 8 June 2020, https://www.express.co.uk/news/uk/1292846/bbc-news-defund-the-bbc-campaign-group-black-lives-matter.

69 Dan Wootton, 'Fury over the BBC's hypocritical coverage of violent protests is real', *Sun*, 8 June 2020, https://www.the-sun.com/news/950688/fury-bbc-hypocritical-coverage-violent-protests/.

70 James Bickerton, 'New campaign to "Defund the BBC" sees explosion in support after launch", *Daily Express*, 11 June 2020, https://www.express.co.uk/news/uk/1294308/BBC-News-Campaign-Defund-the-BBC-licence-fee-payments.

71 A Crewe-based writer of a blog called Zelo Street summarized these initial responses: Tim Fenton, 'Defund The BBC – who's paying?', Zelo Street blog, 9 June 2020, https://zelo-street.blogspot.com/2020/06/defund-bbc-whos-paying.html.

72 The Conversation, Steven Barnett and Doug Specht, '#Defund the BBC: the anatomy of a social media campaign', 10 June 2020, https://theconversation.com/defundthebbc-the-anatomy-of-a-social-media-campaign-140391.

73 Rebecca Perring, 'BBC crisis: "Defund the BBC" campaign raises £30k in boycott bid – "Not fit for purpose!"', *Daily Express*, 15 July 2020, https://www.express.co.uk/news/uk/1309908/bbc-news-defund-bbc-tv-licence-row-bbc-latest.

74 See https://order-order.com/2020/07/06/defund-the-bbc/.

75 Including the three already quoted: McGleenon, 'BBC crisis: 30,000 sign up to Twitter campaign to "DEFUND THE BBC" – "It's time!" '; Bickerton, 'New campaign to "Defund the BBC" sees explosion in support after launch"; Perring, 'BBC crisis: "Defund the BBC" campaign raises £30k in boycott bid – "Not fit for purpose!" '; Emily Ferguson, 'BBC licence fee poll: would you pay a BBC subscription if current funding model scrapped?', *Daily Express*, 22 June 2020, https://www.express.co.uk/news/uk/1299324/bbc-licence-fee-defund-the-BBC-subscription-service-poll; Paul Withers, 'BBC licence fee MUST be decriminalised – warning pensioners are terrified of legal threats', *Daily Express*, 18 July 2020, https://www.express.co.uk/news/uk/1311056/bbc-tv-licence-fee-over-75s-free-tv-licence-decriminalise-non-payment-defund-the-bbc; James Bickerton, ' "Defund the BBC" campaign SAVAGES Gary Lineker in anti-licence fee billboard campaign', *Sunday Express*, 19 July 2020, https://www.express.co.uk/news/uk/1311107/BBC-News-Defund-the-BBC-campaign-billboards-BBC-licence-fee-Gary-Lineker-Maitlis; David Maddox, ' "BIASED BBC" is systematically pro-EU and has FAILED Britain, Ofcom told', *Sunday Express*, 19 July 2020, https://www.express.co.uk/news/politics/1311484/bbc-bias-shock-ofcom-twitter-european-union. The latter refers to a complaint to Ofcom by News-watch.

76 For a start, he was treasurer of the Glasgow University Conservative & Unionist Association (see https://www.facebook.com/permalink.php?id=511362172281580&story_fbid=3145214278896343) and had recently published an article on the hard-right Free Market Conservatives site about how to increase Conservative representation in universities (Free Market Conservatives, James Yucel, 'How do we encourage more Conservative representation in universities?', 8 February 2020, https://freemarketconservatives.org/how-do-we-encourage-more-conservative-representation-in-universities/). Something of a political obsessive, on the eve of the 2019 election, he had also published a detailed analysis in the Glasgow University student newspaper of the DUP's likely post-election strategy

(James Yucel, 'What will the DUP do next?', *Glasgow Guardian*, 10 December 2019, https://glasgowguardian.co.uk/2019/12/10/what-will-the-dup-do-next/).

77 indy100, Joanna Taylor, 'Meet the man behind the hilarious "Tory Hunger Games" account that's about to go viral', 17 January 2020, https://www.indy100.com/article/tory-twitter-hunger-games-piers-morgan-julia-hartley-brewer-9288961; The Tab, Eiran Jane Prosser, 'Student sets up bizarre Hunger Games tournament for Twitter Tories, 22 January 2020, https://thetab.com/uk/2020/01/22/student-sets-up-bizarre-hunger-games-tournament-for-twitter-tories-139006.

78 Tim Fenton, '"Student" BBC Basher WORKS FOR THE TORIES', Zelo Street blog, 9 June 2020, https://zelo-street.blogspot.com/2020/06/student-bbc-basher-works-for-tories.html.

79 Paul Geater, 'Watch: Tom Hunt signs in as Ipswich MP – and joins Conservatives in ERG', *Ipswich Star*, 18 December 2019, https://www.ipswichstar.co.uk/news/tom-hunt-joins-erg-1-6431460).

80 Westmonster, James L. Yucel, 'It's time to defund the BBC – the people have had enough', 8 June 2020, https://westmonster.com/its-time-to-defund-the-bbc-the-people-have-had-enough. Westmonster was co-founded in 2017 by Arron Banks and Nigel Heaver, a former press adviser to Nigel Farage: Jasper Jackson, 'Arron Banks launches Breitbart-style site Westmonster', *The Guardian*, 19 January 2017, https://www.theguardian.com/media/2017/jan/19/arron-banks-launches-breitbart-style-site-westmonster.

81 Martin Amis, *The Moronic Inferno and Other Visits to America*, Jonathan Cape, 1986. Amis took the phrase 'moronic inferno' from a line in Saul Bellow's *Humboldt's Gift* (see Martin Amis, 'The Moronic Inferno', *London Review of Books*, 4, 6, 1 April 1982, https://www.lrb.co.uk/the-paper/v04/n06/martin-amis/the-moronic-inferno): Bellow had in his turn borrowed it from Wyndham Lewis.

82 See Ofcom, 'Annual report on the BBC', 24 October 2019, p. 3, https://www.ofcom.org.uk/__data/assets/pdf_file/0026/173735/second-bbc-annual-report.pdf.

Conclusion: We Have a Choice

1 Quoted in Ben Woods, 'BBC spooked by ghosts from past and future', *Sunday Times*, 22 December 2019, https://www.thetimes.co.uk/article/bbc-spooked-by-ghosts-from-past-and-future-wnr3f9lnm.

2 These democratic checks and balances include Parliament, the judiciary, Westminster lobby journalists, other media (including the BBC, ITV and Channel 4) and the Civil Service. Mrs Thatcher was highly critical of the Civil Service, in particular, but we think she showed more respect for its independence than the current Number Ten.

3 Peter Stubley, 'Dominic Cummings: Timeline of alleged lockdown breaches', *Independent*, 23 May 2020, https://www.independent.co.uk/news/uk/politics/dominic-cummings-latest-news-lockdown-timeline-when-travel-durham-a9530116.html.

4 Rowena Mason, 'Dominic Cummings thinktank called for "end of BBC in its current form"', *The Guardian*, 21 January 2020, https://www.theguardian.com/politics/2020/jan/21/dominic-cummings-thinktank-called-for-end-of-bbc-in-current-form.

5 Matt Honeycombe-Foster, 'Boris Johnson and Dominic Cummings "split over scrapping BBC licence fee"', *Politics Home*, 18 February 2020, https://www.thetimes.co.uk/article/no-10-tells-bbc-licence-fee-will-be-scrapped-hzwb9bzsx.

6 See the Introduction.

7 These include – among other factors – our ageing population, the increase in lifestyle diseases such as Type 2 diabetes, the growing cost of drugs and medical equipment, and the inherently labour-intensive nature of healthcare, social care and elderly care.

8 However, this may change: we await, with some nervousness, the post-Brexit trade negotiations with the USA. The US healthcare and pharmaceutical companies would certainly like these to include higher UK drug prices and better commercial access to the NHS.

9 Deborah Summers and Lee Glendinning, 'Cameron rebukes Tory MEP who rubbished NHS in America', *The Guardian*, 14 August 2009. The Conservatives' 2019 election manifesto's main promises were to 'get Brexit done' and to strengthen the NHS: Steven Swinford, 'Conservative manifesto: Boris Johnson places NHS at heart of "critical" election', *The Times*, 25 November 2019, https://www.thetimes.co.uk/article/conservative-manifesto-boris-johnson-places-nhs-at-heart-of-critical-election-qrogjqsnj; https://www.express.co.uk/news/uk/1208694/Conservative-manifesto-general-election-2019-news-Boris-Johnson-NHS-nurses.

10 Daniel Hannan, 'When even Nicky Morgan thinks we should end the licence fee, its time is up', *Sunday Telegraph*, 20 October 2019. What Morgan actually said, in response to a question from a Conservative member of the DCMS committee asking her to consider replacing the licence fee with subscriptions, was that she was open-minded and would look at the evidence, adding that, 'What I haven't seen is any evidence, either way, what a subscription-based service would do in terms of revenue' (Rowena Mason, 'Nicky Morgan open to replacing BBC licence fee with Netflix-style subscription', *The Guardian*, 16 October 2019), https://www.theguardian.com/media/2019/oct/16/nicky-morgan-open-minded-about-bbc-licence-fee-future. Our analysis in Chapter 10 and Appendix D suggests that any review of subscription funding that looks at the evidence, as Morgan suggests, will reject it.

11 Politics Home, Matt Honeycombe-Foster, 'Boris Johnson to put NHS spending vow into law as he eyes major Cabinet shake-up', 15 December 2019, https://www.politicshome.com/news/uk/political-parties/conservative-party/news/108569/boris-johnson-put-nhs-spending-vow-law-he; Guardian staff, 'From the NHS to Brexit: what can we expect from Johnson's government?', *Observer*, 15 December 2019, https://www.theguardian.com/politics/2019/dec/15/from-the-nhs-to-brexit-what-can-we-expect-from-johnsons-government.

12 'Ex-IPSO chairman Sir Alan Moses says BBC "far too wet" in face of Government criticism', *Press Gazette* and PA Mediapoint, 3 January 2020, https://www.pressgazette.co.uk/ex-ipso-chairman-sir-alan-moses-says-bbc-far-too-wet-in-face-of-government-criticism/.

13 As usual with such announcements, there was some ambiguity about exactly what this meant in terms of additional funding, e.g. whether it includes the capital cost of new hospitals, but it is certainly a large real (inflation-adjusted) increase, estimated at 3.4 per cent per annum: Guardian staff, 'From the NHS to Brexit, what can we expect from Johnson's government'.

14 Its total expenditure was £152.9 billion. Almost 99 per cent of this was funded by general taxation and National Insurance contributions, the rest being from patient charges, mainly for prescriptions (in England) and dentistry. House of Commons, Library, Briefing paper, Rachael Harker, 'NHS funding and expenditure', 23 October 2019.

15 BBC, 'BBC annual report and accounts 2018–19', https://downloads.bbc.co.uk/aboutthebbc/reports/annualreport/2018-19.pdf.

16 The NHS had 1,396,000 full-time-equivalent (FTE) staff in 2017, including in GPs' surgeries: see https://fullfact.org/health/how-many-nhs-employees-are-there. The total FTE headcount of the BBC, including its commercial operations, was 22,401 on 31 March 2019. See 'BBC group annual report and accounts 2018–19', p. 83, https://downloads.bbc.co.uk/aboutthebbc/reports/annualreport/2018-19.

17 GOV.UK, William Hague's speech, 'Marking 80 years of the BBC's World Service', 2 March 2012, https://www.gov.uk/government/speeches/marking-80-years-of-the-bbc-world-service.

18 One implication of the imbalance between the BBC's huge, central role in British culture, society, politics and everyday life and its modest financial scale is that policy about it should no longer be so dominated by economists. Of course, there are economic issues, although even these are always closely bound up with others such as changing technologies, consumption behaviours and

practicalities such as 'information leakage' between bidders in franchise auctions. But most of the important issues are not about finance and economics. This recommendation is strengthened by the way some economists have got much of the economics wrong! In addition to their role in the Project Kangaroo fiasco and the disproportionate regulation imposed on the BBC's ability to innovate, other examples include the Peacock Committee's recommendations on ITV franchise auctions – seen by most, including us, as another fiasco (Appendix C). Economists – especially sensible ones who understand the limitations of their discipline – have a valid role in broadcasting policy analysis, but it should no longer be the dominant one.

19 The Commission for the Determination of the Financial Needs of Broadcasters (KEF), initially set up in 1975, is a group of sixteen independent experts nominated by the German states (*Länder*). Their role is to determine the funding level of the German PSBs (ARD, ZDF and Deutschlandradio), over the following four-year period: http://www.ard.de/home/die-ard/fakten/Kommission_ zur_Ermittlung_des_Finanzbedarfs____/480154/index.html.

20 David Clementi, speech at the Voice of the Listener and Viewer annual conference, 20 November 2019, https://www.bbc.co.uk/ mediacentre/speeches/2019/clementi-vlv.

21 Ibid.

22 BBC, Media Centre, 'BBC international audience soars to record high of 426 million', 18 June 2019, https://www.bbc.co.uk/ mediacentre/latestnews/2019/bbc-international-audience- record-high.

23 LSE Media Policy blog, Edda Humprecht, 'Why resilience to online disinformation varies between countries', 8 April 2020, https://blogs.lse.ac.uk/medialse/2020/04/08/why-resilience-to- online-disinformation-varies-between-countries/.

24 Cummings' other recommendation was political advertising – another big feature of US politics. See Mason, 'Dominic Cummings thinktank called for "end of BBC in its current form" '.

25 BBC, Media Centre, Clementi, speech at the Voice of the Listener and Viewer annual conference, 20 November 2019.

26 See Chapter 10. Four months after the government's consultation on decriminalization closed, it has yet to publish a summary of the responses: https://www.gov.uk/government/consultations/consultation-on-decriminalising-tv-licence-evasion/consultation-on-decriminalising-tv-licence-evasion.

27 See Patrick Barwise and Peter York, Chapter 25: 'It's the Money, Stupid', in John Mair and Tom Bradshaw (eds.), *Is the BBC STILL in Peril? Advice to the New Director-General, Tim Davie*, Bite-Sized Books, 2020.

28 Hilaire Belloc, 'Jim, Who Ran Away from His Nurse and Was Eaten by a Lion', in *Cautionary Tales for Children*, Houghton Mifflin Harcourt, 2002.

29 As discussed in Chapter 10, the Peacock Committee unanimously rejected advertising funding in the 1980s because of (i) the risk of distorting the BBC's priorities and (ii) the negative impact on commercial broadcasters' revenue. The case against it is even stronger today because traditional advertising-funded media – print media even more than commercial broadcasters – are under much greater financial pressure. There are also big disadvantages Peacock did not even consider, including viewers' and listeners' preference for avoiding commercial interruptions and also the substantial hidden 'collection costs' of advertising funding – much higher than for the licence fee.

30 At www.vlv.org.uk.

Appendix A: The 'BBC Deprivation' Study

1 Andrew Ehrenberg and Pam Mills, 'Viewers' willingness to pay for the BBC', London Business School, 1990.

2 Opinion Leader Research, report prepared for the BBC Governance Unit, 'BBC governors' licence-fee-bid forum', March 2006,

http://downloads.bbc.co.uk/bbctrust/assets/files/pdf/our_work/govs/olr_citizensforum.pdf.

3 The households were offered an incentive to participate, as is usual in market research studies that make significant demands on the participants.

4 The other 3 per cent of households were those who responded 'Don't know' in the initial survey.

5 MTM, 'Life without the BBC: household study', August 2015, https://downloads.bbc.co.uk/aboutthebbc/reports/pdf/lifewithoutthebbc.pdf.

Appendix B: The Academic Research on BBC Bias

1 For instance, as to whether, as is sometimes asserted, the BBC's coverage is systematically anti-business, anti-American, anti-Israel, unduly alarmist about climate change and excessively supportive of immigration, multiculturalism, gay rights and other liberal causes.

2 A comprehensive review of the academic research on the BBC's bias/impartiality would need to look at work by scholars at many institutions. As well as Cardiff, these include Aston; Birkbeck, University of London; Brunel University London; East London; Glasgow; Goldsmiths, University of London; Imperial College London; King's College London; Loughborough; the LSE and maybe others in the UK or elsewhere.

3 Centre for Policy Studies, Oliver Latham, 'Bias at the Beeb? A quantitative study of slant in BBC Online reporting', 15 August 2013, https://www.cps.org.uk/research/bias-at-the-beeb/.

4 Martin McElwee and Glyn Gaskarth, *The Guardian of the Airwaves? Bias and the BBC*, Policy Exchange, 2003.

5 Centre for Policy Studies, Peter Oborne and Frances Weaver, 'Guilty men', 2011.

6 The New Culture Forum, Ed West, 'Groupthink: Can we trust the BBC on immigration?', 2013.

7   The New Culture Forum, Dennis Sewell, 'A question of attitude: the BBC and bias beyond news', 2012.

8   Centre for Policy Studies, Latham, 'Bias at the Beeb?', p. 2.

9   Ibid., p. 3.

10 Tim Groseclose and Jeffrey Milyo, 'A measure of media bias', *Quarterly Journal of Economics*, 120, 4, November 2005, pp. 1191–1237.

11 Note, this is about the BBC's *online* news, not its TV or radio news.

12 It may now be possible to do this at scale using AI-based text analysis, which would make the Groseclose and Milyo method more reliable.

13 Centre for Policy Studies, Latham, 'Bias at the Beeb?', p. 6.

14 The Centre for Social Cohesion was set up by Civitas in 2007, became independent of Civitas in 2008, and became part of the Henry Jackson Society in 2011. Its director was the neoconservative journalist and author Douglas Murray and it shared its premises with Civitas and Policy Exchange. One critic, David Shariatmadari, described it as 'the thinktank that does exactly the opposite of what it says on the tin' and 'relentlessly Islamophobic', *The Guardian*, 2 April 2009, https://www.theguardian.com/commentisfree/belief/2009/apr/01/islam-social-cohesion-university-funding. (Note that, because this criticism was in *The Guardian*, Dr Latham's algorithm will have treated it as evidence that the Centre for Social Cohesion was *left*-leaning). It was dissolved in 2013.

15 Centre for Policy Studies, Latham, 'Bias at the Beeb?', Table Two, p. 8.

16 Ibid., p. 1. Note that, because of the very large sample size, several of the results in the full statistical analysis are statistically 'highly significant', meaning that, directionally, they are highly unlikely to have arisen by chance. But the relatively small difference between the two correlation coefficients means that their practical significance is limited. In plain English: the BBC citations are almost certainly, but only slightly, more similar to *The Guardian*'s than to the *Telegraph*'s.

17 Including the IPPR, which earlier analysis had ranked as the fifth most *right*-leaning one.

18 Including the IEA, which earlier analysis had ranked as *left*-leaning.

19 Centre for Policy Studies, Latham, 'Bias at the Beeb?'

20 Lucy Osborne, 'BBC "is twice as likely to cover Left-wing news stories than Right-wing ones" claims study', *Daily Mail*, 12 August 2013, https://www.dailymail.co.uk/news/article-2389589/BBC-twice-likely-cover-Left-wing-news-stories-Right-wing-ones.html; Hayley Dixon, 'BBC is biased towards the left, study finds', *Sunday Telegraph*, 11 August 2013, https://www.telegraph.co.uk/culture/tvandradio/bbc/10235967/BBC-is-biased-toward-the-left-study-finds.html.

21 Justin Lewis and Stephen Cushion, 'Think tanks, television news and impartiality', *Journalism Studies*, 20, 4, 26 October 2017, pp. 480–99, https://orca.cf.ac.uk/105302/1/Think%20Tanks%20Television%20News%20and%20Impartialityb.pdf. Although *Journalism Studies* is an international peer-reviewed journal – now with an editor-in-chief at Vienna University – in 2017 the editor-in-chief was the authors' Cardiff University colleague Professor Bob Franklin, who had founded it before joining the Cardiff group in 2008.

22 See BBC, Commissioning, 'New archive search tool: discover, preview, report', 8 May 2019, https://www.bbc.co.uk/commissioning/news/articles/new-bbc-archive-search-tool-may-2019.

23 Andrew Rich, *Think Tanks, Public Policy, and the Politics of Expertise*, Cambridge University Press, 2004.

24 Richard Murphy, 'The Institute for Fiscal Studies fisked', *The Guardian*, 19 August 2008, https://www.theguardian.com/commentisfree/2008/aug/19/tax.taxandspending; Mainly Macro: Comment on Macroeconomic Issues, Simon Wren-Lewis, 'But do the numbers add up?', 17 May 2017, https://mainlymacro.blogspot.com/2017/05/but-do-numbers-add-up.html.

25 However, on Brexit, the IFS – like the great majority of economists – saw, and continues to see, the long-term economic costs as likely to outweigh the economic benefits. So, although it might be seen as right-leaning on fiscal policy (its speciality) and macroeconomic policy (on which its expertise is contested), on the EU it was and remains at odds with the small minority of right-leaning pro-Brexit economists, who might therefore regard it as left-leaning.

26 As opposed to the CPS' *indirect* measure of selection bias: the BBC's mentions are slightly more highly correlated with those in *The Guardian* than with those in the *Telegraph*.

27 However, the IFS accounted for almost three-quarters of the 'neutral' mentions – 434 out of 604 (72 per cent). If it were classified as right-leaning rather than neutral, the overall distribution would be strongly biased to the right (573/926 = 62 per cent of all mentions in 2009), versus 16.5 per cent on the left.

28 Again, the IFS dominated, with 1,126 out of the 1,585 'neutral' mentions (71 per cent). If it were classified as right-leaning, the bias to the right in 2015 would increase markedly to 70 per cent, versus only 8.5 per cent on the left.

29 From 7 May 2015 onwards, the Conservatives had an absolute majority rather than leading a coalition government.

30 Lewis and Cushion, 'Think tanks, television news and impartiality'.

31 The Trust was the BBC's governing body and regulator during 2007–17. It was operationally independent of BBC management and its stated aim was to make decisions in the best interests of licence-fee payers.

32 This study had been commissioned by the BBC Governors in 2006 before they were replaced by the Trust.

33 John Bridcut, 'From seesaw to wagon wheel: safeguarding impartiality in the 21st century', a report commissioned by the BBC Trust, June 2007, p. 5, http://news.bbc.co.uk/1/shared/bsp/hi/pdfs/18_06_07impartialitybbc.pdf.

34 BBC News, 'BBC Trust issues impartiality follow-up', 2 August 2012, https://www.bbc.co.uk/news/entertainment-arts-19091530.

35 The results of the Prebble Review were reported in 'A BBC Trust review of the breadth of opinion reflected in the BBC's output', July 2013, http://downloads.bbc.co.uk/bbctrust/assets/files/pdf/our_work/breadth_opinion/breadth_opinion.pdf.

36 A second Cardiff content analysis explored the breadth of topics and views in selected broadcast news programmes on the BBC, ITV and Channel 4 in the same two years, 2007 and 2012.

37 Under the current Charter, these roles are now split between Ofcom (regulation) and governance (BBC Board) – see Chapter 1.

38 Mike Berry, 'The *Today* programme and the banking crisis', *Journalism*, 14, 2, 2012, pp. 253–70.

39 Steve Jones, 'A review of the impartiality and accuracy of the BBC's coverage of science', for the BBC Trust, July 2011, https://downloads.bbc.co.uk/bbctrust/assets/files/pdf/our_work/science_impartiality/science_impartiality.pdf; Felicity Mellor, Stephen Webster and Alice R. Bell, 'Content analysis of the BBC's science coverage', Appendix A/Annex 5 to Professor Steve Jones' report, for the BBC Trust, March 2011, http://downloads.bbc.co.uk/bbctrust/assets/files/pdf/our_work/science_impartiality/appendix_a.pdf.

40 James Stanyer, David Deacon, John Downey and Dominic Wring, Loughborough Communication Research Centre, 'Rural areas in the UK impartiality review: a content analysis' for the BBC Trust, May 2014, https://repository.lboro.ac.uk/articles/report/Rural_areas_in_the_UK_impartiality_review_a_content_analysis_for_the_BBC_Trust/9471095.

41 The Conversation, Mike Berry, 'How biased is the BBC?', August 2013, https://theconversation.com/hard-evidence-how-biased-is-the-bbc-17028.

42 Berry, 'The *Today* programme and the banking crisis', p. 257.

43 Tom Mills, *The BBC: Myth of a Public Service*, Verso, 2016, p. 139.

44 See Adrian Renton and Justin Schlosberg, 'Reporting the newspapers: evidence of bias skew in the BBC's selection of titles, stories and guest discussants of newspaper coverage, 18 April–21 May 2017', 5 June 2017, on the Media Reform Coalition website,

https://www.mediareform.org.uk/wp-content/uploads/2017/06/BBC-NEWSPAPERS-REPORT-FINAL.pdf.

45 Including freelancers, UK-based foreign media journalists, magazine writers and some others (those working in public relations, consultants, etc.).

46 Conservative: the *Sun*, *Mail* (and *Mail on Sunday*), *The Times* (and *Sunday Times*), *Telegraph* (and *Sunday Telegraph*), *Star* and *Financial Times*; Labour: the *Sunday People*, *Mirror*, *The Guardian* and *Observer*; and for other parties, first, UKIP: the *Express* (and *Sunday Express*); secondly, the Liberal Democrats: *Independent*; and lastly, those with no endorsement: the *i*, *Independent on Sunday* and *Metro*.

47 Ofcom, 'Ofcom's rules on due impartiality, due accuracy, elections and referendums', 9 March 2017, https://www.ofcom.org.uk/__data/assets/pdf_file/0030/98148/Due-impartiality-and-elections-statement.pdf.

48 Renton and Schlosberg, 'Reporting the newspapers: evidence of bias skew in the BBC's selection of titles, stories and guest discussants', p. 2.

49 Maxwell McCombs, *Setting the Agenda: Mass Media and Public Opinion*, Polity Press, 2004.

50 Stephen Cushion, Richard Thomas, Allaina Kilby, Marina Morani and Richard Sambrook, 'Interpreting the media logic behind editorial decisions: television news coverage of the 2015 UK general election campaign', *International Journal of Press/Politics*, 21, 4, 2016, pp. 472–89.

51 Stephen Cushion and Richard Sambrook, 'How TV news let the Tories fight the election on their own terms', *The Guardian*, 15 May 2015, https://www.theguardian.com/media/2015/may/15/tv-news-let-the-tories-fight-the-election-coalition-economy-taxation.

52 The *Telegraph/Sunday Telegraph*, *The Times/Sunday Times*, the *Mail/Mail on Sunday*, the *Sun/Sun on Sunday* and the *Express/Sunday Express*.

53 The *Independent/Independent on Sunday*, *The Guardian/Observer* and the *Mirror/Sunday Mirror*.

54 Stephen Cushion, Allaina Kilby, Richard Thomas, Marina Morani and Richard Sambrook, 'Newspapers, impartiality and television news: intermedia agenda-setting during the 2015 UK general election campaign', *Journalism Studies*, 2016, Table 3 (p. 11). Published online at https://www.tandfonline.com/doi/full/10.1080/14616 70X.2016.1171163. The sum of the unweighted averages across the four non-BBC broadcasters for items covered by Conservative-supporting papers was 60.7 per cent versus 39.3 per cent for those covered by Labour- or Liberal Democrat-supporting papers.

55 They may well also drive much of the social media news agenda, but that question falls outside the scope of the research we have reviewed and of this book.

56 A report commissioned by the BBC Governors, 'BBC news coverage of the European Union: independent panel report', January 2005, p. 2, http://downloads.bbc.co.uk/bbctrust/assets/files/pdf/our_work/govs/independentpanelreport.pdf.

57 Ibid., p. 4.

58 Related criticisms were that the BBC tended to oversimplify EU issues (e.g. describing all EU institutions as 'Brussels') and to favour both studio interviewees and 'vox pops' that reflected extreme views.

59 A report commissioned by the BBC Governors, 'BBC news coverage of the European Union', p. 7.

60 Ibid., p. 8.

61 Now that the UK has 'taken back control', we shall see if its 'political and daily life' will really change as much as has been suggested.

62 For the results of the Prebble Review, see, 'A BBC Trust review of the breadth of opinion reflected in the BBC's output', July 2013.

63 *BBC News at Ten*, *ITV News at Ten*, *Sky News at Ten*, *Channel 4 News* at 7 p.m. and *Channel 5 News* at 6:30 p.m.

64 See Justin Lewis and Tammy Speers for a further account of the reporting on the MMR vaccine, 'Misleading media reporting? The MMR story', *Nature Reviews Immunology*, 3, 11, 2003, pp. 913–18.

65 Stephen Cushion and Justin Lewis, 'Impartiality, statistical tit-for-tats and the construction of balance: UK television news reporting of the 2016 EU referendum campaign', *European Journal of Communication*, 32, 3, 2017, pp. 220–21.

66 The Conversation, Berry, 'How biased is the BBC?'

Appendix C: The Peacock Committee and Its Wider Legacy

1 House of Commons, Home Office Committee, 'Report of the committee on financing the BBC [Peacock Report]', Cmnd. 9824, July 1986, p. 1, https://tvlicensingnews.com/TVLicensingNews/Home_files/Peacock%20Report.pdf.

2 The release of Cabinet papers in 2014 under the thirty-year rule confirmed this: Jim Pickard and Barney Thompson, 'Archives 1986 & 1986: Thatcher questioned BBC licence fee', *Financial Times*, 30 December 2014, https://www.ft.com/content/4c72a9b0-8535-11e4-bb63-00144feabdco.

3 Steven Barnett and Andrew Curry, *The Battle for the BBC*, Aurum Press, 1994, p. 36.

4 By putting more resources into programmes that delivered the most valuable audiences for a given programme budget and time of day, i.e. a programme with high ratings and attractive demographics (for example, one with an audience with a relatively high proportion of upscale young men).

5 House of Commons, Home Office Committee, 'Report of the committee on financing the BBC [Peacock Report]', pp. 99–101.

6 Even more so after taking into account the additional reasons for rejecting BBC advertising discussed in Chapter 10: (i) viewers and listeners prefer to avoid commercial interruptions and (ii) advertising involves significant hidden costs (agency fees, etc.) –

which are *much* higher than the collection and evasion costs of the licence fee.

7 Those voting in favour were *Financial Times* columnist Samuel Brittan, Alan Peacock, philosopher Lord Quinton and businessman Peter Reynolds; those voting against were presenter and travel journalist Judith Chalmers, journalist Alistair Hetherington and economist and businessman Jeremy Hardie.

8 The regulator, the Independent Television Commission, introduced (i) a 'quality threshold' to ensure sufficient investment in quality programming and (ii) a business plan test to exclude 'winner's curse' bids based on unrealistically optimistic revenue projections.

9 The wide range of the bids suggests that the auction was something of a lottery because of the uncertainty of the revenue projections, and also that some incumbents may have had intelligence that there were no other bidders in their areas. It's also possible that some bidders in other areas knew more about their competitors' bids than is assumed in economists' auction theories, which are predicated on no information 'leakage'.

10 Maggie Brown, 'Margaret Thatcher was the architect of controversial changes to TV and press', *The Guardian*, 12 April 2013, https://www.theguardian.com/media/media-blog/2013/apr/12/margaret-thatcher-television-press. Kathy Gyngell, who founded News-watch in 1999 and the Conservative Woman in 2014, and is associated with some of the right-wing think tanks in the Tufton Street cluster (see Chapter 8), is Bruce Gyngell's widow.

11 Adam Smith Institute, 'Omega Report: communications policy', 1984, p. 42, https://static1.squarespace.com/static/56eddde762cd9413e151ac92/t/5aec3b3603ce641d8ca79b18/1525431566365/communication.pdf.

12 House of Commons, Home Office Committee, 'Report of the committee on financing the BBC [Peacock Report]', p. 152.

13 Ibid., p. 1.

14 These include, 'pay per view', short-term rentals and 'download to own'.

Appendix D: The Trouble with Subscriptions

1 And those with over-seventy-fives on Pension Credit who currently receive a free TV licence.

2 Ofcom, 'The international communications market 2017: TV and audio-visual', December 2017, p. 86, https://www.ofcom.org.uk/__data/assets/pdf_file/0027/108909/icmr-2017-tv-audio-visual.pdf. The penetration of pay TV has slightly fallen since then as some SVoD subscribers have cancelled their pay-TV subscriptions. The reduction in pay-TV penetration is expected to continue, see: 'Analyst: UK pay TV in continued decline', *Advanced Television*, 17 October 2019, https://advanced-television.com/2019/10/17/analyst-uk-pay-tv-in-continued-decline/.

3 1.40 x 75 per cent = 1.05; 1.4 x 80 per cent = 1.12.

4 £103 million out of £3,690 million ('BBC annual report and accounts 2018–19', pp. 61, 208, https://downloads.bbc.co.uk/aboutthebbc/reports/annualreport/2018-19.pdf).

5 Sky, 'Annual report: 2018', p. 91. Sky's non-consumer income comes from advertising, sales to pubs, bars and content sales.

6 This excludes the additional possibility of the evasion rate also increasing: we have no information on whether the proportion of households with unlawful access to pay TV is higher or lower than the 5.5-per-cent current evasion rate for the licence fee.

Appendix E: Research on the BBC's Market Impact

1 Strictly speaking, the issue was *first* raised in the 1920s, when it was agreed, mainly in response to lobbying by the newspapers, that the BBC would not carry advertising.

2 This is actually happening over time because of cumulative funding cuts and programme and technology cost increases, but this type of long-term change is much harder to evaluate than a sudden shock.

3 BBC, 'Public and private broadcasters across the world: the race to the top', December 2013, https://downloads.bbc.co.uk/aboutthebbc/insidethebbc/howwework/reports/pdf/bbc_report_public_and_private_broadcasting_across_the_world.pdf. The fourteen countries were Australia, Brazil, Denmark, France, Germany, Italy, Japan, Netherlands, Norway, Portugal, Spain, Sweden, the UK and the US. The methodology partly replicated that of an earlier study by McKinsey & Company for Ofcom, 'Review of public service broadcasting around the world', September 2004, https://www.ofcom.org.uk/__data/assets/pdf_file/0018/34236/wp3mck.pdf.

4 The correlation coefficient across the fourteen countries was +0.65. (The correlation coefficient is the most widely used statistical measure of the extent to which two variables tend to go up or down together. It can fall anywhere in the range –1 to +1.) A correlation coefficient of +0.65, even with a small sample, would generally indicate a strong positive association, one unlikely to have occurred by chance. However, some of the correlation in this case is likely to have reflected differences in per capita GDP, e.g. Sweden versus Brazil: because Sweden's per capita GDP is much higher than Brazil's, it's not surprising that both its public TV and its commercial TV systems should also have higher per capita revenue than the equivalent systems in Brazil, strengthening the correlation between the two measures across different countries.

5 The correlation coefficient between BBC One and ITV is +0.53.

6 News and information, culture, science, education, religion and children's programmes. The analysis was limited to the eight European countries for which data were available. The correlation coefficient was +0.83.

7 The percentage of respondents rating the quality of the main public and commercial TV channels (all those with an audience share of at least 5 per cent) as 'very good': weighted averages by audience share. The correlation coefficient was, again, +0.83.

8 BBC, 'Public and private broadcasters across the world: the race to the top', p. 1.

9   KPMG, 'An economic review of the extent to which the BBC crowds out private sector activity', for the BBC Trust, October 2015, https://assets.kpmg/content/dam/kpmg/uk/pdf/2017/02/bbccrowdingwebaccess.pdf.

10 Ibid., p. 1.

11 Multiple linear regression with logarithmic independent and dependent variables. The study used a number of additional techniques to test or improve model performance, reliability and interpretability. Some more complex models, with lagged variables and different functional forms, were also tested but did not affect the conclusions. See ibid., Appendix 2.

12 Real GDP per capita had a small *negative* coefficient: TV is cheap entertainment, especially at the margin (e.g. if you either are, or are not, a pay-TV subscriber). When the economy is doing well, people watch less.

13 An additional variable was used to compensate for the switch to a new, more representative, audience measurement panel in 2010, which led to an increase in reported viewing figures.

14 These used one or both of two measures of quarterly BBC activity: the number of BBC entertainment TV broadcast minutes and a (rather dodgy) measure of the BBC's spend per minute of entertainment TV.

15 KPMG, 'An economic review of the extent to which the BBC crowds out private sector activity', p. 28.

16 Ibid., p. 3.

17 Steven T. Berry and Joel Waldfogel, 'Public radio in the United States: does it correct market failure or cannibalize commercial stations?' *Journal of Public Economics*, 71, 2, February 1999, pp. 189–211.

18 KPMG, 'An economic review of the extent to which the BBC crowds out private sector activity', p. 14.

19 Oliver & Ohlbaum Associates Ltd and Oxera Consulting LLP, for the DCMS: 'BBC television, radio and online services: an assessment of market impact and distinctiveness', February 2016, https://assets.publishing.service.gov.uk/government/uploads/

system/uploads/attachment_data/file/504012/FINAL_-_BBC_market_impact_assessment.pdf.

20 O&O and Oxera, for the DCMS: 'BBC television, radio and online services: an assessment of market impact and distinctiveness', p. 9.

21 Internet Advertising Bureau, 'UK advertising spend passes £20bn as growth hits five-year high', press release, 25 April 2016, https://www.iabuk.com/press-release/uk-advertising-spend-passes-ps20bn-growth-hits-five-year-high.

22 O&O and Oxera, for the DCMS: 'BBC television, radio and online services: an assessment of market impact and distinctiveness'. In Patrick Barwise's view, even these low estimates are optimistic, for two reasons. First, he thinks O&O and Oxera overestimated the extent to which increased TV, radio and online commercial exposures would lead to increased advertising revenue. (This is about the 'price elasticity' of advertising exposures, a measure of the extent to which increasing the number of exposures reduces the average price advertisers pay for each exposure, discussed later in this appendix). Secondly, he believes that, since TV, radio and online services partly compete against each other for advertising revenue, the total increase in advertising would be less than the £58 million to £86 million sum of the three separate estimates. For instance, some of the increased TV revenue when the TV advertising market is analysed separately would be captured from radio and online advertising, and vice versa.

23 Internet Advertising Bureau, 'UK advertising spend passes £20bn as growth hits five-year high'.

24 As Mandy Rice-Davies might have put it, 'They would say that, wouldn't they?'

25 Gurjit Degun, 'Commercial radio boosted by 33% rise in online listening', *Campaign*, 6 February 2020, https://www.campaign-live.co.uk/article/commercial-radio-boosted-33-rise-online-listening/1673081.

26 O&O and Oxera for the DCMS: 'BBC television, radio and online services: an assessment of market impact and distinctiveness', pp. 11–12.

27 The indirect cost to consumers of T V advertising depends on the 'counterfactual'. The Reuters Institute study, discussed shortly, assumed that this was a market economy with advertising (you can't have the first without the second), but without TV advertising – as in the UK before 1955 or, broadly, Sweden as recently as 1992 (Patrick Barwise and Robert G. Picard, 'What if there were no BBC television? The net impact on UK viewers', Reuters Institute for the Study of Journalism, Oxford University, February 2014, pp. 33–4, https://reutersinstitute.politics.ox.ac.uk/sites/default/files/2017-06/What%20if%20there%20were%20no%20BBC%20TV_0.pdf). In this situation, companies' marketing budgets would presumably be much the same, but the money currently invested in T V advertising would instead go into some combination of (i) other media advertising, (ii) price cuts and promotions and (iii) other marketing activities such as PR and events. Some of these would significantly benefit consumers either directly (price cuts and promotions) or indirectly (better or cheaper print media); others would be of no consumer value beyond their entertainment value, if any, or information content, if relevant (poster campaigns, most PR). On this basis, TV advertising does have a cost (strictly speaking, an opportunity cost) to consumers, but that cost is somewhat less than the total amount advertisers spend on it, which equates to commercial broadcasters' net advertising and sponsorship revenue plus another 15 to 20 per cent to cover the cost of commercial production and agency fees.

28 Barwise and Picard, 'What if there were no BBC television? The net impact on BBC viewers', p. 4. See also p. 10, pp. 57–61, and Appendix D, which discuss the implications for a wide range of alternative policy options.

29 Ibid., pp. 23, 29.

30 Ibid., pp. 31–2.

31 I T V is now also a significant programme producer, including for the BBC (e.g. *Bodyguard*). Its production revenue, which was much lower in 2012, falls outside the Reuters Institute analysis

but would certainly be lower if the BBC's funding, and therefore programme commissioning, were cut.

32 This so-called 'price elasticity' effect is not in dispute although the exact numbers are unknown and contested. Some estimates even suggest that an increase in the total viewing of advertising-funded TV would lead to a *reduction* in total TV advertising revenue as it would enable advertisers to achieve their audience reach objectives at a lower cost. See Barwise and Picard, 'What if there were no BBC television? The net impact on UK viewers', Appendix A.

33 The evidence suggests not, but the Reuters Institute study optimistically assumed that subscriptions might be significantly higher if there were no competition from the BBC.

34 The impact on consumers would vary between different types of household. See Barwise and Picard, 'What if there were no BBC television? The net impact on UK viewers', pp. 39–42.

35 Ibid., pp. 57–9.

36 The O&O and Oxera report for the DCMS, 'BBC television, radio and online services: an assessment of market impact and distinctiveness' (p. 50), stated that the Reuters Institute study's conclusions were, in O&O and Oxera's view, 'directionally correct but numerically overstated'. We believe that this mainly reflects different views of the price elasticity of TV advertising.

Acknowledgements

This book is about hostile forces external to the BBC, although it also touches on its output, people and internal processes. It's mainly based on published sources (documented in the endnotes) but we also conducted over a hundred interviews to get extra insights, check facts, test our ideas and interpretations and add colour, and received helpful comments on the draft manuscript from over forty 'critical friends'. Because the issues are so political (in all senses) and the BBC's enemies include some very powerful people and institutions, we've chosen not to name any of these primary sources. But we're immensely grateful for their time, knowledge and support, without which this would have been a rather shorter but much less well-researched book.

We would, however, like to name some other people without whose help this book would not exist.

At the BBC, Clare Sumner, Myrna MacGregor and Andrew Scadding leant on their busy colleagues (contrary to the claims of the Beeb-bashers, everyone at the BBC really is constantly busy) for information to answer our endless requests. Helen Moor and Nick North also helped us with audience data.

We would like to thank Katie Hollier and Alice Meehan for research support, our agent Adrian Sington, our editorial consultant Ananda Pellerin, our copyeditor Louisa Watson, and Maria Bedford, Matt Hutchinson, Ruth Pietroni and Louise Willder at Penguin Random House. And, above all, the team at SRU: Maxine Ostwald, Juliette Jackson, Georgina Jackson and Liz Hills.

For Patrick, the roots of this book go back to the late 1970s when he first started working on TV audience behaviour with the late Professor Andrew Ehrenberg at London Business School, funded by the Markle Foundation in New York. The book that came out of that research (*Television and its Audience*, Sage 1988) has never been out of print. He would also like to acknowledge his time as a visiting fellow at Oxford University's Reuters Institute in 2012–14, working with Professor Robert Picard on the economics of television in a digital world and the 'What If There Were No BBC Television?' counterfactual study of the BBC's market impact. Last but not least, he would like to thank his wife, the social historian and author Catherine Horwood, and apologise for any obsessive-compulsive behaviour he may have exhibited in the course of researching and writing this book.

For Peter, the roots go back to conducting group discussions all around the country since the 1970s, but particularly in 'red-wall' northern constituencies. He always started by asking people about their media diets and what they'd seen on TV recently!

Finally, we would like to thank Jane Frost, chief executive of The Market Research Society, who first persuaded us both to become MRS Patrons and then to hand out the prizes as a double act at the Society's annual awards event. It was our conversations at those events that led us to collaborate on this book. If you don't like it, she's the person you should blame.

Index